P9-CEZ-080

Longstreet's Assault—
Pickett's Charge

The Lost Record of Pickett's Wounded

By

Donald J. Frey

BURD STREET PRESS

This White Mane Books publication
was printed by
Beidel Printing House, Inc.
63 West Burd Street
Shippensburg, PA 17257-0152 USA

In respect for the scholarship contained herein, the acid-free paper used in this book meets the guidelines for permanence and durability of the Committee on Production Guidelines for Book Longevity of the Council on Library Resources.

For a complete list of available publications
please write
White Mane Books
Division of White Mane Publishing Company, Inc.
P.O. Box 152
Shippensburg, PA 17257-0152 USA

Library of Congress Cataloging-in-Publication Data

00-039742

High Tide at Gettysburg

A thousand fell where Kemper led;
A thousand bled where Garnett led;
In blinding flame and strangling smoke
The remnant through the batteries broke
And crossed the works with Armistead.

"Once more in glory's van with me!"
Virginia cried to Tennessee:
"We two together, come what may,
Shall stand upon these works today!"

William H. Thompson
4th Ga.

Dedicated to those who wore shades of Gray and imperial blue.

Also by Donald J. Frey

In the Woods Before Dawn: The Samuel Richey Collection of the Southern Confederacy
Grandpa's Gone: The Adventures of Daniel Buchwalter in the Western Army 1862–1865

Contents

Illustrations

Preface

GLORY means remembrance, something to talk about: Babe Ruth in 1927; the 101st Airborne in 1944; Neil Armstrong in 1969; the Cincinnati Reds in 1976; Ronald Reagan in 1980; Pickett's Charge... Death and glory embraced Confederates who charged Cemetery Ridge on a sweltering Friday afternoon in July 1863. Lee's men fought for the most basic of beliefs: "Home, home, boys! Remember, home is over beyond those hills!" an officer cried.[1] Soldiers of the Army of the Potomac were not motivated by the ideal to end the evil of slavery.[2]

Beyond biographies and campaign histories, reminiscences and unit histories, the great attraction for Civil War enthusiasts remains the abiding "what if?" What if Bragg outflanks the Hornet's Nest? What if Franklin supports Meade at Fredericksburg? What if Loring supports Bowen at Champion Hill? What if Smith is more aggressive at Petersburg? **GETTYSBURG**, the war's transcendent *what-if*, attracts pilgrims to Cemetery Ridge and Little Round Top like Rome lured Peter and Paul, Marcion, Jerome, Augustine, Pelagius...

My recollection of interest in the Battle of Gettysburg begins around 1964 when my parents gave me the juvenile book *Gettysburg* written by MacKinaly Kantor. An illustration of the Louisiana Tigers assaulting Cemetery Hill seized my imagination. The decision to compose a work on Gettysburg, thereby tampering with the Holy Grail of Civil War study, originates with a ledger book acquired by the Cincinnati Historical Society in February 1941. Its existence remained unknown until I visited Union Terminal to survey the society's Civil War collection. Chief Surg. Edward Rives, George E. Pickett's division, listed the names of 369 Confederates in the ledger. He treated 249 members of the division at the field hospital. The Virginians participated in Pickett's Charge or like Sgt. Maj. David E. Johnson, 7th Virginia, were wounded during the preliminary bombardment. Three soldiers from Georgia and North Carolina were listed by Rives as "Stragglers." Hospital personnel number 52. Surgeon Rives, a native of Cincinnati, also recorded the names of 60 Virginians cared for by Federal surgeons at the III Corps hospital, located northeast of the John Trostle farmhouse.[3] The last four names on the document are "Deaths heard of."

The Rives document is *sui generis* because no divisional hospital records exist from any Civil War battle. Twenty-three names listed as members of Pickett's division are previously unknown. These names are printed in bold: **William Hubbard**. Surgeon Rives spelled names phonetically; many are incorrect. Spelling has been corrected based on the roster compiled by David Busey in *Nothing But Glory: Pickett's Division at Gettysburg*. Thus, Knuckles becomes Nuchols. Correct ranks have also been noted.

The narrative is intended to provide the campaign and battle with a fresh perspective. This work is not intended to be a definitive account since Edwin Coddington's nonpareil study, *The Gettysburg Campaign: A Study in Command*, constitutes the acknowledged masterwork on the subject. I do not treat every controversy, the record of every regiment or the experience of every noteworthy individual. The participation of one patriotic old soldier, a citizen of Gettysburg, merits particular notice.

John Burns, a 70-year-old veteran of the War of 1812, fought with the immortal Iron Brigade and the Pennsylvania Bucktails, July 1, 1863, on McPherson's Ridge.[4]

> ...I [Lt. Col. John Callis, 7th Wisconsin] sent out my skirmish line—when both sides seemed to take a breathing spell, while here an old man approached us from the rear, with a blue swallow-tailed coat, rolling collar, and brass buttons carrying a long small bore rifle and an old plug hat on, with tight striped pants. I thought he was a 'Yank' by his dress. He came up to me and said in a feeble but resolute voice, 'Sir, are you in command of this regt.?,' I answered, 'yes,' and he said, 'will you allow me to fight in your Regt.?,' to which I replied 'old man you had better go to the rear or you might get hurt. The Rebels are very careless about how they shoot and you are liable to get killed any moment; see the bullets are flying pretty thick now.' But 'tut,' said the old man, 'I've heard the whistle of bullets before.' 'Well then if you will fight you must have a gun that will do some good,' handing him a nice silver mounted rifle that I had captured, he looked at it and said, 'that does look better than my squirrel gun, I will try it.' He took it and started out in front of our line which was laying down at the time, and said he, 'I want to get a sight at one of them.' I then looked in front of him and saw a confederate officer riding at full speed towards us; the old man saw him and fired. Off went the man and on came the horse into our lines without his rider. This old man was John Burns, of whom so much has been said and written.[5]

The invasion of Pennsylvania culminated in Robert E. Lee's victory or death effort to crush the Army of the Potomac decisively. Lee's defeat did not doom the Confederacy since the war was lost (or won) in the West.[6] The war's turning point was not attained by the twin Confederate defeats at Gettysburg and Vicksburg since the Southerners never possessed sufficient military assets to invade and subjugate the North. Nonetheless, a successful invasion of Pennsylvania that included the capture of Harrisburg and Philadelphia would have weakened Lincoln's presidency and perhaps produced a political settlement of the war. The fall of Atlanta in September 1864, which guaranteed Abraham Lincoln's reelection, emerged as the Civil War's *climactic* turning point, the Emancipation Proclamation notwithstanding, because the South's last hope was the election of George B. McClellan, the peace candidate.[7] The bloodiest three days of combat in American history, Gettysburg, did not impact Abraham Lincoln's reelection.

Acknowledgments

A sterling band of individuals, members of the Cincinnati Civil Round Table, have supported me in this effort by allowing access to their libraries and their wealth. These gentlemen are Alan Hoeweler, Tom Breiner, Dan Reigle, and Dave Smith. Wiley Sword, noted scholar, arms collector and Wolverine fan, evaluated my manuscript to provide me with suggestions that improved my work. George Skoch, an outstanding cartographer, executed the superb maps that illustrate this book. Col. Jim Enos of Carlisle photographed the images from *Battles and Leaders*. The work of David Busey, in collaboration with Kathy Georg Harrison in *Nothing But Glory*, made it possible for me to understand the significance of the record left by Edward Rives. I must also acknowledge the publisher of *Gettysburg Magazine*, Bob Younger. Dozens of fine articles that he has published afforded me a better understanding of the Battle of Gettysburg and served as an invaluable source. When we are dust, Bob's magazine will certainly be a collector's item. The Hamilton County Public Library, one of our nation's finest, possesses an exceptional Civil War collection. The availability of such periodicals as *Southern Bivouac* and *Confederate Veteran* along with regimental histories on microfiche allowed me to attempt and complete my work. I wish to acknowledge my years of friendship with Doug Magee of the History Department who permitted me to take out reserved material.

Cost of photographing the hospital record of Pickett's division is prohibitive. The pages that are reproduced from microfiche are intended to demonstrate its existence. The two medical pathological sketches included with the printed list are intended to demonstrate the damage done to the human body by Civil War missiles. They were drawn by Surg. Daniel S. Young, 21st Ohio Volunteer Infantry, in the Western Theatre. They are also unique and are part of a collection at the Cincinnati Medical Heritage Center, University of Cincinnati. Dir. Billie Broaddus kindly allowed their publication in this work.

The late historian of the 57th Massachusetts, Warren Wilkenson, advised me in 1991 that it is impossible to avoid mistakes. Those that may exist in my work are entirely my responsibility. Mr. Edwin C. Bearss volunteered to edit the entire manuscript, including the notes. His contribution to this work is both generous and characteristic of him.

My conclusions about the battle are derived from my understanding of events as well as my knowledge of the military art, for which I paid a price in 1978 while serving as a member of the 259th Military Intelligence Company. As a final note, it is a singular coincidence that Peter Frey, no relation, owned the land called Cemetery Ridge, where Pickett's division met its doom and earned its eternal glory. It would seem I was meant to discover the invaluable record left by a fellow Cincinnatian, Edward Rives. **GO BUCKS**.

Chapter 1
Lee's Decision

...sir, we did whip them at Gettysburg...
Robert E. Lee

Seeds of Southern sorrow in Pennsylvania were sown in Virginia during the Battle of Chancellorsville, May 2, 1863, when Lt. Gen. Thomas Jonathan "Stonewall" Jackson's surprise attack routed the Army of the Potomac's XI Corps. A characteristic of Jackson's legendary generalship was pursuit of a defeated foe. Around 9:00 P.M., as he and his staff reconnoitered beyond the Confederate skirmish line to maintain the momentum of the attack, the 18th North Carolina fired on horsemen that approached from the direction of the enemy. Jackson was wounded severely though not mortally. Taken to the plantation office of Thomas C. Chandler at Guiney Station, General Jackson recuperated from the amputation of his left arm but developed pneumonia. As he wished, the most feared Southern general passed from this world on a Sunday, May 10.[1] The cost of Gen. Robert E. Lee's magnificent victory at Chancellorsville was his most effective subordinate. Lee admitted to his son Custis: "It is a terrible loss. I do not know how to replace him."[2] With the loss of Jackson, "...Lee faced the daunting task of attempting to replace an irreplaceable asset. He never came close to succeeding."[3]

An apostle of the bold, unexpected offensive, Jackson had advocated an invasion of the North since April 1861. Jackson explained his views to General Lee in July 1862, after the Army of the Potomac had been defeated in the series of battles called the Seven Days. In September, following another victory over the Federals at Second Manassas, Lee implemented Jackson's strategy.[4] On September 3, Lee suggested to Pres. Jefferson Davis that a "propitious time" existed to take advantage of the demoralized and weakened Federal forces operating in Virginia by entering Maryland.[5] The army needed subsistence for its men and animals in country untouched by war[6] and drawing the enemy north of the Potomac River, according to Lee, would "aid the citizens of Maryland in any efforts they might be disposed to make to recover their liberties."[7] Foreign recognition also influenced Lee's decision to enter Maryland. Public opinion in Great Britain favored the North but a few influential patricians in Queen Victoria's Cabinet sided with the South. Napoleon III, the emperor of France, would support British policy. Lee also reasoned that a resounding success north of the Potomac River would strengthen the Democratic Party in fall elections. Peace Democrats resented Abraham Lincoln's unconstitutional policies in prosecution of the war; perhaps they would recognize the sovereignty of the Southern Confederacy.[8] On September 4, the Army of Northern Virginia began trickling into Maryland at White's Ford.[9] Four days later, Lee revealed to Brig. Gen. John G. Walker the scope of his ambitious campaign.

> 'In ten days from now,' he continued, 'if the military situation is then what I confidently expect it to be after the capture of Harper's Ferry, I shall concentrate the army at Hagerstown, effectually destroy the Baltimore and Ohio road, and march to this point,' placing his finger at Harrisburg, Pennsylvania. 'That is the objective point of the campaign. You remember, no doubt, the long bridge of the Pennsylvania railroad over the Susquehanna, a few miles west of Harrisburg. Well, I wish effectually to destroy that bridge, which will disable the Pennsylvania railroad for a long time. With the Baltimore and Ohio in our possession, and the Pennsylvania railroad broken up, there will remain to the enemy but one route of communication with the West, and that very circuitous, by way of the Lakes. After that I can turn my attention to Philadelphia, Baltimore, or Washington, as may seem best for our interests.'[10]

Lee's army was nearly overwhelmed by superior numbers in the fields around Antietam Creek at Sharpsburg, Maryland. September 17, 1862, became the bloodiest day in American history as the Army of Northern Virginia withstood a series of uncoordinated assaults to frustrate the Army of the Potomac. Lee retreated into Virginia two days later.[11]

During the winter of 1863 Lee and his mighty right arm, "Stonewall" Jackson, must have discussed the probability of a summer campaign north of the Potomac River. Even before Jackson had concluded his celebrated June 1862 campaign in the Shenandoah Valley, Lee had written to Pres. Jefferson Davis: "After much reflection I think if it was possible to reinforce Jackson strongly, it would change the character of the war...Jackson could in that event cross Maryland into Pennsylvania." In February 1863 Jedediah Hotchkiss,

Jackson's chief engineer, received secret orders to prepare a map of the Shenandoah Valley extended to Harrisburg and Philadelphia. Compiled from county maps of Maryland, Virginia, and Pennsylvania, this large-scale drawing "noted farmhouses, with names of occupants."[12]

Before the Chancellorsville clash, General Lee had resisted suggestions from his superiors to reinforce the Department of the West, commanded by Gen. Joseph E. Johnston. Two vital communications centers, Chattanooga and Vicksburg, were Johnston's responsibility to defend.[13] Gen. Braxton Bragg's Army of Tennessee confronted the more numerous Army of the Cumberland in central Tennessee. Lee believed that an aggressive posture by his own army would bring relief to Bragg.[14] While Lee and Jackson thrashed Maj. Gen. Joseph Hooker's Army of the Potomac at Chancellorsville, the Army of the Tennessee, commanded by Maj. Gen. Ulysses S. Grant, invaded Mississippi to threaten Vicksburg, the last major Southern stronghold on the Mississippi River. Vicksburg linked Texas, Arkansas, and most of Louisiana with the other Confederate States. The fall of Vicksburg would cut off armies serving east of the Mississippi from resources and manpower available west of the river.[15]

Following his dazzling victory at Chancellorsville, General Lee traveled to Richmond to confer with President Davis and the cabinet concerning the summer campaign in the East. Lee argued that supplies for his army were available north of the Potomac River.[16] The Virginian wanted to expel the Federals from the Shenandoah Valley and "if practicable to transfer the scene of hostilities beyond the Potomac." At a minimum he expected to disrupt enemy plans for their own summer campaign.[17]

Secretary of War James A. Seddon had lost faith in Joe Johnston, an obstinate and defensive-minded general. Seddon's opinion influenced President Davis, a Mississippian. On May 16, the cabinet reversed its previous commitment to reinforce the West in favor of Lee's design to operate north of the Potomac River, hoping that Lee's army could maneuver to threaten Baltimore, Washington, and Philadelphia.[18]

Arguments Lee offered his superiors to support his proposal for an offensive reflected the true strategic situation in the East as he assessed it. Victories at Fredericksburg in December and at Chancellorsville depressed him because they "had accomplished nothing; we had not gained a foot of ground, and I knew the enemy could easily replace the men he had lost...I considered the problem in every phase and to my mind it resolved itself into one of two things—either retire to Richmond and stand a siege, which must ultimately have ended in surrender, or to invade Pennsylvania. I chose the latter."[19] On May 10, Lee calculated the "aggregate force" commanded by Gen. Joseph Hooker as "more than 159,000 men."[20] Viewing the disparity in military power realistically, Lee recognized that eventual defeat loomed for the Confederacy. At the onset of the Gettysburg Campaign, he authored a frank appraisal of the manpower situation to his president.

> Conceding to our enemies the superiority claimed by them in numbers, resources, and all the means and appliance for carrying on the war, we have no right to look for exemptions from the military consequences of a vigorous use of these advantages...We should not therefore conceal from ourselves that our resources in men are constantly diminishing, and the disproportion in this respect between us and our enemies, if they continue united in their efforts to subjugate us, is steadily augmenting. The decrease of the aggregate [strength] of this army as disclosed by the returns affords an illustration of that fact. Its [combat] effective strength varies from time to time, but the falling off in its [total] aggregate shows that its ranks are growing weaker and that its losses are not supplied by recruits.[21]

Again, the destination of the Army of Northern Virginia during the Gettysburg Campaign was Harrisburg. Lee certainly desired to encourage the Northern peace party, but his true policy in carrying the war across the Potomac was to cross the Susquehanna. After the war he explained to one of General Jackson's staff officers that his desire was to divert the Federal government's attention away from the capture of Richmond and toward the security of Washington. According to William Allan: "He expected therefore to move about, to manoeveur & alarm the enemy, threaten their cities, hit any blows he might be able to do without risking a general battle, & then towards Fall return nearer his base."[22]

Lt. Gen. James Longstreet, Lee's unchallenged senior subordinate, harbored reservations about an offensive into Pennsylvania. He believed that proper policy was to reinforce Johnston, presumably in command with troops from Virginia. Combined with the Army of Tennessee, Johnston could "crush" the Army of the Cumberland then march for the Ohio River, thereby "drawing Grant's army from Vicksburg to look after and protect his own territory." In discussion with Lee, Longstreet opined that an invasion of Maryland and Pennsylvania would not produce the same result because it "would require more time and greater preparation than one through Tennessee and Kentucky." Confronted with Lee's determination to assume the risk, Longstreet "assented" if an offensive strategy was pursued with defensive tactics. "This point was urged with great persistency. I suggested that, after piercing Pennsylvania and menacing Washington, we should choose a strong position, and force the Federals to attack us, observing that the popular clamor throughout the North would speedily force the Federal general to attempt to drive us out."[23] Ten years later, Longstreet elaborated on this policy in a revealing letter to a former subordinate.

> The ruling ideas of the campaign may be briefly stated thus. Under no circumstances were we to give battle, but exhaust our skill to [xx] in trying to force the enemy to do so in a position of our own choosing. The 1st Corps to receive the attack and fight the battle. The other Corps, to then fall upon and try to destroy the Army of the Potomac.[24]

As the campaign developed, the absence of the Army of Northern Virginia's principal cavalry force rendered this plan unworkable.[25] Concerning James Ewell Brown Stuart's absence, General Lee averred: "Had my cavalry been in place my plans would have been very different, and the result I think very different."[26]

Losses in the recent Battle of Chancellorsville compelled General Lee to fill command vacancies in the army, but his overall objective was a new organization. He had long recognized that four or more divisions were difficult to control under battlefield conditions by his corps commanders, Longstreet and Jackson. As he elucidated to President Davis: "These are more than one man can properly handle & keep under his eye in battle in the country that we have to operate in. They are always beyond the range of his vision, & frequently beyond his reach. The loss of Jackson from the command of one half of the army seems to me a good opportunity to remedy this evil." Lee reorganized the Army of Northern Virginia from two corps into three, composed of three divisions each to facilitate field operations. Lt. Gen. Richard S. Ewell received Jackson's former command, the Second Corps. The First Corps (Longstreet) lost Maj. Gen. Richard H. Anderson's division which formed part of the newly created Third Corps led by Lt. Gen. Ambrose Powell Hill. Lee thought Anderson to be an excellent officer who could command a corps "if necessary."[27]

The Light Division, Hill's former command, formed the nucleus of the Third Corps. It was assigned to the newly promoted major general William Dorsey Pender, "an excellent officer, attentive, industrious & brave." Two of Pender's brigades were detached to comprise a new division commanded by Maj. Gen. Henry Heth, of whom Lee had "a high estimate..." A brigade of North Carolinians and one of Mississippians rounded out Heth's division.[28] As senior commander, Longstreet retained control of the First Corps.[29] Lee considered division commander Maj. Gen. John B. Hood a "capital" officer capable of corps command[30] but found fault with the performance of Maj. Gen. Lafayette McLaws during the recent campaign for lack of aggression.[31] Maj. Gen. George E. Pickett had performed creditably as a brigade commander but had never led his division in battle.[32] General Ewell's senior division commander, Maj. Gen. Jubal A. Early, had proven reliable. Before his death, Jackson had commended to General Lee's "particular attention" the service of Maj. Gen. Robert E. Rodes at Chancellorsville.[33] Maj. Gen. Edward "Allegheny" Johnson commanded the Stonewall Division. He had served under Jackson during the Valley Campaign and was wounded May 8, 1862, at the Battle of McDowell while leading his brigade. Johnson's distinguished service impressed General Jackson who wished to employ him as a division commander. General Johnson spent the balance of 1862 in Richmond recovering from his wound and returned to the field following Chancellorsville.[34]

To promote efficiency, the Army of Northern Virginia's artillery batteries had been reorganized in February into battalions and alloted to corps commanders Longstreet and Jackson. Previously, batteries had been assigned to brigades and divisions, which hindered "unity and concentration in battle."[35] The novel arrangement had worked well at Chancellorsville; the Confederate artillery exercised "a direct influence upon the issue of events at every point..."[36] Arrangement of the army into three corps required reshuffling the various battalions and batteries to provide a complement for the Third Corps.[37] Each of the army's nine divisions received a battalion while two others were designated as a corps reserve.[38] Maj. Gen. J.E.B. Stuart remained commander of the cavalry division, composed of five brigades[39] and a battalion of horse artillery.[40]

Few changes had taken place in the reduced First Corps. Its command structure at the brigade and division level was "well organized." In the Second Corps, three new faces led brigades in Johnson's division. Brigade commanders in the divisions of Early and Rodes were generally competent. The Third Corps possessed many experienced and seasoned brigade commanders as well as a large question mark, Joseph R. Davis, nephew of the president, who had never led troops in combat. Generals Hill and Ewell, tested division leaders, were unproven in their new position as corps commanders.

> Of the nine Divisional chiefs, four could be counted as definitely experienced—McLaws, Anderson, Hood and Early. Two were new in their posts, Johnson and Pender; two had been briefly in acting command of Divisions, Rodes and Heth; and one, Pickett, though administering a Division for some months, had never led it in combat. Among the thirty-seven Brigadier Generals of infantry, twenty-five had a measure of experience

at their grade, though neither in experience or ability were they uniform. Six brigades had new leaders; six others were in charge of Colonels. Even with these men of inexperience or doubtful capacity, it was an army command of much prowess under a superlative General-in-Chief...but it lacked Jackson."[41]

Prompted by "Stonewall" Jackson's demise, Lee's reorganization of his divisions became the "turning-point" in the Army of Northern Virginia's history.[42] Though the Army of Northern Virginia remained a potent instrument of war, a critical element, "Stonewall" Jackson's lethal celerity, was missing.

While the Army of Northern Virginia rested and reorganized, General Lee and President Davis corresponded concerning affairs in the West. Writing to Lee on May 26, Davis expressed optimism concerning Vicksburg, even though Grant now besieged the garrison.[43] General Lee replied in a positive vein. "I am glad to hear that the accounts from Vicksburg continue encouraging—I pray & trust that Genl Johnston may be able to destroy Grant's army—I fear if he cannot attack soon, he will become too strong in his position— No time should ever be given them to fortify. They work so fast."[44] Despite receiving heavy reinforcements from Bragg's army and the Department of South Carolina, Georgia, and Florida, Johnston refused to move against Grant.[45] Informed by Davis that Johnston had not yet attacked Grant,[46] Lee replied: "I still hope that General Johnston will be able to demolish Grant, and that our command of the Mississippi may be preserved."[47] A myth associated with the Gettysburg Campaign is the contention that Lee invaded Pennsylvania to influence events in the Mississippi River Valley. Correspondence and reports do not disclose this as a primary purpose for Lee's decision to carry the war into enemy territory.

On June 3, General Hood's division left the Rapidan River line with orders to march north to Culpeper Court House.[48] McLaws' division left the Rappahannock River line the same day. Ewell's Second Corps departed in stages over the next two days.[49] Hill's Third Corps remained around Fredericksburg "to deceive the enemy, and keep him in ignorance of any change in the disposition of the army." A demonstration by a VI Corps brigade at Hamilton's Crossing, south of Fredericksburg, caused Lee to tarry with Hill in order to ascertain Hooker's intentions. He concluded that General Hooker "had discovered the withdrawal of our troops from Fredericksburg and wished to detain us until he could make corresponding changes." The Confederate commander departed Fredericksburg on June 6 and reached Culpeper Court House the next day.[50]

By June 7, Longstreet and Ewell had concentrated their divisions at Culpeper[51] where J.E.B. Stuart had established his headquarters on May 20.[52] Learning of the Confederate concentration of cavalry about Culpeper, General Hooker became concerned that it "may mean mischief...I am determined, if practicable, to break it up in its incipiency."[53] Hooker directed his cavalry commander, Brig. Gen. Alfred Pleasonton, to cross the Rappahannock and attack the Confederate cavalry. At dawn on June 9, the Federals surprised Stuart. The *Beau Sabreur* brought up reinforcements to thwart Brig. Gen. John Buford's First Division and reestablished his line facing east. Pleasonton's Third Division, led by Brig. Gen. David McM. Gregg, moved in from the south and succeeded in capturing Stuart's headquarters on Fleetwood Hill. The Yankee triumph was brief. After disposing of the threat posed by Buford, Stuart galloped south to engage Gregg. Brig. Gen. Wade Hampton's brigade shattered Col. Percy Wyndham's Second Brigade. Gregg's First Brigade counterattacked to retake Fleetwood Hill and achieved fleeting success. Wade Hampton rallied his men, gained reinforcements, then returned to the fight and chased the broken Federals to Brandy Station, whereupon Gregg withdrew his battered division. Pleasonton ordered a general withdrawal of his cavalry corps and by midafternoon the battle ended.[54]

Casualties at Brandy Station (or Fleetwood Hill), the largest cavalry battle waged in North America, were modest by Civil War standards. Stuart, who could claim that he held the field, lost 523 men. The Federal cavalry suffered higher losses including 486 prisoners along with 450 killed and wounded.[55] Though forced to withdraw, Pleasonton's yellowlegs bragged for days "to anyone in earshot that they had surprised, jolted and embarrassed the cream of the Southern cavalry, fighting Stuart to a standstill for half the day and coming within an ace of routing him utterly."[56] Brandy Station's chief result was the bruise administered to J.E.B. Stuart's ego.

The Gettysburg Campaign began with the taste of defeat for Robert E. Lee's proud cavalrymen. After two years of marked inferiority, the Union cavalry emerged from the joust with fresh confidence. According to historian Edward Longacre, the near defeat "had made Stuart's cavaliers, and the Beau Sabreur himself, look bad..."[57] J.E.B. Stuart, who had made the Army of the Potomac's former commander, George B. McClellan, seem inept,[58] "was humiliated more deeply than ever he had been in his campaigning, humiliated and, if not disillusioned, disconcerted. The Federal cavalry...had given as good as they had taken." Even in his own army "there was sarcastic talk of an exposed rear and of a surprise!"[59]

Though he retained Lee's support, critics of Stuart within the army and the Southern press abounded. Acutely conscious of his

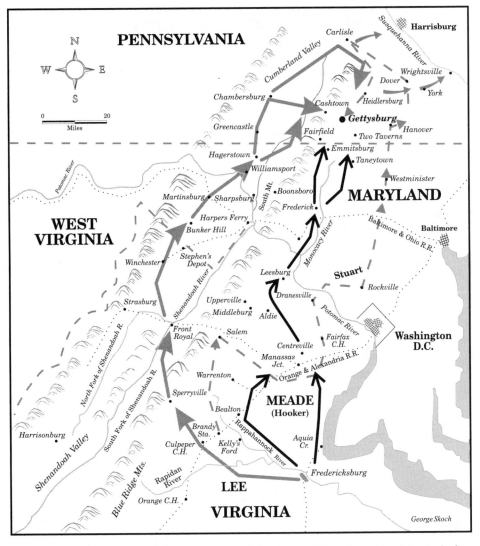

Movements of the Army of the Potomac and the Army of Northern Virginia, including Stuart's cavalry, June 1863

public image, Stuart composed his report on the action to read as though he "had orchestrated the entire day, instead of being twice surprised by enemy columns and recovering only at the cost of desperate fighting."[60] In a postwar letter to Stuart's former adjutant, Henry McClellan, Wade Hampton judged: "Stuart managed badly that day, but I would not say so publicly."[61] Though relieved of his command before month's end, Hooker's decision to confront Stuart's cavalry became an important factor in the outcome of the summer's campaign in the East.

The trek to Pennsylvania commenced June 10. Two days later, Second Corps reached Cedarville, south of Winchester, which was defended by two brigades under Maj. Gen. Robert H. Milroy's command.[62] On June 13, Robert Rodes' division, accompanied by Brig. Gen. Albert G. Jenkins' mounted infantry, moved on Berryville, 10 miles east of Winchester. Detecting Rodes' approach, Col. Andrew T. McReynolds evacuated Berryville and rejoined Milroy at Winchester with his small brigade.[63] Reconnaissance south of Winchester toward Front Royal proved inconclusive to Milroy. He "deemed it impossible" that any part of Lee's army was present, believing that Hooker's headquarters would have informed him if the Army of Northern Virginia had "escaped from the Army of the Potomac..." A captured Louisiana Tiger from Early's division changed Milroy's mind on the evening of June 13; his scattered units consolidated around Winchester.[64]

On June 14, several Confederate brigades attracted Milroy's attention to the south and east while Jubal Early deployed his division against Milroy's principal earthwork, West Fort.[65] Company L, 5th U.S. Artillery, occupied the rather weak bastion with a company from the 116th Ohio and the entire 110th Ohio. Early deployed an artillery battalion behind a ridge to pound the position before assaulting it. Near sunset, with preparations complete, the Rebel artillerists rolled their cannon forward "and opened a terrible fire..."[66]

Taken by surprise, the defenders hugged the ground "and scarcely a head was discovered above the ramparts." The Regulars fired their pieces "wildly..." The Louisiana Tigers, led by Brig. Gen. Harry T. Hays, advanced "slowly and steadily" against scattered fire.[67] The Regulars loosed lethal canister against the attackers "but so overwhelming was their force that it did not appear to have a particle of effect." As the Butternuts stormed the fort, the cannoneers fled—18 escaped. The Ohio infantry resisted briefly before being overwhelmed and withdrew, leaving 40 casualties behind. Capt. Frederick H. Arkenoe, 116th Ohio, "was killed while nobly urging on his men, his face to the foe."[68]

Shortly after West Fort fell, Milroy called a council of war with his brigade commanders. The beleaguered officers resolved to abandon their artillery and wagons, then leave Winchester at 1:00 A.M.[69] As Milroy's men slipped away from the fortifications, "Allegheny" Johnson's three brigades marched to intercept their retreat at Stephenson's Depot, five miles north of Winchester. During the dawn action, the Federal column nearly cut its way through a thin Rebel line. Milroy never coordinated his attacks to allow the full weight of his superior numbers to push aside the Confederates barring escape along the Valley Pike. With the Stonewall Brigade en route and troops running low on ammunition, Johnson exhibited confidence which encouraged his two brigades to remain steadfast against punishing blows on their front and both flanks. "Not realizing that he had the Confederates partially encircled and faltering...Milroy determined to break off the action and retreat." The hour long engagement ended in disaster for Milroy, who escaped to Harpers Ferry. Eleven stands of colors and more than 2,500 prisoners, including officers' wives, fell into Confederate hands. General Johnson contributed to the haul by capturing a group of 30 Yankees. His division lost less than one hundred men.[70]

For an aggregate loss of 269 men, Richard Ewell's corps captured two 24-pounder howitzers, four 20-pounder Parrott rifles, and seventeen 3-inch rifles. Hundreds of loaded wagons and horses were also taken. These captures enabled Second Corps batteries to replace inferior cannon with superior weapons for future combat.[71] General Milroy's total loss of manpower constituted nearly half of the nine thousand soldiers in his division.[72] General Rodes also swept up substantial spoils. Following McReynolds' retreat, Rodes advanced on Martinsburg, which he occupied after a brief skirmish. His command captured a battery, six thousand bushels of grain along with a modest amount of small arms and ammunition.[73] By June 21, with Early at Shepherdstown, Rodes at Hagerstown, and Johnson camped at Sharpsburg, the Second Corps was poised to invade the North.[74] General Ewell's exploit held promise for future success during the incursion into Pennsylvania.

Prior to the fall of Winchester, General Hooker had informed his government that the major portion of Lee's army was marching for the Shenandoah Valley, while Gen. A.P. Hill remained south of the Rappahannock River.[75] On June 5, President Lincoln advised the Army of the Potomac's commander to avoid the temptation of attacking Fredericksburg if Lee left "a rear force" while moving north of the Rappahannock.[76] Five days later Lincoln suggested:

> If left to me, I would not go south of Rappahannock upon Lee's moving north of it. If you had Richmond invested to-day, you

would not be able to take it in twenty days; meanwhile your communications, and with them your army, would be ruined. I think Lee's army, and not Richmond, is your sure objective point. If he comes toward the Upper Potomac, follow on his flank and on his inside track, shortening your lines while he lengthens his. Fight him, too, when opportunity offers. If he stays where he is, fret him and fret him.[77]

Lincoln's sound advice demonstrates his growing grasp of the military art.

Denied freedom of action to assume the initiative against Hill,[78] Hooker divided his army on June 13 into two wings to relocate his line of operations northward for the protection of Washington.[79] By June 15, the Army of the Potomac had concentrated around Fairfax Station, minus II and VI Corps, which marched behind the lengthy wagon train. On June 16, Hooker informed Lincoln of his desire to attack Hill, now moving toward Culpeper, to prevent a junction with Ewell and Longstreet.[80]

The First Corps, strengthened by the addition of Pickett's division, departed Culpeper on June 15 for Winchester. Stuart's cavalry shielded Longstreet's right flank.[81] The Third Corps began withdrawing from the vicinity of Fredericksburg, June 15.[82] A week later the divisions of Longstreet and Hill were encamped about Berryville.[83]

Lee had directed Stuart "to hold the mountain passes with part of his command as long as the enemy remained south of the Potomac, and with the remainder to cross into Maryland and place himself on the right of General Ewell. Upon the suggestion of the former officer [Stuart] that he could damage the enemy and delay his passage of the river by getting in his rear, he was authorized to do so, and it was left to his discretion whether to enter Maryland east or west of the Blue Ridge, but he was instructed to **lose no time** in placing his command on the right of our column as soon as he should perceive the enemy moving northward."[84]

During mid-June, Confederate cavalrymen engaged their Union counterparts in a series of engagements east of the Blue Ridge in Loudoun Valley beginning at Aldie on the seventeenth.[85] An interesting affair occurred at Middleburg that evening where Stuart had established his headquarters. Caught off guard by Col. Alfred N. Duffié's 1st Rhode Island Cavalry around 4:00 P.M., the *Beau Sabreur* was forced to flee with his escort of two squadrons. With the brigades of Wade Hampton and Brig. Gen. William E. "Grumble" Jones on the Rappahannock, Stuart recalled the three brigades operating in Loudoun Valley. The Virginian soon returned with Brig. Gen. Beverly Robertson's nine hundred men to settle the score. The Federals barricaded a barnyard and resisted three attacks. Scouts informed

Colonel Duffié that the countryside swarmed with Rebels. Around 3:30 A.M., Duffié pulled out. He managed to find friendly lines at Fairfax Court House along with four officers and twenty-seven men: two hundred members of the regiment were lost.[86]

The following day, Hooker ordered Pleasonton "to find out where the enemy is, if you have to lose men to do it."[87] Stuart's cavalry division, minus Jones and Hampton, established a line west of Middleburg, June 18. The next day the Rebels faced General Gregg's division which failed to crack the center of Stuart's line. At day's end, Stuart leisurely withdrew his brigades toward Upperville.[88]

Determined to persevere with his mission, Pleasonton decided to throw his corps "at once upon Stuart's whole force, and cripple it up." Pleasonton's goal was Ashby's Gap, west of Upperville. His request for infantry support was answered by Maj. Gen. George G. Meade, who dispatched three brigades of the First Division, V Corps. Pleasonton planned to employ the infantry to engage Stuart's "dismounted sharpshooters" on the Little River Turnpike above Middleburg, east of Upperville. The infantry would clear the way for Gregg's division which would pin Stuart while Buford's brigades outflanked the Confederates north of the turnpike. If Pleasonton's plan succeeded, his combined brigades could force Ashby's Gap and confirm that Rebel infantry no longer operated east of the Blue Ridge.[89]

Col. Strong Vincent's Third Brigade fulfilled the first part of the plan perfectly on June 21. While the 16th Michigan, 44th New York, and 20th Maine skirmished with Stuart's "carbineers" who were protected by stone walls, the 83rd Pennsylvania turned their flank. The dismounted cavalry "fled in confusion," followed closely by the 16th Michigan. The Wolverines captured a disabled Blakely rifle which belonged to Capt. J. F. Hart's South Carolina Artillery.[90]

Stuart intended to withdraw past Upperville to avoid a fight and civilian casualties, but Brig. Gen. Judson Kilpatrick's First Brigade (Gregg) engaged his rear guard. The 5th North Carolina (Robertson) scattered on the streets and a force led by Wade Hampton counterattacked. The Southerners prevailed momentarily until the Northerners rallied to renew the contest. A regiment of Regulars attempted a charge but distance and "marshy ground, intersected by a most difficult ditch," caused their horses to tire before they could reach Hampton's hilltop position. Kilpatrick maintained the pressure on Robertson's brigade and eventually routed the North Carolinians. Stuart led his bloodied battalions away at sundown toward Ashby's Gap, confident that "the enemy lacked the necessary light to peer into the Shenandoah toward Lee's camps."[91]

General Buford's First Division experienced difficulty, north of Upperville, below Goose Creek. Recent rain muddied the trails hampering movement and "Grumble" Jones' unexpected appearance, combined with the water barrier, prevented Buford from turning Stuart's left flank. Buford ordered a countermarch. The Federals recrossed Goose Creek around noon following the receipt of orders to locate Stuart's flank.[92]

Anticipating withdrawal toward Ashby's Gap, Stuart recalled Jones and Brig. Gen. W.H.F. "Rooney" Lee's brigade, commanded by Col. John R. Chambliss Jr. The 11th and 12th Virginia (Jones) delayed Buford's advance but in mid-afternoon his troopers reached the vicinity of Upperville. A Confederate wagon train presented a target of opportunity and Buford ordered Col. William Gamble's First Brigade to attack. Gamble's troopers were stopped by artillery fire and Jones counterattacked fiercely with three regiments driving back the Federals. Col. Thomas C. Devin's Second Brigade engaged the Virginians in turn and forced them to retreat. "Grumble" Jones led his command toward Ashby's Gap followed by John Buford.[93]

> By following Jones toward the mountains at day's close, he managed to place some of his men within hailing distance of Ashby's Gap...several Federals scaled one of the slopes in the fading light and gained the summit. Peering into the valley beyond, they gazed upon a Confederate infantry encampment..."[94]

During the Loudoun Valley engagements, General Stuart did not exhibit his usual behavior in battle. Accustomed to leading by example under fire, "Stuart...was conspicuously absent from the decision-making at the front lines..." His purpose may have been to give combat experience[95] and glory to his subordinates, but Stuart believed that he was a marked man. "It would seem that Stuart's faith in himself may indeed have wavered. So he chose to rest upon past laurels rather than seek new ones."[96] Unfortunately for the Confederacy, Stuart's decision to seek fresh laurels during his next assignment proved pivotal in contributing to the Army of Northern Virginia's most significant defeat.

General Stuart succeeded in his task to screen the Army of Northern Virginia's movements during the opening of the Gettysburg Campaign.[97] The Army of the Potomac made no preparations to follow Lee,[98] even though Hooker knew by June 21 that Confederate troops had entered Maryland "in considerable force..."[99] On June 22, General Meade confided to XI Corps commander, Maj. Gen. Oliver O. Howard: "I don't know what we are going to do. I have had no communication from headquarters for three days."[100] The same day Pleasonton informed Hooker that Buford's scouts "saw a rebel infantry camp about 2 miles long...just below Ashby's Gap."[101] Buford's scouts saw McLaws' division. Receipt of the requested intelligence failed to energize Hooker. Not until June 24, when confirmation that Rebel infantry had entered Pennsylvania reached his head-quarters,[102] did "Fightin' Joe" Hooker issue orders. His army began crossing into Maryland at Edwards Ferry on the morning of June 25.[103] The brigades of Wade Hampton, Brig. Gen. Fitzhugh Lee, and "Rooney" Lee (Chambliss), along with a battery of artillery, were also moving toward the Potomac. After a rendezvous at Salem on June 25, J.E.B. Stuart led his division first southeast and then west through Fairfax Court House. The cavalry column crossed the river at Rowser's Ford at 3:00 A.M., June 28. That night Lee learned from a civilian that the Army of the Potomac was moving north to intercept his army.[104]

OBSERVATION

Multiple objectives influenced Lee's decision to direct his army into Northern territory. He yearned to clear the Shenandoah Valley of invaders, disrupt enemy plans for their summer offensive, and sustain his army upon the untouched farms of Pennsylvania. Another crucial consideration was his desire to remain active rather than allow divisions from his army to reinforce Johnston in Mississippi. The overall objective, however, remained the same as in 1862. Lee wanted to influence Northern public opinion with his army's bayonets. In order to achieve these goals, it was unnecessary to engage in a major battle, but Longstreet's conversations with Lee suggest that possibility was not precluded.

General Lee's decision to assume the offensive involved two distinct choices: attack the enemy in Virginia with two unseasoned corps commanders, or draw the Army of the Potomac into a defensive battle in Pennsylvania. Another Virginia victory would produce a casualty list, and headlines, but would not effect peace. Suitable success in Pennsylvania could open the road to independence. The choice was clear for Lee because the ability of the Confederacy to sustain the war effort was diminishing while Northern manpower and capabilities were increasing. Previous triumphs, the condition of his army, and the goal justified Lee's calculated risk of invasion.

Chapter 2
Stuart's Decision

An army weak in cavalry rarely achieves great success.
Napoleon

General Ewell received orders "to take Harrisburg" on June 21. The next morning his corps entered Pennsylvania's verdant Cumberland Valley. By June 27, they were established in Carlisle, after lingering in Chambersburg for a day "to secure supplies."[1] General Lee intended to employ Ewell's command as a vast mobile force that would "scoop up supplies at a furious pace..."[2] In the van of the army, Ewell's quartermasters harvested the agricultural bounty of south central Pennsylvania without incident.[3] Lee had issued orders to prevent the indiscriminate destruction of public and private property by his army.[4] Though livestock was appropriated and pantries were pillaged, schools, houses, and barns were not torched in the invaders' path for amusement or to retaliate for devastation visited upon the South. Wells and springs were not poisoned. Confederate quartermasters paid for purchases with their government's money. Few Pennsylvania citizens were robbed by the Rebels. Widespread murder and assaults were not reported.[5]

Ewell's soldiers enjoyed their Pennsylvania excursion. A veteran of the Stonewall Brigade recalled:

> ...our quartermasters managed to gobble up everything they came to. They would take the citizens' horses and wagons and load them up with provisions and goods from the stores, consequently we accumulated an immense train. The cavalry were in front, and on our flanks, and they had a good chance for plundering and getting good horses. They made good use of it, too, and came out well supplied; but the infantry got nothing but what we could eat, but we got plenty of that.

Cherries were ripe and plentiful. Rebels on a lark stripped trees of their branches laden with fruit, leaving the trunks.[6]

Operating independently of Ewell's main body, Early's division crossed South Mountain on June 26 to cut the railroad running from Baltimore to Harrisburg and to secure bridges crossing the Susquehanna River. While marching on York, Early—on June 26— caused the iron works owned by Congressman Thaddeus Stevens, a Radical Republican, "to be burnt by my pioneer party." West of Cashtown, Early divided his division. He sent Brig. Gen. John B. Gordon's brigade on a mission to Gettysburg, accompanied by Lt. Col. Elijah V. White's 35th Virginia Battalion (Jones). The other three brigades proceeded east to Mummasburg, a few miles northwest of Gettysburg.[7] "Lige" White's "Comanches" and Gordon's Georgians approached Gettysburg along the Chambersburg Pike, or Cashtown Road. Col. William Jennings, 26th Pennsylvania Militia, saw the enemy in the distance and quickly issued orders for his Sunday soldiers to break camp. Soon the home guards were marching away from Gettysburg. The 17th Virginia Cavalry, detached from Jenkins, caught the 26th toward evening. A skirmish broke out but the emergency men showed the white feather and disappeared.[8]

Early arrived in Gettysburg to find the town under Gordon's control.[9] With an 1860 population of 2,390, Gettysburg had been established by James Gettys 80 years previous. A mid-nineteenth-century writer characterized the town as "unsurpassed for its beautiful scenery and salubrious air. It has ever been esteemed as one of the healthiest districts of Pennsylvania." Seat of Adams County, Gettysburg was "little more than a small market town..." Wheat, barely, corn, oats, and silk were among the county's agricultural products. Apples, cherries, and peaches were plentiful in the summer of 1863.[10] Gettysburg's most important military feature was the network of roads that converged there. "From these unusual facilities for the movement and concentration of large bodies of troops, together with the conformation of the surrounding hills and fields, it would seem as if Gettysburg had been designed by nature for a battle-field."[11]

The Rebels found little at Gettysburg to enlarge their commissary, "but [according to a soldier's faulty recollection] Early did notice a shoe factory in the village and sent word of it to the rear..." Rations intended for the 26th Pennsylvania were issued to Gordon's regiments.[12] Early's division, with Gordon still detached, continued the march on York, June 27.[13] On June 28, John Gordon's brigade passed through York, ignoring the mayor and leading citizens who wished to make a formal surrender of the city. Gordon did send a provost guard to take down the Stars and Stripes displayed on the principal street. The Georgian's destination was Wrightsville on the Susquehanna River. Three or four miles outside of Wrightsville, more Pennsylvania militia were encountered. Unable to outflank the entrenched home guards, Gordon brought up the Courtney (Virginia)

Artillery to shell them out. A "few well-aimed shots" sent the Pennsylvanians flying across the bridge which they fired with inflammable materials placed for the purpose. Gordon's men pursued but were ill-equipped to extinguish the flames that consumed the mile-long span. Part of the town near the bridge caught fire and the Southerners saved Wrightsville from a conflagration.[14] Jubal Early regretted the destruction of the bridge "very much." He wanted to cross the Susquehanna, mount his division on the numerous horses that had accumulated in the vicinity of Lancaster, then move on Harrisburg from the rear as General Ewell approached from the west. "Gettysburg might have been Harrisburg or Philadelphia but for the burning of a bridge."[15]

Back at York, Jubal Early levied a requisition for shoes, socks, hats and rations as well as $100,000. The food, apparel, and most of the shoes were furnished but the authorities provided only $28,600 in cash. Early "was satisfied they made an honest effort to raise the amount called for."[16] As citizens of York and Wrightsville experienced the consequences of war, the First and Third Corps rested around Chambersburg. In 1913, a First Corps veteran, Howard Malcolm Walthall, Co. D, 1st Virginia, recorded his recollection of that period. "...the inhabitants treated us with great respect, and when approached by a dirty, ragged private, invited him to sit at his table for a good square meal. I didn't hear of any aggravated vandalism, but can't vouch for the fate of any pig or rooster who wouldn't get out of the way...the private soldier couldn't unravel the general trend of movements, but if there was anything serious coming on he could sniff it in the air...they would begin to joke about possible results; this one was going to rob every Yankee of his greenbacks, and this one never expected to come out alive, and so on, but generally we were in exuberant spirits..."[17]

The following letter, written by a member of the Third Corps, Col. William S. Christian, 55th Virginia, to "My Own Darling Wife," doubtless expressed the thoughts of many Southern soldiers:

> You can see by the date of this [June 28], that we are now in Pennsylvania. We crossed the line day before yesterday, and are resting to-day near a little one-horse town [Greenwood] on the road to Gettysburgh, which we will reach to-morrow. We are paying back these people for some of the damage they have done us, though we are not doing them half as bad as they done us. We are getting up all the horses, etc., but there are strict orders about the interruption of any private property by individual soldiers.
>
> Though with these orders, fowls and pigs and eatables don't stand much chance. I felt when I first came here, that I would like to revenge myself upon these people for the desolation they

have brought upon our own beautiful home; that home where we could have lived so happy, and that we loved so much, from which their vandalism has driven you and my helpless little ones. But though I had such severe wrongs and grievances to redress, and such great cause for revenge, yet when I got among these people I could not find it in my heart to molest them...I have invariably endeavored to protect their property, and have prevented soldiers from taking chickens even in the main road; yet there is a good deal of plundering going on, confined principally to the taking of provisions. No houses were searched and robbed, like our houses were done, by the Yankees. Pigs, chickens, geese, etc., are finding their way into our camp; it can't be prevented, and I can't think it ought to be. We must show them something of war. I have sent out to-day to get a good horse; I have no scruples about that, as they have taken mine. We took a lot of negroes yesterday. I was offered my choice, but as I could not get them back home I would not take them. In fact my humanity revolted at taking the poor devils away from their homes.

They were so scared that I turned them all loose. I dined yesterday with two old maids. They treated me very well, and seemed greatly in favor of peace. I have had a great deal of fun since I have been here. The country that we have passed through is beautiful, and every thing in the greatest abundance. You never saw such a land of plenty. We could live here mighty well for the next twelve months, but I suppose old Hooker will try to put a stop to us pretty soon. Of course we will have to fight here, and when it comes it will be the biggest on record. Our men feel there is to be no back-out. A defeat here would be ruinous. This army has never done such fighting as it will do now, and if we can whip the armies that are now gathering to oppose us, we will have every thing in our own hands. We must conquer a peace. If we can come out of this country triumphant and victorious, having established a peace, we will bring back to our land the greatest joy that ever crowned a people. We will show the Yankees this time how we can fight.[18]

"Old Hooker" no longer commanded the Army of the Potomac. While the Federal army was concentrating around Frederick, Longstreet's and Hill's divisions were encamped two days' march away in the vicinity of Chambersburg.[19] Hooker's intentions remain unclear but he probably intended moving against vulnerable enemy communications and thereafter govern his movements by Lee's response. To carry out this operation he planned to utilize the garrison at Harpers Ferry under Maj. Gen. William H. French, stationed on Maryland Heights, as well as Maj. Gen. Henry W. Slocum's XII

Corps.[20] On June 26, Hooker telegramed General in Chief Henry W. Halleck and suggested that Maryland Heights be abandoned and French's two brigades reinforce his army. "It must be borne in mind that I am here with a force inferior in numbers to that of the enemy, and must have every man available to use in the field."[21] Hooker inspected Harpers Ferry on June 27. At 10:30 A.M., "Old Brains" Halleck sent Hooker a telegram that emphatically rejected abandonment of Maryland Heights, "except in the case of absolute necessity."[22] Around 2:00 P.M., General Hooker responded to Halleck's telegram regarding Harpers Ferry:

> I find 10,000 men here, in condition to take the field. Here they are of no earthly account. They cannot defend a ford of the river, and, as far as Harper's Ferry is concerned, there is nothing of it. As for the fortifications, the work of the troops, they remain when the troops are withdrawn. No enemy will ever take possession of them. This is my opinion. All the public property could have been secured to-night, and the troops marched to where they could have been of some service. Now they are but bait for the rebels, should they return.

Shortly afterward Hooker fired off another telegram "earnestly" requesting relief "from the position I occupy."[23]

Following his fiasco at Chancellorsville, the Washington government as well as its soldiers lost confidence in Hooker, "and an army does not fight well under a commander in whom it has no faith."[24] General Halleck had cleverly outmaneuvered Hooker and forced a showdown over the latter's authority and freedom of action.[25] Acting swiftly, President Lincoln accepted Hooker's resignation that night and replaced him with a Pennsylvanian, George G. Meade, who carried solid though unspectacular credentials. The Harpers Ferry garrison was placed under Meade's "direct orders."[26] Lincoln gambled by switching horses in midstream during a major campaign and though he was shelved, General Hooker had already contributed to the campaign's successful conclusion by concentrating the Army of the Potomac. His most important contribution to the outcome of the campaign, Pleasonton's foray against Stuart, served to limit Lee's ability to make sound decisions based on timely intelligence because J.E.B. Stuart followed the lure of glory rather than the rule of duty.

General Meade learned of his appointment at 3:00 A.M., June 28.[27] According to Brig. Gen. John Gibbon, the apprentice army commander, "surprised" by his appointment, felt "very heavily" the unsolicited responsibility thrust upon him but "was cheered by the assurances he received of the confidence felt in his ability by the army and the predictions that we would now defeat Lee whenever the armies came in contact." Meade's strategic problem was determining a course of action. "If Lee proposed to invade Pennsylvania he would probably move his whole force northeast and cross the Susquehanna at Harrisburg. If on the contrary, his intention was first to attempt to take Baltimore, with the idea of perfecting afterwards the work of invading Pennsylvania he would move his army southeast." Though complicated, Meade's quandary was mitigated by Stuart's cavalry then threatening Washington, which simplified his need to acquire intelligence concerning Lee's location.[28]

During the last days of June, whenever General Lee encountered General Heth, he invariably inquired about Stuart. "Have you heard anything about my cavalry? I hope no disaster has overtaken my cavalry."[29] On June 23, General Lee had issued instructions to his cavalry chieftain:

> If General Hooker's army remains inactive, you can leave two brigades to watch him, and withdraw with the three others, but should he not appear moving northward, I think you had better withdraw this side of the mountains tomorrow night, cross at Shepherdstown next day, and move over to Frederickstown.

> You will, however, be able to judge whether you can pass around their army without hindrance, doing them all the damage you can, and cross the river east of the mountains. In either case, after crossing the river, you must move on and feel the right of Ewell's troops, collecting information, provisions, &c [etc.].

The commanding general concluded: "...I think the sooner you cross into Maryland, after to-morrow the better...Hill's first division [Anderson] will reach the Potomac to-day, and Longstreet will follow tomorrow."[30]

Evidently, Lee desired his cavalry to perform its customary role of screening infantry divisions and artillery battalions as well as providing intelligence.[31] On June 22, Stuart had received a less ambiguous directive from headquarters. "Do you know where he [the enemy] is and what he is doing? I fear he will steal a march on us, and get across the Potomac before we are aware. If you find that he is moving northward, and that two brigades can guard the Blue Ridge and take care of your rear, you can move with the other three into Maryland, and take position on General Ewell's right, place yourself in communication with him, guard his flank, keep him informed of the enemy's movements, and collect all the supplies you can for use of the army. One column of General Ewell's army will probably move toward the Susquehanna by the Emmitsburg route; another by Chambersburg."[32]

Stuart, however, interpreted his orders differently. Prior to receiving his orders, Stuart had suggested to his superior the desirability of operating east of the Blue Ridge, independent of the main body, where "he could confuse the Yankees as to its whereabouts and intentions, while harassing Hooker in rear and flank and cutting his communications."[33] In a message to Lee, Longstreet condoned Stuart's passing "by the enemy's rear if he thinks that he may get through."[34] In order for the cavalry to link up with Ewell on the Susquehanna, Lee allowed Stuart discretion. Stuart *alone* made the final decision that determined the route and role of the Army of Northern Virginia's principal cavalry element during the campaign's opening. As previously described, Hooker remained *inactive* June 24 and issued marching orders June 25. Clearly, Lee wanted his indispensable cavalry commander to conform his movements to those of the infantry and artillery, yet J.E.B. Stuart pursued a personal agenda to remove tarnish on his record.[35]

General Stuart chose to leave behind the brigades of Robertson and Jones. Robertson, the senior general,[36] received explicit instructions from Stuart.[37] With an undistinguished record, Robertson was thought to be "entirely unpredictable in battle." "Grumble" Jones, an outstanding outpost officer,[38] resented Stuart's seniority; their relationship was not harmonious.[39] It was logical to assign them an inglorious task; Jones had performed similar duty along the Rappahannock with Wade Hampton's brigade the week before.[40]

The problem of seniority should have been resolved and future criticism would have been muted if Stuart had obeyed General Longstreet's *command.* The senior corps commander wrote: "...and order General Hampton—whom I suppose you will leave here in command—to report to me at Millwood..."[41] Wade Hampton, who outranked Beverly Robertson by two weeks,[42] was a superior soldier. Even though "Stuart, like any commander wanted his most competent officers..."[43] to facilitate the success of *his* mission, the South Carolinian could have been spared for the overall good of the expedition into Pennsylvania. Col. Lawrence S. Baker, 1st North Carolina, could have been appointed by Stuart as temporary commander of Hampton's brigade.[44] As events unfolded, Robertson failed to follow the letter of his orders. He ignored communicating with Longstreet; more importantly, he neglected to inform Lee that Hooker was moving north. When the Army of the Potomac left Virginia, Robertson remained on picket duty until June 30. Stuart had instructed Robertson: "...follow the [Confederate] army, keeping on its right and rear." Presumably, Wade Hampton would not have faltered, which explains why Longstreet wanted him left behind.[45] "So Stuart rode on June 25, assuming that Robertson, commanding about 3,000 men, would follow Lee, keep on his right flank, and perform all the tasks Stuart would have if he had been there."[46]

If Robertson failed to follow his instructions from Stuart correctly, the *Beau Sabreur* also ignored the spirit of his own orders.[47] At the beginning of the expedition, the cavalry column encountered Maj. Gen. Winfield S. Hancock's II Corps marching north from Thoroughfare Gap in the Bull Run Mountains toward Gum Springs, Stuart's own destination.[48] At this point, "as Stuart's orders stipulated," the Confederate cavalry should have turned back and crossed the mountains to support the main body.[49] Instead, Stuart unlimbered his artillery to harass Hancock's infantry which deployed and advanced. Satisfied with his show of force, and since "Hancock had the right of way on my road," the Virginian sent Fitzhugh Lee's brigade on a scout. The rest of his horse soldiers spent the day grazing their mounts. Stuart did send a dispatch to headquarters, which was intercepted, "leaving Lee ignorant of Hooker's rapid pursuit."[50]

Had Stuart rejected his notion of a raid, it is probable that he could have reached Emmitsburg, June 29.[51] Even if he had not detected the Army of the Potomac's approach, part of his force would have clashed with Buford's two brigades and perhaps I Corps.[52] This undoubtedly would have changed the course of the campaign. At least one of his brigades would have contributed to earlier success against the Union cavalry on July 1 at Gettysburg. In fairness to Stuart, following Longstreet into the Cumberland Valley would have limited the effectiveness of any reconnaissance. The principal cavalry element, however, would have remained in contact with the main body.[53]

General Lee granted permission to "pass around their army" to disguise the Army of Northern Virginia's advance with the condition: "without hindrance." Hooker had positioned his army from Leesburg to Thoroughfare Gap, therefore, until "the morning of June 25th it was perfectly practicable for Stuart to have done so...Stuart's success depended on preserving the *status quo* of the Federal army until he could get through it. *Hooker was on the defensive waiting for his adversary to move*...When on the morning of the 25th he reached Hooker's rear he found his whole army moving to the Potomac and all the roads occupied by his troops." Hooker's movement was not Stuart's responsibility but he alone decided to proceed with his personal agenda which put his command two days behind the Army of the Potomac.[54] Forced to take a wide detour that delayed the column's entry into Maryland,[55] the Jeff Davis Legion, 10th Virginia, and 2nd South Carolina, were cutting telegraph wires near Washington[56] while the Army of the Potomac was "situated in and around" Frederick.[57] How invaluable to Robert E. Lee would intelligence concerning the approach of the enemy host have been? If Lee had established a defensive position at Gettysburg or Cashtown while Ewell captured Harrisburg, the ensuing clash of arms may have favored the Confederacy with Stuart's cavalry in pursuit of broken Union divisions a la Murat after the Battle of Jena. Those *orders* became J.E.B. Stuart's license to conduct an "independent adventure..." According to Douglas S. Freeman, in Stuart's mind:

> What was possible was permissible. That, as Stuart saw it, was the substance of his orders. So far as the records show, he did not define "hindrance" rigidly in terms of days and hours. He did not realize that he would be hindered most seriously were he delayed in crossing the Potomac to "feel the right of Ewell" and to collect information and provisions.[58]

Stuart's selfishness resulted in a rendezvous with Federal supply wagons at Rockville on June 28. The "one hundred and twenty-five best United States model wagons"[59] became Stuart's "stumbling-block." According to Col. Robert L. T. Beale, 9th Virginia (Chambliss): "The wagons were brand new, the mules fat and sleek and the harness in use for the first time. Such a train we never saw before and did not see again."[60] On June 29, Stuart's raiders[61] moved slowly[62] on and had a brief encounter with home guards. Stuart's troopers tore up tracks of the Baltimore and Ohio Railroad at Hood's Mill and burned a bridge at Sykesville. Though no trains were taken, Stuart boasted in his report: "We remained in possession of the Baltimore and Ohio Railroad nearly all day." In the afternoon, the Confederates[63] trotted toward Westminster where a skirmish flared with two companies of the 1st Delaware Cavalry, which were destroyed. By 5:00 P.M., the town was under Southern control. Stuart decided to remain there long enough to secure forage, parole prisoners, and care for the wounded.[64] He spent the night at Union Mills north of Westminster. During the dark hours scouts discovered enemy cavalry encamped near Littlestown, Pennsylvania. Early in the morning the march to Hanover resumed with Chambliss in the lead followed by the captured wagon train. Hampton's brigade accompanied the wagons while Fitz Lee's regiments watched the left flank.[65]

In the wake of Brandy Station, General Buford retained command of the First Division. The Third Division was combined with Gregg's Second Division.[66] Maj. Gen. Julius Stahel, a Hungarian, commanded the Department of Washington's cavalry. General Pleasanton engineered his removal and the assignment of his division to the Army of the Potomac.[67] Stahel's regiments, reorganized as the Third Division, were given to Judson Kilpatrick.[68] Assuming command on June 29, Kilpatrick's division departed Frederick and proceeded into Pennsylvania, camping for the night at Littlestown. On the morning of June 30, Kilpatrick's two brigades "marched to find the enemy."[69] The Third Division was passing through Hanover around 10:00 A.M. when Stuart's advance guard struck Kilpatrick's rear guard. Initially, Stuart's cavalry confronted only the 18th Pennsylvania and 5th New York,[70] but Brig. Gen. Elon J. Farnsworth returned with the First Brigade reinforcements to support the threatened regiments.[71] Farnsworth led a charge that expelled the Rebels from Hanover[72] and during the rout Stuart was nearly captured. Confederate cavalry regrouped on high ground southeast of Hanover as artillery deployed to check pursuit. Unable to reinforce Chambliss, Stuart waited for his other two brigades to arrive.[73] He admitted in his report on the campaign: "Had it not been for those captured wagons, all three of the Brigades would have been together and could have ended the action quickly."[74]

Wade Hampton's regiments reached the field around 2:00 P.M. to secure Stuart's right flank against Farnsworth. Meanwhile, Fitz Lee encountered the Second Brigade under Brig. Gen. George A. Custer. The Wolverine Brigade, in particular the 6th Michigan, occupied Lee's attention. Dismounted as skirmishers, the 6th Michigan skirmished severely with their foe. Custer and Kilpatrick were unable to organize a concerted attack to break the Rebel line. Content to maintain his lines and unwilling to commit his troops to an attack, Stuart remained on the defensive. He required the cloak of night to disengage his command, then move on toward York, where he expected to find Jubal Early. "Stuart, his timetable more warped now than ever, could not afford another long halt short of Early's headquarters." Fortunately for the Southerners, the Federals broke off the action and encamped.[75]

Stuart's original decision to bring along the U.S. wagons on his excursion had been illogical.[76] Now, in case of an emergency, Stuart grouped his tangible trophies together to destroy them.[77] Still, in this desperate hour, when the fateful battle for the Confederacy would be decided on the ridges around Gettysburg, he was determined to protect his booty, even though he acknowledged in his report that the "wagon train was now a subject of serious embarrassment... "[78] An apologist for Stuart, Mark Nesbitt, imbued with singular insight insists: "He would have burned it then and there, but for Lee's orders. There were those orders. Always those orders."[79] This observation ignores Lee's intentions for Stuart's mission, as expressed to General Ewell:

> I also directed Genl Stuart, should the enemy have so far retired from his front as to permit of the departure of a portion of

the cavalry, to march with three brigades across the Potomac, and place himself on your right, & in communication with you, keep you advised of the movements of the enemy, and assist in collecting supplies for the army...I also directed [Brig. Gen. John D.] Imboden, if opportunity offered, to cross the Potomac, and perform the same offices on your left.[80]

Clearly, Stuart's priority was to acquire intelligence and report same to his superiors. Collecting supplies was a secondary matter.

Undoubtedly, General Lee was concerned about gathering food for his army,[81] but General Meade shared his counterpart's interest in timely and accurate intelligence.

HEADQUARTERS ARMY OF THE POTOMAC,
June 30, 1863.

Commanding Officer Cavalry Corps:

The major-general commanding directs me to say that it is of the utmost importance to him that he receives reliable information of the presence of the enemy, his forces, and his movements...His instructions require him to cover Baltimore and Washington, while his objective point is the army under Lee. To be able to find if this army is divided, and to concentrate upon any detached portion of it, without departing from the instructions which govern him, would be a great object. People in the country are so frightened that he must depend solely on the cavalry for all the information he can gain. He looks to you to keep him informed of their movements, and especially that no force concentrates on his right, in the vicinity of York, to get between him and the Susquehanna, and also that no force moves on his left toward Hagerstown and the passes below Cashtown. Your cavalry force is large, and must be vigilant and active. The reports must be those gained by the cavalry themselves, and information sent in should be reliable. The duty you have to perform is of a most important and sacred character. Cavalry battles must be secondary to this object...[82]

The proximity of Kilpatrick's division, as well as the cumbersome wagon train, necessitated a detour east toward Jefferson in order to reach York.[83] At daylight on July 1, the Confederates arrived in Dover. Stuart allowed his weary command to rest while scouts were sent out to obtain facts concerning Early's whereabouts. Before noon the column was on the march. Stuart had learned that Early's division had left York the day before, moving west for Shippensburg, "which the best information I could get seemed to indicate as the point of concentration for our troops." Hoping to contact part of Ewell's corps north of Shippensburg at Carlisle, Stuart pushed on.[84] Kilpatrick failed to intercept Stuart's column on July 1.

The next day he received orders to move toward Gettysburg and his division "proceeded rapidly across the country in the direction of the firing."[85]

In the evening Stuart's raiders made Carlisle. No Army of Northern Virginia units were there but a force of militia lurked in ambush. Learning of the ruse, Stuart demanded surrender, which Maj. Gen. William F. "Baldy" Smith refused. Stuart repeated his demand and deployed his artillery to emphasize the point. A second refusal to comply with his demand caused Stuart's cannon to open fire. As the horse artillery bombarded Carlisle to no purpose, Stuart's exhausted soldiers slept. Two weeks later, George W. Beale, son of Colonel Beale, described the state of Stuart's command in a letter:

> It is impossible for me to give you a correct idea of the fatigue and exhaustion of the men and the beasts at this time. From great exertion, constant mental excitement, want of sleep and food, the men were overcome, and so tired and stupid as almost to be ignorant of what was transpiring around them. Even in line of battle, in momentary expectation of being made to charge, they would throw themselves upon their horses necks, and even the ground, and fall to sleep...Weak and helpless as we now were, our anxiety and uneasiness was painful indeed. Thoughts of saving the wagons now, were gone, and we began to consider only how, we, ourselves, might escape; but that was not so with that "lady's man," Stuart. He seemed neither to suppose that his train was in danger or that his men were not in a condition to fight.

During the night Stuart received a dispatch from Lee which informed him that there had been fighting at Gettysburg. Stuart ordered his brigades to Gettysburg and rode ahead to rejoin the army.[86]

As Stuart's column threatened Carlisle, Jubal Early's division swept around the right flank of XI Corps to conquer at Gettysburg on July 1. The contribution to the campaign's success by General Stuart's three brigades had been insignificant. If the *Beau Sabreur* had chosen to burn the wagons at Rockville, kept the mules, and refrained from wrecking the railroad, Stuart "could have made Hanover instead of Westminster at a reasonable hour on June 29." After food and rest, it is probable Stuart would have intercepted Early on his march away from York. Instead, Stuart finally returned to the Army of Northern Virginia "on the afternoon of July 2, over sixty hours late, and found himself, rightly or wrongly, in the position of a person who had betrayed a sacred trust."

No individual general in gray caused the Confederate defeat at Gettysburg, yet for many J.E.B. Stuart became the scapegoat.[87] Unquestionably, close contact with the army would have changed

Lee's conduct of the campaign from an intelligence perspective, but not necessarily altered the result of the ensuing battle. Discussion concerning the number of cavalry available to Lee prior to July 1, minus Stuart, clouds the issue, as it is meant to do.[88] General Imboden's small brigade operated against the Baltimore and Ohio Railroad, burning "important bridges" as far west as Cumberland. The Chesapeake and Ohio Canal also received its share of attention from the designated raiders. When Longstreet and Hill reached Chambersburg, General Imboden was ordered back to the army and to collect supplies en route. After relieving Pickett's division at Chambersburg on July 1, Imboden's brigade rejoined the main body at noon, July 3.[89] Though Roberston proved unsuited in the role Stuart assigned him, his failure is a shared responsibility.

> The instructions he received from Stuart misled him. They attempted to cover all sorts of contingencies. In certain points they lacked precision. No stress was laid on the fact that those two brigades were to act as screens to the army, nor was it anywhere indicated that close contact with the army was above all things essential. In fact, the main point was lost sight of, or obscured by references to less important objects, which might well have been left to the initiative of the recipient. If his judgment could not be trusted, he was not a man to whom the command of a detached force, and so important a duty, should have been assigned.[90]

The number of horsemen retained by Lee and available to him is not the issue, since Stuart—not Imboden, Robertson, Jones, or Jenkins—counted as the eyes of the army.

OBSERVATION

J.E.B. Stuart's cavalry division failed in its primary duty to screen the Second Corps and provide the army's commander with intelligence concerning the Army of the Potomac's movements. General Stuart defined his mission in terms of opportunity to raid the enemy concomitant with a personal agenda that tainted his judgment. Stuart's misguided foray in Maryland fundamentally handicapped General Lee's capability to establish his army in a defensive position of his own choice and accept battle.

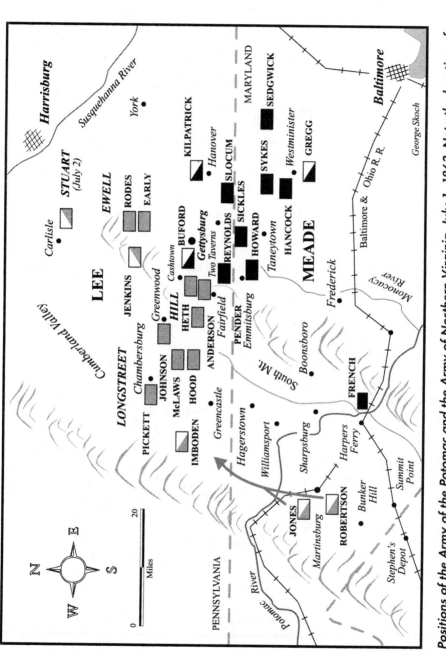

Positions of the Army of the Potomac and the Army of Northern Virginia, July 1, 1863. Note the location of Stuart's cavalry on July 2.

Chapter 3
Reynolds' Decision

*Now boys, raise my head up, give me a drink of water
and go out to your work.*

Maj. Thomas Chamberlin
150th Pa.

Prior to the commencement of the campaign while at Culpeper, General Longstreet provided gold to Henry Thomas Harrison. The spy or scout entered Washington where he socialized with Union officers and followed the Army of the Potomac north. Harrison was arrested by Confederate pickets on the night of June 28.[1] Recognized and escorted to Longstreet's headquarters, Harrison brought startling and vital news. The Army of the Potomac had crossed the river into Maryland. Three Union corps were around Frederick while two others were located near South Mountain. This information animated Longstreet who sent his agent to army headquarters accompanied by Maj. John Fairfax. Accounts differ whether or not Lee actually met with Harrison but he certainly learned the contents of his report.[2] Based on Longstreet's authority, Fairfax vouched for Harrison's reliability, to which Lee responded: "I do not know what to do. I cannot hear from General Stuart, the eye of the army."[3] Five days previous Lee thought that Hooker "was preparing to cross Potomac."[4] The tidings from Harrison, however, were the first solid evidence the principal enemy force in the East was reacting to the Pennsylvania invasion.[5] In this instance, Lee and his army were poorly served by Robertson, who should have provided this information on his way to Pennsylvania. Robertson and Jones rejoined the main body on July 3.[6]

In *Battles and Leaders of the Civil War*, "Old Pete" Longstreet described his army's situation with regard to the fresh intelligence about the enemy:

We then found ourselves in a very unusual condition: we were almost in the immediate presence of the enemy with our cavalry gone. Stuart was undertaking another wild ride around the Federal army. We knew nothing of Meade's movements further then the report my scout had made. We did not know, except by surmise, when or where to expect to find Meade, nor whether he was lying in wait or advancing.[7]

Plans for the Second Corps to capture Harrisburg on June 29 were canceled. To prevent the interdiction of his communications in the Cumberland Valley through Maryland back to Virginia, General Lee ordered his army to concentrate east of South Mountain. He ordered A. P. Hill to move his corps on Cashtown followed by First Corps the next day.[8] Pickett's division remained at Chambersburg to watch the rear while a battery and brigade were detached from Hood's division to picket the road from New Guilford to Emmitsburg.[9] This duty, the proper function of cavalry, would have been assigned to Stuart had he followed Longstreet into the Cumberland Valley.

From Chambersburg, at 7:30 A.M., General Lee's military secretary composed the following dispatch to General Ewell:

GENERAL: I wrote you last night, stating that General Hooker was reported to have crossed the Potomac, and is advancing by way of Middletown, the head of his column being at that point in Frederick County. I directed you in that letter to move your forces to this point. If you have not already progressed on the road, and if you have no good reason against it, I desire you to move in the direction of Gettysburg, via Heidlersburg, where you will have turnpike most of the way, and you can thus join your other divisions to Early's, which is east of the mountains. I think it is preferable to keep on the east side of the mountains. When you come to Heidlersburg, you can either move directly on Gettysburg or turn down to Cashtown. Your trains and heavy artillery you can send, if you think proper, on the road to Chambersburg. But if the roads which your troops take are good, they had better follow you.[10]

Heth's division, leading the Third Corps, reached Cashtown, eight miles northwest of Gettysburg on June 29. Due to the lack of shoes in his division and the false report of a supply at Gettysburg, Heth sent Brig. Gen. J. Johnston Pettigrew's North Carolinians to snatch them.[11] Upon reaching the outskirts of Gettysburg on June 30, Pettigrew observed enemy troops. Unwilling to hazard an attack against a force of unknown size, Pettigrew withdrew and returned to Cashtown.[12] That evening Pettigrew delivered his report to Heth as Hill rode up. Heth instructed his subordinate to repeat his account to the corps commander. Hill and Heth discounted the report of an enemy presence at Gettysburg, "except possibly a small cavalry vedette." Heth declared to Hill, "If there is no objection, I will march my division tomorrow, go to Gettysburg and secure those shoes. Hill replied: 'Do so.'"[13] Hill sent a courier to Lee and also informed Ewell that "I intended to advance the next morning and discover what was in my front."[14] General Hill's decision to reconnoiter toward Gettysburg "was made of his own motion..."[15]

At day's end, June 30, the advantage of position was with Lee. His army, 69,000 strong, was concentrating north and west of Gettysburg. Pender and Heth were camped at Cashtown. Rodes' division rested at Heidlersburg, nine miles from Gettysburg, while Early's troops lay three miles east of that village. "Allegheny" Johnson's division was at Scotland, northeast of Chambersburg. Anderson's men bedded down at Fayetteville, six miles west of Cashtown; the brigades of Hood (minus one) and McLaws were nearby. Pickett's three brigades remained at Chambersburg.[16] Lee's army was massed "in the vicinity of Cashtown, where it would have held a very strong defensive position...if attacked."[17]

On the eve of the battle, June 30, General Meade believed that the disposition of Lee's three corps indicated an advance on Gettysburg.[18] Pettigrew's brief appearance within a mile of Gettysburg on the Chambersburg Pike had been observed by Buford's cavalry division; the intelligence was forwarded to Army of the Potomac headquarters.[19] Thanks to his cavalry, General Meade could alert his corps commanders that the invaders were moving southeast "probably in strong force, on Gettysburg."[20] With his army of 90,000 scattered across northern Maryland, from Emmitsburg to Manchester, Meade ordered his corps commanders to "hold their commands in readiness...to march against the enemy..."[21] Anticipating a clash with Lee, Meade directed his engineers to select a defensive position that could be occupied "by rapid movement of concentration, in case the enemy should cross South Mountain." The point chosen was Pipe Creek, near Taneytown, where Meade established his headquarters on June 30.[22] General Buford, meanwhile, prepared to meet the expected enemy advance on the ridges northwest of Gettysburg.[23]

At 9:00 A.M. on July 1, Heth's division reached the vicinity of Gettysburg via the Chambersburg Pike. Heth deployed his lead brigades on either side of the pike, Davis on the left (north) and Archer on the right (south). Brig. Gen. James J. Archer's Tennesseans and Alabamians were veterans who had rendered distinguished service at Chancellorsville. General Davis commanded a brigade of Mississippians and a regiment of North Carolinians.

Pettigrew's North Carolinians and Col. John M. Brockenbrough's Virginians were held in reserve. The Confederates advanced to "feel the enemy...and determine in what force the enemy were..."[24]

Davis and Archer became embroiled in a fire fight with Buford's First Brigade under Colonel Gamble, supported by Lt. John H. Calef's Company A, 2nd U.S. Artillery. Defenders of McPherson's Ridge "having the advantage of position" resisted stubbornly but were overpowered by numbers after two hours and were relieved by I Corps, led by Maj. Gen. Abner Doubleday.[25]

Maj. Gen. John F. Reynolds, who directed the army's left wing, I, XI and III Corps,[26] reached Gettysburg around 10:00 A.M.[27] At the Lutheran Seminary he consulted Buford, who pledged to hold McPherson's Ridge until infantry support arrived. Returning to the Emmitsburg Road, Reynolds waited for his troops to come up. He sent a dispatch to General Meade that advised his superior he intended to make a stand northwest of Gettysburg. "I will fight him inch by inch, and if driven into the town, I will barricade the streets, and hold him back as long as possible."[28] Reynolds' calculated decision to oppose superior numbers purchased time with blood.[29] If I Corps had been forced to deploy south of Gettysburg on Cemetery Hill, the result "would, in all probability, have been disastrous." With 10 hours of daylight remaining and several divisions converging on Gettysburg, the Rebels would in all likelihood have driven the Federals from their position. With control of roads leading to Gettysburg from the west and north, the triumphant Confederates could have defeated the Army of the Potomac in detail as it marched to the sound of the guns.[30] Indeed, General Lee had anticipated the unfolding scenario according to Maj. Gen. Isaac R. Trimble, who conversed with him on June 25:

> Our forces...can be concentrated on any point east of South Mountain in forty eight hours or less. My plan is to throw an overwhelming force against the enemy's advance, as soon as I learn the road they take, crush them and following up the sweep, beat them in detail, and in a few hours throw the whole army into disorder...I am hourly expecting to hear from Gen. Stuart and our cavalry, and to learn where the enemy crosses the Potomac and what route they take.[31]

Trimble's account contradicts Longstreet but is believable because Lee tended to handle his army aggressively. Though a defensive battle was preferable, Lee's generalship was flexible enough to include a change of plans according to circumstances.

The I Corps began filtering through the fields west of Gettysburg around 10:30 A.M.[32] To contain Davis' brigade, General Reynolds placed the 2nd Maine Battery, Capt. James Hall, between the

Chambersburg Pike and an unfinished railroad bed that cut through McPherson's Ridge. Three regiments of Brig. Gen. Lysander Cutler's Second Brigade, Brig. Gen. James S. Wadworth's First Division, were deployed to the right of the battery north of the railroad cut while the 84th (14th Brooklyn) and 95th New York formed a line on the battery's left, south of the Chambersburg Pike.[33]

The 55th North Carolina (Davis) overlapped the right flank of Cutler's northern element and "moved forward virtually unopposed." Col. John K. Connally's regiment swept on toward the Federal flank and rear.[34] Yankees found themselves in a tight spot. Scores were captured by the 2nd and 42nd Mississippi Regiments. The 56th Pennsylvania lost a flag as well.[35] General Wadsworth ordered the exposed regiments to retreat but the 147th New York remained on the field. Lt. Col. Francis C. Miller could not issue the order "being wounded at the moment of receiving it." As the 56th Pennsylvania and 76th New York regrouped on Seminary Ridge, the 147th New York continued fighting. According to Lt. J. Volnay Pierce of Company G: "We were now nearly surrounded and the fight was very hot—" Before being relieved, the Empire State regiment lost 207 men, in half an hour.[36]

During the advance across winding Willoughby Run and the ascent of McPherson's Ridge, General Archer's four regiments separated into two wings. The 1st Tennessee (Provisional Army) and 13th Alabama, accompanied by General Archer, were on the right. The 7th and 14th Tennessee comprised the line's left. "...Archer being dismounted, the brigade was without a commander. The general could direct what he could see, but his view was restricted."[37] He neglected basic tactics and led his troops into a trap because a skirmish line did not precede the main line to detect danger.[38] This fundamental failure of leadership, repeated a few hours later by another Confederate brigade commander, resulted in disaster and grief for families in North Carolina.

While Cutler's brigade contended with Confederates north of the Chambersburg Pike, Brig. Gen. Solomon Meredith's Iron Brigade (Doubleday) appeared on the field. General Reynolds challenged the 2nd Wisconsin, shouting: "Forward men, forward for God's sake and drive those fellows out of the woods..."[39] Without hesitation, the veterans of First Manassas and Antietam Creek "charged with the utmost steadiness and fury..."[40]

Lieutenant Calef's battery came under fire from Archer's left wing which had infiltrated McPherson's Woods.[41] When the 2nd Wisconsin reached the ridge's crest, the regiment received a volley from a distance of less than 50 yards that dropped "many officers and men," including Lt. Col. George H. Stevens who fell mortally wounded.[42] Undaunted, the Badgers pressed forward into the timber to tangle with the 14th Tennessee, Archer's most advanced regiment.[43] General Reynolds, trailing the 2nd Wisconsin,[44] "was shot through the head, as was supposed, by a Rebel sharpshooter, and died shortly afterwards."[45]

The 2nd Wisconsin continued advancing "in the face of a most terrific fire of musketry..." Lucius Fairchild, colonel of the regiment, suffered a shattered left elbow.[46] The Rebels found themselves outflanked on the right[47] by the 7th Wisconsin which broke the Tennessee line.[48] Maj. John Mansfield, now leading the 2nd Wisconsin, refused to allow the Tennesseans time to reform and ordered pursuit. The regiment "captured a large number of prisoners," including an "exhausted" General Archer.[49] Patrick Mahoney, Company G, collared the first general captured from Lee's army since he had assumed command.[50]

Archer's right wing suffered the same fate as the left wing when the 24th Michigan and 19th Indiana swept across their right flank.[51] To W. H. Bird, Company C, 13th Alabama: "It seemed to me there were 20,000 Yanks down in among us hallowing surrender...and of course I had to surrender." Other Alabamians fled in the direction of the 1st Tennessee. Shoved back by the Hoosiers and Michiganders, the Rebel regiments ran down the ridge.[52] The 7th Wisconsin rushed after them in conjunction with the 19th Indiana and 24th Michigan.[53] Dozens of Rebels fell into their hands as Archer's survivors sought safety on Herr Ridge where the rest of the division remained.[54]

General Doubleday assumed command on the field when John Reynolds fell. As the contest for McPherson's Ridge evolved, Doubleday retained the 6th Wisconsin under Lt. Col. Rufus R. Dawes and the brigade guard, two officers and one hundred men, as a reserve.[55] His decision proved prudent for the Iron Brigade and the Union. Flushed with victory, Davis' brigade surged after the 76th New York and 56th Pennsylvania. The 2nd Mississippi closed in on the 2nd Maine Battery and captured a gun. "At this critical moment Davis lost control of his brigade and the pursuit quickly became disorganized. Two of his three regimental commanders were down, and the pursuit was directed by exuberance more than discipline."[56]

Doubleday sent orders for Dawes to contain the developing threat to the Iron Brigade's rear with his reinforced regiment. The Yankees ran toward the Chambersburg Pike and resting their rifles on a fence, fired a volley that ripped through the Southern ranks.[57] Maj. Alfred H. Belo, 55th North Carolina, was "impressed with the fact that the side charging first would hold the field..."[58] The flight of fatal missiles "checked" the Rebels, who "rallied, and made a run

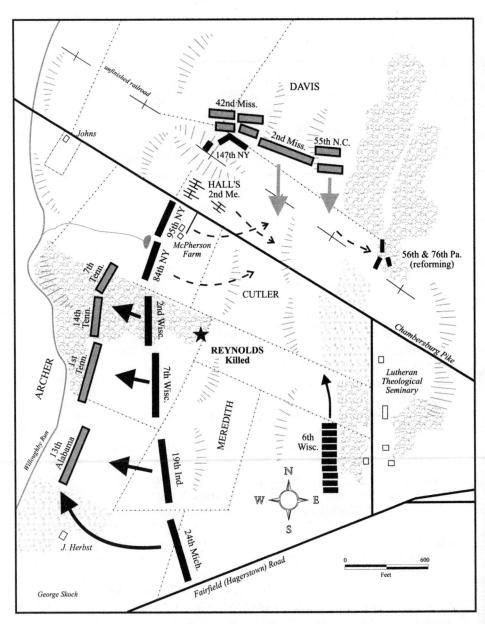

Repulse of Davis and Archer by the I Corps, northwest of Gettysburg, July 1, 1863

for the cover of the Railroad Cut from which they opened...a murderous fire." Knowing that his command could not prevail in a duel of musketry, Dawes chose to charge. Shouting: "Forward double-quick Charge," "Align on the Color..." Dawes' force climbed two fences to close with the enemy, "a sure test of metal and discipline." To the left and rear of the 6th Wisconsin, elements of the 84th and 95th New York contributed their numbers to the attack.[59]

Within the deep de facto trench, Maj. John A. Blair, 2nd Mississippi, attempted to organize a defense from jumbled companies.[60] In moments, Blair and his soldiers learned the "dreadful limitations" their sanctuary provided.[61] Adj. Edward P. Brooks, 6th Wisconsin, "with promptness and foresight," directed a detachment to plug the south end of the cut, trapping Confederates.[62] As Federals closed on the cut from the west, a group rushed toward William B. Murphy who carried the 2nd Mississippi's flag. The color guard shot down more than a dozen attackers before being eliminated. Murphy tore the flag from its staff[63] but Cpl. Francis A. Weller, Company I, 6th Wisconsin, seized Murphy and claimed his colors.[64] When the line of Yankees reached the edge of the cut, "all shouted, 'surrender,' 'throw over your arms.'" Dawes entered the cut and received the sword of Major Blair, along with swords from six other officers.[65] Maj. John F. Hauser turned over to the provost guard "7 officers and about 225 men."[66]

Most of Davis' troops escaped the Railroad Cut. Due to its "shattered condition" the brigade saw little action again that day. In his report on his division's performance up to that point, General Heth noted: "The enemy had now been felt, and found to be in heavy force in and around Gettysburg." Heth established another line of battle on the right side of the pike and waited for reinforcements to renew the contest.[67]

Davis' rout around noon "saved" the 147th New York,[68] which reformed on the Chambersburg Pike near Seminary Ridge and later returned to the fight.[69] General Doubleday re-established the First Division's initial battle line[70] as Brig. Gen. John C. Robinson's Second Division and the Third Division, Brig. Gen. Thomas A. Rowley, came up, accompanied by a brigade of artillery. Initially, Robinson's regiments remained near the seminary in reserve while Col. Roy Stone's three Pennsylvania regiments (Rowley) extended the right flank of the Iron Brigade on McPherson's Ridge. The 19th Indiana anchored the brigade's left flank; Col. Chapman Biddle's four regiments (Rowley) were *en echelon* behind the Western men.[71]

During the early afternoon lull, more Union troops arrived to strengthen the defense of Gettysburg. General Howard, senior to Doubleday, assumed command of troops on the field, including his own XI Corps. He directed his Second Division under Brig. Gen. Adolph von Steinwher to hold Cemetery Hill as a "rallying point" in case of a reverse. Howard's decision demonstrated discernment as well as foresight. The First Division, Brig. Gen. Francis C. Barlow, and Third Division, Brig. Gen. Alexander Schimmelfennig, were deployed north of Gettysburg under the overall direction of Maj. Gen. Carl Schurz. The two divisions held a weak position because the four brigades were insufficient to maintain an extended line. Col. George von Amsberg assumed command of Schimmelfennig's First Brigade.[72]

On the morning of July 1, General Lee rode from Greenwood to Cashtown, where he intended to establish his headquarters, and "probably" learned of the engagement at Gettysburg from the sound of artillery fire.[73] Upon reaching Cashtown about 11:00 A.M., he consulted with Hill, who provided "few answers to Lee's inquires." Hill hastened to Gettysburg to obtain facts concerning the unsettling situation. Lee then spoke with General Anderson, whose division had arrived at 10:00 A.M.:

> I cannot think what has become of Stuart; I ought to have heard from him long before now. He may have met with disaster, but I hope not. In the absence of reports from him I am in ignorance as to what we have in front of us here. It may be the whole Federal army, or it may only be a detachment. If it is the whole Federal force we must fight a battle here; if we do not gain a victory, those defiles and gorges through which we passed this morning will shelter us from disaster.

The Confederate commander set off for Gettysburg to investigate the artillery fire's significance.[74] Unaware Heth had stumbled into the Army of the Potomac, Lee "*could not believe it*, as Stuart had been specially ordered to cover his (Lee's) movement & keep him informed of the position of the enemy, & he (Stuart) had sent no word."[75] In the afternoon Anderson received orders to move on Gettysburg, which indicates that morning Hill had not expected serious resistance to his reconnaissance.[76]

Two more battle-tested divisions, both from Ewell's corps, were converging on Gettysburg. Jubal Early's division approached from the northeast on the Heidlersburg Road while Robert Rodes' division, marched along the Middletown Road.[77] General Rodes' regiments arrived on Oak Hill, formed by the conjunction of Oak Ridge and McPherson's Ridge, around noon.[78] He deployed his division on Oak Ridge and observed an opportunity to strike the I Corps flank.[79] Apparently, Rodes personally reconnoitered his avenue of approach against his intended target, Stone's brigade on McPherson's Ridge.[80] "The situation seemed ideal. Rodes was pointed squarely at a vulnerable

Federal point, he had a wooded ridge to cover his approach, and the height of his protecting ridge assured him of a commanding position whenever he established hostile contact."[81]

Warned by cavalry of Rodes' approach, General Doubleday[82] sent one of Robinson's brigades to hold Oak Ridge, an extension of Seminary Ridge, on Stone's left. Due to the advanced position of XI Corps, a "wide interval" existed between the two corps.[83] Brig. Gen. Henry Baxter's Second Brigade established a line shaped like an inverted *V*. Three regiments, the 83rd New York, 90th and 88th Pennsylvania, were posted along the Mummasburg Road to form the right shank of the *V*. The 12th Massachusetts held the apex of the *V*. The 11th Pennsylvania and 97th New York formed the left shank and enjoyed the advantage of being behind a stone wall. Brigaded for only six weeks, Baxter's regiments had never fought together.[84] Fragments of Cutler's brigade occupied the woods below Baxter's position, perpendicular to his left flank.[85]

General Rodes arranged his attack carefully, sending Georgians under Brig. Gen. George P. Doles to contain the XI Corps and secure the left flank. Next to Doles, Col. Edward A. O'Neal's Alabamians were in line and to their right were the North Carolinians commanded by Brig. Gen. Alfred H. Iverson Jr. Another Tar Heel brigade, under Brig. Gen. Junius Daniel, was positioned on the extreme right of Rodes' battle line with the intent of supporting Iverson or attack as circumstances directed. A third brigade of North Carolina troops led by Brig. Gen. Stephen D. Ramseur remained in reserve.[86] Rodes retained the 5th Alabama as a reserve to occupy the space between O'Neal and Doles. O'Neal evidently believed that the 3rd Alabama was also under the division commander's direct control. Consequently, O'Neal's dispersed brigade confronted Baxter's six regiments with only the 6th, 12th, and 26th Alabama Regiments. Compounding the confusion, Colonel O'Neal chose to remain in the rear with the 5th Alabama. He did not supervise his brigade, which failed to move in the direction Rodes had personally indicated and "enfilade the Federal position."[87] Rodes' attack commenced at 2:30 P.M.,[88] but Alabama's participation was brief. Baxter's right regiments engaged O'Neal's three regiments as did the left wing of the 45th New York (von Amsberg), acting as skirmishers on the extreme left flank of the XI Corps. Company I, 1st Ohio Artillery, Capt. Hubert Dilger, added to the agitation among the Alabamians.[89]

Seeing his attack faltering, Rodes ordered the 5th Alabama forward in support,[90] but the 6th Alabama on the brigade's left was exposed to the fire of the 45th New York and fell back. Their withdrawal caused the 12th and 26th to follow. The Alabamians rallied[91] near the McClean Farm. Four companies of the 45th New

York, covered by heavy artillery fire, charged the concentration of demoralized Rebels.[92] Samuel B. Pickens, colonel of the 12th Alabama, stated in his report: "It was impossible for us to hold the position we had gained any longer without being cut to pieces or compelled to surrender, the enemy having advantage of us in numbers and position."[93]

The Alabamians were driven back before Iverson's brigade stepped off which deprived the Carolinians of support on their left flank.[94] According to historian Warren Hassler: "The fact that these two Confederate brigades did not attack Baxter simultaneously probably saved the Federals from defeat at this time."[95] From right to left, the 12th, 23rd, 20th, and 5th North Carolina Regiments advanced as evenly as though on parade. After disposing of O'Neal, Baxter shifted his regiments to counter this new threat and formed a continuous line.[96] Iverson, who also remained in the rear, did not employ a screen of skirmishers to steer his brigade. With each stride across the meadow, the unsuspecting Confederates inserted themselves deeper into a killing zone.[97] Deprived of a general to maintain their alignment, the brigade closed on the stone wall in oblique fashion, the left being closer to the quiescent Yankees than the right.[98] In the opinion of a survivor from Company F, 12th North Carolina: "Iverson's men were uselessly sacrificed. The enemy's position was not known to the troops. The alignment of the brigade was a false one, and the men were left to die without help or guidance."[99]

Baxter's people waited until the Southern line rose from a swale, then opened fire on their unwary targets at less than one hundred yards. Cutler's regiments also fired with effect.[100] At close range, Yankee bullets hit both flanks and the brigade front with "a pitiless fire."[101] Bullets from a thousand muskets left hundreds of men dead or wounded, lying "on a line as straight as a dress parade..."[102] In the 5th North Carolina, which had lost its field officers at Chancellorsville, the four surviving captains went down.[103]

Watching from a safe distance, General Iverson thought he saw "handkerchiefs raised," in token of surrender.[104] He reported to General Rodes that one of his regiments had "gone over to the enemy..."[105] Actually most of the prone figures were dead or wounded, "and the ones doing the feeble signalling were the trapped survivors trying to give up."[106] Perceiving an opportunity, the 83rd and 97th New York charged along with the 88th Pennsylvania. Many prisoners were taken as well as three flags.[107] Captives and captors soon scurried back to the stone wall. Another Confederate attack was developing. As Baxter's brigade resumed its place on Oak Ridge, Brig. Gen. Gabriel R. Paul's First Brigade (Robinson) began deploying[108] to protect Baxter's flanks.[109]

The 5th, 20th, and 23rd North Carolina had been "almost annihilated..."[110] Because of its position on the brigade's right flank, the 12th North Carolina suffered less than the other regiments.[111] Lt. Col. William S. Davis moved his men away from the slaughter "by the right flank to a little bottom in a wheat field." Later Davis attached his companies to Ramseur's brigade.[112] When General Rodes ordered Ramseur to support both Iverson and O'Neal,[113] Col. Cullen A. Battle "offered" Ramseur the 3rd Alabama.[114] The 2nd and 4th North Carolina went to O'Neal's assistance while the 14th and 30th North Carolina "prepared to carry the stone wall." Two of Iverson's line officers explained to Ramseur how to avoid the enfilade fire that had wrecked their brigade.[115]

General Paul's five regiments prepared to meet the next assault alone since Baxter's brigade, low on ammunition, had left the area.[116] The First Brigade's line had assumed the shape of an inverted *V*. Two regiments, the 104th New York and 13th Massachusetts, faced east. The 107th Pennsylvania, 16th Maine, and 94th New York held the stone wall.[117] Ramseur's first attack "was hurled back with loss."[118] Ramseur regrouped his regiments, including Iverson's remnants and O'Neal's command, to renew the effort. His second attack routed the Federals. The 14th and 30th closed on the stone wall perpendicularly, then wheeled to the left on the run while the 2nd and 4th swept forward on the right rear to catch the Federals while changing front.[119] Despite Rodes' inability to synchronize the attack of Iverson and O'Neal, his division cleared Oak Ridge, thanks to Ramseur's tactical dexterity.[120]

Historians contend that keeping Ramseur's crack brigade in reserve during the initial attack instead of substituting it for either Iverson or O'Neal proved a costly mistake.[121] Considering the stubbornness of Robinson's division, that is uncertain but Ramseur would have employed skirmishers and avoided Iverson's disaster. As commander of the 26th Alabama, Edward O'Neal's "gallant conduct" at Malvern Hill and "gallantry" at Antietam had been noted in reports by his superiors.[122] O'Neal led Rodes' old brigade at Chancellorsville. In his May battle report, General Rodes stated that O'Neal "deserves especial notice for his gallantry."[123] A commission for Colonel O'Neal's promotion to brigadier general dated June 6 was received at Lee's headquarters. Prior to the invasion, however, General Rodes blocked the promotion and President Davis subsequently canceled it.[124]

Alfred Iverson had been recommended for promotion by "Stonewall" Jackson and Maj. Gen. Daniel Harvey Hill, who wrote in his endorsement: "Colonel Iverson is in my opinion the best qualified by education, courage, and character of any colonel in the service for the appointment of brigadier general."[125] Iverson received his promotion in November 1862.[126] During the Battle of Chancellorsville Iverson led his brigade until "I received a contusion from a spent ball which made walking very painful..." Near the end of the action, Iverson left the field while his brigade was still under fire. His officers, who disliked the Georgian, broadcast he was a coward. At Carlisle, Iverson became drunk. "It was possibly the first time his brigade had seen him drunk and probably the last, but the impression of his overindulgence was lasting..." Iverson was not a coward nor was he drunk at Gettysburg. "He was most likely in the process of conferring with General Daniel as to the direction of the assault when his brigade received the sudden and devastating volley and went to ground."[127]

Both O'Neal and Iverson, like Archer, were capable combat officers who acted incompetently at Gettysburg. This condition afflicted the Confederate officer corps throughout the campaign. The former commander of Rodes' division, D. H. Hill, would have cleared Oak Ridge of Yankees precipitately and stormed into Gettysburg. According to one Confederate general, "There was never a harder fighter than Gen. D. H. Hill."[128] Hill left the Army of Northern Virginia because he irritated Lee and his brother-in-law, "Stonewall" Jackson, to assume command of the Department of North Carolina.[129] During the Maryland Campaign a vital dispatch addressed to Hill was lost which disrupted Lee's plans. Lee was of the opinion that "D.H. Hill had such a queer temperament he could never tell what to expect from him, & that he croaked."[130] Hill's transfer may have contributed heavily to Confederate defeat at Gettysburg.

Ramseur's success aided the effort of Junius Daniel[131] who had failed to drive Colonel Stone's brigade. Arrayed along the Chambersburg Pike to defend the Railroad Cut, the Pennsylvanians had repelled three attacks, assisted by Cutler's survivors.[132] A line of batteries organized near the seminary by Col. Charles S. Wainwright, I Corps chief of artillery, demolished Daniel's attacks with "a destructive fire of canister and shell."[133]

As Robinson's men resisted Rodes' continuous attacks, the defenders of McPherson's Ridge faced a renewed onslaught backed by overwhelming artillery superiority.[134] Brockenbrough's Virginians advanced upon the Iron Brigade's right flank. Pettigrew's brigade brought the fight to the 24th Michigan and 19th Indiana as well as Chapman Biddle's brigade. While the 11th and the 26th North Carolina pressed the Iron Brigade's left and center, the 47th and 52nd North Carolina shattered Biddle's line with musketry "at a distance not greater than 20 paces."[135] Biddle's position, *en echelon* behind the Iron Brigade, allowed the 11th North Carolina to outflank the 19th Indiana which suffered heavily.

Private Wes Payton was struck by a musket ball in the abdomen, turning him in a series of somersaults. His eyes bulged

out and he called to his friend, Private Moore, "Robe, I'm shot!"
He looked down, expecting to find a gaping fatal wound, and
saw that the bullet had struck a brass button on his frock coat,
saving his life.[136]

The Hoosiers held their line "until the fire of the flanking column on
our left had almost annihilated the regiment."[137]

The 24th Michigan engaged in a sanguinary duel for control of
the high ground with the 26th North Carolina who "came on with
rapid strides, yelling like demons." Due to the 19th Indiana's withdrawal, the 24th Michigan's left flank became exposed.[138] Forced to
fall back due to the tactical disadvantage, the Wolverines established successive lines of resistance. They inflicted extremely heavy
casualties upon their antagonists but were in turn dropped in rows
of blue. Losses mounted in the 26th Carolina as the color guard fell
to a man. To sustain the momentum of his stalled attack and rally
his regiment, Col. Henry K. Burgwyn Jr. carried the colors until he
received a mortal wound.[139] Burgwyn's regiment, eight hundred
strong, lost 549 men; Company C was wiped out.[140] The 24th Michigan lost 67 killed and a total loss of 363 men, the greatest total
number of any Union regiment during the three days at
Gettysburg.[141] General Heth also became a casualty when a bullet
passed through his new, oversized hat. A paper lining "broke the
outer coating of my skull and cracked the inner coating, and I fell
senseless."[142]

In contrast to I Corps, which fought for hours and chewed up
successive Confederate units, XI Corps crumbled quickly.[143] Upon
"arriving in sight" of Gettysburg, General Early immediately ordered
forward artillery and his infantry went into line.[144] Gordon's brigade, assisted by Doles, pummeled Barlow's division and sent it reeling rearward, its "regimental organizations having become destroyed."
Barlow fell trying to rally his men, paralyzed by a bullet. Col. Wladimir
Krzyzanowski's Second Brigade (Schimmelfennig) came up and formed
a line to arrest the Confederate advance. The Georgians commanded
by Doles and Gordon overwhelmed them with musketry. The 75th
Pennsylvania lost 111 killed and wounded in 15 minutes. Survivors
of the brigade retreated to the town's northern limits.[145] Another
brigade of three regiments (von Steinwher) led by Col. Charles R.
Coster established a line behind a partial stone fence on the outskirts of Gettysburg "to cover the retreat."[146]

Jubal Early observed this obstacle to Gordon's further advance
"and ordered him to remain stationary" as Hays' Louisianians and
Hoke's North Carolinians, led by Col. Isaac E. Avery, assailed Coster's
weak brigade.[147] The 27th Pennsylvania, 154th and 134th New York
occupied a brickyard below a slope that afforded the attackers a
tactical edge. Advantage accrued to the Rebels because their line

extended beyond the defender's left flank. Though momentarily halted by canister blasts from Company K, 1st Ohio Artillery, and "very destructive fire" from Coster's men, the onrushing Rebels closed with the Federals. Fighting became hand to hand as the 57th North Carolina swept around the 134th New York's rear and smashed it with gunfire. Under orders from Coster, the 27th Pennsylvania pulled out leaving the 154th New York to its fate. When the survivors of the 154th rallied on Cemetery Hill, a jaded squad of 18 officers and men remained.[148]

Coster's rout ended organized resistance by XI Corps northeast of Gettysburg and coincided with the final attack against I Corps when Hill ordered forward Dorsey Pender's fresh division.[149] Due to the XI Corps collapse and Rodes' advance, Robinson's division faced destruction on Oak Ridge. Outflanked on the right and left, General Robinson ordered his brigades to retreat around 4:15 P.M.[150] The 16th Maine (Paul) conducted a heroic rear guard action to delay the enemy and sacrificed themselves for the Union. Their "suicide stand" allowed Robinson's battered division to retreat on Cemetery Hill relatively unmolested; the 16th lost more than 160 prisoners.[151] The 13th Massachusetts (Paul), running out of ammunition, waited for orders as XI Corps dissolved to their right.

> The order was given to rally on Cemetery Hill. While some of the boys fell back along the railroad cut, others went directly through the town to the hill. Those who went through the town were obliged to run the gauntlet of the side streets, already filled with the men of Ewell's corps...Over fences, into yards, through gates, anywhere an opening appeared, we rushed with all our speed to escape capture. The streets swarmed with the enemy, who kept up an incessant firing, and yelling, "Come in here, you Yankee ——— ——!"
>
> The great trouble was to know where to run, for every street seemed to be occupied by the "rebs," and we were in imminent danger of running into their arms before we knew it. There was no time to consider; we must keep moving and take our chances; so on we went until at last, completely blown, we reached the hill occupied by the batteries of the Eleventh Corps. In spite of our efforts, ninety-eight of the Thirteenth were captured.[152]

Lysander Cutler's brigade joined the general exodus. Receiving fire on both flanks, the New Yorkers and Pennsylvanians "suffered severely..."[153] Lt. Clark Scripture established a section of Dilger's battery near the "Diamond" to assist the retreating regiments.[154] The XI Corps retreated in relatively good order until the Federals found themselves confounded by the unfamiliar streets. In the chaos that followed, hundreds were captured.[155] At the college, the 45th

New York covered the Third Division's retreat, withdrawing when "it was evident that to stay much longer would be certain destruction." Panic overtook a column of fugitives when the 45th was in the middle of the "Diamond." In an attempt to extricate themselves from the confusion, the New Yorkers went several blocks east. Heading into an alley, they received a searing fire. "Unfortunately this alley led into a spacious yard surrounded by large buildings, which only offered an entrance, but no way to pass out, excepting a very narrow doorway, to freedom and heaven; but the enemy's sharpshooters had already piled a barricade of dead Union soldiers in the street in front of this doorway. About 100 of the Forty-fifth Regiment extricated themselves from this trap, ran the gauntlet and arrived safely at the graveyard."[156] The 45th New York lost 178 missing and captured, the greatest amount for any Union regiment engaged at Gettysburg.[157]

General Schimmelfennig's horse was shot down in alley off Baltimore Street. With Rebels in sight, the general cleared a fence and hid for the next two days behind a woodpile.[158] At least three thousand other Federals were captured or missing, most from I Corps.[159]

The Iron Brigade's last stand occurred at "the barricade," 40 yards below Seminary Ridge, "a slight breastwork of loose rails" that Robinson's division had thrown together before entering the fight.[160] Biddle's brigade occupied the area south of the seminary. The Western men held the center while Stone's battered brigade, now led by Col. Edmund L. Dana, 143rd Pennsylvania, defended the line up to the East Railroad Cut.[161]

With Brig. Edward L. Thomas' brigade in reserve,[162] Pender's division charged the I Corps survivors. On Pender's right, dismounted cavalry held "a portion of a stone wall...under cover of trees." Five North Carolina regiments under Brig. Gen. James H. Lane were neutralized by William Gamble's cavalry brigade.[163] On the opposite flank near the Chambersburg Pike, North Carolinians led by Brig. Gen. Alfred M. Scales were "raked" by enfilade fire directed from Company B, 4th U.S. Artillery, Lt. James Davison.[164] Describing his brigade's experience on July 1, Scales wrote:

> ...the brigade encountered a most terrific fire of grape and shell on our flank, and grape and musketry in our front. Every discharge made sad havoc in our line, but still we pressed on at a double-quick until we reached the bottom, a distance of about 75 yards from the ridge we had just crossed, and about the same distance from the college, in our front. Here I received a painful wound from a piece of shell, and was disabled. Our line had been broken up, and now only a squad here and there marked the place where regiments had rested.[165]

Many companies lost their officers. Heavy casualties among field officers contributed to brigade disorganization.[166] Sheltered by "the feeble barricade of rails" parts of I Corps continued resisting the attackers in a single line, with no reserves.[167]

Col. Abner Perrin's South Carolinians achieved the decisive breakthrough in the center. Ordered not to fire their weapons during the advance, Perrin's people endured "a furious storm of musketry and shells..." Having checked Scales' brigade, the Federals directed their fire toward the South Carolinians, who received an intense blast of musketry within two hundred yards of the barricade. Every color sergeant in the brigade perished; it seemed as though the 14th South Carolina "was entirely destroyed." Discarding their knapsacks and blankets, the Carolinians were inspired by their mounted leader's "courage as defied the whole fire of the enemy, (naturally drawn to his horse, his uniform, and his flashing sword) the brigade followed, with a shout that was itself half a victory."[168] Unscathed, Perrin noticed a gap between Gamble's cavalry and Biddle's line; he exploited the weak spot with two regiments. The 12th South Carolina poured lead pills into the 121st Pennsylvania's flank. Rallying on their colors, the Pennsylvanians fled for Gettysburg, followed by the rest of the brigade.[169] Masses of enemy troops now threatened I Corps on three sides. Abner Doubleday recognized the end had come; he ordered retreat about 4:30 P.M.[170] The 7th Wisconsin suffered its largest losses of the day covering the division's retreat,[171] allowing valiant I Corps soldiers fighting south of the Chambersburg Pike to fall back "in some order." This portion of John Reynolds' glorious command retreated around Gettysburg's western outskirts.[172]

By 5:00 P.M., I and XI Corps survivors had rallied on Col. Orland Smith's Second Brigade (von Steinwehr) which covered the northern face of Cemetery Hill.[173] Though panic was not evident, according to Rufus Dawes: "It is likely that if fresh troops had attacked us then, we would have fared badly. The troops were scattered over the hill in disorder, while a stream of stragglers and wounded men pushed along the Baltimore Turnpike toward the rear. But this perilous condition of affairs was of very short duration."[174] A slit of golden opportunity existed for Confederates to storm Cemetery Hill, sending the Army of the Potomac in defeat back into Maryland but momentum had been lost in the Gettysburg streets. Fatigue, casualties, and thousands of prisoners impaired the combat capability of many regiments.[175] Jubal Early, however, controlled relatively fresh brigades which could have attempted an assault on Cemetery Hill.[176] He explained in his memoir that fences on Gettysburg's outskirts obstructed an advance while enemy batteries would have enfiladed his troops as they formed in the streets. "I, therefore, could not make an advance from my front with advantage, and thought it ought to be made on the right."[177]

Convinced that his single division could not capture the high ground unaided, Early sought Ewell and Hill to urge "an immediate advance upon the enemy before he should recover from his evident dismay..." Before locating the lieutenant generals, Early learned that the army's rear was threatened by an enemy force advancing along the York Pike. Early sent Gordon's brigade to support Brig. Gen. William "Extra Billy" Smith's brigade east of Gettysburg in the area of the York Road.[178] Though Early discounted the report of Federals on the York Road, the First Division, XII Corps, was within two miles of Gettysburg on the Hanover Road.[179] Smith's alarm may have been caused by friendly forces seen on the York Road.

While Early considered Ewell's next move,[180] Winfield Scott Hancock, who had arrived some time after 4:00 P.M.,[181] began organizing a defense. Remnants of I and XI Corps were reforming on the Taneytown Road and Baltimore Pike respectively. Hancock assumed command of both corps vice Howard as General Meade's personal representative. Assisted by his staff, Howard, Buford, and others, a battle line was established on Cemetery Hill.[182] The *parousia* of Hancock was a pivotal event for it transformed discouraged soldiers into veterans once again ready for battle.[183]

> It gave the troops a new inspiration. They all knew him by fame, and his stalwart figure, his proud mien, and his superb soldierly bearing seemed to verify all the things that fame had told about him. His mere presence was a reinforcement, and everybody on the field felt stronger for his being there.[184]

According to Hancock's chief of staff, Lt. Col. Charles Morgan: "A line of battle with skirmishers out was plainly seen east of the town, making its way towards Culp's Hill, and so far as I could see we had not even a skirmisher to meet it."[185] Morgan had observed the Louisiana Tigers advancing a half mile east of Gettysburg along the York Road to Rock Creek. They then followed the course of the stream south and settled in a field. General Hays continued forward "with a number of men," watching the retreating blueclads.

> ...Hays would have moved his brigade and occupied Culp's Hill had it not been that he and Gordon had received positive orders from General Ewell, through Early, not to advance beyond the town if they succeeded in capturing it.
>
> General Hays sent for Early and pointed to him the importance of moving the whole division on Culp's Hill, and occupying not only it, but the Baltimore pike. General Early then said: 'I am satisfied you are right; it should be occupied on the spot,

but I can not disobey orders,' and then, turning away from us
a few steps said, more to himself than Hays, 'If Jackson were on
the field I would act on the spot.' General Hays then spoke a few
animated words to Early, when the latter said, 'You are right
General, you are right. I'll send to Ewell for orders at once.'[186]

Jubal Early neglected to mention this interlude with Harry Hays in
his memoir, which focuses on Cemetery Hill and Richard Ewell.

When the 7th Indiana (Cutler) arrived at 5:00 P.M., the Hoosiers were sent to Culp's Hill and "immediately commenced the construction of a temporary breastwork."[187] Three large untried
regiments belonging to the Second Vermont Brigade under the command of Brig. Gen. George J. Stannard reached the field with the
7th Indiana and "took position on Cemetery Hill, in rear of our line
of battle..."[188] By 5:25 P.M., Hancock was confident that the force
on Cemetery Hill could withstand a frontal attack. His primary concern was for the left because the position held by I and XI Corps
could be flanked by an enemy advance on Cemetery Ridge. Two XII
Corps brigades from Brig. Gen. John W. Geary's Second Division
solved the problem by deploying on the ridge. The 5th Ohio and
147th Pennsylvania, First Brigade, Col. Charles Candy, were sent
to occupy "a range of hills south and west of the town..."[189] As time
passed in "comparative quiet..." XI Corps was disposed to defend
Cemetery Hill with I Corps divisions in support on both flanks. General Slocum, commanding XII Corps, reached Cemetery Hill near
7:00 P.M.[190] Shortly thereafter lead regiments of III Corps appeared
south of Gettysburg marching up the Emmitsburg Road. Hancock
transferred command to Slocum and returned to army headquarters at Taneytown where General Meade had been evaluating intelligence from Gettysburg. Meade's belief that Lee's "whole army" was
moving on Gettysburg plus favorable reports concerning "the character of the position" resulted in orders for his army to concentrate
at Gettysburg.[191]

Robert E. Lee reached Gettysburg around 2:00 P.M. He hesitated before allowing Heth to advance in support of Rodes because
Longstreet's corps was not on the field and Lee was reluctant to
bring on a general engagement. In the company of Hill on Seminary
Ridge he witnessed Federals streaming toward Cemetery Hill.[192]
Unlike General Meade, the absence of cavalry placed General Lee at
a great disadvantage.[193] Prisoners revealed the presence of two corps
but Lee remained ignorant of actual enemy strength on the field
and which units were approaching Gettysburg. Richard Anderson's
fresh division began arriving about 4:30 P.M. and went into camp
"as a reserve in case of disaster."[194]

James Longstreet reached the field on July 1 at 3:30 P.M.[195] He
found Lee on Seminary Ridge studying the concentration of Federal

troops on Cemetery Hill. Longstreet examined the enemy position "and made a careful survey as I could from that point." He concluded that the enemy position presented a clear opportunity to effect the defensive strategy he thought had been agreed upon. Longstreet suggested to Lee that the Army of Northern Virginia could "interpose" itself between Washington and the Army of the Potomac on the morrow by shifting toward the right. Lee could then receive an attack with the advantage of position. Should the enemy army not behave as expected, Lee could then maneuver in the direction of Washington and establish his army in a choice position. The Federals would certainly attack when they realized Washington and the Army of the Potomac's rear were threatened. General Lee responded to Longstreet's suggestion emphatically: "No, the enemy is there, and I am going to attack him there."[196] Longstreet pressed his case, arguing against Lee's resolve to take the offensive:

> I called his attention to the fact that the country was admirably adapted for a defensive battle, and that we should surely repulse Meade with crushing loss if we would take position so as to force him to attack us, and suggested that, even if we carried the heights in front of us, and drove Meade out, we should be so badly crippled that we could not reap the fruits of victory; and that the heights of Gettysburg were, in themselves, of no more importance to us than the ground we then occupied, and that the mere possession of the ground was not worth a hundred men to us. That Meade's army, not its position, was our objective. General Lee was impressed with the idea that, by attacking the Federals, he could whip them in detail. I reminded him that if the Federals were there in the morning, it would be proof that they had their forces well in hand...[197]

General Lee sustained his conviction and would not be persuaded. "No; they are there in position, and I am going to whip them or they are going to whip me." Sensing "further argument" would be fruitless, Longstreet "determined to renew the subject the next morning. It was then about 5 o'clock in the afternoon."[198] Lee's decision to ignore Longstreet's advice may have been influenced by the lack of intelligence from Stuart concerning the Army of the Potomac's proximity to his own army.

Soon after reaching the town square or "Diamond," about 5:00 P.M., General Ewell received a message from Lee that instructed him "to carry the hill occupied by the enemy, if he found it practicable..." Lee also cautioned Ewell to avoid bringing on a general engagement until the army had further concentrated.[199] Ewell instructed Rodes and Early to prepare for an assault then investigated the probability of carrying it out. He discovered that suitable positions were unavailable for his batteries to support an attack. His divisions would be "extremely vulnerable" to close range artillery fire from Cemetery Hill as they deployed into line from the streets. Ewell concluded that he required troops from Third Corps to assist Early and Rodes but he could not communicate with Hill.[200] Circumstances compelled Ewell to cancel renewal of the battle on July 1.

> Ewell had not acted in an indecisive manner; to the contrary, his decision not to assault Cemetery Hill was a determination based upon his assessment of the situation upon the battlefield. It was made after Ewell had surveyed the battlefield, conferred with his two division commanders, and had conducted a close reconnaissance of the Federal position.[201]

General Ewell's failure to seize the heights on July 1 became one of the chief reasons tendered by Confederates for their Gettysburg defeat. As his stepson Maj. G. Campbell Brown explains, Ewell made a sensible decision.

> It was now within an hour & a half of dark—the enemy's force on the hill already showed a larger force than the combined lines of our two divisions—they were a mile and a quarter away, & the town had to be turned by our troops if any advance was made—one division going on each side of it, the line then re-uniting in the open valley, within easy cannon shot & in open view of an enemy in superior numbers and advantageously posted...Ewell finally decided to make no direct attack—but to wait for Johnson's division coming up & with his fresh troops seize & hold the high peak to our left of Cemetery Hill.[202]

Though Cemetery Hill presented a prickly problem for an attacker, Culp's Hill would have fallen with ease before 5:00 P.M. Richard Ewell's failure to establish Confederate control of this high point, east of Cemetery Hill, represents his true failure on July 1. General Trimble, who served in the Second Corps as a supernumerary officer, thought Ewell "moved about uneasily, a good deal excited, and seemed to me to be undecided what to do next." Trimble had also reconnoitered and noting the conspicuous elevation which dominated Cemetery Hill,[203] "strongly advised the occupation of Culp[']s Hill at once."[204] Ewell expressed doubt and though Trimble assured him that the position was vital, the corps commander remained unconvinced. Trimble exploded in frustration: "'Give me a Brigade and I will engage to take that hill.' Ewell was unmoved by Trimble's appeal. 'Give me a good regiment and I will do it!' When Ewell shook his head, Trimble stalked off. He would not serve, even as a volunteer aide, under such an officer!"[205] This exchange between Trimble and Ewell occurred before the 7th Indiana began fortifying Culp's Hill. In 1865, General Meade admitted to Ewell that

occupation of Culp's Hill would have forced I and XI Corps to withdraw from Gettysburg.[206]

As related previously, Ewell planned to utilize General Johnson's
division, on the march from Scotland and delayed by the First Corps
wagon train,[207] "to take possession" of Culp's Hill.[208] Ewell directed
Lt. Thomas T. Turner of his staff and a civilian, Robert D. Early, to
reconnoiter Culp's Hill. The pair rode to the summit of the "rugged
and rocky mountain," without encountering the enemy and returned
to deliver their report.[209] Meanwhile, Ewell and Early encountered
Johnson west of Gettysburg on the Chambersburg Pike around 6:30
P.M. Johnson informed Ewell that his division was an hour behind
him. This news upset the corps commander's plan and he instructed
Early to take Culp's Hill. Early claimed his division could not carry
out the order due to its condition following a day of marching and
fighting. Ewell withdrew his order to Early and the meeting broke
up "about an hour before sunset." The generals parted; Early set off
to inspect his troops while Ewell established his headquarters in a
house on the Carlisle Road.[210]

A short time later, General Lee arrived at Ewell's headquarters
to determine the Second Corps' situation and discuss operations
for the next day. Ewell summoned Early who soon presented himself[211] and dominated the discussion, which included Robert Rodes.
In response to a proposal from Lee that Second Corps should attack
at daylight, Jubal Early argued against it while Rodes and Ewell
remained mute. Early believed the enemy would concentrate during
the night against Ewell. The ground south of Gettysburg, he argued, favored an attack and capture of the Round Tops would allow
the Army of Northern Virginia to dominate the battlefield. Ewell and
Rodes concurred with Early's view and after further conversation,
Lee inquired:

> Then perhaps I had better draw you around towards our right,
> as the line will be very long and thin if you remain here, and
> the enemy may come down and break through?'
>
> Again it was Early who answered, not Ewell, and it was
> pride, not tactics, that shaped his reply. He felt that his men
> had won a victory and that they would consider their success
> empty if they were ordered to give up the ground they had
> gained...Lee not need fear, he asserted, that the enemy would
> break through. The Second Corps could hold its own against
> any troops that might be sent down the hills to attack it.

The opinion of three senior commanders forced Lee to modify his
nascent plan to resume the engagement on the morrow. Longstreet's
corps must deliver the main attack.[212] Early correctly identified the
best point for offensive action but his obstinate attitude regarding

redeployment of the Second Corps rendered the task of defeating the Army of the Potomac more difficult. Ewell's command remained in an "awkward place...where there was no reasonable probability of his accomplishing any good on the enemy's line in his front & where his artillery was of no service..." The lengthy line established by the Confederates exacerbated communication and coordination of attacks.[213]

Leaving Ewell's headquarters, General Lee felt "perplexed, almost stunned," over the defensive posture favored by his subordinates. Rodes and Early rejoined their divisions while Lieutenant Turner and his companion reported to Ewell.[214] Johnson's four brigades had tramped along the Railroad Cut through Gettysburg and the division bivouacked northeast of town.[215] At midnight, Ewell instructed Johnson "to take possession" of Culp's Hill, "if he had not already done so." After forming a line of battle, Johnson dispatched a "reconnoitering party" to investigate "the position of the enemy in reference to it."[216] Col. Ira G. Grover, 7th Indiana, had assembled eight companies of his regiment in a small area on the wide hill which accounts for the failure of Turner and Early to notice them earlier.[217] When the scouts returned with a detachment, Company B, on picket at the eastern base of the hill, ambushed them. A lieutenant from the 25th Virginia was captured as his companions were driven off. "So ended Johnson's effort to occupy Culp's Hill and Lee's opportunity to pry the Federals from their Gettysburg position without making a full-scale and bloody attack." On the way back to friendly lines, the Rebels apprehended a Union courier.[218] Lieutenant Turner brought an enemy dispatch to Ewell which contained valuable intelligence. Two divisions of V Corps were only four miles away; they would resume their march to Gettysburg at 4:00 A.M. The message also confirmed that XII Corps was on the scene.[219] Dawn was breaking and though General Lee desired an attack to commence early in the morning, it would be late afternoon when James Longstreet chose to unleash his divisions.

OBSERVATION

Once Lee turned from the Susquehanna, perhaps it was inevitable that the impetuous A. P. Hill brought on a meeting engagement. More aggressive than Longstreet or Ewell, beginning the battle seems to have been Hill's defining role on July 1-3, 1863. John Reynolds, who could have commanded the Army of the Potomac, died on defensive ground he chose. By thwarting Heth's initial thrust, thereby buying time for the Union army to concentrate, Reynolds reversed the "ruling ideas of the campaign..." giving General Meade the opportunity to defeat the Army of Northern Virginia in detail due to Pickett's absence.

Five of Hill's 13 brigades and Rodes' division incurred heavy losses overcoming the I Corps. Jubal Early's division, in the right place at precisely the right time, suffered modest losses sweeping the XI Corps from the field, assisted by Doles. Though Early's casualties were light, his procrastination and failure to occupy Culp's Hill when Nike beckoned, imposed a heavy burden on Lee. Early increased the odds against his army by offering poor advice to Lee, who should have rejected it and moved "Allegheny" Johnson's division to the right. Perhaps the absence of cavalry on his left flank influenced Lee's decision to leave the Stonewall Division attached to the Second Corps.

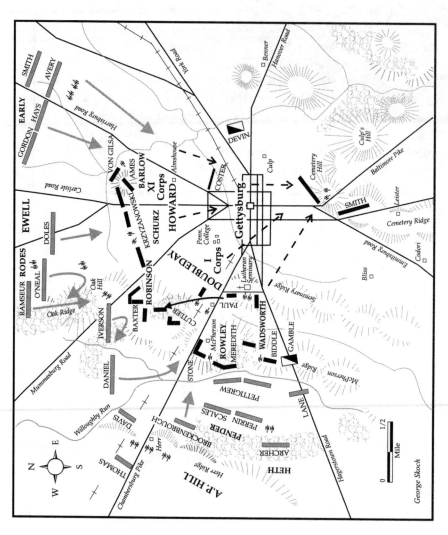

Confederate attacks on the I Corps and XI Corps resulted in the retreat to Cemetery Hill, July 1, 1863.

George Skoch

Chapter 4
Anderson's Inaction

Dear Father: I have not long to live. I have tried
to be a faithful soldier, and I die for the flag.

Pvt. Martin J. Coleman
5th Mass. Battery

George Gordon Meade set foot on Cemetery Hill after midnight on July 2. At the Evergreen Cemetery gatehouse he conferred with senior officers including Howard, Slocum and Maj. Gen. Daniel E. Sickles, III Corps. The confidence of his senior generals regarding the strength of the army's position must have confirmed in Meade's mind his original determination "to give battle..."[1] Throughout the night Meade prepared for the day's work; just prior to daybreak he set out to survey the ground. Accompanied by his chief of artillery, Brig. Gen. Henry J. Hunt, General Howard, and an engineer, Capt. William H. Paine, Meade rode from Cemetery Hill to the vicinity of Little Round Top, then north to Culp's Hill and back to headquarters at Lydia Leister's cottage, west of the Taneytown Road. Along the way, Captain Paine sketched the terrain and Meade indicated the position each corps should take. Copies were made and sent to corps commanders. Meade's survey showed that both flanks were secured by steep and rocky hills. Southwest of Cemetery Ridge broken ground well suited for defense extended almost to the Emmitsburg Road. Overall the position presented "some real advantages" for determined and experienced troops. The greatest Federal advantage was the convex line, shaped like a *J* which permitted rapid reinforcement along interior lines for any hard-pressed point.[2]

While General Meade acquainted himself with the ground his army would defend, General Geary's division left its bivouac on Cemetery Ridge and marched off to reinforce the right flank.[3] The Second Division rejoined the First Division to defend Culp's Hill and helped extend the line east to Rock Creek and the Baltimore Pike. Two regiments from Baltimore, the 150th New York and 1st Maryland, Potomac Home Brigade, were attached to the First Division as the Second Brigade under Brig. Gen. Henry H. Lockwood. Brig. Gen. Thomas H. Ruger, Third Brigade, now commanded the First Division in place of Brig. Gen. Alpheus S. Williams, who directed XII Corps.[4] A few hours later, II Corps replaced the divisions of Robinson and Doubleday on Cemetery Ridge, extending the XI Corps line south from Cemetery Hill.[5] The Third Division under Brig. Gen. Alexander Hays occupied the right flank near the cemetery while the First Division led by Brig. Gen. John C. Caldwell held the left flank. In the center, Gen. John Gibbon's Second Division was distributed with Brig. Gen. Alexander S. Webb's Second Brigade on the right and the Third Brigade under Col. Norman J. Hall on the left. Brig. Gen. William Harrow's First Brigade was in reserve.[6] From Culp's Hill to the Round Tops, right to left, the Army of the Potomac's main line was the XII, I, XI, II, and III Corps.[7]

Conferring with his brigade commanders, Geary expressed disdain for the practice of constructing "rifle-pits" because "it unfitted men for fighting without them." Brig. Gen. George Sears Greene, Third Brigade, countered "that the saving of life was of far more consequence to him than any theories as to breastworks, and that, so far as his men were concerned, they would have them if they had time to build them."[8] Persuaded by Greene, Geary relented and Second Division troops began throwing up breastworks.[9] Greene's brigade "fell to work...with unaccustomed heartiness...Right and left the men felled the trees, and blocked them up into a close log fence. Piles of cordwood which lay nearby were quickly appropriated." Labor on the breastworks continued until a virtual fortress had been constructed by noon. Similar defenses were erected by the First Division.[10] A Confederate participant in the subsequent attack recorded that the works "were built of heavy logs, with earth piled against them to the thickness of five feet, and abatis in front."[11] General Greene's sagacity in this instance has been neglected, if not forgotten. His determination to dig in saved Culp's Hill for the Union and was perhaps the most important contribution made by any brigade commander at Gettysburg.

For much of the morning General Meade's main concern was his right flank. Around 8:00 A.M., V Corps, Maj. Gen. George Sykes, was posted in line with XII Corps, east of Rock Creek. Meade considered going on the offensive from that point pending arrival of VI Corps, but a negative report from Slocum and Brig. Gen. Gouverneur K. Warren, chief of engineers, describing the rugged terrain, dissuaded him.[12] General Slocum was briefly designated commander of V, VI, and XII Corps to orchestrate the contemplated attack. "This irrelevant command arrangement continued to live in Slocum's mind, however, and he illogically considered himself a wing commander for the rest of the battle."[13] By noon the Army of the Potomac's concentration at Gettysburg was completed,[14] except for VI Corps, on the march from Manchester, more than 30 miles away. When Maj. John Sedgwick's corps arrived at 2:00 P.M., Meade shifted his strategic reserve, V Corps, from the Baltimore Pike to the center behind Cemetery Ridge "some time after three o'clock."[15]

General Sickles' III Corps was assigned the area vacated by Geary's division. Capt. George G. Meade, sent by his father to obtain a report concerning the disposition of Sickles' corps, rode back to headquarters with unwelcome news. The III Corps had yet to move because Sickles was unsure where to place his divisions. Annoyed by Sickles' dilatory behavior, General Meade reiterated instructions that III Corps' right should connect with II Corps' left on the line Geary's division had held the night before. Returning to Sickles' headquarters near the Abraham Trostle House, Captain Meade delivered the message. Around 7:00 A.M., III Corps deployed on Cemetery Ridge as the commanding general desired, "to the foot of Little Round Top." Pickets advanced up to the Emmitsburg Road, about a mile away from the main line.[16] Sickles deplored the location of his corps on Cemetery Ridge because high ground east of the Emmitsburg Road dominated it. Moreover, artillery assigned to the First Division, Maj. Gen. David B. Birney, had a poor field of fire.[17] During the Battle of Chancellorsville, Sickles had been ordered to evacuate Hazel Grove, an elevated clearing that "was an excellent position for artillery and for infantry defense." The Confederates promptly crowned the plateau with a battalion of artillery and proceeded to pound III Corps.[18] This experience influenced Sickles' reaction to his assigned position at Gettysburg.

Dan Sickles' appearance at army headquarters around 11:00 P.M. switched Meade's attention toward the army's more vulnerable left flank and his most irksome subordinate.

> Sickles reported his continuing uncertainty about the position assigned his corps. Meade repeated that the Third Corps should extend its line southward on Cemetery Ridge from the left of the Second Corps through Geary's old position toward the Round Tops. Apparently satisfied, Sickles asked Meade if he might post his two divisions according to his own discretion. Meade responded affirmatively, with the caveat that his lieutenant observe the general defensive scheme already outlined.[19]

Accompanied by General Hunt, Sickles left Meade and rode up to the Peach Orchard east of the Emmitsburg Road. Sickles described the new line he proposed. Hunt recollected that it "constituted a favorable position *for the enemy* to hold. This was one good reason for our taking possession of it." He noted benefits and drawbacks between the position Sickles desired and the one designated by Meade. The new position's particular weakness involved III Corps' available manpower, but Hunt judged it was "tactically the better line of the two, provided it were strongly occupied, for it was the only one on the field from which we could have passed from the defensive to the offensive..." Around this time, with Meade's approval, General Pleasanton withdrew John Buford's cavalry screening the army's left flank. Perhaps for this reason, Hunt suggested that reconnaissance of the woods beyond the Peach Orchard was appropriate.[20]

Following Hunt's departure, Sickles ordered Birney's division to send out a reconnaissance party. Col. Hiram Berdan's 1st United States Sharpshooters drew the assignment. Companies D, E, F and I, along with the 3rd Maine (Second Brigade), crossed the Emmitsburg Road and scouted west along the Millerstown (Wheatfield) Road to Pitzer's Woods. Around noon a sharp skirmish broke out between the Yankees and a brigade belonging to Anderson's division. During the short scrap casualties were about even but in the face of far superior numbers, the Federals "quickly retired to the Peach Orchard while Berdan reported that there were indeed Confederates in the woods in front of the Union line."[21] Sickles' fears were confirmed and he reacted to the perceived threat to his corps by preparing to receive an attack.

General Lee subsequently claimed in his January 1864 report concerning the Gettysburg Campaign that he had not intended "to deliver a general battle so far from our base, unless attacked..."[22] This explanation is partially disingenuous because the Army of Northern Virginia was not attacked. Lee could never have contemplated a campaign in Pennsylvania without a battle because it would be "politically if not strategically imperative for the Union army to take the offensive..."[23] Stuart's failure to keep him apprised of Meade's movements coupled with Hill's rash foray dashed his hope "to select a favorable position, where he could receive the attack which the enemy would be compelled to make, and from which, if successful, he could seriously threaten the Federal capital."[24]

Retreat from Gettysburg was an option for Lee but in his mind "to withdraw through the mountains with our extensive trains would have been difficult and dangerous. At the same time we were unable to await an attack, as the country was unfavorable for collecting supplies in the presence of the enemy...A battle had, therefore, become in a measure unavoidable, and the success already gained gave hope of a favorable issue."[25] Lee's determination to retain the initiative[26] imposed upon him development of an attack plan. Around 4:00 A.M., Capt. Samuel R. Johnston of Lee's staff, accompanied by a few others, reconnoitered the Union right, south of Cemetery Hill. Riding along Seminary Ridge, they observed no enemy pickets or units in the area around the Peach Orchard. According to historian Harry Pfanz, this was "an inexplicable thing, for there should have been many to see." Continuing on, they crossed the Emmitsburg Road and examined the Round Tops. Seeing nothing to excite further interest, the scouts returned to Lee's headquarters.[27]

Relying on Captain Johnston's flawed intelligence, Lee eventually formulated a plan to deliver his "principal" attack against the Union left executed by Longstreet with the divisions of McLaws and Hood. Tactically, Lee wanted McLaws to form his division perpendicular to the Emmitsburg Road and lead the attack against the vulnerable Union flank. Hill was ordered to threaten the Army of the Potomac's center with Heth and Pender while Anderson's division cooperated with Longstreet. Ewell's role was to demonstrate against the Union right, "to be converted into a real attack should opportunity offer."[28]

Following R. E. Lee's death in 1870, biased critics of James Longstreet claimed he had been ordered to attack at dawn. His failure to follow this spurious order became the chief cause in the minds of Jubal Early, John Gordon, and Fitzhugh Lee for the Gettysburg defeat, even though Meade outnumbered Lee at 8:00 A.M.[29] Longstreet himself mustered testimony from Lee's former staff officers that refuted this assertion,[30] which has been proven baseless.[31]

General Longstreet was in the saddle before sunrise. By 5:00 A.M., he had joined Lee on Seminary Ridge and renewed his proposal to turn the Army of the Potomac from its position at Gettysburg to avoid a costly assault. Lee again rejected Longstreet's recommendation. Discussion of the forthcoming attack included Hood, Hill, and Heth.[32] Longstreet remarked to Hood: "The General is a little nervous this morning; he wishes me to attack; I do not wish to do so without Pickett. I never like to go into battle with one boot off."[33] When General McLaws arrived, Lee and Longstreet quarreled over the placement of his division. Longstreet wanted the division parallel to the Emmitsburg Road. He also refused McLaws' permission to reconnoiter the ground. Lee rode over to confer with Ewell concerning final details of the day's operation. Around 11:00 A.M., Lee returned and Longstreet was ordered to begin moving his corps.[34]

During Lee's absence, Longstreet delayed the movements of his seven available brigades; he was missing a sock as well as a boot. Brig. Gen. Evander M. Law's brigade (Hood), on picket duty at New Guilford, rejoined the division at noon, following a march of 20 miles in eight hours.[35] Though Longstreet subsequently asserted that Lee assented to the postponement of his opening movements,[36] the commanding general became agitated waiting for the battle to begin.[37] Further delay ensued as Confederate commanders sought a route that would conceal their flanking maneuver from enemy observation.[38] Undoubtedly, Longstreet procrastinated because he disagreed with Lee's desire to give battle—his petulant attitude contributed to his performance at Gettysburg. In the opinion of an officer who served on Longstreet's staff for three years: "There was apparent apathy in his movements. They lacked the fire and the point of his usual bearing."[39] According to a recent biographer, Jeffrey Wert: "The chief characteristics of Longstreet's generalship— thoroughness, initiative, careful attention to detail—were all absent on the morning of July 2."[40] Longstreet's failure to discharge his duty with verve cost the lives of troops under his command and handicapped the Confederate cause he served. His divisions could have occupied the ground Lee desired to control without a fight.[41]

After marching then countermarching over roads and through fields southwest of Gettysburg, Longstreet's troops arrived at their assembly areas. Around 3:00 P.M., McLaws' division came within sight of the Peach Orchard. His lead brigades under Brig. Gen. Joseph B. Kershaw and Brig. Gen. William Barksdale formed behind a stone wall. Behind the South Carolinians and Mississippians were the Georgians of Brig. Gens. Paul J. Semmes and William T. Wofford.[42] General McLaws rode forward to inspect his front where he expected to pinpoint the enemy's vulnerable flank. Dismounting, he entered a line of trees "and took a good look at the situation, and the view presented astonished me, as the enemy was massed in my front, and extended to my right and left as far as I could see." McLaws viewed III Corps which had advanced from Cemetery Ridge to the Emmitsburg Road.[43]

Colonel Berdan's warning had sparked Sickles into action. The forward position he coveted must be occupied quickly to avoid repeating the Chancellorsville experience. Sickles believed that advantages of a salient line outweighed the disadvantages; he acted precipitately without consulting Meade. In apparent anticipation of the contemplated movement, a few units had already moved forward. At 2:00 P.M., the corps advanced in a spectacular display of military splendor.[44] Brig. Gen. Andrew A. Humphrey's Second Division took up a position along the Emmitsburg Road. Col. George C. Burling's Third Brigade, serving as corps reserve during the battle, never fought as a unit. Brig. Gen. Joseph B. Carr's First Brigade held the right flank of the corps while Col. William R. Brewster's

Second Brigade connected with Birney's division at the Peach Orchard. Brig. Gen. Charles K. Graham's Pennsylvanians of the First Brigade protected a segment of the Emmitsburg Road south of the Millerstown Road. Behind Graham, the Third Brigade under Col. Philippe Regis De Trobriand formed in a section of the Rose Woods around "Stony Hill." In De Trobriand's rear, Brig. Gen. J. H. Hobart Ward's Second Brigade was positioned in Rose Woods and prolonged the III Corps line into Devil's Den.[45]

Potentially strong, III Corps' final position could be maintained if both exposed flanks were supported sufficiently. Humphrey's division stood a half mile in front of II Corps which presented a gap in the Union line. Though Ward's forward position on Houck's Ridge shielded Little Round Top, none of his regiments occupied it. Critics insist that Dan Sickles "failed to recognize the importance of Little Round Top..." George Meade apparently experienced the same lapse of judgment since Sickles never received a positive order to occupy the eminence.[46] Had Sickles remained glued to Cemetery Ridge as Meade wished, Little Round Top would still have remained unoccupied. In the opinion of chief historian emeritus of the National Park Service, Edwin C. Bearss, "He can't extend his left from the Pennsylvania Monument to Little Round Top because he doesn't have the manpower, and he would have had nothing on Little Round Top."[47] Devil's Den and the Wheatfield would have fallen to Confederate bayonets with minimal casualties.[48] The III Corps would have been flanked[49] and likely routed. Redisposition of III Corps provided Birney's division with the tactical advantage of cover behind rocks and stone fences,[50] which would have not been the case in an open field fight on the crest of Cemetery Ridge. John Haley, Company I, 17th Maine, who experienced the violence of the Confederate attack, offered his opinion in 1882 of Sickles' decision to establish the forward line.

> ...I think of the stubbornness of the conflict, and length of time we held a much heavier force in check. And although it has been claimed by many that Sickles' line was exceedingly faulty on that day (which no one denies) still, in my judgment, it was Providential, if there ever was anything of this nature; for he held the rebels in check, and exhausted them...I believe that if Birney's division had been formed originally as Meade said he intended on the general line or ridge running to Round Top, the rebels would have gone through it like an egg shell...[51]

Comrade Haley describes a cardinal military principle: defense in depth. Birney's three brigades traded space for time, which consumed the power and momentum of the Confederate attack. The previous day, I Corps had fulfilled this precise purpose.[52] Critics of

Dan Sickles overlook the fact that if III Corps had been pushed from Cemetery Ridge, V Corps formations in support would have been disrupted by fleeing men and riderless horses.[53] Any V Corps counterattack would have been delayed and Confederate colonels could have reorganized their regiments to consolidate their position.

Another participant in the contest at Gettysburg, who directed Longstreet's artillery, Col. Edward Porter Alexander, judged in retrospect that "it was no harm to Meade to have our charge expend its fury upon an advanced line in front...Sickles claims that his advanced position is what gave Meade the victory, and in my opinion he has reasonable grounds for thinking doing so."[54] Students of Gettysburg seem obsessed with the romance of Little Round Top's defense, the so-called *key* to the battlefield. In point of fact, a direct assault upon Cemetery Ridge would have enjoyed a greater probability of success due to the absence of natural and man-made obstacles as well as greater artillery support afforded by occupation of the Peach Orchard. Had Lee's brigades established dominance on Cemetery Ridge, the Federal center, Meade would have been forced to withdraw from Gettysburg. The VI Corps, largest organization in the Army of the Potomac's order of battle, in all likelihood would have prevented a rout on the magnitude of Second Manassas. In summary, occupation of Little Round Top by a fraction of III Corps as an extension of the Cemetery Ridge line would have been detrimental and as will be explained, the obsession of Evander Law for attacking it, robbed the Army of Northern Virginia of supreme prospects for victory on July 2.

At 3:00 P.M., when Lafayette McLaws detected Union troops where they were not expected to be, General Meade summoned his principal commanders to headquarters.[55] Before Sickles' arrival, General Warren notified Meade that III Corps had left Cemetery Ridge.[56] As Sickles rode to the Leister cottage, Longstreet's artillery announced that the battle was under way. Meade, meeting Sickles at the doorway, told him not to dismount. Taking this cue, Sickles galloped back to his command. Shortly afterward, General Meade rode up to Sickles and scrutinized his deployment.

> 'Are you not too much extended, general?' said Meade. 'Can you hold this front?' 'Yes,' replied Sickles, 'until more troops are brought up; the enemy are attacking in force, and I shall need support.' General Meade then let drop some remark showing that his mind was still wavering as to the extent of ground covered by the Third Corps. Sickles replied, 'General, I have received no orders. I have made these dispositions to the best of my judgment. Of course, I shall be happy to modify them according to your views.' 'No,' said Meade, 'I will send you the

Fifth Corps, and you may send for support from the Second
Corps.' 'I shall need more artillery,' added Sickles. "Send to the
Artillery Reserve for all you want,' replied Meade; 'I will direct
General Hunt to send you all you ask for.' The conference was
then abruptly terminated by a shower of shells, probably directed at the group, and General Meade rode off. Sickles received no further orders that day.[57]

General Sickles applied to the Artillery Reserve for reinforcements
and received four batteries. Lt. Col. Freeman McGilvery brought forward his First Volunteer Brigade and posted it in line facing south
along the Millerstown (Wheatfield) Road behind the Peach Orchard.
Positioned east to west were the 9th Massachusetts Battery, Capt.
John Bigelow; 5th Massachusetts Battery, Capt. Charles A. Phillips;
15th New York Light Artillery, Capt. Patrick Hart; Companies C and F
(Consolidated) Pennsylvania Light Artillery, Capt. James Thompson.[58]

Confronted by this unexpected situation, the prospect of a frontal assault instead of the anticipated envelopment of the Union flank,
Longstreet suspended the attack with Lee's approval. McLaws was
instructed to wait until Hood's brigades had moved to the far right.
Hood's division became the lead attack element while McLaws assumed a supporting role.[59] Upon reaching the Emmitsburg Road,
General Hood made three requests to Longstreet for permission to
move his division around Big Round Top because his "picked Texas
scouts" had informed him that the enemy flank and rear "were badly
exposed to our attack in that direction." Hood mistakenly believed
the Round Tops were occupied and feared flanking fire upon his
troops as they struggled to pass through the jagged terrain below
the high ground. General Law, also with an eye on the Round Tops,
sent out scouts. A runner returned with news that Big Round Top
was unoccupied which caused Law to consider a flanking movement would be successful. He conveyed his views to Hood, who
maintained his orders were to conduct a frontal attack when McLaws
was in position. Law and Hood protested in vain for Longstreet was
in no mood to change General Lee's orders to attack up the
Emmitsburg Road. As the brigades were moving forward, Longstreet
found Hood who appealed for the movement around the Round Tops.
Longstreet simply stated the obvious: "We must obey the orders of
General Lee."[60]

Confident in their prowess, the Texas Brigade advanced toward Houck's Ridge around 4:00 P.M. with the 3rd Arkansas on the
left flank.[61] The 1st and 4th Texas were in the center of the brigade
while the 5th Texas held the right flank. To their right, Law's brigade continued Hood's forward line of attackers. From left to right
were the 4th, 47th, 15th, 44th, and 48th Alabama Regiments. Brig.

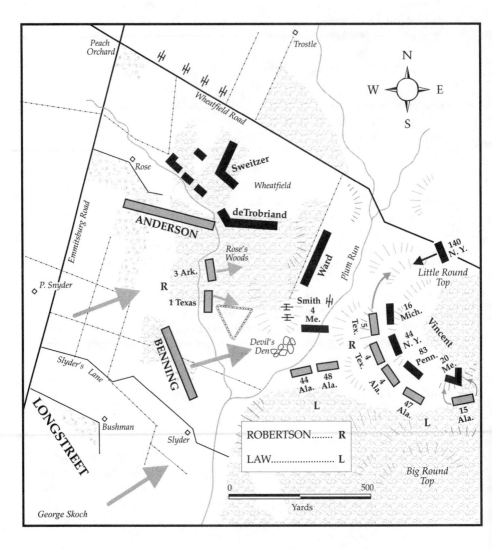

Confederate attack on the Federal left on July 2, 1863.
Note the scattered regiments of Robertson and Law.

View of Devil's Den

Gettysburg: The Pictures and the Story, Ohio Historical Society

Gen. Henry L. Benning's Georgians followed Law while Brig. Gen. "Tige" Anderson's four Georgia regiments supported Brig. Gen. Jerome B. Robertson's Texans and Arkansans.[62] During the advance, Robertson's regiments and the Alabamians endured "a heavy and destructive fire"[63] of case shot and shell from the 4th New York Battery, the extreme left of the Union line. Capt. James E. Smith had placed four 10-pounder Parrotts on the ridge above Devil's Den. Two other cannon were ready for action behind the ridge, aimed down the Plum Run Gorge.[64] Hood had instructed Robertson explicitly "to keep my left on the Emmitsburg road and in no event to leave it unless the exegency [sic] of the battle made it necessary or proper, in which case I was to use my judgment." Robertson believed the Alabamians were unleashed "prematurely a full mile from the enemy's battle line..."[65] As the attack developed, the 3rd Arkansas attempted to maintain contact with the road as the 1st Texas remained on its right flank. Closing up on the 4th Alabama, the 4th and 5th Texas drifted away from the 1st Texas which cleaved the Texas Brigade into two wings. This maneuvering impaired the impact of Robertson's effort, crippling the division's mission to attack up the Emmitsburg Road, because Law blundered by charging for the high ground. Kathy Georg Harrison, a Park Service historian at Gettysburg National Military Park, offered this evaluation of Laws' independent decision.

> Evander M. Law pulled Robertson off of the Emmitsburg Road anchor by his movements toward Big Round Top; his sweeping arc was obviously wider than anticipated by Lee...Yet Law insisted before the attack that the Round Tops were the key and should be taken; one wonders whether Law stretched the meaning of his orders, or perhaps disobeyed his instructions, to pursue his individual campaign.[66]

Twenty minutes after his division began advancing, General Hood was wounded by shell fragments in the left arm. Lee's "key" division commander was carried from the field. A Southerner remarked: "The loss of his consumate daring and leadership in attack at such a crisis may not be measured. But it is easily imaginable that it was of seriously adverse affect."[67] Had the plan that Lee envisioned been carried out under Hood's supervision, the futile attacks upon Little Round Top may have been avoided. In all probability the Texas Brigade would have clashed with De Trobriand's brigade north of the Wheatfield while the Alabamians would have confronted Ward's brigade north of Devil's Den in the Rose Woods. With the support element of Anderson and Benning assisting Robertson and Law, Birney's division could not have averted eventual disaster.[68] Col. Strong Vincent's brigade (V Corps), which occupied Little Round Top after

4:30 P.M.,[69] would have observed the unfolding debacle, unable to intervene.

Scanning the ground below Little Round Top, General Warren discerned danger to his army. No troops occupied Little Round Top except for signalmen and Rebel regiments, if not countered, would outflank Sickles. With no time to lose, he sent messengers flying for reinforcements, then he decided to find General Sykes himself. Fortunately for the Union, Warren found him promptly and explained the situation to him. Sykes sent aides in search of Brig. Gen. James Barnes, First Division, with an order to dispatch a brigade to the threatened point. Colonel Vincent encountered one of Sykes' aides and upon inquiry, learned of the crisis. Risking his career, Vincent led the Third Brigade to the high ground and glory. His selfless decision was "key" to the Union defense of Little Round Top.[70]

Evander Law assumed command of the division after Hood was wounded and exercised little control of succeeding events. Law's initial decision, however, to direct his own brigade toward the Round Tops established the chain of events that embroiled much of the division in the struggle for Devil's Den and culminated in the epic fight for Little Round Top. To neutralize Smith's cannon on Houck's Ridge, Law peeled off the 48th and 44th regiments from his right flank and sent them toward Devil's Den at the foot of Little Round Top. The 15th Alabama, led by Col. William C. Oates, now formed the brigade's right flank; the 47th Alabama covered Oates' left flank. Oates controlled both regiments. Law instructed Oates to continue forward, then wheel to the left and drive toward Devil's Den across the lower slope of Little Round Top. Companies A, D, and F, 47th Alabama, with A and H, 48th Alabama, were detached as skirmishers to protect the brigade's right from the annoying 2nd U.S. Sharpshooters. "During the remainder of the afternoon the five companies acted as two uncoordinated units." This improvised battalion loitered around Big Round Top and played no part in the battle.[71]

On the extreme left of Hood's leading line, the 3rd Arkansas could make no headway.[72] The Arkansans were opposed by the 20th Indiana, 86th New York, and 99th Pennsylvania (Ward). The 17th Maine (De Trobriand), positioned behind a stone wall in the Wheatfield, north of Devil's Den, fired into their flank.[73] Lt. Col. Philip A. Work's 1st Texas encountered the 124th New York (Ward) and was checked attempting to capture Smith's deadly cannon.[74] The "Orange Blossoms" defended the eastern wall of a triangular plot on Houck's Ridge in support of Smith's Parrotts. Twice the Texans charged but failed to drive the New Yorkers.[75] In tribute to Texas tenacity, Lt. Col. Francis M. Cummins of the 124th wrote: "The troops we fought must have been old veterans; never saw braver men...that was not their first fight I know."[76]

As the 4th Alabama, 4th and 5th Texas traversed the saddle between the Round Tops to keep their appointment with the 16th Michigan, 44th New York, and 83rd Pennsylvania on Little Round Top's western section,[77] a potentially decisive action was taking place behind Devil's Den involving the 44th and 48th Alabama.

The Plum Run gorge became the soft underbelly of the Union line and the best possible place for the Confederates to exploit a breakthrough which could take Smith's guns from the rear and outflank Ward, and its defense thus became a necessity if the Union line as advanced by Sickles was to remain intact. If Sickles' left fell before supports arrived, it could have meant defeat for Meade's Union army.[78]

Unconcerned about his front, Captain Smith requested Col. Elijah Walker to situate the 4th Maine on his left.[79] Walker refused and Smith applied to General Ward for resolution of the dispute. Ward sent a staff officer with an order for the 4th Maine to occupy Devil's Den. Walker "remonstrated with all the power of speech I could command, and only (as I then stated) obeyed because it was a military order—The enemy was near, there was no further time for argument. I must obey and suffer the results, or disobey and take the consequences."[80]

Soon after the 4th Maine settled in amid the jumbled boulders, the 44th Alabama attacked. As the Alabamians and New Englanders traded shots for about 20 minutes, the 48th Alabama attempted to outflank Walker's regiment.[81] Although he had received a "painful" wound during the initial gunfire, Colonel Walker alertly refused his regiment's left flank.[82] Fire from Devil's Den defenders proved unbearable to many of the exposed 48th, who fell back.[83] Due to fatigue among his men, Col. William F. Perry, 44th Alabama, hesitated to order a charge.[84] Battling for their lives, Walker's people noticed a brigade filing across Little Round Top's northern slope, "not more than 300 yards to their left." Walker expected the newcomers to secure his threatened flank, but their work lay on the heights. Strong Vincent's brigade had arrived.[85] William Oates was in the wrong place to deliver a decisive blow against the Union line.

Farther north on Houck's Ridge, the 124th New York counterattacked the 1st Texas and sent them reeling. The 15th Georgia (Benning) had reached the combat zone and the combined firepower of the two regiments stunned the "Orange Blossoms." The hardfighting New Yorkers were forced back. To the 15th's right, the 20th Georgia continued up the ridge as the remainder of Benning's brigade moved right toward Devil's Den.[86] John W. Lokey, Company B, 20th Georgia, recounts his experience on Houck's Ridge.

After firing several shots I became aware that about a dozen of us were in an exposed position and in advance of the regiment. So I dropped back down the hill a few yards; but finding that I couldn't do much good there, I advanced up the hill to the right. In ascending to the right I passed Col. [John A.] Jack Jones, of my regiment, lying on his back with about half his head shot off...I passed on to the top of the hill, and, throwing up my old Enfield rifle, I was taking deliberate aim at a Yankee when a Minie ball passed through my right thigh. I felt as if lightning had struck me. My gun fell, and I hobbled down the hill. Reaching the timber in the rear, I saw a Yankee sergeant running out in the same direction, being inside our lines. I called to him for help. Coming up, he said; "Put your arm around my neck and throw all your weight on me; don't be afraid of me. Hurry up; this is a dangerous place." The balls were striking the trees like hail all around us, and as we went back he said: "If you and I had this matter to settle, we would soon settle it, wouldn't we?" I replied that he was a prisoner and I a wounded man, so I felt that we could come to terms pretty quick.[87]

The shattered 124th New York could no longer protect Smith's guns above Devil's Den. Union reinforcements arrived but Benning's numbers determined the outcome of the fight for Houck's Ridge and Devil's Den.[88] The 2nd Georgia, 17th Georgia, and 44th Alabama caused the 4th Maine to abandon the Den and climb the ridge to assist their brigade. Captain Smith's crews left their pieces on the ridge and quickly manned the two remaining guns behind Devil's Den aimed down the gorge. The 6th New Jersey (Burling) and 40th New York (De Trobriand) supported Smith's new position.[89]

Exhaustion and lack of ammunition caused General Ward to order the 20th Indiana, the 86th and 124th New York to fall back.[90] Their departure allowed the 1st Texas and the 15th Georgia to finally claim Smith's torrid cannon on Houck's Ridge. The 4th Maine assisted by the 99th Pennsylvania (Ward) counterattacked Rebel occupiers of Devil's Den. The withdrawal of Ward's right wing, however, rendered the Houck's Ridge line indefensible; the 99th and 4th soon withdrew to rejoin the brigade.[91] Captain Smith continued resisting Hood's division northeast of Devil's Den, below Little Round Top. He fired "obliquely" with his reserve section[92] and "the terrible fire...swept down the gorge."[93] Deadly discharges of canister compelled the Rebels to fall back three times. The 40th New York, aided by the 6th New Jersey's musketry, charged through the gorge and most Confederates sought safety in Devil's Den or on the western slope of Little Round Top, away from the "Slaughter Pen."[94] After suffering terrible losses trying to dislodge the Rebels from Devil's

Den, Col. Thomas W. Egan, 40th New York, ordered a withdrawal to avoid a flanking movement. The 6th New Jersey likewise retired and Captain Smith ordered his survivors to the rear.[95]

Above the Slaughter Pen, from right to left, the 16th Michigan, 44th New York, 83rd Pennsylvania, and 20th Maine defended Little Round Top.[96] Resolute, sweat-covered soldiers of the 4th Alabama, along with the 4th and 5th Texas Regiments, scrambled up the steep slope and slipped around lofty boulders to focus their assaults on the center of Vincent's brigade. Hundreds pressed to within 50 feet of the Yankees before falling back.[97] After regrouping at the base of the "rocky hill," the Rebels again tried to storm the natural bastion though it is unlikely that any field officer directed their effort. Yankee balls picked them off, but their own rounds frequently found flesh. A member of the 44th New York, Pvt. Richard C. Phillips, "...felt a terrible shock...I thought that my whole shoulder had been torn off, but seeing it still there, and the pain going to my thumb and two fingers, I concluded that I was only badly hurt and began to groan terribly."[98] Lt. Charles E. Hazlett's Company D, 5th U.S. Artillery, opened fire from the 16th Michigan's right rear which encouraged Vincent's people, even though the artillery rounds were more effective against the figures swarming around Devil's Den.[99]

Stalled by the sharp fire, most of the Rebels faded from Vincent's front. Reinforced by the 48th Alabama, the Texans infiltrated the area vacated by Smith's reserve section and its supports to threaten the 16th Michigan on Vincent's right flank. Without any formation, the mass of Texans and Alabamians streamed up the steep slope of loose stones to close with the Michiganders.[100]

> The third Confederate attack could not have been timed better
> as far as Vincent's right was concerned. Three companies of
> the 16th Michigan and the regimental colors were being with-
> drawn to higher ground as the Texans and Alabamians neared
> their positions. Panic ensued and some men in the 16th began
> to run towards the rear.

The critical situation required leadership: Colonel Vincent fell mortally wounded trying to rally the Wolverines.[101]

Brig. Gen. Stephen W. Weed's Third Brigade (V Corps) was marching to support III Corps when General Warren found it. Warren rode up to the senior colonel of the brigade, Patrick Henry O'Rorke, 140th New York, and shouted: "Paddy give me a regiment." O'Rorke explained the brigade's orders to Warren who replied: "Is that the 140th? If so take your regiment immediately up the hill and form a junction with Vincent on the left. There is a gap there that must be filled without delay, or the position is gone."[102]

View of the Valley of Death from Little Round Top

Gettysburg: Past and Present, Ohio Historical Society

Unhesitatingly, Colonel O'Rorke led his men toward the threatened point on the hill's northern slope. Gleaming sword in hand he yelled: "Down this way, boys!" and turned to watch the progress of his troops. A ball pierced his neck and the heroic O'Rorke fell without a sound. The 140th New York scrambled down the hill and formed in the shape of an *L* with two companies aligned on the 16th Michigan's right.[103] The fortuitous appearance of O'Rorke's regiment quickly ended danger to Vincent's flank. Their flaming muskets disheartened the Rebels who sensed victory. "Many of them dropped their arms and surrendered, others were shot in their attempt to retreat." The balance sought shelter among rocks in the "Valley of Death" where they maintained a desultory fire.[104] After briefly supporting Company I (Watson's), 5th U.S. Artillery, the rest of Weed's brigade came up to secure Little Round Top's right extremity.[105] On the opposite end of Vincent's line, the day's most famous action flared.

Instead of obeying Law's order to wheel toward Little Round Top, the 15th Alabama scaled Big Round Top. During the arduous climb a detachment from the 2nd U.S. Sharpshooters harassed the Alabamians; Oates feared "that in executing the movement he would expose his flank and rear to the elusive foe."[106] The 47th Alabama further complicated compliance because it "was crowding me on my left, and running into my regiment, which had already created considerable confusion."[107] Lt. Col. Michael J. Bulger's 47th Alabama stormed up Little Round Top's slope toward the Union line where they fought hand to hand with the 20th Maine. Bulger was wounded in the chest and his regiment fell back when an assault by the 4th Alabama failed, uncovering the 47th's left flank. Though the 47th Alabama exchanged long range fire with the Yankees,[108] its withdrawal isolated the 15th Alabama. After allowing his tired men a respite, Oates proceeded down the north face of Big Round Top. The tense Alabamians met no opposition until they encountered "a ledge of rock constituting a perfect breastwork...we received from behind it a most destructive fire."[109] Sizing up the situation, Oates decided to attack, confident that the Yankees could be driven from the ledge. Success would assist the 47th Alabama, "enfilade the whole Federal line, and drive it from the hill."[110]

Col. Joshua L. Chamberlain's 20th Maine controlled the position Colonel Oates wanted. Though the Confederates outnumbered his regiment, "Chamberlain offset this superiority with strength of position, iron determination, and better tactics."[111] Encouraged by their colonel, the Alabamians attempted repeatedly to drive the New Englanders, who counterattacked savagely. Frequently, the fighting became hand to hand. Oates picked up a musket and fired in frustration and Chamberlain mounted a lofty rock to better observe the enemy.[112] Chamberlain watched a "considerable body of the enemy" maneuvering to outflank his left. He stretched his regiment in that direction, then refused his left wing nearly perpendicular to his right wing, which connected with the 83rd Pennsylvania. The flanking column "burst" upon the relocated left wing and advanced to within 10 paces before falling back beset by heavy musketry. Undaunted, the Confederates charged again to renew the fight along the 20th's entire front. Chamberlain described the edge of the fight as rolling "backward and forward like a wave."[113] Time after time the 20th Maine countercharged the 15th Alabama but neither regiment would yield the contest until the fifth effort forced the "Yellow Hammers" down the slope.[114] "The ground was strewed with dead and wounded men of both sides, promiscuously mingled."[115]

After more than an hour of combat, ammunition ran short in the 20th Maine. Those soldiers with no rounds remaining in their cartridge boxes prepared to wield their muskets as clubs. Certain that his boys could not withstand another assault, Chamberlain decided to take the offensive. As the right wing held fast, the left wing swept forward in a bayonet charge. When the left wing came abreast of the right wing, the entire regiment stormed down the hill. Colonel Chamberlain's inspired tactic was "almost miraculously successful."[116] The irresistible wave of Yankees drove the Rebels toward the Sharpshooters and Company B, which had been detached to prevent a surprise; dozens of Alabamians were captured. Colonel Oates ran with the rest of his men. He collapsed from exhaustion and was carried off Big Round Top on a stretcher.[117]

Shortly after Hood fell, "Tige" Anderson "was ordered in to the left of Law[']s brigade, but...I failed to connect with Law by some distance..."[118] The 59th Georgia went into action against Ward's brigade on the 3rd Arkansas' left flank as the 8th and 9th Georgia clashed with the 110th Pennsylvania and 5th Michigan (De Trobriand) posted on Stony Hill, north of the Wheatfield. In the center, the 11th Georgia withdrew and regrouped after grappling with the 17th Maine.[119]

Around 5:00 P.M., General Kershaw's seasoned brigade (McLaws) crossed the Emmitsburg Road. From right to left, the units were the 15th, 7th, 3rd, 2nd, 3rd Battalion, and 8th South Carolina.[120] Stony Hill, beyond the Rose farm, became the right wing's mark while the left wing headed for McGilvery's concentration of guns near the Peach Orchard[121] "from which the enemy were pouring a deadly fire..." Despite canister slugs and shell fragments that tore through their ranks,[122] the left wing moved steadily toward the cannon causing the artillerists to flee. General Kershaw, who

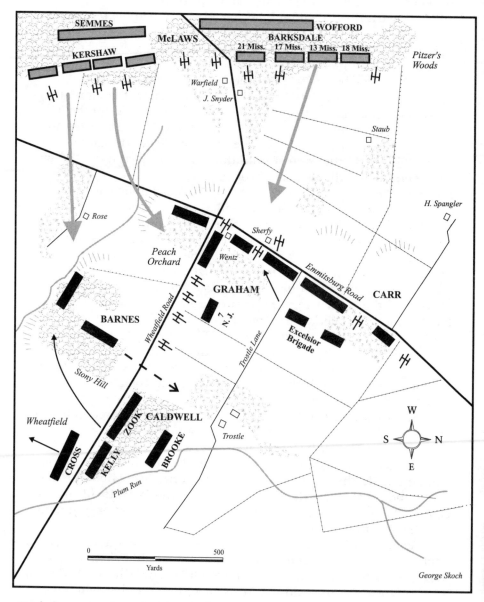

Confederate attack against the Peach Orchard and the Emmitsburg Road, July 2, 1863

accompanied the other wing, ordered the 7th South Carolina to move toward the right. The command carried along the brigade's line and the left wing complied, leaving the smoking guns "at the moment of perfect success..."[123]

Kershaw had expected General Barksdale's brigade to move simultaneously "and conform to my movement."[124] Barksdale's absence on Kershaw's left had permitted Union artillerists to concentrate on the Carolinians and pummel them.[125] If Barksdale's Mississippians had advanced promptly to neutralize this nest of cannon and crippled the Union defense, close support of Anderson and Kershaw by Confederate artillery would have been expedited. Eager to engage the enemy, the Mississippians were "temporarily delayed" nearly half an hour. Formations were broken while passing through the batteries on their front.[126] Once they had recovered, their advancing alignment from right to left was the 21st, 17th, 13th, and 18th Mississippi. The Mississippians "crushed all opposition in their irresistible sweep."[127] Barksdale's people shattered Graham's brigade and swept away Burling's regiments in support.[128] Barksdale exhorted his troops: "Forward, men, forward!"[129] The 17th, 13th, and 18th wheeled north which corresponded to General Lee's design and advanced until they were "temporarily halted by the well-directed fire of the 120th New York."[130]

Assisted by the 8th South Carolina and 3rd South Carolina Battalion, the 21st Mississippi cleared the Peach Orchard. Among their prisoners was General Graham, who had been severely wounded. Emerging from the Peach Orchard, the 21st Mississippi continued straight ahead.[131] The 7th New Jersey (Burling) folded under simultaneous pressure from the South Carolinians and Mississippians depriving McGilvery's gun line of its last infantry support.[132] The Union batteries along the Wheatfield Road now in jeopardy began withdrawing from the jubilant 21st Mississippi.[133] McGilvery conceived forming another artillery line "on the rising ground across the swale" north of the Trostle House.[134]

The 21st Mississippi, their approach covered by a knoll, advanced upon the 9th Massachusetts Battery south of the Trostle House. Captain Bigelow had been ordered "to hold his position as long as possible at all hazards..."[135] A stone wall made it nearly impossible for the Bay Staters to withdraw their guns. Doses of canister obliged the 21st to outflank the battery which enabled the infantrymen to bring a crossfire on the artillerymen. Two artillery pieces escaped the trap. Bigelow was wounded at the stone wall trying to extricate the battery's four remaining guns. Fighting became hand to hand as the Mississippians overwhelmed the gun crews. Lts. George Kempton, of Company I, and W. P. McNeily, Company E, straddled tubes to claim captures for their respective companies.[136] Bigelow's sacrifice allowed McGilvery to assemble a formidable line of artillery that included more than a dozen cannon from his own command as well as two fresh batteries: Company F, 6th Maine Artillery, and Company B, 1st New York Artillery.[137] When no organized body of infantry was available to repair the rupture in the III Corps line, Freeman McGilvery provided decisive leadership the crisis demanded.[138]

Two diminutive brigades of General Barnes' division occupied Stony Hill and extended De Trobriand's line from the Wheatfield toward the Peach Orchard. No troops were in line connecting with McGilvery's improvised gun line.[139] Kershaw's right wing attacked Stony Hill while Anderson's brigade once again assailed De Trobriand's position along with Stony Hill. Rebels threatened to outflank the 118th Pennsylvania on the right of Col. William S. Tilton's First Brigade (Barnes). This menace caused Tilton to withdraw his regiments north across the Wheatfield Road away from Kershaw's Carolinians. Col. Jacob B. Sweitzer's Second Brigade (Barnes) followed Tilton's movement and settled in the Trostle Woods. The 3rd and 7th South Carolina claimed Stony Hill.[140]

Tactically, the departure of Tilton and Sweitzer along with the earlier withdrawal of Ward left De Trobriand's brigade vulnerable to envelopment on both flanks and being surrounded. Colonel De Trobriand led his battered regiments away from the fight. Strategically, his brigade's exit from the field "meant that the whole left wing of Sickles's line had been smashed and that its right wing along the Emmitsburg Road was in jeopardy." Without additional troops to contest Confederate domination of the Wheatfield, General Lee's plan to sweep north toward Cemetery Hill could still succeed.[141]

Fortunately for the Union, Brig. Gen. John C. Caldwell's First Division was dispatched by Hancock "to the scene of the conflict."[142] The fight resumed around 5:30 P.M. when Caldwell's four brigades advanced into the Wheatfield. The First Brigade, Col. Edward E. Cross, led the way. Much of the brigade stood in the open receiving fire from Kershaw's Carolinians as well as Anderson's Georgians now defending the stone wall previously held by the 17th Maine. The 5th New Hampshire with most of the 148th Pennsylvania were on the left in the woods. They dueled with Anderson's brigade along with the 1st Texas and the 15th Georgia.[143]

The Third Brigade under Brig. Gen. Samuel K. Zook advanced on Stony Hill as Col. Patrick Kelly's Irish Brigade approached a gap between Anderson and Kershaw.[144] "Tige" Anderson had been wounded and General Kershaw regarded the approaching storm with apprehension. He ordered the 7th South Carolina to refuse its right flank, then hastened to bring up Semmes' Georgians.[145] The 3rd and 7th South Carolina focused on Zook's people to their front and Cross's right regiments which allowed the Irish Brigade to approach within 20 yards before being detected.[146] The Irish Brigade fired a few volleys, then charged the 7th South Carolina. Outflanked, the regiment fell back to the vicinity of the Rose House. The 3rd South Carolina, now Kershaw's right, maneuvered to meet the attack of Caldwell's Second and Third Brigades.[147]

On Anderson's front, Colonel Cross was shot, and command of the brigade devolved on H. Boyd McKeen. The colonel of the 81st Pennsylvania advised General Caldwell that the brigade was running low on ammunition. Caldwell ordered his reserve brigade under Col. John R. Brooke into action. The Fourth Brigade replaced the First Brigade on the field, though the 5th New Hampshire and three companies of the 148th Pennsylvania remained on the firing line.[148] Brooke's brigade drove Anderson's weary regiments from the stone wall and proceeded into Rose Woods. Many Georgians were captured but the brigade made a stand on Houck's Ridge.[149] Combat continued swirling around Stony Hill as the 3rd South Carolina, reinforced by the 50th Georgia (Semmes), stalled Zook's advance. The 15th South Carolina with a portion of Semmes' brigade defended the gap between Anderson and Kershaw's weak right wing. General Semmes was mortally wounded as the Irish Brigade and Brooke's battalions drove back his Georgians. Kershaw then ordered the 3rd South Carolina to fall back on the 7th.[150] Caldwell's whole line advanced to possess Stony Hill and he requested support from Barnes.[151]

Colonel Brooke's forceful advance exposed both his flanks; he sent an aide to Caldwell with an appeal for assistance.[152] General Caldwell obtained Sweitzer's regiments from General Barnes, then found two brigades of regulars under Brig. Gen. Romeyn B. Ayres (V Corps) to support his feeble left flank. "Thus far everything had progressed favorably. I had gained a position which, if properly supported on the flanks, I thought impregnable from the front. General Ayres was moving forward to connect with my left, but I found on going to the right that all the troops on my right had broken and were fleeing to the rear in great confusion."[153]

Like a sand castle undermined by the surge of the sea, Caldwell's division collapsed. William Wofford's spirited regiments utilized the Millerstown (Wheatfield) Road as an avenue of approach against Caldwell's unsupported right flank. The fresh brigade "intimidated" Federals on Stony Hill and in the Wheatfield. "Its appearance gave new life and hope to Kershaw's and Semmes's men on its right, and its advance carried them in its wake."[154] On the extreme right of the division, Col. Richard P. Roberts' 140th Pennsylvania (Zook) felt renewed Rebel fury first. Roberts was killed trying to refuse his line to withstand the attack and his successor,[155] Lt. Col. John Fraser, anxiously sought instructions from Zook, who had been mortally wounded. Groups of men on the regiment's left running rearward convinced Fraser "that a large portion of our division was actually retreating." He sacrificed his command to "keep the enemy at bay as long as possible."[156] The 140th Pennsylvania lost 241 officers and men from a strength of 560 on July 2, twice the loss of any other regiment in Caldwell's division.[157]

Lt. J. Jackson Putnam numbered among the 140th's casualties.

As we fell back through the Wheatfield, we suffered dreadfully, losing more, I think, than on the advance. It was then I was wounded. Stopping to assist an imploring man, whose leg was crushed, to a less exposed position between two rocks, I fell considerably behind my retreating company, and into proximity with the enemy, who were now advancing with cheers and cries of 'Halt, halt, you damned Yankee, halt!' which I had no disposition to do. When the 24th Georgia (of Semmes brigade) [Wofford] was within about twenty-five yards of me, I received a minie ball in my left leg, just above the ankle, crushing both bones, and bringing me down instantly. The regiment charged over me...[158]

Colonel Brooke believed his bullies could hold their ground but with their ammunition nearly consumed, "I thought it wise to get out..."[159] Though the disordered condition of Anderson's and Semmes' regiments hampered effective pursuit, Wofford's indomitable Georgians rendered Caldwell's retreat a rout.[160] Colonel Kelly reported that the Irish Brigade "narrowly escaped being captured."[161] Sweitzer's brigade advanced again into the Wheatfield and was nearly surrounded. Fighting became hand to hand as they retreated toward the bulwark provided by Company L, 1st Ohio Artillery.[162] On the southern end of the Wheatfield, the U.S. Regulars were hit in the right flank by heavy fire delivered by Wofford's triumphant warriors. Bullets cut the 2nd U.S. Infantry's flag staff; the colors fluttered into the color bearer's hands. Perceiving the peril from the Georgians approaching his rear, General Ayres ordered his division to face about and positioned them on the right of Weed's brigade north of Little Round Top.[163]

Despite a paucity of leadership at the division level and by Longstreet,[164] the Confederates had crushed the Army of the Potomac's left flank. No enemy troops remained in the Wheatfield or below Little Round Top. Four frayed Butternut brigades, Semmes, Kershaw, Anderson, and Benning plus Wofford's relatively intact brigade, flowed toward the north slope of Little Round Top[165] but a fresh Union unit was forming to deny fruits of victory. Nine regiments of the Pennsylvania Reserves under Brig. Gen. Samuel W. Crawford (V Corps) "swept through the Valley of Death" and shoved Longstreet's depleted brigades back to the Rose Woods and the Peach Orchard.[166] Capt. George Hillyer, 9th Georgia (Anderson), remembered the repulse differently and more romantically:

> ...our line arrived at the foot of this noted locality, the Round Top. It was a rocky hill and about one hundred and fifty or two hundred feet high, sloping so that a person could climb it; but with difficulty. On this crest were fifteen or twenty Federal cannon, a line of their Zouaves just in front of them down the hill towards and facing us; and back of them another line equally strong. Their combined fire was almost resistless. Our line emerged from the stumpy brush through which we had charged and came out into a long, narrow but nearly straight opening, which skirted the foot of Little Round Top and the elevated plateau which stretched away on our left towards Cemetery Hill...We had then been fighting for over three hours. Although strengthened by McLaws on our flank, yet neither he nor Hood had any more than a single line, and, of course, by time this was greatly thinned. I could see to the right and left along the opening I have mentioned, thirty-five or forty battleflags, and only from thirty to fifty men with each. On crossing this opening and going a little way up on the rocky slope...we saw that no one was nearer to the enemy's position than we were, and that our little attacking column hesitated. They were all veterans in the highest sense. I heard no order to retreat and gave none, but everybody, officers and men, seemed to realize that we could not carry the position, the enemy outnumbering us probably ten to one, and we exhausted and our ranks thinned as they were. By common consent we fell back to a point where there was a stone wall.[167]

Though the Confederate tide around Little Round Top and the Wheatfield receded, the battle raged unabated on Cemetery Ridge.

Around 6:20 P.M., a cannonball clobbered Dan Sickles in the right leg.[168] Command of III Corps passed to General Birney, who ordered General Humphreys "to throw back my left, and form a line oblique to and in rear of the one I then held..." Birney envisioned a line that would extend to Little Round Top in front of the artillery line McGilvery was organizing. Despite misgivings, Humphreys complied with the impractical order.[169] The 11th New Jersey (Carr) redeployed perpendicular to the Emmitsburg Road along with most of Colonel Brewter's Excelsior Brigade to oppose Barksdale's Mississippians who had blasted Graham's brigade and its supports into chaos.[170]

Volleys from the Mississippians quickly disposed of the 71st and 72nd New York.[171] The Jerseymen, fashioned from sterner stuff, lost their colonel, major, and three senior captains in 10 or 12 minutes, yet remained an organized body of fighting men. Adj. John Schoonover assumed direction of the regiment.

> The fire of the enemy was at this time perfectly terrific; men were falling on every side. It seemed as if but a few minutes could elapse before the entire line would be shot down, yet the galling fire was returned with equal vigor. Slowly and stubbornly the regiment fell back, keeping up a continual fire...[172]

Protected by a stone wall, the 120th New York remained steadfast on the 11th's left flank and "brought the Mississippians to a halt a few rods in their front." Flanked by fresh enemy troops, the 11th New Jersey and 120th New York fell back with the remainder of Carr's brigade, unable to withstand a new Confederate onslaught.[173]

Longstreet's corps, now fully engaged, required assistance from Hill's corps to maintain the momentum of its intrepid attack. Around 6:00 P.M., three brigades belonging to Anderson's division advanced on the Emmitsburg Road.[174] Brig. Gen. Cadmus M. Wilcox's Alabamians struck Carr's front and were sustained by three regiments of Floridians led by Col. David Lang.[175] The Floridians, who engaged the Federals from three hundred yards, "flanked the right of Carr's brigade and did much to make the Emmitsburg Road line untenable." Assailed in front by Wilcox, on the left by Barksdale, and outflanked by Lang, the condition of Carr's line deteriorated rapidly.[176] At one point, the 11th Massachusetts received fire from three different directions. Carr intended to initiate a counterattack but was overruled by Birney, who ordered a retreat.[177]

Beaten but not broken, the First Brigade retreated in relatively good order along with fragments of other regiments and two supporting batteries. General Humphreys was conspicuous as he encouraged his men to face about and return fire from the advancing Rebels.[178] General Hancock sent the 19th Massachusetts and 42nd New York (Hall) to aid the hard-pressed First Division. Forming a line, the regiments fired two volleys, then retreated "to avoid capture, the enemy's line outflanking us on the right and left hundreds of yards to each side, and very near—so near, indeed, that both regiments captured several prisoners."[179] Describing the successful advance of his brigade across the open fields, Colonel Lang wrote: "...I do not remember having seen anywhere before, the dead lying thicker than where the Yankee infantry attempted to make a stand in our front."[180]

Crossing the Emmitsburg Road, the Alabamians and Floridians directed their advance on Cemetery Ridge.[181] The Floridians

View of Emmitsburg Road. Note fences on both sides of the road.

Gettysburg: The Pictures and the Story, Ohio Historical Society

advanced rapidly to capture three cannon belonging to Company C, 5th U.S. Artillery, abandoned when their horses and limber drivers were shot down.[182] Continuing forward, they were confronted by the 19th Maine (Harrow). Col. Francis E. Heath observed the 8th Florida's color bearer before his regiment and "ordered one of my men to 'drop him' and he did..."[183] Both Confederate brigades continued in pursuit of Humphreys' broken division and worked their way to the Plum Run swale, at the foot of Cemetery Ridge[184] while Barksdale's braves changed direction to follow Wilcox and Lang toward the crest. Determined to conquer or die, the Mississippian refused to halt his regiments and allow them to reform, telling his colonels: "Crowd them—we have them on the run."[185]

Brig. Gen. Ambrose R. Wright's Georgians, the northernmost brigade of Anderson's trio, joined the action preceded by the 2nd Georgia Battalion, acting as skirmishers. As his line approached the Emmitsburg Road with the 3rd Georgia in the center, 22nd Georgia on the right, and 48th Georgia on the left, Wright noted that Brig. Gen. Carnot Posey's regiments on his left flank had not advanced. He dispatched Capt. R. H. Bell to inform General Anderson of his brigade's endangered flank.[186] The Rebels engaged the 82nd New York (Harrow), posted along the Emmitsburg Road, forward of the main Union line. Struck in the front, enveloped on both flanks, and menaced in their rear, the New Yorkers fell back after suffering heavy losses.[187] Deprived of support on its left flank, the 15th Massachusetts (Harrow) endured a "deadly fire," then "retired in some disorder, being pressed so closely that we lost quite a number of prisoners..."[188] Some faint-hearted Yankees ran for safety into the Rebel ranks.[189] Company B, 1st Rhode Island Artillery, had bolstered the forward line but now experienced "a most severe infantry fire" which resulted in the loss of two cannon.[190] Colonel Hall, whose brigade held a section of stone wall shaded by a clump of trees to the Georgian's left, described their advance as "irresistible, its regularity surprising, and its rapidity was fearful."[191] General Gibbon was alarmed by the "impetuosity" of Wright's storming column which "came quite through a vacancy in our line."[192] Wright's brigade, threatening the Union right center, now dominated a section of Cemetery Ridge. The Army of Northern Virginia was poised for victory.

Gibbon referred to the gaping hole in the Army of the Potomac's battle line now defended by Humphreys' withered division which was "scarcely equal to an ordinary battalion...being composed of the fragments of many shattered regiments." McGilvery's line of artillery also remained in action and obtained the support it sorely needed. General Hancock deployed Col. George L. Willard's brigade (Hays) north of the "Plum Run Line" in the zone where Excelsior

Brigade survivors "were running back before the enemy as if they were but a line of skirmishers." Hancock requested additional troops from Meade to connect with Gibbon's division to fill the gap.[193] On the 126th New York's left front, William Barksdale cursed and exhorted his scattered men, trying to hold them in line for a push past Plum Run toward perceived victory. He shouted: "Brave Mississippians, one more charge and the day is ours!"[194] Barksdale fell mortally wounded west of Plum Run and was left behind.[195]

Brigade command passed to the 18th Mississippi's colonel, Thomas M. Griffin, who strived to rally his command. The 125th and 126th New York advanced on the Rebels with the 111th New York slightly to the rear of the 126th. Despite heavy losses, the New Yorkers kept moving forward as the Butternuts fired rapidly. From a strength of 390, the 111th lost 185 killed and wounded in less than 20 minutes. A final volley delivered at close range did not deter the Yankees who pressed ahead into the swale[196] where a "short but terrible contest ensued..." At the point of the bayonet, many Mississippians "threw down their arms and lay down in ranks..." Colonel Griffin, understanding further resistance would be "fruitless," ordered retreat.[197] Concerning his brigade's action on July 2, Pvt. Robert A. Moore, Company G, 17th Mississippi, recorded in his diary: "...were forced to fall back for lack of support."[198]

After overwhelming the worn Mississippians, the New Yorkers advanced across open ground to encounter a "murderous" fire on the left from Confederate artillery now posted along the Emmitsburg Road and musketry on the right. They progressed four hundred yards up the hill and recaptured abandoned artillery but were beyond any flank support. Colonel Willard, "finding his brigade unable to stand so severe a fire, ordered the regiments to retire..." As his brigade recrossed Plum Run, Willard was struck by an artillery round that mangled his head.[199] Meanwhile, the 39th New York, detached as a reserve on the brigade's left rear, advanced on the 21st Mississippi.[200] Col. Benjamin Humphreys saw Kershaw's troops "give way and Wofford was retiring toward the Peach Orchard...I saw my safety was in a hurried retreat."[201]

Humphreys' decision to withdraw may have been prompted by the arrival of Lockwood's brigade as well. In response to Hancock's request for reinforcements, General Meade issued[202] an "urgent" order to Slocum some time after 5:00 P.M. to send "all the troops he could spare..." General Slocum ordered Williams to send a division. The Michigander started out with the First Division because it was "nearest to the line of march." On the way, General Williams found Slocum and suggested that Geary's division stay behind "to cover the whole line..." Slocum agreed[203] but at 7:00 P.M., General Geary received an order from Slocum to follow the First Division, leaving

Greene's brigade "to occupy the whole of the entrenchments previously occupied by the Twelfth Army Corps..."[204]

General Williams found an excited Freeman McGilvery who reported no available infantry support and the loss of Bigelow's cannon. General Lockwood received an order from Williams to charge and recapture the guns. The 21st Mississippi, already retreating, responded weakly and Lockwood's men recovered three cannon. The crisis on the left flank had receded when the First Division arrived and never became engaged; it retraced its steps at dark.[205] John Geary's First and Second Brigades wandered away from the battle, unable to find the rest of the corps.[206] On the Federal left, General Meade avoided disaster because fifteen of his brigades absorbed the offensive power of seven Confederate brigades. In the center, one Union regiment saved the day.

About 5:00 P.M., the 1st Minnesota (Harrow) had been ordered to support Company C, 4th U.S. Artillery on Cemetery Ridge. The Minnesotans had watched the Confederate onslaught overwhelm their III Corps comrades who were "driven back in some confusion, the enemy following in heavy force."[207] Hundreds of discouraged survivors stumbled through the Minnesotan's ranks. By Hancock's order, Col. William Colvill "undertook to stop and put them in line; but found it impossible, and demoralizing to my own regiment to do so." Company C opened fire when Sickles' people cleared their front, as the rampant Alabamians paused to reform their lines in the Plum Run swale. General Hancock, who had just left Andrew Humphreys, discerned the Rebels must be checked. He needed five minutes and seeing the Minnesotans exclaimed to Colvill: "'My God! Are these all the men we have here?...Advance Colonel and take those colors...'"[208] Instantly Colvill put his men in motion. A participant described the determination of the First Manassas veterans as they descended the ridge at the double-quick.

> It seemed as if every step was over some fallen comrade. Yet no man wavers; every gap is closed up—and bringing down their bayonets, the boys pressed shoulder to shoulder and disdaining the fictious courage proceeding from noise and excitement, without a word or cheer, but with silent, desperate determination, step firmly in unbroken line...forward.[209]

The 1st Minnesota, 262 strong, unleashed a volley from thirty yards that shattered the opposing brigade's first line. The second enemy line returned the compliment and Colvill ordered a charge driving back the Rebels. Hastily, the Yankees took cover and opened a sustained fire on Wilcox's Alabamians who were reluctant to close with their antagonists. Superior numbers allowed the Rebels to envelop both of the regiment's flanks simultaneously as the Minnesotans fought

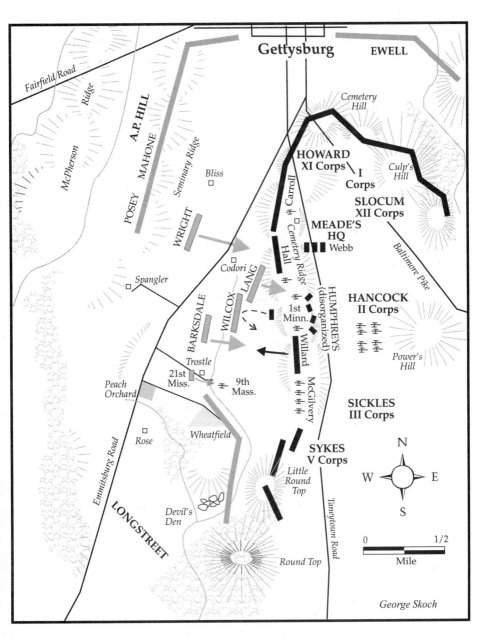

Confederate attack on Cemetery Ridge, July 2, 1863

desperately to sustain their position. Vermont troops on the left and the 82nd New York on the right relieved Colvill's heroes, who captured numerous prisoners and "upon the fire ceasing...We took the colors."[210] When the order to "fall back" was relayed, according to Sgt. Patrick H. Taylor, Company E, "about 50 of us rallied on our regimental colors..." Though the 1st Minnesota's ordeal was brief, about 15 minutes, their timeless valor purchased precious time and possibly preserved the Army of the Potomac's position at Gettysburg.[211]

The stinging setback prompted General Wilcox to reassess his chances of storming the Union "stronghold" without additional troops. He sent an officer "to the division commander, to ask that support be sent to my men, but no support came."[212] Two additional brigades under Anderson's command were available to aid the balance of his division for the assault on Cemetery Ridge. General Posey's brigade had replaced Scales' weak brigade as skirmishers in the no-man's-land between Seminary Ridge and Cemetery Ridge. The 48th and 19th Mississippi scuffled with the Second Brigade (Hays) for control of the Bliss farm. Between 5:00 and 5:30 P.M., the 12th New Jersey (Hays) expelled the Mississippians from the farm and they fell back to a fence. Wright's advance stirred the Mississippians into action. The 16th Mississippi abetted the 48th and 19th in the recovery of the Bliss buildings. Together they "advanced in a spontaneous and disorganized fashion without proper alignment or in full strength." Posey remained in the rear with the 12th Mississippi, unaware of the state of affairs at the front. Individual Mississippians crossed Emmitsburg Road[213] but Wright's gallant rush was deprived of effective support because Posey's brigade was "unable to advance as a unit."[214]

The fifth brigade under Anderson's command, led by Brig Gen. William Mahone, never entered the battle. Anderson sent the messenger from Wilcox to Mahone with an order to advance, but the Virginian refused to budge. Mahone apparently interpreted his brigade's role as confined to artillery support.[215] Posey's and Mahone's failure to become involved in the main attack was Anderson's definite responsibility. According to Lt. Col. G. Moxley Sorrel of Longstreet's staff, Anderson "was a very brave man, but of a rather inert, indolent manner for commanding troops in the field, and by no means pushing or aggressive."[216] A "breakdown in command" occurred. If Anderson had exerted himself and his staff to exercise proper control of the division, opportunity to achieve victory would have been enhanced, though not guaranteed. Inclusion of Posey's Mississippians and Mahone's Virginians as elements of the *en echelon* attack against Cemetery Ridge "would merely have broadened the front but not the depth of the attack."[217] Nonetheless, Anderson's failure to utilize his full division had consequences on another part of the field for it permitted unengaged Federal troops to be employed elsewhere.[218]

Near twilight, Maj. Gen. John Newton, who had replaced Doubleday, received an order to send the Second and Third Divisions toward the potentially fatal gap beyond Gibbon's division.[219] The I Corps "established themselves on the line, meeting the enemy at once, and doing good execution."[220] The 13th Vermont's right wing under Col. Francis V. Randall led the advance.[221] Randall encountered General Hancock "who was encouraging and rallying his men to hold on to the position." Hancock pointed out Company C's cannon in the distance and asked Randall if his battalion could retake them. Randall replied that he would try, then deployed his five companies into line.[222] At the double-quick, the Vermonters set off with their leader ahead. Randall's horse went down and the line paused while a few men lifted the animal off their commander's leg. Continuing forward, the Green Mountain Boys received a volley from the 22nd Georgia, "which did us very little injury, when my men sprang forward with the bayonet with so much precipitancy that they appeared to be taken wholly by surprise..." Dozens of Rebels fell to the ground in surrender as Randall's men rushed over them to reclaim Lt. Gulian V. Weir's guns. Unsatisfied with this achievement, the Vermonters persisted on to the Emmitsburg Road, which alarmed Ambrose Wright[223] and inspired Humphreys' division.[224]

Unable to exploit advantages they had gained or maintain their advanced positions without supports, Lang, Wilcox, and Wright were forced to withdraw.[225] Perceiving the imminent encirclement of his three regiments, Colonel Lang ordered a retreat back to Emmitsburg Road. Finding the new position untenable, the Floridians returned to their assembly point on Seminary Ridge.[226] General Wilcox found that his brigade had become isolated, unsupported on either flank. He withdrew his men from the field "to prevent their entire destruction or capture."[227] General Webb's Second Brigade counterattacked Wright's men on Cemetery Ridge.[228] With both flanks exposed, the Georgians "were now in a critical condition. The enemy's converging line was rapidly closing upon our rear; a few moments more, and we would be completely surrounded; still, no support could be seen coming to our assistance...we...prepared to cut our way through the closing lines in our rear." Wright extricated his command from near disaster "with immense loss."[229] The 48th Georgia, which bore the brunt of Webb's counterattack, lost its colors and more than 100 prisoners, including 16 of 23 field officers.[230] A Pennsylvania recorded that Wright's brigade retreated as "a dispirited mob."[231] Colonel Randall's bold foray became a catalyst for renewed action by Humphreys' division. Colonel Brewster rallied 150 men from his five New York regiments and followed the fleeing Confederates. Sgt. Thomas Hogan, 72nd New York, picked up the abandoned colors of the 8th Florida and presented it to General Humphreys.[232] Carr's brigade rushed back to its former position on the Emmitsburg Road and captured numerous Rebels along the way who had been playing possum.[233] The I and II Corps also participated in the forward movement. Except for the area around the Peach Orchard and Devil's Den, the Army of the Potomac recovered the ground it had forfeited in a battle still to be won.[234] Though Cemetery Ridge and "Round Top Ridge" remained under Union control, Cemetery Hill and Culp's Hill remained threatened by Butternut brigades.[235]

OBSERVATION

Four superb hours of combat directed at the Union left and center brought the Confederates inconsequential gains. Thanks to Warren and Hancock, Longstreet's corps was outnumbered, not outfought. Rapid fragmentation of Hood's division produced separate attacks which lacked the cohesion necessary to deliver a decisive blow. Evander Law bears particular responsibility for this condition due to his fixation on the high ground. Below Little Round Top lay the best opportunity to achieve victory. If the 4th and 5th Texas along with the 4th, 44th, and 48th Alabama had focused their effort on the gorge behind Devil's Den, it is unlikely that the 4th Maine and two artillery pieces would have successfully resisted a brigade-sized attack. Consequently, the retreat of Ward's brigade would have uncovered Sickles' flank. The III Corps' rear would have become vulnerable to attack from the Wheatfield as Hood's division exploited its advantage, before Caldwell's intervention. General Lee's plan to roll up the Army of the Potomac, now in motion, may have succeeded when McLaws and Anderson crossed the Emmitsburg Road.

No matter where Sickles established his main line, Little Round Top was vulnerable—without V Corps intervention it would have fallen. By delaying his attack, General Longstreet allowed V Corps to support III Corps and ultimately determine the day's outcome on the Union left. He should have mastered his misgivings and advanced without waiting on Law's brigade, trusting that the Alabamians would catch up. A vigorous movement by Longstreet in the early afternoon which resulted in the occupation of the Peach Orchard area would have pinned Sickles to

Cemetery Ridge. In conformity to Lee's plan, III Corps could have been outflanked, and forced to fight at a disadvantage. Stone walls utilized by Union brigades below Little Round Top would have been unavailable, therefore the outcome of this scenario is based upon manifest Rebel success in the open field against the Federal brigades.

Capture of Little Round Top, unsuited as an offensive outpost, offered no tactical advantage to the Confederates. Any threat posed by Hood's disorganized brigades could have been contained by V or VI Corps, supported by the ample reserve artillery and organic batteries. A strong defensive position, Confederate domination of Little Round Top may have caused Meade to consider withdrawal to Pipe Creek due to the length of his line, lack of strong reserves, and the weakness of his center. Due to the absence of strong opposition, Anderson's advance upon the Union center held great promise. The rout of Caldwell and dispersal of Humphreys by McLaws rendered Meade's position very critical. Employment of the 1st Minnesota by Hancock to buy time maintained a pattern throughout the battle as Union units appeared at pivotal points to parry Rebel thrusts.

Chapter 5
Early's Call

It is all right now.

George G. Meade

Around 3:00 P.M., as Generals Hood and McLaws deployed their divisions, George Pickett's three brigades arrived "within cannon shot of the battlefield."[1] Thirteen hours earlier the Virginians had departed Chambersburg and after an "unceasing" march, reached Willoughby Run.[2] Tired and hungry, the men "scattered" seeking food, water, and rest, then exchanged rumors.[3] Maj. Walter Harrison of Pickett's staff reported to General Lee and informed him "that with two hours' rest, they could be at any part of the field he might desire to use them." Lee declined Pickett's offer and told Harrison: "Tell Gen. Pickett I shall not want him this evening..."[4] Only three miles from Gettysburg, the Virginians were "all anxious to go in, but word came we were not needed then."[5] Lee's decision not to employ Pickett's division on July 2 was a mistake. Marengo and Waterloo are two examples where French and Prussian troops respectively determined the outcome of a battle after fatiguing marches.[6] Though speculation is not fact, it seems Pickett's division would have been best employed in support of Anderson.[7]

Prior to Longstreet's attack against Sickles, Richard Ewell and Jubal Early sited several batteries "to fire on Cemetery Hill and the wooded [Culp's] hill."[8] In compliance with Lee's order to assist Longstreet with a diversion, Ewell avowed in his report: "I made the necessary preparations..."[9] In fact this was untrue because Ewell "gave no explicit instructions to Rodes and Early and Johnson regarding their co-operation." He left the details to his division commanders.[10] General Ewell's neglect foiled any coordinated Second Corps action against the Federal right as intended by the army commander.

As Hood's division advanced toward destiny at Devil's Den and Little Round Top, a fraction of General Ewell's artillery went into

90

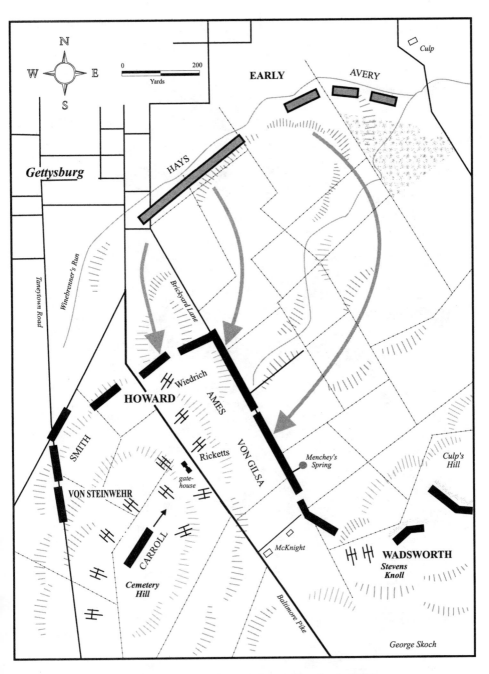

Confederate attack on Culp's Hill, July 2, 1863

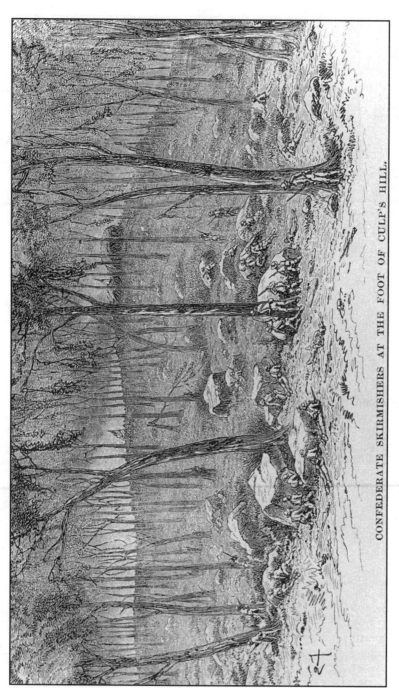

CONFEDERATE SKIRMISHERS AT THE FOOT OF CULP'S HILL.

View of Culp's Hill showing the steep slope and obstacles confronting the attackers.

action.[11] Lt. Col. R. Snowden Andrews' artillery battalion, under the command of Maj. Joseph W. Latimer, attached to Johnson's division, opened on Cemetery Hill from Benner's Hill, an eminence east of Rock Creek, south of the Hanover Road. The "broad crest" of the hill was a poor site from which to engage in an artillery duel. It offered no cover or concealment and the Confederates, unlike the Federals, fought without benefit of prepared positions.[12] The Rebel artillerists, however, were "remarkably accurate, and immediately commanded the attention of the Federal artillery posted on Cemetery Hill."[13] Colonel Wainwright commanded a formidable array of thirteen rifled cannon and six Napoleon smoothbores which responded to the enemy salvoes.[14]

For more than 90 minutes the antagonists traded shot and shell. The 5th Maine Battery, located on the western slope of Culp's Hill, was particularly efficient, inflicting heavy losses in the 4th Allegheny Battery. Amid explosions and whirling metal, chaos prevailed in the Confederate battalion. A witness recorded the singular condition of Latimer's batteries.

> Never, before or after, did I see fifteen or twenty guns in such a condition of wreck and destruction as this battalion was. It had been hurled backward as it were, by the very weight and impact of metal from the position it had occupied on the crest of a little ridge, into a saucer-shaped depression behind it; and such a scene as it presented— guns dismounted and disabled, carriages splintered and crushed, ammunition chests exploded, limbers upset, wounded horses plunging and kicking, dashing out the brains of men tangled in the harness; while cannoneers with pistols were crawling around through the wreck shooting the struggling horses to save the lives of the wounded men.

Man and beast were exhausted. Ammunition was depleted as well. Latimer sent Sgt. Maj. Benjamin Karnes to General Johnson with the message that the position was untenable. Johnson ordered Latimer to withdraw three batteries but leave one behind to cover the advance of his infantry or repel any Federal foray.[15]

Despite the inadequacy of artillery support and the vigorous response by Union batteries in the exchange with Andrews' battalion, around 6:30 P.M., Ewell judged "that the propitious time had arrived for a general advance of his whole corps."[16] Minus the Stonewall Brigade, Johnson's division moved out to attack Culp's Hill.[17] Brig. Gen. James A. Walker's Virginians were providing flank security against Gregg's cavalry on the Hanover Road, "thus seriously weakening the force of the attack."[18] Back on Benner's Hill, Latimer's four cannon roared in support of Johnson's advance "which drew a terrible fire..."[19] A Yankee shellburst killed Latimer's horse as a fragment smashed the teenager's left arm.[20]

By the time the Stonewall Division had waded Rock Creek and deployed into line, the sun had set. In the center, five regiments from Louisiana led by Col. Jesse M. Williams confronted George Greene's lone brigade from the base of the hill. On their right was a brigade of Virginians led by Brig. Gen. John M. Jones. Brig. Gen. George H. "Maryland" Steuart's regiments advanced on the division's left flank.[21] Lt. Col. Logan H. N. Sayler stated that the 50th Virginia "tried again and again to drive the enemy from their position...but the fire was so heavy we could not stand it."[22] Jones' and Williams' people presented little threat to the Federals secure in their lair. A 44th Virginia officer reported: "...it was so dark that it was impossible to distinguish friend from foe. All was confusion and disorder."[23] Loss of the brigade flag and a regimental color to the 60th New York indicates groups of Virginians attempted to press home their attack.[24] The Louisianians likewise failed to cross the enemy works. Four attacks were repulsed and the 1st Louisiana's color bearer was captured.[25] When the heavy attack commenced, General Greene sent messengers to Howard and Wadsworth, whose division connected with the Third Brigade's left flank. Several regiments were quickly dispatched to aid in repelling the Confederates. Regiments sent by General Schurz at the direction of Howard were the 157th New York, 61st Ohio, 45th New York, and 82nd Illinois. These units entered the trenches relieving Greene's regiments.[26]

"Maryland" Steuart's brigade struck the extreme right of Culp's Hill and encountered the least resistance. Though the 1st North Carolina, 3rd North Carolina, and 2nd Maryland Battalion were unable to penetrate the enemy works, Virginians on the brigade's left infiltrated the area on the 137th New York's right.[27] At this critical moment, the 71st Pennsylvania arrived in the 137th's rear. Sent by General Hancock in response to musketry on the XII Corps' front, the "California Regiment" was brought forward by Capt. Charles P. Horton of Greene's staff. After a few shots, to Horton's amazement, Col. Richard Penn Smith ordered his Pennsylvanians to withdraw.[28] Smith apparently feared for his regiment's safety as it received fire from the front, right, and rear. He marched the regiment back to its camp "without orders."[29] The 23rd Virginia traded shots with the 137th New York from works left unoccupied by the departure of Brig. Gen. Thomas L. Kane's Second Brigade (Geary). Col. David Ireland pulled his New Yorkers out of the exposed position to avoid the enfilade fire. Ireland's men tumbled into a "solid traverse" excavated on General Greene's order which protected the brigade's right flank.[30]

The New Yorkers maintained a "steady fire" from their strong position, checking their attackers.[31] Reinforcements reached the army's endangered right flank as the 147th New York piled into the Third Brigade's rifle pits and fought with the 149th New York.[32]

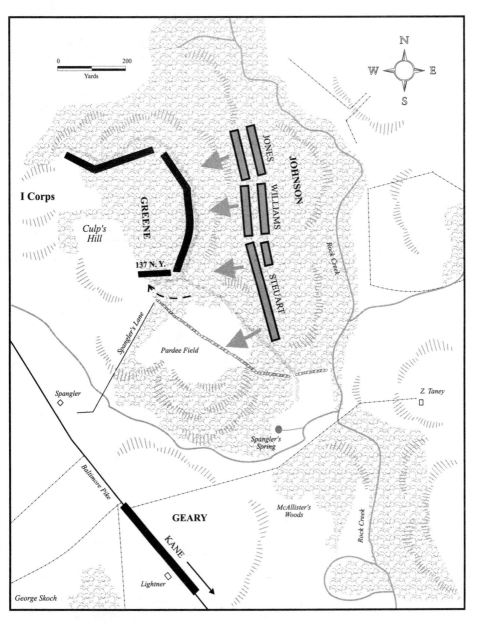

Confederate attack on Cemetery Hill, July 2, 1863

Silently the 6th Wisconsin went "up the hill over the hill and down the hill like a whirlwind without provoking a shot..."[33] Along with the 84th New York, the Wisconsin men slammed into Steuart's left flank and sent the 10th Virginia reeling from a section of captured works.[34]

Though the Rebels retained control of the First Division's works along with a stone wall east of Greene's position, by 10:00 P.M. the fight for Culp's Hill had ended.[35] Shortly after the Confederate assaults ceased, Kane's brigade returned to secure Greene's right, thus relieving the 137th New York,[36] which had suffered the same percentage of loss as did the 20th Maine on the opposite flank.[37] The First Division attempted to recover its works but a "considerable portion" were possessed by Steuart's men. Trenches on the far right, free of Rebels, were retaken by the Third Brigade. The remainder of the division fell back to cover the Baltimore Pike and wait for daylight to again confront the Rebels.[38]

The Stonewall Division's assault failed because determined defenders enjoyed the advantage of prepared positions and the slopes of Culp's Hill were strewn with boulders that practically precluded any successful attack. Had the Stonewall Brigade joined the attack, it "could have pushed all the way to the Baltimore Pike."[39] Alternately, the Virginians could have taken Greene's brigade in the rear, erasing Federal control of Culp's Hill and thereby endangering Meade's entire defensive position. One of these scenarios could have eventuated with perhaps fatal results for the Army of the Potomac if only J.E.B. Stuart had abandoned those wagons!

Cemetery Hill remained in Union control because the Confederate effort to capture it was limited and uncoordinated. When Johnson's division became "warmly engaged," Jubal Early ordered forward Hays' Louisiana Tigers and Avery's North Carolinians to "carry the works" on East Cemetery Hill, so-called because the Baltimore Pike separates it from the Evergreen Cemetery.[40] The Louisianans issued from a field on Gettysburg's outskirts below Stratton Street with the Carolinians on their left. Utilizing Hays' brigade as a pivot point, Avery wheeled his three regiments to strike the Federals head on. Federal infantry awaited the certain clash below East Cemetery Hill behind a stone wall that followed both sides of Brickyard Lane.[41] Early's blow was directed at the First Division (XI Corps), commanded by Brig. Gen. Adelbert Ames.[42] Col. Andrew L. Harris, senior officer of the Second Brigade, did not expect the assault and was surprised when the Rebels appeared. He admired their courage as the batteries on Cemetery Hill opened on the Rebel lines. When the range closed, the infantry greeted the attackers with musketry. "They moved forward as steadily, amid this hail of shot[,] shell and minnie ball, as though they were on parade far removed from danger."[43]

Darkness and smoke obscured advancing Tigers and Tar Heels. Most of the artillery fire passed overhead; in clear daylight, the two brigades would have suffered "horrible slaughter." Small arms fire did not break them as they approached the foot of the hill.[44] Though the Federals aimed poorly, Colonel Avery presented a conspicuous target on horseback and he received a mortal wound.[45] Due to the shorter distance they crossed to close with the enemy, the Tigers struck first. Hays' right regiments hit Harris' Ohio Brigade between the 107th Ohio and 25th Ohio "and soon all along my whole line the fighting was obstinate and bloody. The bayonet, club-musket, and anything in fact that could be made available was used, both by the assailing and their assailers."[46] Louisianans rammed through a gap between the 25th Ohio and 75th Ohio in Harris' right center. The 107th Ohio and 25th Ohio were forced to fall back on Capt. Michael Wiedrich's Company I, 1st New York Artillery. Volleys from the 17th Connecticut and 75th Ohio slowed down the attackers and few passed them to threaten the batteries on the hill's crest.[47]

Leaderless, the North Carolina brigade achieved similar success. On the extreme right of Ames' line, the 57th North Carolina pushed past the 33rd Massachusetts (Smith) despite heavy losses. The 21st and 6th North Carolina drove back the 68th and 54th New York of Col. Leopold von Gilsa's First Brigade (Ames) along with the 41st New York's left battalion.[48] Darkness, disorder, and casualties prevented the Tar Heels from charging up the hill in an organized body. Maj. Samuel M. Tate, 6th North Carolina, led a "portion" of his regiment plus a dozen members of the 9th Louisiana toward Capt. R. Bruce Ricketts' Companies F and G (Consolidated), 1st Pennsylvania Artillery. The cannoneers remained steadfast and "stood with a tenacity never before displayed by them..."[49] Resolved to keep their guns and hold their important position, Ricketts' men resisted with revolvers, handspikes, and rammers. Though one piece was spiked in the melee around his left and center sections, Ricketts maintained fire with his right section.[50] With Buckeye assistance, Wiedrich's crewmen also defended their pieces courageously. To inspire the battery's defense, Lt. Peter F. Young, Company B, 107th Ohio, raced forward firing his revolver. Shooting down the 8th Louisiana's color bearer, he retrieved "the vile rag...These in one hand and revolver in the other, I was in the act of turning towards our men, when a rebel bullet pierced my *left lung and arm*; the turning saved me from falling and rebel bayonets undoubtedly, for I kept on my feet till I reached our men..." A Rebel lieutenant following Young was about to strike him with his sword when Lt. Fernando C. Suhrer, also of Company B, cut down the assailant with his own blade.[51]

General Howard reacted tardily to the threat posed by Early's sudden attack. He ordered General Schurz to dispatch two regiments from Krzyzanowski's brigade to assist Wiedrich. Adelbert Ames stated the 58th and 119th New York "were of no service [and] in fact were not engaged."[52] Again, Winfield Scott Hancock exercised initiative to save the day. When heavy fire "broke out on Howard's front, General Hancock, knowing how little dependence was to be placed on the Eleventh Corps," ordered General Gibbon to send Howard support.[53] "Send a brigade, send Carroll!" Hancock shouted.[54]

General Gibbon, who now directed II Corps because Hancock had replaced Birney as III Corps commander,[55] sent Col. Samuel S. Carroll's First Brigade (Hays) "to the sound of the firing."[56] If Hill's Corps, in particular the brigades of Posey and Mahone, had been more pugnacious, Carroll "could not have been spared to Howard.—"[57] The First Brigade had spent the afternoon supporting batteries around Ziegler's Grove[58] and though he lacked "precise orders" concerning the enemy's location,[59] Carroll responded "immediately" to the emergency[60] and "arrived at a very critical time..."[61] His three regiments sprinted over the murky battlefield to deliver a decisive blow against the Army of Northern Virginia. The 14th Indiana, leading the brigade, charged toward Ricketts' battery with fixed bayonets.[62]

Major Tate sent for support in vain[63] as Harry Hays reorganized his troops in anticipation of certain counterattack. A column of infantry emerged from the gloom and fired a volley at one hundred yards. General Hays hesitated to order fire in reply because he thought the unidentified troops could be friends. The flash from two more volleys identified the onrushing troops as hostile and Hays saw two more lines, the 4th Ohio and 7th West Virginia, behind them.[64] Savage hand-to-hand combat broke out as Carroll's men closed with the Confederates.[65] Capt. David E. Beem, Company H, 14th Indiana, recounted the action in a letter to his wife:

> We arrived just in the nick of time. They had already surrounded one gun. The Artillerists defended—their pieces bravely but nearly lost them...When we approached, the officers of the battery threw their hats in the air and shouted for joy. We pushed right on to the rebel horde and got right among them, but they did not long stand our volleys. They ran pell mell...in thirty minutes the attack was repulsed and the battery saved.[66]

Hays ordered a withdrawal to the bottom of Cemetery Hill because his command was "beyond the reach of support..."[67] The First Brigade confronted the Butternuts at the stone wall where they made a short stand. Carroll deployed his regiments into line and after loosing "two or three volleys" the Rebels faded away. By 10:20 P.M., the musketry had subsided; Colonel Carroll advanced skirmishers to cover his front.[68]

Angry Louisiana Tigers drifted through the Gettysburg streets, cursing their officers, and related details of their failure to a Union sergeant:

> They said they went up the hill before the gunners had time to depress their pieces, to fire at them, and drove the gunners

away and were trying to turn the pieces, when the infantry supports of the batteries came up and they had a short hand to hand conflict. But our boys were too many for them, and they, not receiving any support, were driven back with considerable loss.[69]

As had been the case for Ambrose Wright an hour before, "Hays had to retreat for lack of help at the decisive moment."[70] General Hays had expected support on his right from Rodes,[71] who misjudged the time required to deploy his division in order to attack simultaneously with Early. Though Rodes succeeded in making contact with Pender's division on his right, the promising North Carolinian no longer commanded it.[72] Pender had been wounded in the leg by a shell fragment;[73] command of his division passed to General Lane, who prepared to support Rodes.[74] General Ramseur, assigned by Rodes to direct the proposed assault in support of Early, examined Cemetery Hill from the northwest at a distance of two hundred yards. He detected a daunting double line of infantry behind "stone walls and breastworks" backed by artillery. After consulting with General Doles, the pair appealed to Rodes for "further instructions." Rodes recalled his lead brigades because Early had suspended the attack.[75]

"Old Jube" had advanced Gordon's brigade to assist the Carolinians and Louisianans but chose to halt the Georgians "because it was ascertained that no advance was made on the right, and it was evident that the crest of the hill could not be held by my two brigades supported by this one without any assistance, and that the attempt would be attended with a useless sacrifice of life." Early's rationalization is disputed by Harry Pfanz who argues the opinionated Virginian "forfeited" the opportunity to control Cemetery Hill by withholding Gordon's six regiments from the fight.[76] In Douglas Freeman's opinion, the blunder may have rested with Rodes because an attack by his division would have surprised XI Corps.[77] Freeman asserted:

> The whole of the three days' battle produced no more tragic might-have-been than this twilight engagement on the Confederate left. For Early's right regiments had been within 400 feet of the flank of the Federal batteries commanding the approaches to the hill from Rodes's front. Had Rodes's 5000 been at hand to support Early for even an hour, the Federal guns could have been captured and turned on the enemy. Cemetery Hill would have been cleared, and the ridge to the south could have been so enfiladed that the Federals would have been compelled to evacuate it.[78]

Rodes' and Early's failure to coordinate their divisions characterizes the entire Confederate effort on July 2. In the words of a Civil

War centennial historian: "The Confederate operations of July 2 re-
sembled the performance of an orchestra playing a symphony from
a blurred score and without a conductor."[79] During the course of
the battle General Lee lingered near the Seminary, which limited
his ability to oversee events on a line of battle that stretched five
miles.[80] An English observer, Lt. Col. Arthur Fremantle, Coldstream
Guards, observed Lee and states in his memoir that the commanding general sent one message throughout the day.[81]

Every Confederate division involved in the overpowering attacks on Meade's position captured ground. The most significant
attacks, Early's and Anderson's, ultimately floundered. Their gains
were not exploited because their respective superiors failed to adequately supervise or coordinate the action of their divisions. Ewell
"turned in a performance that was less than mediocre."[82] Hill's
management of the Third Corps throughout the entire battle remains rather mysterious "and none of his actions are more enig-
matic than those of the late afternoon of 2 July."[83] Hancock's
dynamism and decisiveness contrasts distinctly with the passivity
of Lee, Ewell, and Hill. Warren's alert reaction to the threat posed to
Little Round Top by Longstreet saved that position. Walter H. Taylor, Lee's adjutant general, wrote: "The whole affair was disjointed.
There was an utter absence of accord in the movements of the several commands, and no decisive results attended the operations of
the second day."[84]

The Army of Northern Virginia had established a presence across
Emmitsburg Road on the right and clung to enemy works on the left
while the Army of the Potomac's center, its most vulnerable point,
remained intact. Lee possessed Pickett's division as a strategic reserve while Meade retained VI Corps for the third day's trial. Around
9:00 P.M., General Meade assembled his corps commanders at the
Leister cottage for a council of war. The company included Gouverneur
Warren, who fell asleep. After discussing the battle, the army's condition and the merits of its position, Maj. Gen. Daniel Butterfield, chief
of staff, posed a question to the pride of generals. "Under existing
circumstances, is it advisable for this army to remain in its present
position, or to retire to another nearer its base of supplies?"[85] General Slocum expressed the consensus of opinion: "Stay and fight it
out." As the council broke up, General Meade remarked to Gibbon:
"'If Lee attacks to-morrow, it will be in *your front*.' I asked him why he
thought so, and he replied, 'Because he has made attacks on both
our flanks and failed, and if he concludes to try it again it will be on
our center.' I expressed the hope that he would, and told General
Meade, with confidence, that if he did we would defeat him."[86] For
the Confederates, hope for decisive victory, that flared brightly on
July 2 then dimmed, was extinguished July 3.

OBSERVATION

General Lee's attack broke down because Anderson failed to commit Posey and Mahone. Due to the Confederate line's length, cooperation and coordination between division and brigade commanders were essential for the utmost employment of mass and force on the offensive. The result of R. H. Anderson's delinquency was Carroll's decisive counterattack on East Cemetery Hill which Harry Hays was unable to thwart. General Meade's ready reserve was displaced, returning from the left flank to reinforce Culp's Hill. Excluding Colonel Carroll's three regiments, sufficient manpower to prevent Confederate conquest of (East) Cemetery Hill, which dominated the Army of the Potomac's center and right, was unavailable. Control of this integral position by Early would have exposed the XI Corps to a rear attack. Had Rodes' division advanced, Howard's corps might have collapsed quickly, threatened front and rear in the dark, leaving the Confederates in command of Cemetery Hill. General Meade would have been forced to withdraw that night or disengage the next day and fight a rear guard action.

Richard S. Ewell allowed the Federals to occupy Culp's Hill unmolested on July 1, with the cosequence that the Stonewall Division's offensive power was wasted. Natural obstacles along with strong works rendered the hill secure from frontal attack. The small measure of success gained by Steuart's brigade on the right flank was due to the previous withdrawal of the defenders. General Greene's foresight in constructing strong works with a traverse prevented exploitation of the modest gain before reinforcements arrived.

Ewell's decision to attack Culp's Hill was taken under his own responsiblity. Orders from Lee did not dictate a full-scale assault. Perhaps Ewell wished to rectify an earlier error. The inescapable truth is that the Stonewall Division was squandered: it contributed nothing to the outcome of the battle. This condition resulted from Lee's misplacement of Johnson's division and leaving it under Ewell's control. General Lee's key tactical mistake during the battle was leaving a division east of Gettysburg instead of deploying it to attack more favorable ground south of town. Despite this disadvantage, Lee succeeded in breaking Meade's line on Cemetery Ridge and forced his counterpart to commit his ready reserve to restore the Army of the Potomac's left flank. Lee in turn chose to retain Pickett in reserve thereby negating the advantage achieved on Cemetery Ridge—the knockout punch, was delivered a day too late.

Maj. Gen. James Ewell Brown Stuart, commanded cavalry division

His decision to conduct a raid instead of supplying intelligence crippled Lee's strategy to fight the Army of the Potomac in detail.

Battles & Leaders

Gen. Robert Edward Lee, commander, Army of Northern Virginia

He failed to control his army on July 2 thereby allowing it to conduct uncoordinated attacks.

MOLLUS, United States Army Military History Institute

Lt. Gen. Richard Stoddert Ewell, commanded Second Corps

He failed to occupy Culp's Hill on July 1, then ordered an unnecessary attack to capture it on July 2.

Battles & Leaders

Maj. Gen. George Gordon Meade, commander, Army of the Potomac

In his first battle as an army commander, he inflicted the second defeat on the Army of Northern Virginia.

Battles & Leaders

Maj. Gen. Joseph Hooker

Replaced as commander of the Army of the Potomac on the eve of battle

Battles & Leaders

**Lt. Gen. Ambrose Powell Hill,
commanded the Third Corps**

He began the battle with a forced reconnaissance to Gettysburg on July 1.

Battles & Leaders

**Maj. Gen. Jubal Early, commanded
a division in the Second Corps**

He failed to advance supporting troops
to hold Cemetery Hill on July 2.

Battles & Leaders

**Maj. Gen. Winfield Scott Hancock,
commanded the II Corps**

His dogged leadership throughout
the battle proved crucial in defeating
the Confederates.

Battles & Leaders

**Maj. Gen. John Fulton Reynolds,
commanded the left wing,
Army of the Potomac**

He decided to defend Gettysburg at
the cost of his life.

Battles & Leaders

Lt. Gen. James Longstreet, commanded the First Corps

His controversial role as senior corps commander at Gettysburg contributed to Confederate defeat.

Battles & Leaders

Maj. Gen. Richard Heron Anderson, commanded a division in the Third Corps

He failed to utilize his entire division during the attack on Cemetery Ridge on July 2.

Battles & Leaders

Brig. Gen. Evander McIvor Law, commanded a brigade in Hood's division

His fixation on the Round Tops prevented Hood's division from attacking the III Corps in the rear.

Battles & Leaders

Maj. Gen. Daniel Edgar Sickles, commanded the III Corps

On July 2, his troops absorbed the power of Longstreet's attack when they advanced from Cemetery Ridge to Emmitsburg Road and Rose Woods.

Battles & Leaders

Brig. Gen. George Sears Greene,
commanded a brigade in the XII Corps

His determination to fortify Culp's Hill proved decisive in its defense on July 2.

Battles & Leaders

Maj. Gen. George Edward Pickett,
commanded the First Corps Division

His division was sacrificed because Longstreet failed to foresee its need for immediate support.

Battles & Leaders

Col. E. Porter Alexander,
commanded the First Corps Artillery

He gave the order for Pickett's division to advance on July 3.

Battles & Leaders

Howard Malcolm, left, *and Robert Ryland Walthall,* right

These brothers from Richmond, photographed in 1861, both participated in Longstreet's Assault as members of Companies D and G, 1st Virginia. Robert was slightly wounded. At the Battle of Drewry's Bluff, May 16, 1864, Robert exposed himself to Federal fire "when a ball crashed through his brain and he fell fluttering in my arms and had fought his last fight." Howard survived the Siege of Petersburg and died in 1924.

Photograph courtesy of Grace Turner Karish

**Brig. Gen. John Gibbon,
commanded a division in the II Corps**

First commander of the Iron Brigade, his division defended Cemetery Ridge on July 2 and July 3.

Battles & Leaders

**Brig. Gen. Lewis Addision Armistead,
commanded a brigade
in Pickett's division**

He led remnants of the division over the stone wall near the Angle.

Battles & Leaders

**Edward Rives, Surgeon in Charge,
Pickett's division, 1863**

Daniel Drake and His Followers

Chapter 6
Longstreet's Assault

...overwhelmed on the flanks & by reinforcements...

Porter Alexander

During the second day of battle at Gettysburg, the Army of Northern Virginia inflicted approximately 10,000 casualties on the Federals for a loss of 6,800 without achieving a single major objective.[1] The "partial successes" attained by Ewell and Longstreet[2] induced General Lee's belief "that, with proper concert of action, and with the increased support that the positions gained on the right [Peach Orchard] would enable the artillery to render the assaulting columns, we should ultimately succeed, and it was accordingly determined to continue the attack." Ewell and Longstreet would attack simultaneously. The Stonewall Division, augmented by two brigades from Rodes and one from Early, would attempt to "dislodge" the enemy from Culp's Hill. Reinforced by Pickett's division, Longstreet would hurl his entire corps against Cemetery Ridge.[3]

The early morning offensive originally envisioned by Lee never unfolded. "General Longstreet's dispositions were not completed as early as was expected, but before notice could be sent to General Ewell, General Johnson had already become engaged and it was too late to recall him."[4] Again, Longstreet's dilatory attitude embarrassed General Lee's strategy. During the night Longstreet neglected to bring up Pickett's division to deploy for action at daylight. This oversight forced Lee to scrap his original plan for a simultaneous "daylight" attack by Ewell and Longstreet.[5]

Under cover of darkness, General Walker's Stonewall Brigade rejoined its division. The brigades of Junius Daniel and four of Edward O'Neal's regiments also reinforced Johnson. "Extra Billy" Smith contributed two regiments, the 49th and 52nd Virginia.[6] At 4:30 A.M., Union artillery opened on Ewell's corps and fired for 15 minutes,[7] which precipitated a series of Confederate assaults against

Geary and Greene. Johnson's reinforced division assailed Culp's Hill unsupported by artillery. The Stonewall Brigade and Williams' Louisianans made the first attempt, followed by O'Neal's Alabamians at 8:00 A.M. Walker's Virginians conducted a second assault an hour later "which was done with equally bad success as our former efforts..."

> The scenario for each rush up the hill was remarkably the same...Bursting shells broke and splintered trees, chipped the rocks and boulders covering the slope, and took down men. As the Southerners closed on the brow of the hill, the air was filled with minie balls, as volley after volley was fired by the Union defenders from behind the log fortifications. The Federals shot so fast and so often that the Southerners could only hear a single deafening noise...The Confederates ran from boulder to boulder seeking cover. Not able to reach the top of the hill because of the intense fire, many Rebels could not retreat and were trapped behind trees and rocks. Wave after wave of assaulting infantrymen broke against the unyielding defense.[8]

The 66th Ohio played a notable part in repelling the Confederate assaults in a manner duplicated by the 8th Ohio in the afternoon. Pursuant to orders from Colonel Candy, Lt. Col. Eugene Powell moved his regiment over the works where I Corps connected with Greene's New Yorkers. After driving away Jones' Virginians at dawn, Powell's people took a position directly in front of the 60th New York, perpendicular to Greene's earthworks.[9] The Buckeyes occupied "a perfect location to deliver an enfilading fire on the advancing columns." Throughout the long morning of unequal combat, the Rebels never attempted to drive out the exposed unit.[10]

The final Confederate attack occurred on the opposite end of Geary's division, away from the 66th Ohio. General Steuart's brigade left the log breastworks they had occupied the previous 14 hours and formed for the assault. General Daniel's North Carolinians settled into the works vacated by Steuart's men. At 10:25 A.M., Steuart flashed his sword and set his line in motion through the woods and into a field.[11] A member of the 2nd Maryland Battalion described the outcome.

> As the line, well preserved, passed into the opening just beyond, a burst of flame and shot and shell seemed to sweep the devoted band from the earth. To advance was impossible— the odds ahead were too fearfully apparent; to remain was simple madness. There was no alternative, and so the order to retire was given...the survivors looked around with wonder that even they were left alive.[12]

The "Cincinnati Regiment" (5th Ohio) and 147th Pennsylvania (Candy) allowed the Rebels to approach within one hundred yards before dropping their hammers. On the left of Steuart's line, the Virginians and 1st North Carolina faltered, then fell back. On the right, the 2nd Maryland Battalion and 3rd North Carolina continued forward.[13] The 29th and 109th Pennsylvania (Kane) opened fire at a distance of 60 yards. A few Marylanders advanced to within forty paces before the battalion broke for the rear[14] which left the 3rd North Carolina "alone moving to the front, unsupported, when the officers and men were ordered to withdraw, which was done slowly and without confusion...This last charge on the third day was a cruel thing for the Third. They had borne their full share of the engagement, not even enjoying the protection of the works they had captured from the enemy."[15]

Steuart's survivors regrouped to await a counterattack[16] as General Johnson accepted the verdict of the battlefield: "The enemy were too securely intrenched and in too great numbers to be dislodged by the force at my command."[17] Soon after the last Confederate attack, Brigadier General Ruger's First Division, was ordered by General Williams "to try the enemy on the right...with two regiments, and, if practicable to force him out."[18] A probe by the 2nd Massachusetts and 27th Indiana from Col. Silas Colgrove's Third Brigade, was characterized by Johnson as "a demonstration in force." It was repulsed by the 2nd Virginia and Smith's brigade with heavy losses.[19] This needless action ended the battle on this sector of the field. Ewell's corps recrossed Rock Creek—by noon the sanguinary struggle for Culp's Hill had ended.[20] Scores of wounded from the 2nd Maryland Battalion remained on the slopes.[21] Two hours before Steuart's doomed assault, the 1st Maryland Eastern Shore Regiment returned to Culp's Hill.[22] Col. James Wallace recollected: "We sorrowfully gathered up many of our old friends & acquaintances & had them carefully & tenderly cared for."[23]

While Ewell's corps pursued its hopeless task against XII Corps defenders of Culp's Hill, General Lee reconnoitered the Union line on Cemetery Ridge. He developed a new plan and established a point of attack for an assault conducted by Longstreet. Lee considered the Union line on Cemetery Ridge weak where the Emmitsburg Road passed through a depression. He believed "that by forcing the Federal line at that point and turning toward Cemetery Hill the right would be taken in flank and the remainder would be neutralized, as its fire would be destructive to friend and foe..." Lee also judged the previous two days of combat had weakened the Army of the Potomac's unit cohesion and reduced its defensive capability. Hill and Longstreet listened as General Lee explained his decision. Longstreet pointed out that the right flank of his assaulting column would be vulnerable to Union artillery fire from Little Round Top. Col. Armistead L. Long of Lee's staff countered this objection by assuring Longstreet that artillery fire from Little Round Top "could be suppressed by our batteries."[24]

Longstreet convinced Lee it would be inadvisable to include the divisions of McLaws and Hood in the assault because the opposition could move to crush the right flank of his corps, gain the army's rear, and cut the Confederates off from the Potomac River. He also pointed out, gratuitously, "that the conditions were different from those in the days of Napoleon, when field batteries had a range of six hundred yards and musketry about sixty yards."[25] Determined to "strike" the enemy, Lee relented and told Longstreet that McLaws and Hood would be replaced by two of Hill's divisions. Unconvinced, Longstreet replied: "General, I have been a soldier all my life. I have been with soldiers engaged in fights by couples, by squads, companies, regiments and armies, and should know, as well as anyone, what soldiers can do. It is my opinion that no 15,000 men ever arrayed for battle can take that position." Unmoved, Lee ordered Longstreet to prepare for the assault.[26] General Hill "begged" Lee to be allowed to employ every regiment of his corps. According to Hill's chief of staff, Lee "refused, and said what remains of your corps will be my only reserve, and it will be needed if Gen'l Longstreet's attack should fail."[27]

Substitution of Hill's troops for his own gave Longstreet "substantially the same effective strength" possessed by the First Corps; it seemed the sensible measure for Lee to take under the circumstances.[28] Heth's division and two brigades of Pender's division were designated by Lee to reinforce Longstreet.[29] General Pettigrew had assumed command of the division due to Heth's debility.[30] Choosing this division to participate in the decisive assault was questionable. Though the 11th Mississippi had been absent on July 1 and returned to reinforce Davis' brigade on July 2, the division had lost approximately 40 percent of its effective strength.[31] Moreover, Brockenbrough's brigade of Virginians "was in a chaotic stage of demoralization" and unreliable.[32] On July 2, the division had formed a line of battle in support of batteries on Seminary Ridge. Approximately 9:00 A.M. the following morning, Heth's division shifted its position a quarter mile to the left and deployed in rear of Maj. William J. Pegrams' artillery battalion (Hill).[33]

The decision to employ Scales' North Carolinians was also unfortunate since the brigade had endured ghastly losses on July 1.[34] Only two field officers remained to lead five regiments. Col. William

L. J. Lowrance, 34th North Carolina, commanded the brigade.[35] Lane's brigade was a logical selection since its losses during the previous two days had been "but slight."[36] Apparently, inclusion of Scales in the attacking column was due to the division's deployment. Thomas' and Perrin's brigades, which formed the division's front line on July 3, conducted "very heavy" skirmishing. Lowrance and Lane supported them in the second line. Federal pressure probably prevented the exchange of Scales (Lowrance) for Thomas or Perrin. General Lane, who commanded the division, was ordered by Hill to withdraw the reserve line and report to Longstreet as support for Pettigrew.[37] Around 12:30 P.M., Isaac Trimble took command of Pender's division and assumed control over Lowrance and Lane.[38] The Baltimorean "rode down the line and halted at different regiments and made us little speeches—saying he was a stranger to us and had been sent to command us in the absence of our wounded general and would lead us upon Cemetery Hill [Ridge]..."[39]

When the Virginians approached the rear of Seminary Ridge, Longstreet explained to Pickett where to shelter his troops, the direction Lee intended for the division to take during the assault and its objective, 1,400 yards away.[40] Pickett's division deployed diagonally to the Union line, behind the crest of Seminary Ridge.[41] Brig. Gen. Richard B. Garnett's brigade (8th, 18th, 19th, 28th, and 56th Virginia) composed the left of Pickett's first line while Brig. James L. Kemper's brigade (1st, 3rd, 7th, 11th, and 24th Virginia) held the right. Brig. Gen. Lewis A. Armistead's brigade (9th, 14th, 38th, 53rd, and 57th Virginia) formed in rear of Garnett as a supporting line for an approximate total of 5,800 Old Dominion infantry.[42]

The brigades of General Wilcox and Colonel Lang, intended to protect Pickett's right flank, rested two hundred yards in front of the Virginians, behind the artillery posted on the Emmitsburg Road.[43] General Longstreet did not concern himself with arrangement of the Third Corps troops. Though Lee and Hill share blame for their defective deployment, it was Longstreet's responsibility to oversee them since they had been assigned to him. "Like the day before, Longstreet did as ordered but without spirit and grave concerns."[44]

Pickett's Virginians, confident of success, settled on Seminary Ridge around 9:00 A.M.[45] According to the 53rd Virginia's lieutenant colonel, the division's "*esprit de corps* could not have been better...They felt the gravity of the situation, for they knew well the metal of the foe in their front; they were serious and resolute, but not disheartened. None of the usual jokes, common on the eve of battle, were indulged in...officers and men knew at what cost and at what risk the advance was to be made, but they had deliberately made up their minds to attempt it." Capt. James R. Hutter, Company H, 11th Virginia, observed members of Kemper's brigade shake hands saying: "Boys, many a one of us will bite the dust here today, but we will say to General Lee, if he wants them driven out, we will do it."[46] A III Corps prisoner, who witnessed the assault, recalled: "In spite of the marked incongruity of color and makeup in the uniforms, particularly in the matter of head dress, which often boarded [sic] on the fantastic, there was no mistaking the fact that these men were tried, disciplined veterans."[47]

On Cemetery Ridge, equally determined and experienced troops awaited Pickett, Pettigrew, and Trimble. General Hancock again led the redoubtable II Corps; Gibbon had reverted to his division commander role.[48] General Gibbon's Second Division held the focal point of Longstreet's impending assault, the Copse of Trees. North of Gibbon's position, the Third Division, minus Carroll's brigade, extended to Ziegler's Grove. Col. Eliakim Sherrill now led the brigade of New Yorkers holding the end of the line. General Newton positioned his First Division on Gibbon's left. Defense of Gibbon's and Hays' sector was strengthened by a stone wall that ran south from Ziegler's Grove along the crest of the ridge. At a point about 250 feet from the Copse of Trees, the wall angled west for approximately 200 feet, then stretched south again a few hundred feet before terminating. The perpendicular point where the wall resumed its course toward the trees is remembered as the Angle.[49]

The Philadelphia Brigade (Webb) defended the area around the Angle. Along the wall rested the 69th Pennsylvania. Behind them there was Company A, 4th U.S. Artillery. To their right, up to the Angle, the wall was vacant which allowed the cannon a field of fire. The 71st Pennsylvania was located behind the guns along a portion of the wall running along the crest. In reserve were Companies A and B, 106th Pennsylvania, along with the 72nd Pennsylvania, behind Colonel Hall's Third Brigade,[50] on line next to Webb. Three regiments held the Third Brigade's front line. The 42nd New York and 19th Massachusetts formed a reserve in the right rear. Colonel Harrow's First Brigade continued the line to the left.[51]

Webb's well-tested Pennsylvanians had assisted in the repulse of Wright's Georgians the previous evening.[52] According to Cpl. John Buckley, Company K, members of the 69th Pennsylvania retrieved discarded enemy weapons. The best were selected, reloaded, then leaned against the wall. "The ammunition we found to contain three buck-shot and a ball...We abstracted the buck-shot from the ammunition and reloaded the spare guns putting 12 to the load, and almost every man had from two to five guns loaded that were not used until Pickett got within fifty yards of the wall."[53] Troops unprotected by stone security constructed rail breastworks and "slight" rifle pits one foot deep.[54] Supporting II Corps infantry were five companies. From right to left, beginning in Ziegler's Grove, were: Company I, 1st U.S. Artillery, Lt. George A. Woodruff; Company A, 1st Rhode Island Artillery, Capt. William A. Arnold; Company A, 4th U.S. Artillery, Lt. Alonzo H. Cushing; Company B, 1st Rhode Island Artillery, Lt. T. Frederick Brown; and Company B, 1st New York Artillery, Capt. James McKay Rorty. Lieutenant Brown, wounded July 2, was replaced by Lt. W. S. Perrin. Losses in men and horses had forced two of Brown's guns to be withdrawn and sent to the rear.[55]

In the morning, General Pettigrew had reported to Longstreet:

who directed him to form in rear of Pickett's Division and support his advance upon Cemetery Hill [Ridge], which would be commenced as soon as the fire from our artillery should have driven the enemy from his guns and prepared the way for attack, and I presume that it was in consequence of this having been the first plan settled on that the erroneous report was circulated that Heth's Division was assigned the duty of supporting that of Pickett. But the order referred to was countermanded almost as soon as given, and General Pettigrew was ordered to advance upon the same line with Pickett, a portion of Pender's Division acting as supports.[56]

Pettigrew informed Col. Birkett D. Fry, 13th Alabama, now commander of Archer's brigade, of the planned assault and instructed him "to see General Pickett at once and have an understanding as to the *dress* [alignment] in the advance." Colonel Fry found General Pickett "in excellent spirits." He was supremely confident that his Virginians would be able to drive the Federals from the ridge after they had been "demoralized by our artillery." Garnett agreed to dress on Fry, who returned to Pettigrew and reported the accord.[57] General Lee resolved that infantry preparation should lack nothing. He rode along his lines with Longstreet twice, then repeated the exercise without him.[58] His plan incorporated a preliminary cannonade to silence enemy batteries on Cemetery Ridge. After the Federal artillery had been suppressed, the troops would advance.[59] Lee directed his own batteries "to be pushed forward as the infantry progressed, protect their flanks, and support their attacks closely."[60]

Colonel Alexander, who exercised command of the First Corps artillery, learned that a Copse of Trees on Cemetery Ridge signified the point of attack and thought it was the town cemetery. Around 9:00 A.M., he began repositioning the corps' cannon. Seventy-five artillery pieces were sited on an "irregular line" of 1,300 yards that extended from the Peach Orchard northwest to the edge of Spangler's Woods. Eight pieces remained on the extreme right to support the flank below the Round Tops. While engaged in his preparations, Brig. Gen. William N. Pendleton, chief of artillery, offered Alexander use of short-range howitzers from Third Corps. Colonel Alexander placed the guns commanded by Maj. Charles Richardson to the left rear of his gun line[61] and intended holding their fire from the preliminary cannonade. Richardson's cannon would be kept "under cover & out of view, so that with fresh men, & uninjured horses, & full chests of ammunition, these 9 [7] light howitzers might follow Pickett's infantry in the charge, more promptly, & also, perhaps more *safely* than guns out of the firing line could do."[62]

Sixty additional cannon under Col. R. Lindsay Walker (Hill) extended the Army of Northern Virginia's array of artillery north to the Fairfield Road.[63] Beyond the road were 20 guns belonging to the battalions of Walker and Snowden. Two additional battalions under Lt. Col. Hilary P. Jones and Col. William Nelson (Ewell) were available to contribute to the cannonade. A pair of breech-loading Whitworth rifles imported from Great Britain assigned to an Alabama battery were positioned on "a commanding point north of the railroad cut..."[64] The imposing line of 172 tubes was flawed because 56 cannon remained mute during the cannonade while 80 of the 84 guns involved belonging to the Second and Third Corps "were in the same line *parallel to the position of the enemy...*" A more prudent disposition of the artillery in an arc would have brought Cemetery Hill under a crossfire. General Pendleton was responsible for faulty placement of Lee's artillery.[65]

Preparations for the grand cannonade were complete in the forenoon.[66] At noon, General Longstreet informed Colonel Alexander that when Pickett was ready, he himself would order the batteries to open fire. In the meantime, Alexander found an observation point on the left of Pickett's line and discussed the upcoming assault with General Wright.[67] Confederate witnesses noted that General Longstreet was glum, "listless and despairing."[68] Longstreet admitted after the war that July 3, 1863, was the most depressing day of his life. He believed Pickett's men would be sacrificed in a hopeless charge. Unwilling to bear the "entire responsibility" for ordering the charge, he sent an exculpatory note to Colonel Alexander. "If the artillery fire does not have the effect to drive off the enemy or greatly demoralize him, so as to make our efforts pretty certain, I would prefer that you should not advise General Pickett to make the charge. I shall rely a great deal on your judgment to determine the matter, and shall expect you to let Pickett know when the moment offers."[69]

The senior lieutenant general's message provided the colonel with a "sudden shock."[70] The tone of his commander's words suggested to Alexander "that there was some alternative to the attack and placed on me the responsibility of deciding the question."[71] Colonel Alexander replied that he could judge the effect of his fire only by the enemy's counterfire. Smoke would obscure the field and the condition of the enemy infantry would be unobservable. Sufficient ammunition was at hand for only one attempt to break the Federal line on Cemetery Ridge. General Longstreet's second note to Alexander read:

> Colonel. The intention is to advance the infantry, if the artillery has the desired effect of driving the enemy's off, or having other effect such as to warrant us in making the attack. When the moment arrives advise Gen. Pickett, and of course advance such artillery as you can use in aiding the attack.[72]

Colonel Alexander felt the weight of responsibility because he did not believe his guns alone would rout the enemy. He entertained "a vague hope that with Ewell's and Hill's cooperation something might happen..."[73]

The artillery colonel handed the paper to General Wright, who remarked: "'He has put the responsibility back upon you.' I said, 'General, tell me exactly what *you* think of this attack.' He said, 'Well, Alexander, it is mostly a question of supports. It is not as hard to get there as it looks. I was there yesterday with my brigade. The real difficulty is to stay there after you get there—for the whole infernal Yankee army is up there in a bunch.'" Alexander realized the final decision to conduct the charge must be made before the bombardment began because battlefield conditions would prevent accurate assessment of the enemy's condition. General Lee expected the assault to go forward and he had presumably resolved the question of supports, therefore Alexander interviewed Pickett and "felt his pulse..." Satisfied with Pickett's optimism and Wright's encouragement, Alexander wrote Longstreet: "General. When our artillery fire is at its best I shall order Gen. Pickett to charge."[74]

Shortly before 1:00 P.M. the order to open the bombardment reached Maj. Benjamin F. Eshleman, who commanded the renowned Washington Artillery of New Orleans. At 1:00 P.M., a discharge from the Third Company shattered the summer stillness in Adams County. A faulty friction primer was quickly replaced and a second discharge followed. Smoke soon billowed above the Rebel batteries as cannoneers worked their pieces in the mightiest artillery exchange ever heard in the Western Hemisphere.[75] The volume of Union counterfire from 80 guns escalated slowly but within five minutes the entire line from Little Round Top to Cemetery Hill seemed volcanic in its intensity.[76] A Tennessean recollected: "It seemed as though the demons of demolition were turned loose, but no imagination can adequately conceive of the magnitude of this artillery duel. It surpassed the ordinary battery fire as the earthquake, or some convulsion of nature, surpasses the mutterings of an ordinary thunderstorm. As if to heighten the scene of terror and dismay, out from the devoted farm-houses rushed old men, women, and children."[77]

General Hunt, observing the Confederates redeploying their artillery, believed the "unbroken mass" of batteries indicated an assault on the Union center. He ordered his own battery commanders to hold their fire when the enemy cannonade began, for 15 or 20 minutes, to avoid exhausting their own ammunition. Hunt wanted to break up and repel the Rebel infantry formations "or at least bring them to our lines in such condition as to make them easy prey." When the Union artillerists opened, they were instructed to concentrate moderate fire on the most destructive enemy batteries. The cannonade commenced as Hunt imparted his instructions to Hazlett's battery on Little Round Top, now commanded by Lt. Benjamin F. Rittenhouse.[78] General Hancock, in command of the defensive line on Cemetery Ridge, interfered with Hunt's purpose to conserve long-range ammunition. He insisted that enemy artillery fire be returned to encourage his infantry, reasoning that short-range canister was sufficient to defeat the impending assault. Hunt's program to break up the Confederate charge before it reached the Union line was forsaken.[79]

Most Rebel rounds passed over the prone II Corps infantry to impact a thousand yards behind Cemetery Ridge. The Leister cottage was struck repeatedly. Ambulances loaded with wounded traveling the Taneytown Road became targets and hospitals "were riddled." Crazed horses bounded through the fields.[80] Confederate artillerists elevated their pieces too high[81] and cut fuses too long[82] which caused shells to explode caissons or limbers beyond Cemetery Ridge rather than burst above Meade's prone regiments. The chief effect of this misdirected fire was to drive the reserve artillery and the ammunition train beyond the Taneytown Road.[83]

Roaring cannon and bursting shells were so continuous that individual reports became indistinguishable.[84] Large, round shells were plainly visible as they curved in their trajectory toward Taneytown Road but projectiles from rifled cannon were invisible unless they tumbled in flight. A bursting shell would throw "its fragments about in a most disagreeably promiscuous manner, or, first striking the ground, plough a great furrow in the earth and rocks, throwing these last about in a way quite as dangerous as the pieces of the exploding shell."[85] Though members of the 19th Massachusetts hugged the ground around boulders, many were hit in the back. "Men were constantly seen hobbling off, with blood streaming from their wounds."[86] South of the Copse of Trees, a member of the 1st Minnesota recounted his experience.

> The air seemed to be filled with the hissing, screaming, bursting missiles, and all of them really seemed to be directed at us. They knew our exact position, for before we lay down they could with the naked eye plainly see us, and where our lines were, and tried to explode their shells directly over us; but fortunately most of them went just far enough to clear us, while many struck in front of us and bounded over us. We lay behind a slight rise of ground, just enough, by lying close, to hide us from the view of the rebels. A good many shell and pieces struck mighty close to us, and among us, but strange to say, none of us were injured, while the troops that lay behind us had many killed and wounded...I kept thinking, surely they cannot fire much longer; their guns will get so hot they will have to stop...[87]

General Gibbon crossed the ridge line and beheld "the most infernal pandemonium it has ever been my fortune to look upon." Very few infantrymen could be seen, but the legs of Cushing's cannoneers serving their guns were perceptible beneath the pall of smoke. Walking past the Copse of Trees to the stone wall where his infantry sought shelter, Gibbon tried to detect enemy movements. Smoke obscured his line of sight and he determined that the passage of innumerable enemy projectiles signified either a retreat or an assault.[88] North of the Copse of Trees on Hays' front, the 14th Connecticut huddled with the 1st Delaware, protected by the stone wall. Because the wall had been constructed on a ledge, short rounds bounded off the outcropping instead of driving into the ground and exploding. The regiment received little damage but Arnold's battery on their left "sustained a more serious loss." One of the three-inch rifles was directly behind Sgt. Major William B. Hincks. The concussion of each discharge threw gravel on him "and I could not only see and smell the thick cloud of burning powder, but could taste it also." Hincks' perspiration formed mud in the dusty soil.[89] The 108th New York, in support of Woodruff's battery, "suffered fearfully." Woodruff, loosing 75 percent of his horses, soon depleted his long-range ammunition. The New Yorkers assisted the artillerists in moving the guns to the rear to await Rebel infantry. Unintimidated by the shot and shell, General Hays rode in front of his regiments "exhorting the 'boys' to stand fast and fight like men."[90] Forward of the main line, the 8th Ohio (Carroll) lay in a ditch along the Emmitsburg Road. The Buckeyes were caught between the fire of both armies.[91]

> Nothing more terrific than this storm of artillery can be imagined. The missiles of both armies passed over our heads. The roar of the guns was deafening, the air was soon clouded with smoke, and the shriek and startling crack of exploding shells above, around, and in our midst; the blowing up of caissons in our rear; the driving through the air of fence-rails, posts, and limbs of trees, the groans of dying men, the neighing of frantic and wounded horses, created a scene of absolute horror.[92]

Pickett's division waited the fateful order to advance beneath the "whirl and whiz of shot and shell." Many soldiers were struck by shell fragments while others were prostrated by the heat.[93] Lacking tools, the Virginians could not dig gopher holes for temporary protection. According to Howard Walthall, 1st Virginia, the noise was "terriffic, and with the rays of the sun was enough to weaken the bravery of the strongest in the ranks. The shells were exploding over our heads and hurling death in the ranks, the two men on my right and left were struck. One Davy Edwards, was killed outright; and the other, Jas. Norton was sadly disfigured. It was Hell as Sherman subsequently said war was. I know I felt almost paralized, and would have dug a hole in the ground to escape if it had been possible, but I kept as calm as possible..."[94]

The ground shook—in every direction "might be seen guns, swords, haversacks, heads, limbs, flesh and bones in confusion or dangling in the air or bounding on the earth." Five men were killed in the 8th Virginia. Maj. Edmund Berkeley's hat was "plastered" by the brains of Pvt. Albert J. Morris, who was decapitated.[95] The 3rd and 7th Virginia were particularly hard hit.[96] Sgt. Maj. David E. Johnston of the latter regiment witnessed eight men killed or wounded by one blast. Johnston raised his head "to get, if possible, a breath of fresh air." The next moment another explosion tore the heads off two men and wounded two others. Johnston suffered broken ribs and a contusion to his left lung.[97] Company F, 3rd Virginia, "suffered terribly." Lts. Patrick H. and John C. Arthur were lost. "Nearly every minute the cry of mortal agony was heard above the roar and rumble of the guns."[98] Armistead's brigade "suffered but slight loss,"[99] though Col. William R. Aylett, 53rd Virginia, became a casualty "and retired from the field."[100] At the peak of the bombardment, a frantic fox that bolted in the direction of Lane's brigade was surrounded. Capt. J. McLeod Turner, 7th North Carolina, killed the critter with his sword.[101] During the bombardment, Pickett's division lost at least 300 and "probably near 500 men."[102]

Anxiously, Colonel Alexander observed the effect of his fire on the Federal artillery because he "had intended fully to start Pickett on his travels after the Arty had been at it about ten minutes, for he had a long ways to go & ammunition burns up very fast in an affair like that. But the fire developed by the Federal line was so perfectly terrific that I did not believe any Infantry could traverse half the necessary distance under it & firmly as I intended to order Pickett forward, at the end of the ten minutes I could not bring myself to do it."[103] He believed that when Pickett began moving, 30 minutes would elapse before the column closed with the enemy. With an ammunition supply sufficient for an hour's firing, he determined to send Pickett forward "at the very first favorable sign..."[104] Alexander hoped "to silence some at least" of the guns on Cemetery Ridge before instructing Pickett to advance.[105]

During the height of the bombardment, General Hancock rode along the ridge crest with an orderly carrying the II Corps standard to inspire the boys. One regimental band began playing the "Star-Spangled Banner." Removing his hat, "Hancock the Superb" waved and smiled at his soldiers, "never showing a trace of concern about the shells and solid shot dropping about him."[106] Exposed on the crest of Cemetery Ridge without the benefit of works, II Corps batteries suffered severe losses in men, horses, and guns.[107] Screaming shells inflicted terrific punishment upon Cushing's battery. A disemboweled artilleryman blew his brains out. Two guns were disabled and wheels on three others were splintered but quickly replaced. Severely wounded in the groin and right shoulder, Lieutenant Cushing refused to quit his post. Captain Rorty was killed and his battery wrecked. Brown's battery was reduced to three pieces.[108] North of Little Round Top, Lieutenant Colonel McGilvery had established 39 guns in the area where he held off Barksdale the previous day. A "slight parapet" protected his cannoneers from harm and few casualties occurred.[109] Shortly after the battle, Captain Phillips, 5th Massachusetts Battery, explained in a letter:

> ...My men were entirely sheltered by our parapet, and about the only damage done was to kill 8 or 10 horses.
> Viewed as a display of fireworks, the Rebel practice was entirely successful, but as a military demonstration it was the biggest humbug of the season.[110]

Once the Confederates had expended an estimated 10,000 rounds, McGilvery ordered "a slow, well-directed fire" concentrated on the opposing batteries.[111]

Approximately 2:30 P.M., General Hunt ordered his batteries to cease fire because ammunition was running low. He judged the danger in bringing up a resupply from the rear as too great. General Meade concurred and Hunt received the commanding general's directive from Capt. Henry H. Bingham, aide to General Hancock.[112] Shortly after the Union cannon ceased firing, the Confederate batteries fell silent. No longer terrorized by thoughts of being torn to shreds by shell fragments, the end of the bombardment brought a feeling of relief to Union soldiers.

Alexander Webb and Alonzo Cushing conferred near the Copse of Trees.[113] Cushing reported that most of his guns were disabled but with more men he could still work his remaining two. Webb agreed to provide men and stated: "Cushing, it is my opinion that the Confederate infantry will now advance and attack our position." Cushing in great pain manfully responded: "I had better run my guns right up to the stone fence and bring all my canister alongside each piece." "All right, do so," Webb answered. Assisted by volunteers from the 71st Pennsylvania, First Sgt. Frederick Fuger wheeled the pieces forward next to Company I, 69th Pennsylvania. Fuger piled canister behind No. 2 gun.[114]

General Hunt called up fresh guns from the Artillery Reserve to replace the crippled batteries of Brown and Arnold, which withdrew from the fight. At least one piece belonging to Arnold's battery remained with a crew near the 14th Connecticut. Capt. Andrew Cowan's 1st New York Independent Battery, in action with Doubleday's division, received orders to move farther right. His six pieces replaced Brown's battery near Webb's brigade. Company K, 1st New York Artillery, Capt. Robert H. Fitzhugh, and Company A, 1st New Jersey Artillery, Lt. Augustin N. Parsons, went into action near the Copse of Trees. The timely arrival of these batteries materially aided the defense of Cemetery Ridge since "...the enemy's infantry were advancing very rapidly."[115]

Scanning Cemetery Ridge, Colonel Alexander sought a sign that enemy artillery fire had diminished. With his own ammunition running out, he knew Pickett must advance soon and sent a note to him that read: "If you are coming at all you must come at once, or I cannot give you proper support, but the enemy's fire has not slackened at all. At least 18 guns are still firing from the cemetery [ridge] itself." Moments later he saw Brown and Arnold leaving the ridge. Cushing's remaining two pieces were silent and Alexander concluded his fire had produced the desired effect. More importantly, he saw no enemy batteries coming up to replace the ones that had withdrawn. This development induced Alexander to dispatch another urgent note to Pickett. "For God's sake come quick. The 18 guns are gone. Come quick or I can't support you." The Georgian sent two copies of the message accompanied by a verbal admonition because "I wanted to get them inspired to disregard everything but getting there."[116] Though four opposing batteries on Cemetery Ridge had been rendered nearly impotent, unbeknownst to Alexander and his superiors, the grand cannonade had failed in its primary objective to demoralize the Union infantry. Webb's brigade lost around 50 men while casualties among the Federals "holding the position did not exceed two hundred."[117]

Upon receiving Alexander's first note, Pickett approached "Old Pete," his friend and patron. Longstreet scrutinized the message without comment, convinced that the outcome of Pickett's advance would be "needless slaughter." Pickett inquired: "General, shall I advance?" Turning his face aside, Longstreet gave no order. Pickett repeated the question. Overcome by his feelings, Longstreet would not speak to avoid betraying his lack of confidence in the assault's success. He sadly bowed his head and turned to mount his horse. "Sir, I shall lead my division forward." General Pickett rode away to set in motion the charge that carried his name into glory.[118]

Unattended, Longstreet rode over to Alexander's position where he could observe Pickett's movement toward the ridge. Alexander revealed to Longstreet that Richardson's howitzers had disappeared and insufficient ammunition remained with the batteries to properly support Pickett. Longstreet responded vehemently. "Go & halt Pickett right where he is, & replenish your ammunition." Alexander explained that the ammunition train was nearly empty and the time necessary to fulfill his order would allow the Federals to recover from the bombardment. He concluded: "Our only chance is to follow up now—to strike while the iron is hot." Examining the enemy position through his field glasses Longstreet replied deliberately. "I don't want to make this attack—I believe it will fail—I do not see how it can succeed—I would not make it even now, but Gen. Lee has ordered & expects it." Sensing that Longstreet would cancel the assault with encouragement, Alexander declined to interfere "in so grave a matter." The pair waited in embarrassed silence until relieved by the appearance of the gallant Virginians. Alexander spoke briefly with his friend Dick Garnett, then hurried off to assemble artillery to accompany the attackers.[119]

General Pickett dashed to his division near 2:50 P.M.[120] and his vibrant voice rang out before Garnett's brigade. "Charge the enemy, and remember old Virginia...Forward! Guide center! March!"[121] He then proceeded along the rear of Kemper's brigade and ordered the men to prepare for the advance.[122] "Up, men, and to your posts! Don't forget today that you are from old Virginia!"[123] A courier informed General Armistead the dreaded moment had

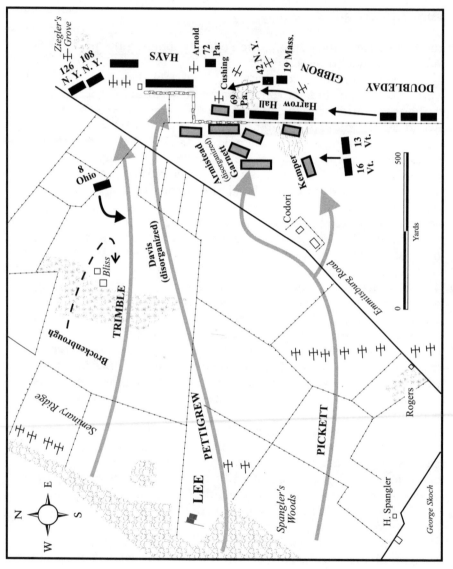

Longstreet's assault, July 3, 1863, focusing on Pickett's division

George Skoch

arrived. "Attention Battalion!" came the command and his men sprang to their feet. Armistead approached the 53rd Virginia's color bearer, Leander C. Blackburn, and asked: "Sergeant, are you going to put those colors on the enemy's works to-day?...I will try, sir, and if mortal man can do it, it shall be done."[124] The general then addressed his brigade: "Remember, men, what you are fighting for. Remember your homes and your firesides, your mothers and wives and sisters and sweethearts."[125] He then gave the command: "Attention, second battalion! battalion of direction forward; guides center; march!" Turning to the front, though his proper place was in the rear, "Lo" strided forward 50 yards before his brigade. He placed his hat on the point of his sword as a standard to be seen by his followers.[126] Generals Kemper and Garnett led their brigades on horseback.[127]

With sweat trickling down their backs and stinging their eyes, Pickett's people stepped off with orders to maintain their ranks with no cheering nor firing.[128] The right regiment in Kemper's brigade was the 24th Virginia, followed in order by the 11th, 1st, 7th, and 3rd. In Garnett's brigade, the 8th Virginia held the right with the 18th, 19th, 28th, and 56th extending the line to the left. Behind them, from right to left, were the 14th, 9th, 53rd, 57th, and 38th Virginia Regiments of Armistead's brigade.[129] As the acrid shroud of smoke lifted,[130] cries of "Here they come! Here they come! Here comes the infantry!" traveled through the 19th Massachusetts. Regiments "shook themselves" to reform their lines as a general's aide shouted: "Up, boys, they are coming!"[131] Lt. Anthony W. McDermott, 69th Pennsylvania, summoned a memory of the defining moment in the life of Pickett's Virginia division: "No holiday display seemed more imposing, nor troops on parade more regular, than this division of Pickett's Rebels. They came steadily arms at a trail, their appearance was truly a relief from that terrible fire of their artillery; not that it was destructive, but the dread it occasioned..."[132]

Arrangement of Pettigrew's division and its supports, perhaps, guaranteed failure of Longstreet's assault. Arrayed from left to right were Brockenbrough, Davis, Pettigrew, and Fry (Archer). The depleted division's two weakest brigades held the vulnerable left flank. Lane and Lowrance (Scales) formed in the rear toward Pettigrew's center could provide little support in the event of disaster. A better deployment would have stacked the North Carolinians *en echelon* behind Brockenbrough to deflect a deadly flank attack. "Through negligence or overconfidence, the organization failed to provide the strongest order of battle its number made possible."[133]

Pettigrew arranged his division in line of regiments. Half the companies composed the first line while the remainder were one hundred yards to the rear.[134] It is likely General Pettigrew ordered his four brigades to advance without receiving word from Longstreet since the latter was reluctant to give his assent to Pickett.[135] The brigde of direction for the entire column, Fry's, began its movement on Pettigrew's order.[136] Pettigrew exclaimed to Col. James K. Marshall, who commanded his own regiments, "Now, Colonel, for the honor of the good Old North State, forward!"[137]

"Look! do you see them coming?" cried the Jerseymen of the Twelfth Volunteers. General Hays rode along the line saying: "'They are coming boys; we must whip them, and you men with buck and ball [smoothbore muskets], don't fire until they get to that fence,' pointing to the fence along Emmittsburg [sic] Road."[138] To Chauncey L. Harris of the 108th New York, Company F, the distant figures looked like statues in the shimmering summer heat.[139]

Union accounts agree that the emergence of the Butternut infantry from the tree line was a remarkable sight to behold, imposing in its portent. Maj. Theodore G. Ellis of the 14th Connecticut reported: "The spectacle was magnificent":[140]

> It was, indeed, a scene of unsurpassed grandeur and majesty...As far as the eye could reach could be seen the advancing troops, their gay war flags fluttering in the gentle summer breeze, while their sabers and bayonets flashed and glistened in the midday sun. Step by step they came, the music and rhythm of their tread resounding on the rock-ribbed earth. Every movement expressed determination and resolute defiance, the line moving forward like a victorious giant, confident of power and victory.[141]

Lt. Frank A. Haskell, aide to General Gibbon, beheld "an overwhelming resistless tide of an armed ocean of men..."[142] To Capt. William Davis, 69th Pennsylvania, it seemed "no power could hold them in check."[143] Col. Dennis O'Kane of the 69th reminded his boys they were fighting on their native soil and charged his regiment "not to fire a shot until the enemy came so close to us that we could distinguish the white of their eyes...and that should any man flinch in our duty, he asked that the nearest man would kill him on the spot."[144]

Pickett's left came under fire first, "the division...at an average of 1100 yards,"[145] from batteries on Cemetery Ridge as well as McGilvery's artillery brigade which hit their flank.[146] According to the 19th Virginia's major, Charles S. Peyton, artillery on Little Round Top "enfiladed nearly our entire line with fearful effect." A single shell killed or wounded as many as 10 men. One explosion "killed three or four men" of the 8th Virginia.[147] Though round shot ricochetted through the ranks and "shells exploded incessantly" overhead or in their midst,[148] gaps in the regiments closed.[149] One of the 8th Virginia's survivors recalled:

> A ponderous shell screams across the valley, striking the ground in front of the advancing line, bursts and "cuts a swath" of ten men out of a company. Four of them all fall flat on their faces, nevermore to rise; five or six others limp away to the rear, or lie moaning and groaning in agony. "Close up men!" shouts the captain and immediately the gap is closed; a new "touch of elbows" is established, and the line moves on without faltering for an instant. "Whizz-z!" whistles a grape shot, and the crashing bones tells that it has found a victim in the same captain who just spoke! "Close up, men" shouts the first lieutenant now in command. Another crash and the regimental major falls dead. "Close up, men!" and we step over the corpse, and march right on.[150]

Crossing the field with a makeshift battalion of artillery on Pickett's right flank, Porter Alexander noticed a doomed man from Kemper's brigade "with the most horrible wound that I ever saw...A solid shot had carried away both jaws and his tongue...nothing, of course, could be done for him."[151] On the skirmish line, amidst the terror of the battlefield, "Monk" Wingfield, Company D, 1st Virginia, made a chilling observation. He asked his pard Charles T. Loehr, "Where are our reinforcements?"

> On looking around nothing was in sight, except the three brigades of Pickett about 300 yards in rear of our skirmish line and now subject to a storm of shells, tearing great gaps into the lines..."Monk I don't see any," on which he replied, "We are going to be whipped, see if we don't." Alas, for the poor fellow, these were his last words, for a bullet ended his life only a few minutes afterward.[152]

Union skirmishers proved obstinate but no obstacle. They fell back when Pickett's main line approached within one hundred yards and were brushed away.[153]

The course of Pickett's column carried the division to the right, south of the Copse of Trees. Pettigrew and Trimble moved in a direct line for the ridge.[154] As the Virginians approached Emmitsburg Road, they executed a 45-degree turn, a "left oblique," in order to join Pettigrew for a simultaneous rush at the Federal position.[155] Emmitsburg Road angled away from Cemetery Ridge, turning even more sharply southwest at the Nicholas Codori farm. Kemper's brigade passed south and Garnett's brigade went north of the farm buildings.[156] Crossing the Emmitsburg Road, "There was a momentary

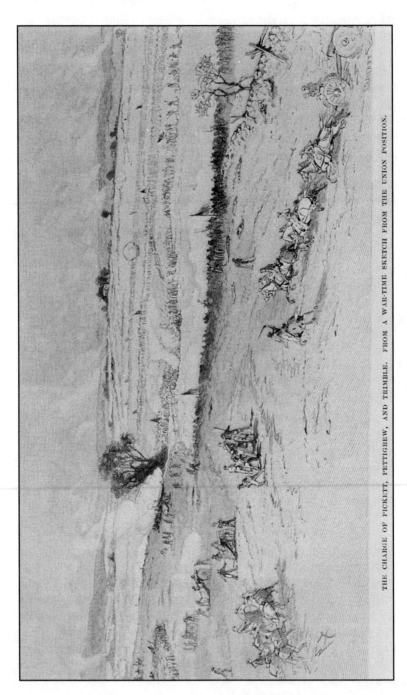

THE CHARGE OF PICKETT, PETTIGREW, AND TRIMBLE, FROM A WAR-TIME SKETCH FROM THE UNION POSITION.

View of Longstreet's Assault

check" as Pickett's two lead brigades lost their formation. Sturdy fences lined both sides of the road. The Rebels began receiving fire from the 69th Pennsylvania as they presented nearly stationary targets squeezing through openings or climbing over the fences.[157] They were granted a momentary respite from the lead singing through the air when they entered a swale, parallel to their new line of advance. Change of direction brought Kemper's regiments closer to the Federal line and they entered the convenient shelter first, followed by Garnett's people. Surviving regimental and company officers reformed ranks before leading their men in the final attempt to reach the Yankees.[158]

With the fearsome Rebel Yell ("yi! yi!") in their throats, Pettigrew's division advanced over undulating ground in measured tread. Ordinarily, raising the Rebel Yell increased ardor as well as speed—not this day. After covering half the distance to the stone wall, Pettigrew's people came under heavy fire, as the Tennesseans connected with Garnett.[159] General Garnett shouted at Colonel Fry: "I am dressing on you!" Moments later, Birkett Fry was prostrated by a bullet in his thigh.[160] A staff officer, Capt. Samuel A. Ashe, remembered: "The piercing cries of the dying and wounded could be heard over the field amid the shriek of shells and the roar of the cannon."[161] Myriad missiles rent the 47th North Carolina's ranks "at almost every five or ten steps but they were immediately filled in by our brave boys."[162] Captain Turner of the 7th recalled: "We pressed rapidly forward and in spite of the numerous obstacles, such as fences, ditches, &c., the whole line remained unbroken until we had passed over at least two-thirds of the distance from the woods to the enemy's line..."[163]

Col. Franklin Sawyer's 8th Ohio crossed Emmitsburg Road to confront the attackers as the supporting artillery opened fire:

> They were at once enveloped in a dense cloud of smoke and dust. Arms, heads, blankets, guns and knapsacks were thrown and tossed into the clear air. Their track, as they advanced, was strewn with dead and wounded. A moan went up from the field, distinctly to be heard amid the storm of battle, but on they went...[164]

Brockenbrough's brigade caught hell. Command confusion caused the 22nd Virginia Battalion and 40th Virginia to start off without the 47th and 55th Virginia, which ran to catch up.[165] Batteries on Cemetery Hill targeted them "with destructive effect..."[166] The 8th Ohio poured bullets into the Virginia brigade from one hundred yards away. Assailed in front and flank, "A panic soon took hold of them and they fled, back to the low ridge."[167] Brockenbrough's brigade disintegrated. Colonel Christian carried the colors as he assisted his color bearer to the rear.[168] When Brockenbrough's Virginians broke, General Trimble ordered his demi-division to close up on Pettigrew's line.[169]

Pettigrew's division began crumbling as the 8th Ohio wheeled and fired into the flank of Davis' brigade[170] which "pushed forward in advance of the general line...and was driven back."[171] All of the colonels in Davis' brigade were killed or wounded. For the Mississippians, it became a soldier's fight with no one in command. Lt. Andrew J. Baker, Company A, 11th Mississippi, led a thin line onward "as individuals rather than as an organization."[172] Capt. William T. Magruder was killed near the Brian barn, close to the stone wall.[173] Soldiers of the 55th North Carolina continued forward toward a section of wall held by New York troops, south of the Brian barn. Lt. T. D. Falls of Company C along with Sgt. J. Augustus Whitley, Company E, reached a point nine yards from the stone wall. Capt. E. Fletcher Satterfield, Company H, fell nearby, wounded by a shell in the chest.[174]

Momentarily lost from view, Pickett's column suddenly "seemed to rise out of the earth, and so near that the expressions on their faces was distinctly seen."[175] General Garnett urged his men onward as a mass of blue appeared to their right, moving at the double quick with their muskets at shoulder shift. Above the din of the battlefield, Capt. Henry T. Owen, 18th Virginia, heard Garnett order: "Faster, men! faster! Close up and step out faster, but don't double quick!"[176] From a range of two hundred yards, Cushing's and Cowan's batteries began dealing doses of canister into the close Rebel ranks.[177] Company C, 5th U.S. Artillery, unlimbered on the ridge, spewing canister slugs.[178] The 20th Massachusetts and 7th Michigan (Hall) opened fire at two hundred yards increasing disorder in Pickett's regiments. Dead Virginians crumpled to the ground while wounded went to the rear. Soldiers remaining in the front ranks crowded together. At one hundred yards, the remainder of the Third Brigade pulled their triggers.[179] Within the Confederate column "the storm of lead and iron seemed to fill the air, as in a sleet storm, and made one gasp for breath...many of the men bent in a half stoop as they marched up the slope, as if to protect their faces, and dodge the balls."[180]

Before Pickett's dogged veterans reached the Emmitsburg Road, General Webb ordered the 71st Pennsylvania forward to the stone wall on the right of Cushing's remaining pieces. Eight companies under Lt. Col. Charles Kochersperger occupied the available space while Colonel Smith deployed the two remaining companies at the wall to the rear with Hays' division.[181] As the intrepid Confederate tide surged closer, portions of Webb's brigade, the 71st in particular, began breaking from the wall, "not because the enemy was upon it, but because it seemed impossible to stay."[182]

OBSERVATION

Limited success on July 2 induced General Lee to continue the battle at Gettysburg. His original battle plan for July 3 included an offensive against the Union center and right. The premature action that flared on Ewell's front forced Lee to improvise another course of action to attain the victory he thought was within his grasp.

The Army of Northern Virginia retained sufficient assets to successfully assault and hold Cemetery Ridge on the afternoon of July 3. The assault failed in Longstreet's execution, not in Lee's conception. In hindsight, Pickett and Pettigrew should have advanced shortly after the artillery opened, thus assuring sufficient ammunition remained in the limbers to support the column when it reached its objective. Proper artillery support could have suppressed any threat to Kemper's flank, enabling Wilcox and Lang to particpate effectively by engaging Federal troops who, as it turned out, flanked the Virginians. Pettigrew, followed by Trimble, should have advanced on the Copse of Trees while Pickett's brigades maneuvered below to avoid stone walls which provided psychological strength as well as physical security for the defenders. Total success for the Pickett-Pettigrew-Trimble Charge depended upon support from Anderson's entire division to hold the ridge.

Chapter 7
Pickett's Charge

Trust in God and fear nothing.

Lewis A. Armistead

As his division persisted in its immortal charge, George Pickett "found himself a mere bystander, an impotent witness to tragedy." He directed Capt. Robert A. Bright of his staff to find Longstreet and relate that the Federal position could be taken. Unless reinforcements came up, however, it would not be held. Bright located General Longstreet sitting alone on a fence and relayed Pickett's message. At that moment the English observer rode up.[1] Colonel Fremantle exclaimed: "I wouldn't have missed this for any thing." Longstreet calmly replied. "The devil you wouldn't! I would like to have missed it very much; we've attacked and been repulsed; look there!" Fremantle saw "small broken parties" of Pickett's men "slowly and sulkily" in retreat. Longstreet watched "troops supporting Pickett and saw plainly that they could not hold together ten minutes longer."[2] Pickett's men had not yet crossed Emmitsburg Road during the interview between the Englishman and American.[3]

Incredibly! Longstreet chose to release Wilcox. He told Captain Bright that Wilcox could be called on for assistance; the staff officer galloped off to locate Pickett.[4] Cadmus Wilcox awaited orders nearly half an hour and now with the assault about to fail in Longstreet's opinion, his Alabamians and the Floridians were sent into the fight. Writing after the war, Wilcox bitterly denounced Longstreet. "Such a reinforcement to Pickett could have availed nothing, could only be sacrificed; and yet it was by his order that it advanced."[5] Bright reported to Pickett who immediately dispatched a brace of staff officers ordering Wilcox "to come in..." Moments later, Bright followed Capt. Edward R. Baird and Lt. Stuart W. Symington with the same message. Upon Bright's approach, Wilcox waved his hands in exasperation saying: "I know; I know."[6] Reluctantly, Wilcox and Lang moved their regiments forward, too late to protect Pickett's exposed right flank from Stannard's Vermonters. Concerning Pickett's advance, Colonel Lang wrote: "...before they had gone far, the wounded and the frightened came running back in large numbers, and it was impossible to tell when the main body came back...As soon as Pickett's division had retired, we were thrown forward (as a forlorn hope I suppose), notwithstanding the repulse of the day before, and the repulse of Pickett's whole division..."[7]

The Vermont Brigade held a position forward of the main line, south of Gibbon, on Doubleday's front. As Pickett's onrushing division approached, General Stannard withdrew the 16th Vermont from the skirmish line and it formed behind the 14th Vermont regiment. As Kemper's battalions passed them, halfway to Emmitsburg Road, the brigade "opened a rapid and destructive fire..." The 13th Vermont changed front 90 degrees and the 16th deployed in line on their left flank. Following in Pickett's wake, the two regiments unleashed a searing series of volleys less than 250 feet from the fraying flank.[8] Stannard's brigade played a very significant role in the repulse of Longstreet's Assault because it dissipated the force of the charge on the Federal center as Kemper's right pressed "down upon the center crowding the companies into confusion."[9] Howitzers husbanded by Alexander might have prevented Stannard's interference but General Pendleton withdrew four of them before the charge and Major Richardson moved the remainder to cover, away from searching Federal shells.[10] Owing to near exhaustion of ammunition, the sustained close artillery support for the attackers Lee envisioned never developed.[11] South of the Codori farm, Porter Alexander's makeshift battalion went into action far from Pickett's right flank.[12] Five pieces under Maj. John C. Haskell's command shelled Federals massed around the Copse of Trees but were quickly neutralized by McGilvery's counterfire.[13]

Kemper's brigade drifted north, parallel to the Union line, away from the furious enfilading fire and volleys to their front delivered by Harrow and Hall. Many mixed with Garnett's right regiments, uncovering Harrow's brigade. Some of Kemper's people found cover on Hall's front among rocky brush-covered knolls, "ideal for skirmishers and sharpshooters."[14] From a distance of less than one hundred yards, Longstreet's old brigade discharged "one well-directed volley..."[15] Pointing toward cannon beyond the wall with his sword, James Kemper shouted: "There are the guns, boys, go for them." The merged brigades "pushed rapidly up the heights."[16] Near the Union line, Kemper was shot down. "Quickly after I fell, a federal officer with several men took possession of me, placed me on a blanket, and started to carry me (as the officer said) to a federal surgeon, when some of my men came up and firing across my body, recaptured me and carried me in the same blanket to our own rear."[17]

Lt. George W. Finley, Company K, 56th Virginia, composed this vivid account that captures the furor as Longstreet's Assault neared its climax:

> Still on and up the slope towards that stone fence our men steadily swept, without a sound or a shot, save as the men would clamor to be allowed to return the fire that was being poured into them. When we were about 75 or 100 yards from that stone wall some of the men holding it began to break for the rear, when, without orders, save from captains and lieutenants, our line poured a volley or two into them and then rushed upon the fence, breaking the line and capturing many of the men, who rushed forward toward us crying "Don't shoot!" "We surrender!" "Where shall we go?" etc. They were told to go to the rear, but no one went with them so far as I saw...

Finley was impressed by the gallantry of artillerists who remained with their pieces, deserted by most of their 71st Pennsylvania supports.[18]

Union troops in front of Cowan's battery, unprotected by the stone wall, suddenly "became panick stricken and broke in confusion." Pulling back 50 yards to avoid being overrun, the battery resumed firing with percussion shell.[19] The 11th Virginia struck this portion of the Union line as "a mass or ball, all mixed together, without company organization." In all there were about three hundred men from three regiments, including the 24th and 3rd. No enemy were visible on their front. Capt. John H. Smith, Company G, 11th Virginia, "expected to see General Lee's army marching up to take possession of the field. As I looked over the work of our advance with this expectation, I could see nothing but dead and wounded men and horses in the field beyond us, and my heart never sank in my life as it did then."[20]

Col. William R. Terry, 24th Virginia, with the assistance of Capt. William T. Fry, a member of Kemper's staff, formed survivors of his own regiment and the 11th Virginia perpendicular to the ridge to oppose Stannard's brigade which threatened to take Pickett's embattled division from behind.[21] Col. Joseph Mayo Jr., 3rd Virginia, "hastily gathered a small band together and faced them to meet the new danger. After that everything was a wild kaleidoscopic whirl. A man near me seemed to be keeping tally of the dead for my especial benefit. First it was Patton, then Collcotte [sic], then Phillips, and I know not how many more...Seeing the men as they fired, throw down their guns, and pick up others from the ground, I followed suit, shooting into a flock of blue coats that were pouring down from the right..."[22]

Pickett's division swirled before the stone wall, a "mingled mass, from fifteen to thirty deep..."[23] The 69th Pennsylvania poured a "destructive fire" into the Rebels which slaughtered them at less than 50 yards. Survivors stood and returned fire while other pressed toward the Angle on the 69th's right.[24]

In the words of his biographer, Kent Masterson Brown, Lieutenant Cushing "fell to his knees, and blood gushed from his nose and mouth, splattering Fuger's boots, trousers, and blouse. Lon's eyes rolled back in their sockets. His kepi fell from his head. A bullet had hit him just below his nose, drilling its way to the base of his brain."[25] Seeing the black tubes poking over the wall, the Rebels realized it meant death or worse for many. Artillerist Christopher Smith "remembered distinctly that they pulled their caps down over their eyes and bowed their heads as men do in walking against a hail storm. They knew what was coming."[26] Lieutenant Finley distinctly felt "the flame of the explosion..." Unscathed, he stepped on the stone wall. To his right, Lt. John A. Lee crossed with the 28th Virginia's colors, the first member of the division to get over the wall. Finley noticed friendly troops to his left...the Tennesseans![27] He bounded over to them and shook the hand of a captain, exclaiming: "Virginia and Tennessee will stand together on these works to-day!"[28]

Two of Woodruff's guns were pushed forward by the 108th New York to enfilade Pettigrew's line. From a range of less than three hundred yards, the cannoneers began discharging canister.[29] Pickett and Pettigrew reached the Emmitsburg Road simultaneously[30] but it was far closer to the Union line, north of the Copse of Trees. Greater casualties from musketry befell Pettigrew's division because the Federals were closer to the road. Many members of the 14th Connecticut were equipped with the Sharps rifle which permitted a higher rate of fire than conventional muzzle-loaders.[31] When the Rebels neared the road and its inhibiting obstacles, fences on both sides, four lines of Federals rose and delivered "a perfect hail-storm of lead..."[32] The first line of Confederates "dropped from the fence as if swept by a gigantic sickle swung by some powerful force of nature...the number of slain and wounded could not be estimated by numbers but must be measured by yards."[33] Struck by two balls in the brain, Colonel Marshall dropped dead at the fence.[34] A Tennessean who survived the ordeal wrote:

> It was not a leaping over; it was rather an insensible tumbling to the ground, in the nervous hope of escaping the thickening missiles that buried themselves in falling victims, in the ground, and in the fence, against which they rattled with the distinctiveness of large rain drops pattering on the roof...Our stay in the road could not be called a halt. In a moment the order to

advance was given, and on we pressed across the next fence, but many of our comrades remained in the road, and never crossed the second fence, many being wounded in crossing the first and in the road.[35]

Lt. John C. Moore of the 7th Tennessee estimated no more than two-thirds of the "charging column" crossed the road, which weakened considerably the assault's impact. The double fences also disrupted their momentum, more so than Pickett's effort, due to the nearness of the flaming Federal line. Many unwounded Rebels remained in the road because its depth of two feet served as a sheltered firing position: "...there seemed to remain a line of battle in the road."[36]

"Steady, men! steady! Don't double quick. Save your wind and ammunition for the final charge!" Garnett yelled.[37] Virginians joined Tennesseans to storm the Angle. Some of Cushing's people stayed put, prepared to resist to the last along with Sgt. Maj. William S. Stockton, who led a staunch set of the 71st. Hand-to-hand combat ruled as men fired at each other from less than 10 feet. "Men fell as leaves fall. There were some cool, deliberate movements on the part of some, while others manifested the most fiery determination. Amid yells and curses men whirled about—falling on their hands and knees—some spinning around like tops while falling, others throwing out their arms and gulping up blood while falling..."[38]

Pvt. James W. Clay, Company G, 18th Virginia, remembered seeing Garnett wave his black felt hat, encouraging his men. Struck in the forehead by a shell fragment, Clay stumbled to the rear "and fell among some rocks, severely injuring my knee and preventing further locomotion." When he collapsed, Clay lost sight of his general but watched the tumult at the Angle. His captain, Archer Campbell, who had a broken arm, joined him. Two Yanks offered to assist them to the rear and related that Garnett "had been killed...Just before these men reached us, General Garnett's black war horse came galloping toward us with a huge gash in his right shoulder, evidently struck by a piece of shell. The horse in its mad flight jumped over Captain Campbell and me."[39]

Momentarily, there were no blueclads at the Angle but on the crest of the ridge opposite, the 72nd Pennsylvania volleyed with the Virginians and Tennesseans. This fire probably brought down General Garnett and caused the Rebels east of the wall to jump back over it and fight from cover. With no one in command to lead them,[40] "just at the point of success," the column hesitated to press their advantage.[41] According to a Federal: "This was the pinch, and the officers knew it."[42]

General Gibbon, trying to mount an attack by swinging out the left of his division, felt "a stinging blow" behind his left shoulder. Faint from the loss of blood, he turned command of the division over to General Harrow and "left the field, the sounds of the conflict still ringing in my ears."[43] Lieutenant Haskell, with the reins of his horse in one hand and sword in the other, attempted to arrest the flight of the 71st Pennsylvania as "the damned red flags of the rebellion began to thicken and flaunt along the wall..." He ordered fugitives to "'halt', and 'face about' and 'fire,' and they heard my voice and gathered my meaning, and obeyed my commands. On some unpatriotic backs of those not quick of comprehension, the flat of my sabre fell not lightly, and at its touch their love of country returned..."[44] Part of the 71st reformed behind the 72nd Pennsylvania and the detachment from the 106th, which had come up under General Webb's order. On foot, Webb tried bringing the 72nd forward to the charge—the men would not budge. In desperation, Webb gripped Sgt. William Finecy's regimental standard but he would not release his grip. Though his general ordered him forward, Finecy remained on line with his regiment. Frustrated and fuming, Webb hurried down the slope to the embattled 69th Pennsylvania. Except for the bold who responded to Webb's call, the 72nd Pennsylvania remained riveted below the crest of Cemetery Ridge and sustained heavy casualties.[45]

Hissing like the "cobra's whisper of death," a shell exploded knocking down Colonel Mayo—his mind went blank. Regaining his feet, with bone splinters and bits of flesh sticking to his uniform, he saw Lt. William T. Taliaferro "jumping like a kangaroo and rubbing his crazy bone and blessing the Yankees..." Colonel Terry, "with a peculiarly sad smile on his face," pointed to the rear "with his sword, and I knew what he meant." George T. Walker, courier to General Kemper, expressed Mayo's own thought: "Oh! Colonel, why don't they support us?" Desperate circumstances called for a decision. Captain Smith, in consultation with other line officers, dispatched "Big Foot" Walker for reinforcements. As Walker left Cemetery Ridge, another courier followed to insure the message got through. "We were so anxious to maintain the position we had gained, that we watched the two men we had sent to our rear across the field, and saw them both, the one after the other, disappear over the ridge from which we had marched forward."[46]

General Longstreet's report states that he ordered Anderson's three remaining brigades forward "to support and assist the wavering columns of Pettigrew and Trimble." Longstreet averred Hill's troops "hesitated" then "broke their ranks and fell back in great disorder, many more falling under the enemy's fire in retiring than while they were attacking." He assumed that Federals on Pettigrew's and Trimble's front would concentrate on Pickett, "before Anderson's division could reach him..."[47] The order was canceled as Anderson was about to move because "it was useless, and only would involve unnecessary loss, the assault having failed."[48] The truth is, Longstreet never planned proper follow-up support for the Virginians,[49] even though logic dictated Pettigrew or Trimble could function in that role.[50] Longstreet sacrificed Wilcox and Lang because he could not refuse Pickett's direct request for support—and expose himself to charges. Had Longstreet performed up to his capability that day, he would have ordered Posey, Mahone, and Wright forward before the Virginians gained the Emmitsburg Road. Posey's brigade *expected* to be included in Longstreet's assault.[51] In a letter to a former Federal officer dated January 4, 1884, Longstreet exposed his monstrous negligence and irrefutable misconduct. "We could not look for anything from Pickett except to break your line. The supports were to secure the fruits of that break."[52] Finally, James Longstreet plainly lied in his report. "Upon riding over to Colonel Alexander's position, I found that he had advised General Pickett that the time had arrived for the attack...I gave the order to General Pickett to advance to the assault."[53] Virginia chauvinism transmuted the role of Pettigrew-Trimble into a secondary, or supporting, role to Pickett's division,[54] though all of Hill's brigades, except Brockenbrough's Virginians crossed the Emmitsburg Road, and "advanced in the *same line*..."[55]

Forsaken by Longstreet, the Virginians, Alabamians, North Carolinians, Mississippians, and Tennesseans pressed their attack against the II Corps. Lt. J. Wiley Jones, Company I, 47th North Carolina, fell with a thigh wound. Waving his sword, he cheered on his men. The 47th's color bearer crossed the second fence but went down with a mortal wound.[56] Unhorsed, General Pettigrew passed over both fences. A ball crushed the bones in his left hand which caused him to retire.[57] According to a Carolinian: "It was a second Fredericksburg affair, only the wrong way."[58] Courageous color bearers brought their tattered banners up the slope and planted them. Color-guards lay down, waiting for their regiments to rally on them and advance.[59] In small groups, their lines broken, the dogged Southerners charged to fall in some places within 20 paces of the flaming muskets.[60] The 14th Tennessee and the 13th Alabama could not reach the Federal line because the stone wall on their front was to the right and rear of the Angle.[61] Trapped in the road or on the slope, they "beckoned" to Trimble's troops.[62] Sergeant Major Hincks of the 14th Connecticut leaped over the wall. Hincks "ran straight and swift" for the 14th Tennessee's flag. With a "terrific yell, he seized the flag and hastily returned to the line." The prize bore a dozen battle honors, including "Seven Pines," "Ox Hill," "Sharpsburg," "Fredericksburg," "Chancellorsville..."[63]

Colonel Lowrance's regiments advanced "until the right of the brigade touched the enemy's line of breastworks, as we marched in rather an oblique line."[64] Seeing Lowrance's brigade coming up, Capt. Joseph J. Davis, 47th North Carolina, encouraged Company G to maintain its order.[65] As the 38th North Carolina reached the first blood-spattered fence, wounded and unwounded of Marshall's brigade ran through their ranks.[66] The 38th reached the second fence in skirmish strength and "kept up a weak fire" through the planks.[67] The 16th North Carolina, on the brigade's right flank, received a blast of canister from Arnold's last operational gun.[68]

Responding to the breakup of Davis and Brockenbrough, Lane advanced his brigade on the oblique to become Pettigrew's front line on Marshall's right.[69] The 7th North Carolina, led by Captain Turner, pushed down the first fence but hesitated at the second obstacle. "...I climbed over on the right and my men were following me rapidly. I had advanced ten yards or more towards the works when I was shot down; the men who had gotten over returned to and laid down in the Pike as did the entire regiment."[70] Relatively few members of Lane's brigade passed beyond the sunken road.[71] The men who made it to the wall found it too high to leap over and were forced to surrender.[72]

Pickett's division kept coming. Following in the wake of Garnett's troops, Armistead's regiment's crossed the road to ascend Cemetery Ridge. General Armistead dropped back into the ranks allowing his men to fire.[73] According to Lt. James W. Whitehead, Company I, 53rd Virginia: "As we got within forty yards of the stone wall, came all along the line the order of charge, and charge we did. From behind the fence the Yankee infantry rose and poured into our ranks a murderous fire. Garnett's brigade and Kemper's had almost entirely disappeared; their brave commanders, their gallant officers, with hundreds of the rank and file, were stretched on the field, and it remained for Armistead's men to finish the work. After a desperate fight the Yankees began to give way and as they fell back our men rushed forward to the stone wall with unfaltering steps, Armistead still leading the charge."[74] Pickett's division crowded together, aiming, firing, reloading, and dying at the stone wall. General Armistead, hat on the hilt of his sword, ran along the 69th Pennsylvania's front toward the Angle, as General Hancock was riding past Hall's reserve line.[75]

Sensing that a halt at the stone wall meant defeat, Armistead shouted at Lt. Col. Rawley Martin of the 53rd. "Martin, we can't stay here, we must go over that wall!" In agreement, Martin yelled: "Forward with the colors." Scaling the wall, Armistead turned to remnants of Pickett's division, hat still on his sword, and uttered immortal words: "Boys, we must use the cold steel, who will follow me?"[76] Cpl. Robert Tyler Jones stepped onto the stones, flaunting the 53rd Virginia's flag, then pitched forward, severely wounded. Lt. Hutchings L. Carter, Company K, retrieved the colors and bounded forward. Following Armistead's footsteps, Maj. John C. Timberlake, 53rd Virginia, mounted the fence and roared: "Look at your General! Follow him!"[77] Hundreds, perhaps five hundred Johnnies, including men from Pettigrew's division, responded to Armistead's example.[78] Some advanced to their right toward the 69th Pennsylvania's rear, the Copse of Trees, while most went straight ahead with their gallant general.[79]

> On swept the column over ground covered with dead and dying men, where the earth seemed to be on fire, the smoke dense and suffocating, the sun shut out, flames blazing on every side, friend could hardly be distinguished from foe, but the division, in the shape of an inverted V, with the point flattened, pushed forward, fighting, falling and melting away...[80]

The 69th Pennsylvania was overrun.[81] While rallying the regiment's hard-pressed right wing, Lt. Col. Martin Tschudy was killed. Before falling, he ordered the three right companies, I, A, and F, to change the front 90 degrees to shield the regiment's flank and rear. Capt. George C. Thompson fell before giving the order to his company. Remaining at the wall, Company F was engulfed; most of its members were captured. Company D, next in line, pulled back from the wall thereby preventing the regiment from being enveloped by Rebels. They fought it out hand to hand. Lashing out left and right, Cpl. Hugh Bradley, a "savage," "powerful man," used his musket as a club. Overpowered, his skull was shattered by a Rebel musket. The 69th's six other companies stepped back from the wall. They merged into a mass of men no longer defending their position but fighting for their colors. Loading and firing as rapidly as possible, to one participant "it looked as though our regiment would be annihilated..." Colonel O'Kane suffered a mortal wound; Maj. James Duffy received a thigh wound.[82]

From Seminary Ridge a Union prisoner witnessed the culmination of Pickett's Charge:

> At last, and after a desperate struggle, the confederates broke over the low irregular stone wall with a chorus of yells, and the men and flags seemed to mingle in a common mass. Our troops rose from the ground like an immense flock of partridges, poured their fire in the faces of their assailants, and a terrific hand to hand struggle seemed in progress. As the volume of smoke rose in blue flakes, our men appeared to be giving way before the onset of the second line, the first having

Panorama of the battlefield with the Round Tops looming in the distance. Monument to General Meade is located to the left, with the Copse of Trees in the center.

Gettysburg: Past and Present, Ohio Historical Society

almost vanished in the fight and its fragments mingled with
the second. A large number of our men appeared as prisoners
in the enemy's rear, the fire for a moment grew fainter, and the
cheers of the confederates made the hills echo.

In that awful moment I feared our line was hopelessly broken, but at this time of peril there opened a fresh and deadly
fire from the little wooded knoll almost on Pickett's flank, that
changed the features of the scene like magic.[83]

Col. Arthur F. Devereaux, 19th Massachusetts, asked Hancock's
permission to attack the Rebels "swarming over the stone wall."
Hancock, "the very embodiment of the god of war...", directed
Devereaux "To get in G-D- quick!"[84] Maj. Edmund Rice of the 19th
saw Hancock pointing at the trees: "Forward, men! Forward! Now is
your chance." With a cheer, the 19th Massachusetts and 42nd New
York "made an impetuous dash, racing diagonally forward for the
clump of trees."[85] Colonel Hall's three other regiments, followed by
Harrow's brigade, as well as the 80th New York and 151st Pennsylvania (Biddle) converged on the Copse of Trees as the Confederates
made a final effort to carry Cemetery Ridge.[86] Though regimental
organization had vanished[87] and officers lost control, Hancock's men
were motivated by the "same spontaneous impulse to meet and hurl
back the foe."[88] Firing as they advanced, the 1st Minnesota fought
ferociously. According to Lt. William Harmon of Company C: "We
were crazy with the excitement of the fight. We just rushed in like
wild beasts. Men swore and cursed and struggled and fought,
grappled in hand-to-hand fight, threw stones, clubbed their muskets, kicked, yelled and hurrahed." Marshall Sherman, Company
C, captured the 28th Virginia's colors.[89] During the melee, General
Hunt rode down the slope to Cowan's battery. He discharged the
loads in his pistol crying: "See 'em! See 'em!" His mount fell dead
and the general was extricated by artillerymen who placed him on a
sergeant's horse. Hunt rode away to urge on Hall's regiments.[90]

Twenty minutes after "Big Foot" Walker set out for reinforcements, "anticipating that we would be attacked, and being in no
condition to resist any serious assault, we soon concluded...to send
the men back to our lines, and we so ordered." Captain Smith ban-
daged his leg with a towel from his haversack while Capt. Robert W.
Douthat, Company F, fired a musket several times. Raising up, Smith
saw a column of blue moving toward them, 70 yards away. Dropping the musket, Douthat observed: "It's time to get away from here."
The twosome remained under fire until they cleared the last fence
at the Emmitsburg Road.[91] Colonel Mayo called to the group around
him to scatter and they too left the ridge.[92]

Confederates continuing forward with Armistead were caught
in a crossfire by the 72nd Pennsylvania and the 69th's right wing.[93]

Leaping off the wall, Lieutenant Colonel Martin was hit in four places, "his thigh shattered and crippled for life."[94] Sgt. Dennis B. Easley, Company H, 14th Virginia, crossed the wall simultaneously with General Armistead on his left. As Armistead advanced up the slope toward Cushing's abandoned rear section, General Webb passed him on his way to the 69th Pennsylvania.[95] Reaching Cushing's second line of guns, Armistead placed his hand upon one. Capt. Benjamin L. Farinholt, Company E, 53rd Virginia, heard Armistead exclaim: "The day is ours. Turn these guns upon them, boys..."[96] The Yankee line loosed a volley: "Armistead fell forward, his sword and hat almost striking a gun." Dropping behind a cannon, Easley's musket flamed at the Pennsylvanians until the ramrod was damaged. "General Armistead did not move, groan, or speak while I fired several shots practically over his body..."[97] The fall of Armistead caused his followers to falter. Many laid down to surrender. Major Timberlake "ordered the men to fall back and get to the stone fence and make the best of the situation they could."[98] Lieutenant Finley went forward until Armistead was wounded. "Seeing that most of the men still remained at the stone fence I returned, and was one of the very few who got back unhurt."[99]

Passing beyond Gibbon's embattled brigades, General Hancock rode over to Doubleday's division.[100]

> ...Just after General Stannard had ordered the Thirteenth and Sixteenth Vermont regiments out on Pickett's flank, General Hancock, followed by a single mounted orderly, rode down to speak to General Stannard...my eyes were upon Hancock's striking figure—I thought him the most splendid looking man I ever saw on horseback, and magnificent in the flush and excitement of battle—when he uttered an exclamation and I saw that he was reeling in the saddle.

Lts. George G. Benedict and George W. Hooker sprang toward Hancock to catch him as he toppled from his horse. General Stannard opened the fallen hero's clothing where blood spurted from a "a ragged hole" in his upper, inner thigh. Alarmed for his life, Hancock pleaded: "Don't let me bleed to death. Get something around it quick." Stannard applied his handkerchief and Benedict assured the corps commander that the flowing blood was not arterial.[101] Hancock refused to leave the field; he remained "long enough to witness the total repulse..."[102]

Major Rice recollected the Copse of Trees, behind the 69th, "was fairly jammed with Pickett's men, in all positions, lying and kneeling...I noticed two men, not a musket-length away, one aiming so that I could look into his musket-barrel; the other, lying on his back, coolly ramming home a cartridge. A little farther on was one

on his hands and knees waving something white in both hands."[103]
Lt. John H. Lewis, Company G, 9th Virginia,[104] described the end
for Pickett's valiant survivors who clung to their hard-won position
at the stone wall:

> ...Death lurks in every foot of space. Men fall in heaps, still
> fighting, bleeding, dying. The remnant of the division, with scarce
> any officers, look back over the field for the assistance that
> should have been there; but there are no troops in sight; they
> had vanished from the field, and Pickett's division, or what is
> left of it, is fighting the whole Federal center alone.
>
> We see ourselves being surrounded. The fire is already from
> both flanks and front; but yet they fight on and die. This can
> not last. The end must come; and soon there is no help at
> hand. All the officers are down, with few exceptions, either killed
> or wounded. Soon a few of the remnant of the division started
> to the rear, followed by shot, shell and musket-balls.[105]

Trapped in a "cul-de-sac-of death" and lacking support or leaders, Pickett's men became disheartened. They began retreating or
showing tokens of surrender, handkerchiefs or white paper.[106] Lieutenant Finley, knew "we could not hold the fence any longer." He
looked back to gauge "chances of withdrawing":

> The men who had began to fall back seemed to be dropping as
> they ran, like leaves...It seemed foolhardy to attempt to get
> back. The Federal line pressed on until our men fired almost
> in their faces. Seeing that it was a useless waste of life to
> struggle longer I ordered the few men around me to "cease
> firing" and surrendered.[107]

Prodded by regiments rushing past the trees toward the wall
along with disorder among the Rebels, the 72nd Pennsylvania moved
forward, led by Sergeant Finecy, who fell from one of the last shots.[108]
Major Timberlake, Armistead's brigade highest ranking surviving
officer, "made up my mind, with the few men I had, to fight as long
as I could, and then, if I must surrender. When the enemy reached
to within twenty yards, I ordered my men to cease firing and
surrender...but some few refused even to do this until they were
about to be bayoneted."[109] Grabbing a rifle, Sergeant Easley loaded
it "but just then I saw three bayonets pointed at my breast, and I
put it down."[110] South of the Angle, desperate close combat continued.[111] The 80th New York shouted at their foe to surrender with
the promise they would be unharmed.[112] Colonel Devereaux reported
that hundreds of Rebels instinctively dropped their arms. "My line
seemed to open as if by magic. It was not flight however, a flood of
unarmed, defenceless men poured through. They almost ran over
me."[113]

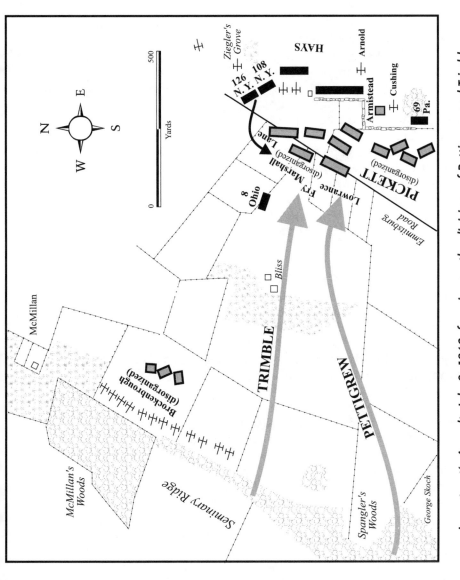

Longstreet's Assault, July 3, 1863, focusing on the divisions of Pettigrew and Trimble

Streams of piercing lead, combined with the fences along the road that broke the assault's momentum, doomed the effort of Pettigrew's and Trimble's troops.[114] General Trimble rode to the front of the 7th North Carolina to encourage the Carolinians over the fence. Wounded in the left leg, Trimble was removed from his horse. At that moment his aide Charles Grogan said: "General, the men are falling back, shall I rally them?" Glancing to his right, Trimble "beheld troops in broken squads falling back. I could plainy see everything like a third or half a mile, and inferred that Pickett and Lane [on the left] had been badly repulsed..." Trimble knew the assault had failed and replied: "No! let them get out of this, its all over." Placed back on his horse, Trimble returned to the rear.[115] When heavy enfilade fire from the left began striking among the North Carolinians, the fiasco ended.[116]

Elements of the 126th and 108th New York, advancing from the main line, wheeled to the right and mowed down Lane's men. Some Butternuts returned fire while others sought to save themselves.[117] General Lane ordered the 33rd North Carolina's colonel to meet the enemy movement. Col. Clarke M. Avery protested: "God General, do you intend rushing your men into such a place unsupported, when the troops on the right are falling back." Comprehending futility in continuing the unequal contest, Lane ordered a retreat to save the survivors.[118]

Unstoppable, the Yankees rolled south. Lt. Col. William G. Morris of the 37th North Carolina recollected: "...we became engaged with a flanking party on our left and was soon surrounded and captured."[119] Marshall's brigade was lashed "by a deadly volley from the left." Maj. John T. Jones, 26th North Carolina, apprehended peril as the assaulting column began breaking up from left to right. "What could we do now?...With no support upon the left, I asked myself what we should do. I had only about sixty men left in my regiment, and that small number diminishing at every moment, (the others had suffered as badly.) The order came from the right to fall back."[120] Some members of the 26th remained in the road firing until they were taken from the rear and captured.[121]

Lowrance's brigade, "now reduced to mere squads," saw no support in the field behind them. "The natural inquiry was, What shall we do? and none to answer. The men answered for themselves, and, without orders, the brigade retreated, leaving many on the field, unable to get off, and some, I fear, unwilling to undertake the hazardous retreat."[122] Fry's Tennesseans and Alabamians, seeing "that it was a hopeless case...fell back." Capt. Archibald D. Norris of Company K tore the 7th Tennessee's flag from its staff and carried it away beneath his uniform.[123] Pvt. John V. McKinney, Company G,

1st Tennessee, surrendered at the rock wall with "a small remnant."[124] First Sgt. Junius Kimble, Company A, 14th Tennessee, reckoned it was time to pull out when his prayer for support was unanswered. Like "lightning" he ran for one hundred yards. "Suddenly I realized that I was a good target for those yelling Yankees, and, having a horror of being shot in the back, I faced about and backed out of range..." In their stampede back to Seminary Ridge, panicked Rebels threw away their accoutrements and knapsacks. An 8th Ohio lieutenant, Thomas F. Galwey recollected: "We dashed in amongst them, taking prisoners by droves...As far [as] the eye could reach, the ground was covered with flying Confederates. They all seemed to extend their arms in their flight, as if to assist their speed."[125]

Lt. Col. Francis E. Pierce ordered the 108th New York to "'cease firing,' and the rebels ran in and gave themselves up as prisoners." Jubilant Yankees rushed onto the field to retrieve trophies. Dead and dying Southerners were everywhere.[126] General Hays noted in his report: "The angel of death alone can produce such a field as was presented."[127] In the excitement of the moment, Hays, smacked his steed with his sword "and dashed down among the rebels, seized a stand of colors, and carrying them back he rode at a gallop along the front of our lines, laughing and trailing the rebel flag in the dust, and then it was that cheer after cheer went up for him..."[128]

Disorganized remnants of once formidable regiments returned to Seminary Ridge.[129] A. P. Hill came down to Posey's skirmish line ordering Pettigrew's people to reform on the rifle pits. The North Carolinians rallied in rear of the artillery.[130] Around five hundred men remained in Joe Davis' brigade[131] and survivors staggered back with no organization. President Davis' nephew drifted slowly down the line of the 16th Mississippi (Posey), sword in hand. David E. Holt of Company K inquired: "'General Davis, where is your brigade?' He pointed his sword up to the skies, but did not say a word, and stood there for a moment knocking pebbles out of the path with the point of his sword. He could not talk, and neither could I. He walked on and I went back to my place."[132] Losses were very heavy. The 11th Mississippi, unengaged on July 1, in gaining Brian's barnyard, lost 312 men from a complement of 592—52.7 percent.[133] Company C, 11th North Carolina, took three officers and 34 men into the fight. Two officers were killed and 30 men failed to return.[134]

No field officers remained with Davis' brigade. Major Jones survived as senior officer in Pettigrew's brigade.[135] General Lee took Lt. Col. Samuel G. Shephard of the 7th Tennessee by the hand and said: "Colonel, rally your men and protect our artillery. The fault is mine, but it will be all right in the end."[136] By Trimble's order, General Lane reformed the division on the same ground it occupied before the advance.[137]

Capt. Benjamin F. Little, Company E, 52nd North Carolina, "was shot when about 50 feet from the enemy's works and where I lay was thickly strewn with killed and wounded, some of them having fallen immediately at the works. I do not think a single one ever got back to the rear, except those who were slightly wounded. And such was the case with the companies on either side of my company."[138] Those who were wounded severely early in Longstreet's Assault could be carried back to Seminary Ridge. The slightly wounded escaped before they got too close to fall back.[139] At the beginning of the charge, Pvt. Robert W. Morgan, Company C, 11th Virginia, was wounded on the right instep. Stopping to examine the wound, he was immediately struck again in the left foot. Morgan hobbled to the rear using a discarded rifle and his own weapon as crutches. His cook and servant, Horace, alternately carried the disabled soldier on his back or accompanied him in an ambulance until they reached home, Pigeon Run, Virginia, below Staunton.[140] Lt. Azra P. Gomer, Company G, 3rd Virginia, severely wounded in the leg managed to make it back to the division field hospital, though he fought at the Angle.[141]

Pickett's survivors returned to their lines in irregular small groups "trailing their arms, and although exposed to a storm of shell that burst behind, among and ahead of them, but few moved faster than a walk."[142] The tragic appearance of Wilcox and Lang on the field diverted the enemy's attention allowing many of Pickett's men to escape.[143] General Wilcox, following his duty, could not see troops he was ordered to support. Crossing the Emmitsburg Road, Alabamians and Floridians "were exposed to a close and terrible fire of artillery."[144] The 16th Vermont moved 80 yards by the left flank, then charged the 2nd Florida, on Lang's left flank.[145] The movement resulted in the capture of several dozen prisoners along with the 2nd's colors.[146] Colonel Lang concluded "our only safety from utter annihilation was in retreat."[147] Observing the threat on his left rear, General Wilcox rode back to obtain artillery support. Succor from the long arm was unavailable because nearby batteries lacked long-range ammunition. Due to the disappearance of Pickett's division from the field, his threatened left flank "and knowing that my small force could do nothing save to make a useless sacrifice of themselves, I ordered them back."[148]

When Pickett's division gained the Cemetery Ridge slope, Maj. William T. Poague prepared to bring six howitzers forward. Perplexed by the increasing number of men he saw retiring, "the awful truth began to force itself upon me that the attack had failed":

> At this very critical moment General Pickett himself appeared on the line of my guns on horseback and near one of them looking intently to the front. Nobody was with him. Though

not acquainted with him, I knew who he was, and at once rode to him and said after saluting, "General, my orders are that as soon as our troops get the hill I am to move as rapidly as possible to their support. But I don't like the look of things up there." He made no reply and didn't even turn his head to see who I was, but continued to gaze with an expression on his face of sadness and pain.

At that instant a Virginia flag was borne rapidly along and in rear of the stone wall by a horseman, and again I said, "General, is that Virginia flag carried by one of our men or by the enemy." No reply. I then said, "What do you think I ought to do under the circumstances. Our men are leaving the hill." "I think you had better save your guns," was his answer and at once rode off.

Major Poague subsequently deployed his howitzers to resist any enemy advance.[149]

Capt. Frank E. Moran, Company H, 73rd New York, captured the previous day by the 13th Mississippi portrayed the cavalier in defeat. "Pickett alone, of all the general officers, appeared unhurt. He came back with his dark dusty begrimed face bowed almost to his saddle and his horse at a walk, his long hair was wet with perspiration, and he returned the greeting of the cheering groups as they passed him, motioning the men towards the rear with his hand. He was entirely unattended."[150]

Shortly after the Confederates had been driven off, General Meade rode up to Cemetery Ridge accompanied by his son. They saw General Hays galloping along with the captured flag. Satisfied that the Rebels had "turned," father and son moved toward the Copse of Trees where Lieutenant Haskell was asked: "How is it going here?" The valiant lieutenant replied: "I believe, General, the enemy's attack is repulsed." Meade exclaimed incredulously: *"What! Is the assault already repulsed?"* Scanning the field he beheld batches of prisoners, captured flags, and receding fugitives. His face brightened. "Thank God." Suppressing a motion to wave his hat, the victor at Gettysburg voiced the emotion of an army. "Hurrah!" Captain Meade waved his cap exuberantly "and roared out three 'hurrahs' right heartily." Imparting instructions to Haskell, General Meade set off to visit other parts of the line.[151]

General Hancock sent a dispatch to Meade urging him to advance V and VI Corps to "win a glorious victory."[152] Conditions on the battlefield and the fatigue of Meade's troops hindered organization of a counterattack. Moreover, the army was in a defensive posture. Presumably V and VI Corps would have led the effort but they would have encountered Law and McLaws. In short, a counterattack was possible but under the circumstances impractical and unnecessary.[153]

General Longstreet expected the enemy to "throw himself against our shattered ranks and try to crush us." Dispersing his staff officers to rally the troops, he rode out to the batteries, the only organized line of defense in the army's left center, determined to throw back any Union sortie. Longstreet judged that his presence among the cannoneers would demonstrate "the necessity of holding the ground to the last extremity."[154] Artillery fire checked a line of skirmishers that disappeared from Longstreet's front. Their withdrawal relieved him of the fear that Meade would try to follow up the repulse.[155]

Defeated yet unconquered, the Army of Northern Virginia still retained faith in its captain. Every soldier who General Lee encountered heard encouraging words. "All this will come right in the end: we'll talk it over afterwards; but, in the mean time, all good men must rally. We want all good and true men..." To Colonel Fremantle he remarked: "This has been a sad day for us, Colonel—a sad day; but we can't expect always to gain victories." Cadmus Wilcox, distraught over his brigade's state, found General Lee, who greeted him blithely with a soothing handshake, saying:

> "Never mind, General, *all this has been* MY *fault*—it is *I* that have lost this fight, and you must help me out of it in the best way you can." In this manner I [Fremantle] saw General Lee encourage and reanimate his somewhat dispirited troops, and magnanimously take upon his own shoulders the whole weight of the repulse. It was impossible to look at him or to listen to him without feeling the strongest admiration, and I never saw any man fail him except the man in the ditch.[156]

Encountering Longstreet, George Pickett lamented: "General, I am ruined my division is gone—it is destroyed."[157] Pickett's division suffered an appalling casualty rate of 44 percent, including 1,500 wounded and unwounded prisoners.[158] The 8th Virginia suffered a casualty rate of 69 percent while the 57th Virginia lost 57 men killed.[159] By comparison, Lane's brigade, lightly engaged on July 1, suffered a casualty rate of 45.7 percent.[160] General Hays estimated at least 1,500 Rebels fell into his division's hands. Presumably, the bulk of this number represents troops from Hill's corps.[161] Losses to Pettigrew and Trimble during Longstreet's Assault are impossible to determine accurately. During two days of battle, these divisions lost approximately six thousand men from a combined battle strength of 14,139.[162] Regarding the controversy concerning which division retreated first, Pvt. Arthur T. Watts, Company A, 16th Mississippi, offered an eyewitness opinion. "The divisions of Pickett and Heth went in together, remained together, and retreated together. It has always been a matter of surprise to me how Pickett's Division was accorded all the glory for that assault, when I knew that Heth's men had gone as far and remained as long as did Pickett's men."[163]

Seeing no reinforcements were coming, Corporal Loehr "'got'" when the Federals recovered their works. Slightly wounded, Loehr joined several hundred of his comrades at a creek behind Seminary Ridge where they bathed their wounds or slaked their thirst. General Pickett rode up and Cpl. Charles P. Belcher waved the 24th Virginia's flag, crying: "General, let us go at them again!" General Kemper, suffering severely, was carried into the crowd and General Lee soon appeared. Pickett, in tears, shook hands with Lee, who told him: "General Pickett, your men have done all that men could do; the fault is entirely my own." Turning to Kemper, Lee said: "General Kemper, I hope you are not seriously hurt, can I do anything for you?" Looking up, Kemper replied: "General Lee, you can do nothing for me; I am mortally wounded, but see to it that full justice is done my men who made this charge." Lee responded affirmatively, then rode away.[164] Wounded below the knee and left arm, General Armistead was carried to the XI Corps hospital. Surg. Henry C. Hendrick, 157th New York, wrote: "He had lost quite a deal of blood, but the wounds were not necessarily fatal. He never rallied, however, and died a little past noon on the Fourth of July."[165]

Captured flags, the standard of decisive victory, were gathered in bunches by the victors. The 19th Massachusetts recovered at least four flags, including those of the 14th, 19th, and 57th Virginia.[166] Besides the 14th Tennessee's flag, the 14th Connecticut claimed flags from the 1st Tennessee, 16th, and 52nd North Carolina.[167] The 8th Ohio took flags from the 38th Virginia and 34th North Carolina.[168] The 1st Delaware reported the capture of three while the 12th New Jersey took two.[169] The 9th Virginia's flag was taken by the 71st Pennsylvania while the 72nd Pennsylvania claimed two captures.[170] Busy sending prisoners to the rear and "looking up" the killed and wounded, the 69th Pennsylvania recovered none of the trophies of victory, which resulted in great measure to their courageous stand.[171]

In the opinion of Isaac Trimble: "Longstreet managed badly, for the troops on our left, Pettigrew and my command, should have been started 20 minutes before Pickett, so as to have thrown all our line against the federal[s] at the same moment. This might have made a different result."[172] Due to faulty brigade deployment and the attack's wretched execution, Longstreet's assaulting column was snared in a classic tactical trap, the double envelopment. Around 12,000 troops, excluding Wilcox and Lang, participated in the assault, a sufficient number to take the position, contrary to Longstreet's opinion, because Pickett's people *did* reach Cemetery Ridge.[173] As General Wright predicted, the problem was staying there. General Pickett's report on Gettysburg "severely criticised the failure to furnish him with the supporting force which had been ordered..." Trimble and Pettigrew were the likely culprits in the Virginian's mind. To avoid "dissensions" General Lee requested Pickett to withdraw his original report and substitute another that embraced the casualties sustained by his division.[174] Historian R. E. Stivers believed that the Virginian "undoubtedly put his finger all too closely on what actually went wrong on that unhappy July 3—and that is unquestionably why Lee asked him to destroy it *for the sake of the morale of the Confederate Army.* We can assume, certainly, that Pickett honorably complied to the extent of doing away with the original report."[175]

Following the repulse of Longstreet's Assault, Gettysburg's last actions involved cavalry. General Kilpatrick ordered Elon Farnsworth to attack Rebels in the woods and broken terrain below Big Round Top. Predictably, the charge resulted in a fiasco. The cavalry brigade suffered 107 casualties and Farnsworth was killed.[176] Another cavalry engagement that went against the Federals occurred near Fairfield, south of Gettysburg, when the 6th U.S. Cavalry was virtually annihilated by "Grumble" Jones and his brigade.[177] The campaign's principal cavalry engagement was a tactical draw. Early in the morning of July 3, J. E. B. Stuart led his cavalry east, away from Gettysburg, looking for a fight. He hoped to either exploit the success of Lee's offensive or create enough havoc in the enemy rear to force the Army of the Potomac's withdrawal from the ground it occupied south of Gettysburg.[178] George Custer's Michiganders and Col. John B. McIntosh's brigade, under the overall command of General Gregg, checkmated Stuart. After preliminary skirmishing, the main bodies clashed around 3:00 P.M. Both sides claimed they drove the other back to their original line.[179] Though the Confederate cavalrymen inflicted higher casualties on their counterparts, Stuart's strategy to reach the Baltimore Pike failed.[180] The chief Southern loss was Wade Hampton, who suffered two sabre cuts to his head and a shrapnel wound.[181]

Longstreet withdrew his infantry and artillery back to Seminary Ridge[182] as General Lee prepared for an immediate withdrawal from Gettysburg and retreat to Virginia.[183] Following a council of war at A. P. Hill's headquarters, Lee summoned General Imboden to his tent. Around 1:00 A.M., Lee approached Imboden, who noted great sadness on his chieftain's face. Attempting to break an awkward silence, Imboden alluded to Lee's fatigue and remarked: "General, this has been a hard day on you." "Yes, it has been a sad, sad day to us." Lee remained silent a minute or two, then declared in an emotional tone:

> I never saw troops behave more magnificently than Pickett's division of Virginians did to-day in that grand charge upon the enemy. And if they had been supported as they were to have been,—but, for some reason not yet fully explained to me, were not,—we would have held the position and the day would have been ours...Too bad! *Too bad!* OH! TOO BAD!

The pair repaired to Lee's tent where he explained to Imboden the role his brigade would play in the retreat. Lee intended to bring as many wounded as possible back to Virginia. He assigned Imboden the task of escorting the army's major wagon train to Williamsport on the Potomac and reinforced him with 17 artillery pieces, including eight guns of the Washington Artillery. Imboden left Lee's headquarters around 2:00 A.M. Fourteen hours later, a 17-mile collection of wagons and ambulances bearing mangled humanity began the return trip to the Confederacy during a severe storm.

Few of the wounded had received medical attention. Shrieks and groans, curses and prayers issued from the jolting vehicles. "Oh God! why can't I die?" "My God! will no one have mercy on me?" "I am dying! I am dying! My poor wife, my dear children, what will become of you?" The wagons could not stop to aid the dying for safety to the many lay in speed. "On! On! We *must* move on." At daybreak the column reached Greencastle where civilians attacked the wagons. A show of force ended this menace but parties of Union cavalry stabbed at unguarded points. General Imboden avoided capture when the 18th Virginia, commanded by his brother, Col. George W. Imboden, rode to the rescue. During the afternoon of July 5 the immense train rolled into Williamsport which was converted into a vast hospital. The Potomac River, having risen 10 feet, closed the ford. Imboden began ferrying ambulatory wounded across the river.[184]

General Imboden armed some seven hundred teamsters and organized them into companies of one hundred men. Wounded line officers, commissaries, and quartermasters commanded the makeshift units. Colonels Aylett and John L. Black led battalions of 250 men each while the remainder served as skirmishers. Imboden retained his own regular units as a mobile reserve.[185] The 54th North Carolina (Avery) and 58th Virginia (Smith), left in Virginia to guard prisoners, augmented Imboden's scratch force.[186] General Buford's division, reunited with its reserve brigade, attacked Imboden's *laager* late on the afternoon of July 6.[187] With no superiority in manpower, the Federals were foiled by Imboden's preparations as well as his advantage in artillery. The First Brigade gained a minor success when Colonel Gamble's men captured a few vehicles.[188] The arrival of Fitzhugh Lee's brigade from Greencastle "settled the contest." Imboden estimated his loss at 125 and claimed the capture of 125 enemy cavalrymen who had fought dismounted and "failed to reach their horses." Maj. William H. Medill was mortally wounded on the skirmish line while commanding the 8th Illinois.[189]

After losing in excess of 23,000 men,[190] the Army of Northern Virginia remained at Gettysburg on July 4, prepared to give battle from Seminary Ridge.[191] That night Lee's army began its retreat with Ewell's corps the last to leave.[192] A week later the Rebel army occupied good defensive ground southeast of Williamsport on an extended line of nearly eight miles and waited to cross the swollen Potomac River. On July 12, they were completing a strong line of earthworks as the Army of the Potomac approached.[193]

The Army of the Potomac's casualties at Gettysburg were more than 23,000.[194] On July 5, General Meade sent VI Corps in pursuit of Lee while the remainder of his army remained at Gettysburg to bury the dead and care for wounded. General Sedgwick followed as far as Monterey Pass, which he did not attempt to force. The next day Sedgwick's command followed the army to Emmitsburg.[195] Handicapped by poor roads, lack of horses, food and footgear, the Army of the Potomac halted at Middletown, Maryland, on July 8 to refit and resupply its thinned ranks. On July 9, Meade's army moved west in three columns toward the waiting, unvanquished Rebels. Meade communicated to General Halleck his conviction that "the decisive battle of the war will be fought in a few days."[196]

Confederate engineers had commenced construction of a pontoon bridge at Falling Waters within their defensive perimeter[197] as the river began falling. Anticipating with confidence an enemy attack, Lee's chief concern was providing flour for the subsistence of his troops.[198] Meade planned an attack for July 13 but a majority of his corps commanders dissuaded him. Informed by General Meade of the delay, Halleck urged action. "Yours of 5 p. m. received. You are strong enough to attack and defeat the enemy before he can effect a crossing. Act upon your own judgment and make your generals execute your orders. Call no council of war. It is proverbial that councils of war never fight. Re-enforcements are pushed on as rapidly as possible. Do not let the enemy escape."[199]

Before receiving Halleck's telegram, Meade ordered II, V, VI and XII Corps to conduct a reconnaissance in force, "The movement to commence punctually at 7 a.m."[200] Around dusk on July 14, the Army of Northern Virginia began retreating across the Potomac.[201] Ewell's corps forded the river at Williamsport while Longstreet, followed by Hill, crossed the pontoon bridge at Falling Waters. Though a severe storm hampered the movement, Ewell completed his crossing by 8:00 A.M., except for the Louisiana Tigers, who accompanied the corps artillery across the pontoon bridge.[202] Longstreet's corps completed its crossing at 9:00 A.M.[203] Anderson's division began crossing followed by Pender, leaving Heth's battered division as rear guard.[204]

Judson Kilpatrick noticed at 3:00 A.M. that Rebel pickets south of Hagerstown were retiring and immediately initiated pursuit. Learning from civilians that the enemy had retired toward Falling Waters, Kilpatrick pressed on until he found further progress blocked by a line of battle.[205] Around 11:00 A.M.,[206] Kilpatrick ordered Custer to attack with the 6th Michigan as the remainder of the Wolverine Brigade came up. Companies B and F dismounted but Kilpatrick wanted a saber charge.[207] Maj. Peter A. Weber led one hundred troopers on a death ride. At first, the Confederates withheld their fire, believing the onrushing horse soldiers belonged to their own army. The cavalrymen passed through the earthworks to assail the 1st Tennessee which fought back with clubbed muskets because most of their rifles were unloaded. Loading and firing, the Rebels emptied enemy saddles. Few Federals regained their lines; Weber was among the slain. This one-sided encounter resulted in scant casualties to the Rebels. General Pettigrew, however, wounded in the left side by a pistol ball, succumbed three days later.[208] Ironically, the Gettysburg Campaign ended as the battle began: Heth's division engaged Union cavalry.

General Hill ordered Heth to cross the pontoon bridge "as speedily as possible..."[209] By 1:00 P.M., the last organized body of Lee's army had returned to Virginia.[210] Absence of another battle "created great dissatisfaction in the mind of the President,"[211] who expected a further "collision" between the armies.[212] Lincoln composed a letter to Meade that read in part: "I do not believe you appreciate the magnitude of the misfortune involved in Lee's escape...Your golden opportunity is gone, and I am distressed immeasurably because of it." Perhaps Lincoln's innate charity caused him to file this letter for it was never signed or sent to Meade.[213]

General Lee accepted responsibility for failure and placed no blame on the army, acknowledging that perhaps he expected "too much of its prowess & valour."[214] Unvarnished truth establishes that Stuart's imprudence, Longstreet's lethargy, Ewell's demeanor, Hill's judgment, Early's attitude, Anderson's inertia, Hood's wound, and Laws' disobedience all contributed to Lee's defeat at Gettysburg. In sum, bad decisions by proven leaders, including Lee, caused the Confederate reverse. Conversely, good decisions by Union leaders, who brought troops to exactly the right place at the decisive moment, produced victory.

At the Battle of Gettysburg, the Army of Northern Virginia's performance was crippled by the absence of astute senior leadership.

After the war, Lee contended: "If I had had Stonewall Jackson with me, so far as man can see, I would have won the battle of Gettysburg."[215] On May 21, 1863, Lee had written a remarkably prophetic letter to General Hood that included: "...I agree with you in believing that our army would be invincible if it could be properly organized and officered. There never were such men in an army before. They will go anywhere and do anything *if properly led.*"[216] In August, pleading poor health, Lee requested that President Davis appoint "a younger and abler man than myself..."[217] Davis of course did not act upon Lee's request; the war continued 21 more months, south to Petersburg and Atlanta, east to Savannah and west to Appomattox Court House.

The Army of Northern Virginia marched into Pennsylvania confident and puissant, expecting another victory. The Southern Confederacy, however, was doomed to defeat; therefore its most formidable force in the field was destined to be defeated, for the Southern states seceded contrary to the dynamic imperative of history which is unity: clans > tribes > nations > kingdoms > states. As expressed below, it is well that Lee's legions lost the Battle of Gettysburg and in their failure merit immutable American glory. Writing to the official government historian Col. John Badger Bachelder in 1890, John B. Gardner, 21st Virginia, offered these trenchant thoughts.

> I was at the reunion at Gettysburg in 1888...I never enjoyed anything so well in my life...The results of the war was a blessing in disguise to the south and I only regret it did not take place fifty years ago. I do believe the country is stronger to day than ever before. The Blood of our fallen Braves will ultimately cement this country together so close that the outside world will have to stand off and admire our greatness.[218]

Writing in 1863, Michael M. Miller, Company K, 1st Regiment Pennsylvania Reserves, also expressed truth. "To divide this country would Be to establish a continual war for generations to come and, while we are at it we had Better end it and let our children Rest in Peace and not have the next generation Suffer as this one has done."[219]

OBSERVATION

Though General Lee managed sufficient military power to defeat the Army of the Potomac in Pennsylvania, critics have argued that the invasion was folly. Victory in the field combined with favorable circumstances may have conceded the capture of Washington to the Army of

Northern Virginia and resulted in peace. Previous victories in Virginia and the mathematical certainty of future defeat warranted the endeavor. Like Napoleon during the Waterloo Campaign, Lee was ill served by senior subordinates. Like Napoleon on June 18, 1815, Lee wasted infantry on July 2, 1863. Vain attacks against the fortified chateau of Hougoumont absorbed too many French battalions. When Marshal Ney (Longstreet) finally broke the British center, infantry support was not readily available. Similarly, Confederate success on July 2 went unexploited because fresh troops were not thrown in at the crucial moment. This paucity of troops was due in part to the Stonewall Division's employment in a futile and needless attack on Culp's Hill.

At Gettysburg, General Lee's style of command betrayed him. Customarily, he would formulate a plan and issue orders for his key commanders to execute, then trust in Providence. Lee's inadequate supervision of Hill and Ewell on July 2 insured their weak performances. His two most able subordinates, Stuart and Longstreet, fell far below plausible expectations. Stuart's raid denied Lee fundamental intelligence concerning the Army of the Potmac's disposition which deprived him of the opportunity to attack elements of it, or to receive an attack on chosen ground. Longstreet's delay on July 2 exacerbated the obstacles his troops encountered during the sweep toward the Union left. His defeatist attitude on July 3 contributed to the reverse but Lee also erred by allowing his troops to assault a point strengthened by stone walls. Lee's failure to avoid this hazard, as well as the awkward assembly of the assault column, is baffling. Had adjustments been made, it is reasonable to conclude that the Army of Northern Virginia would been victorious because V and VI Corps were out of place to prevent the storming of Cemetery Ridge. The crowning irony of the Battle of Gettysburg: "Stonewall" Jackson was absent. Without his genius of maneuver, the army he served brilliantly was frustrated in great measure by stone walls.

General Meade's mistakes did not harm his army. His concern for the right flank on July 2 was countered by Longstreet's delay in attacking. Officers and men serving in the Army of the Potomac responded to the crisis of invasion with determination to triumph—Gettysburg was their finest hour. President Lincoln's decision to replace Hooker with Meade gave the troops an opportunity to defeat the Army of Northern Virginia through a combination of propitious leadership, hard fighting, and fortunate circumstances.

CONCLUSION

Due to circumstances on July 1, Robert E. Lee detected the opportunity to wreck the Army of the Potomac in battle on July 2. Though the Army of Northern Virginia fought successfully during the Seven Days, it failed to function in harmony. The Battle of Malvern Hill represented an attempt by Lee to finish off McClellan's army. After the victory at Second Manassas, "Stonewall" Jackson's pursuit of the Army of Virginia resulted in the Battle of Chantilly and the Federals withdrew into Washington's defenses. Following the standoff of McClellan at Antietam, Lee wanted to attack but the condition of his army prevented renewal of the contest. At Fredericksburg, dominance of the Federal artillery across the river prevented an offensive operation. Lee's determination to punish VI Corps following his victory at Chancellorsville reflects his inclination to inflict casualties on his opponent. Finally, in Pennsylvania, Lee considered the situation presented to him by Providence and chose to attack, regarding the time and place opportune for a showdown. The Army of the Potomac in defeat could not retreat into prepared defenses nor find protection from rivers or gunboats. The calculated risk failed because *everything* had to go wrong, from Little Round Top to Culp's Hill on July 2, and on Cemetery Ridge on July 3, as Pemberton prepared to surrender Vicksburg, and Price planned for an assault at Helena, Arkansas, on July 4.

Chapter 8

Wounded of Pickett's Division at Breame's Mill near Gettysburg, Pennsylvania

...I do believe...that the measure of American greatness can be achieved only under one flag.

George Edward Pickett

Born a patrician in Nelson County, Virginia, Landon C. Rives (October 24, 1790–June 3, 1870) graduated from William and Mary College at age 18. Rives studied medicine at the University of Pennsylvania and graduated in 1821. Eight years later he departed Oak Ridge, his ancestral home in the Piedmont. Rives relocated his family in Cincinnati, established a medical practice, and "owing to the polish and urbanity of his manners...became a very popular physician." The Southern family "made frequent returns to Virginia, and thus kept up a strong bond of affection with old friends and old scenes in the old home."[1]

Edward Rives was born in Cincinnati on August 27, 1833. The youngest of four children, he was the only native Ohioan. He attended the University of Virginia, 1849–1850, and returned to Cincinnati to study medicine in his father's office. Rives completed his study of medicine at the College of Physicians and Surgeons in New York City. He interned at Bellevue Hospital for a year and subsequently spent two years working at Randall's Island Children's Hospital. When the Civil War began, he and his elder brother Landon were practicing in the Virginia mountains.[2] In tribute to Landon and Edward, Margaret Rives King wrote:

> Both my brothers were men of ability, of singularly good manners, and cultivated gentleman. Surgery was the branch of their profession they preferred...As writers and lecturers they distinguished themselves, and left valuable evidence of their literary ability and usefulness in their profession.[3]

Edward Rives enlisted in the Roanoke (Bedford) Greys, designated Company F, 28th Virginia, in August 1861. Throughout 1861 and 1862, Assistant Surgeon Rives served the 28th Virginia's needs. On January 13, 1863, he was appointed surgeon. At the Battle of Gettysburg, Rives attended the wounded of Pickett's division at the field hospital as division surgeon.[4] Taken prisoner on July 5, 1863, Surgeon Rives was transported to Fort McHenry in Baltimore where he remained confined until August 10. Paroled at City Point in November, he was exchanged at month's end. Following a furlough, Rives returned to duty. On May 25, 1864, V. Quisenberry replaced Edward Rives as surgeon of the 28th Virginia. Rives transferred to the 56th Virginia. On June 3, 1864, Rives operated on Samuel F. Abrahams of Company D. Abrahams' right humerus was amputated at the shoulder. He received a furlough on August 10.[5]

Following the war, the ex-Confederate returned to Cincinnati to practice medicine and surgery. He opened an office at 82 East Third Street near Broadway and became professor of physiology. "Dr. Rives prepared the *first* pathological microscopic slides for the magic lantern with which he afterwards demonstrated his lectures at the Medical College of Ohio."[6]

On October 4, 1870, Edward Rives married Marie T. Thompson; they had no children. Following a term as pathologist to the Cincinnati Hospital, 1872–1874, he moved to his wife's home town on account of failing health and "practiced in Hillsboro for a number of years." Surgeon Rives died at his residence on East Main Street at 11:00 P.M. on September 26, 1883, after an extended illness. He is buried in the family plot on a knoll in Cincinnati's Spring Grove Cemetery.[7]

"...the most horrible wound that I ever saw."

Sketch by Daniel S. Young, Surgeon, 21st Ohio Volunteers,
Cincinnati Medical Heritage Center, University of Cincinnati

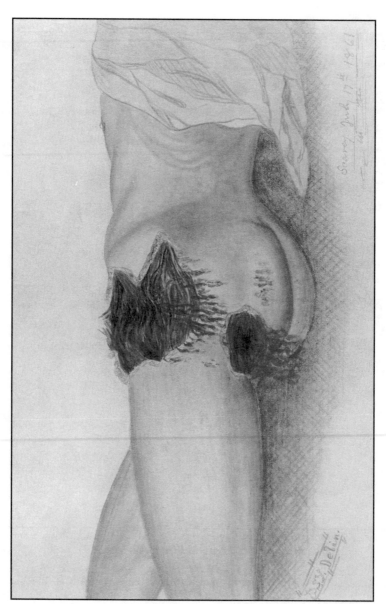

"Somebody's Darling"

Sketch by Daniel S. Young, Surgeon, 21st Ohio Volunteers,
Cincinnati Medical Heritage Center, University of Cincinnati

Name	Rank	Brigade	Regiment	Company	Wound
Loving, Cleophas	Pvt.	Garnett's	8th Va. Inf.	C	abdomen wound; penetrated cavity; died July 7.
Saunders, George	Pvt.	Garnett's	8th Va. Inf.	C	flesh wound to leg; sent off July 25.
Oliver, Elisha D.	Capt.	Garnett's	18th Va. Inf.	I	arm wound; amputated; sent off July 25.
Jones, George W.	Lt.	Garnett's	18th Va. Inf.	I	leg wound; sent off July 25.
Baugh, William A.	Sgt.	Garnett's	18th Va. Inf.	A	arm wound; amputated; sent off July 25.[8]
Lafargue, Henry	Pvt.	Garnett's	18th Va. Inf.	A	facial wound; sent off July 12.
Lipscomb, Junius L.	Pvt.	Garnett's	18th Va. Inf.	C	arm wound; amputated; sent off July 25.
Glenn, Josiah B.	Pvt.	Garnett's	18th Va. Inf.	D	wound to humerus; amputated; sent off July 25.[9]
French, Hugh H.	Pvt.	Garnett's	18th Va. Inf.	E	wounds to testicle and thigh; sent off July 22; July 25.
Webb, Lagiah E.	Pvt.	Garnett's	18th Va. Inf.	G	flesh wound to thigh; sent off July 22.
Fore, Julius L.	Pvt.	Garnett's	18th Va. Inf.	H	wound to perineum (bladder); sent off July 29.
Garrett, Joseph W.	Pvt.	Garnett's	18th Va. Inf.	H	foot wound; sent off July 22.
Harvey, A.	Pvt.	Garnett's	18th Va. Inf.	H	thigh wound; sent off July 29.[10]
Fitzgerald, L.	Pvt.	Garnett's	18th Va. Inf.	I	flesh wound to thigh; sent off July 22.[11]
Roach, W. S.	Pvt.	Garnett's	18th Va. Inf.	K	arm wound; fractured comp[ound] commin[uted]; treated without splints & covering; sent off July 29.[12]
Durrett, John D.	Pvt.	Garnett's	19th Va. Inf.	A	back wound; bronchitis; sent off July 25.
Jones, E. H.	Pvt.	Garnett's	19th Va. Inf.	E	abdomen wound; penetrating cavity; died July 5.[13]
Herndon, Edward J.	Pvt.	Garnett's	19th Va. Inf.	F	right lung and arm wounds; amputated arm; died July 10.
Jennings, L. O.	Pvt.	Garnett's	19th Va. Inf.	I	wound to left lung; emphysema paraeintesis [illegible]; sent off July 25.[14]
Leathers, James A.	Pvt.	Garnett's	19th Va. Inf.	K	ankle wound; amputation 17th July; sent off July 29.

Name	Rank	Brigade	Regiment	Company	Wound
Debo, Reed P.	Sgt.	Garnett's	28th Va. Inf.	G	flesh wound to thigh; sent off July 22.[15]
Tucker, Andrew	Pvt.	Garnett's	28th Va. Inf.	B	flesh wound to thigh; sent off July 23.
Starks, William E.	Pvt.	Garnett's	28th Va. Inf.	C	flesh wound to thigh; sent off July 25.
Camper, Peter, A.	Pvt.	Garnett's	28th Va. Inf.	C	flesh wounds to leg and back; sent off July 25.
Payne, Joseph H.	Pvt.	Garnett's	28th Va. Inf.	D	leg wound; sent off July 23.[16]
Knight, Osson P.	Pvt.	Garnett's	28th Va. Inf.	F	arm wound; radius treated with splints; sent off July 14.
Moorman, William H.	Pvt.	Garnett's	28th Va. Inf.	F	flesh wound to thigh; sent off July 23.
Skinner, James H.	Pvt.	Garnett's	28th Va. Inf.	F	flesh wound to hip; sent off July 23.
Wilson, George W. E.	Pvt.	Garnett's	28th Va. Inf.	F	flesh wound to thigh; sent off July 23.
Wilson, John R.	Pvt.	Garnett's	28th Va. Inf.	F	flesh wound to leg; sent off July 22.
Ailiff, Philip C.	Pvt.	Garnett's	28th Va. Inf.	G	["humerus" written over "shoulder"] humerus wound; amputated July 4 surgical neck; sent off July 25.
Drewry, Carey B.	Pvt.	Garnett's	28th Va. Inf.	G	lung wound; died July 6.
Barker, William H.	Pvt.	Garnett's	28th Va. Inf.	G	flesh wound to leg; sent off July 22.
Hubbard, William	Pvt.	Garnett's	28th Va. Inf.	G	flesh wound to leg and severe wound to buttock; round shot; sent off July 25.[17]
Dowdy, James T.	Pvt.	Garnett's	28th Va. Inf.	G	abdomen wound; ensiform cartilage; passed ball thro' natural passage; sent off July 29.
Vinyard, N. J.	Pvt.	Garnett's	28th Va. Inf.	I	thigh wound; sent off July 23.
Owens, John B.	Pvt.	Garnett's	28th Va. Inf.	I	contusion, abdomen; sent off July 22.
Field, Richard	Sgt.	Garnett's	56th Va. Inf.	E	hip wound; sent off July 22.[18]
Dedman, John H.	Pvt.	Garnett's	56th Va. Inf.	A	leg wound; amputated; sent off July 25.

Name	Rank	Brigade	Regiment	Company	Wound
Williams, David P.	Pvt.	Garnett's	56th Va. Inf.	B	hip wound; sent off July 22.
Purduy, William S.	Pvt.	Garnett's	56th Va. Inf.	B	facial and foot wounds; sent off July 23.
Clark, William C.	Pvt.	Garnett's	56th Va. Inf.	A	thigh wound; sent off July 22.
Trainham, David C.	Pvt.	Garnett's	56th Va. Inf.	C	wound to right lung; sent off July 25.
Brown, Reuben R.	Pvt.	Garnett's	56th Va. Inf.	D	scalp wound; sent off July 22.
Davis, J. J.	Pvt.	Garnett's	56th Va. Inf.	D	thigh wound; sent off July 25.
Denton, John T.	Pvt.	Garnett's	56th Va. Inf.	D	wound to ["breast" lined out] right lung; died July 29.
Williams, Embren E.	Sgt.	Garnett's	56th Va. Inf.	E	arm wound; amputated; sent off July 25.[19]
Craig, John	Pvt.	Garnett's	56th Va. Inf.	H	thigh wound; sent off July 22.
Gibson, H. T.	Pvt.	Garnett's	56th Va. Inf.	H	wound to humerus; frac[tured], treated without splints; sent off July 25.
Blackwell J.	Pvt.	Garnett's	56th Va. Inf.	H	wound to humerus; fractured comp[ound] commin[uted]; sent off July 25.[20]
Lawson, Thomas G.	Pvt.	Garnett's	56th Va. Inf.	I	groin wound; sent off July 22.
Hardiman, John E.	Pvt.	Garnett's	56th Va. Inf.	I	thigh wound; sent off July 22.[21]
Heath, Logan W.	Pvt.	Garnett's	56th Va. Inf.	K	thigh wound; sent off July 25.
Fields, John A.	Pvt.	Garnett's	56th Va. Inf.	K	heel wound; sent off July 12.
Tucker, Bentley H.	Pvt.	Garnett's	56th Va. Inf.	K	wound to humerus; amputated; sent off July 25.[22]
Kemper, James L.	Brig. Gen.	Kemper's	1st Va. Inf.		groin wound; sent off July 29.
Moriarity, John	Sgt.	Kemper's	1st Va. Inf.	C	back wound; sent off July 12.[23]
Miller, William T.	Cpl.	Kemper's	1st Va. Inf.	G	leg wound; amputated – tetanus; died August 5.[24]
Overstreet, John P.	Pvt.	Kemper's	1st Va. Inf.	B	arm and leg wounds; sent off July 22.
Johnson, George W.	Pvt.	Kemper's	1st Va. Inf.	B	arm wound; sent off July 29.[25]

Name	Rank	Brigade	Regiment	Company	Wound
McCary, Benjamin J.	Pvt.	Kemper's	1st Va. Inf.	C	thigh wound; sent off July 12.
Clarke, James D.	Pvt.	Kemper's	1st Va. Inf.	C	scalp wound; sent off July 12.
Davis, Eli M.	Pvt.	Kemper's	1st Va. Inf.	C	wounds to right side & arm; sent off July 12.
Giles, Richard E.	Pvt.	Kemper's	1st Va. Inf.	C	wound to left breast; sent off July 22.
Wingfield, L. R.	Pvt.	Kemper's	1st Va. Inf.	D	chest wound; sent off July 22.
Morton, Tazewell S.	Pvt.	Kemper's	1st Va. Inf.	D	neck wound; sent off July 12.
Keiningham, John C.	Pvt.	Kemper's	1st Va. Inf.	D	neck and mouth wounds; sent off July 22.
Edwards, David S.	Pvt.	Kemper's	1st Va. Inf.	D	arm wound; sent off July 29.
Fergusson, Henry C.	Pvt.	Kemper's	1st Va. Inf.	G	wound to humerus; amputated at joint; sent off July 29.
Hord, Benjamin, H.	Pvt.	Kemper's	1st Va. Inf.	G	wound to chest; sent off July 22.
Anderson, William H.	Pvt.	Kemper's	1st Va. Inf.	H	neck wound; sent off July 12.
Mosby, William B.	Pvt.	Kemper's	1st Va. Inf.	H	wound to side; sent off July 29.
Payne James W.	Pvt.	Kemper's	1st Va. Inf.	H	shoulder wound; sent off July 12.
Neal, S. S.	Pvt.	Kemper's	1st Va. Inf.	I	groin wound; sent off July 29.
Griffin, E. J.	Pvt.	Kemper's	1st Va. Inf.	I	arm and knee wounds; tetanus; died July 18.
Jackson, Thomas B.	Lt.	Kemper's	3rd Va. Inf.	C	flesh wounds to both thighs; sent off July 22.
Guy, Robert F.	Lt.	Kemper's	3rd Va. Inf.	B	wound to right shoulder; no reaction; died July 4.
Gomer, Azra P.	Lt.	Kemper's	3rd Va. Inf.	F	thigh wound; amputated July 3 upper third; sent off July 22.
Ames, Benjamin F.	Sgt.	Kemper's	3rd Va. Inf.	F	abdomen wound; mortally; died July 3. [26]
Tuck, Paul P.	Sgt.	Kemper's	3rd Va. Inf.	K	shoulder wound; sent off July 14. [27]
Murray, William H.	Sgt.	Kemper's	3rd Va. Inf.	K	shoulder wound; sent off July 14. [28]

Name	Rank	Brigade	Regiment	Company	Wound
Jackson, George T.	Sgt.	Kemper's	3rd Va. Inf.	C	chest and thigh wounds; sent off July 22.[29]
Mitchell, Daniel B.	Sgt.	Kemper's	3rd Va. Inf.	C	heel wound; sent off July 22.[30]
Jordan, John C.	Pvt.	Kemper's	3rd Va. Inf.	F	thigh wound; erysipelas; died July 12.
Murray, Elisha	Pvt.	Kemper's	3rd Va. Inf.	F	shoulder wound; contusio[n] tetanus; died July 21.
Pope, Joseph W.	Pvt.	Kemper's	3rd Va. Inf.	G	shoulder and back wounds; died July 11.[31]
West, Henry G.	Pvt.	Kemper's	3rd Va. Inf.	G	lung wound; severe; died July 16.
Wier, John A.	Pvt.	Kemper's	3rd Va. Inf.	K	flesh wound to leg; erysipelas; amputated above knee, tetanus; died July 8.
Houston, David G. Jr.	Capt.	Kemper's	11th Va. Inf.	D	abdomen wound; penetrating cavity; died July 4.
Kelly, John	Cpl.	Kemper's	11th Va. Inf.	E	flesh wound to leg; sent off July 14.[32]
Lec[e?], John	Cpl.	Kemper's	11th Va. Inf.	I	chest wound; sent off July 29.
Rector, Thomas S.	Sgt.	Kemper's	11th Va. Inf.	A	wound to left arm; resection shoulder joint; sent off July 29.[33]
Daniel, John P.	Cpl.	Kemper's	11th Va. Inf.	H	wounds to both ankles; amputation both legs; died July 30.[34]
Embrey, Robert E.	Pvt.	Kemper's	11th Va. Inf.	I	neck wound; sent off July 14.
Moorman, Samuel E.	Pvt.	Kemper's	11th Va. Inf.	B	abdomen wound; penetrating cavity; died July 17.
Dudley, William H.	Pvt.	Kemper's	11th Va. Inf.	B	abdomen wound; contusio[n]; sent off July 14.
Little, James T.	Pvt.	Kemper's	11th Va. Inf.	B	knee wound; sent off July 22.
Morris, James A.	Pvt.	Kemper's	11th Va. Inf.	B	thigh wound; sent off July 22.
Thurmond, Pleasant L.	Pvt.	Kemper's	11th Va. Inf.	B	leg wound; sent off July 14.
Dinguid, Edward S.	Pvt.	Kemper's	11th Va. Inf.	A	chest wound; sent off July 22.
Jones, James C.	Pvt.	Kemper's	11th Va. Inf.	C	elbow wound; amputation July 16th; sent off July 29.

Name	Rank	Brigade	Regiment	Company	Wound
Jones, Lineous	Pvt.	Kemper's	11th Va. Inf.	C	throat and lung wounds; died July 8.
Dunivant, Leroy W.	Pvt.	Kemper's	11th Va. Inf.	C	flesh wound to leg; sent off July 22.
Ammen, John N.	Pvt.	Kemper's	11th Va. Inf.	D	foot wound; sent off July 22.[35]
Tweedy, George D.	Pvt.	Kemper's	11th Va. Inf.	D	knee wound; mortal; died July 3.[36]
Fluke, Abraham W.	Pvt.	Kemper's	11th Va. Inf.	D	shoulder wound; sent off July 22.
Daprato, John	Pvt.	Kemper's	11th Va. Inf.	E	wound to right ankle; amputation secondary; sent off July 29.[37]
Kyle, Robert G.	Pvt.	Kemper's	11th Va. Inf.	F	flesh wound to thigh; ["illegible" lined out] sent off July 22.[38]
Agnew, William H.	Pvt.	Kemper's	11th Va. Inf.	G	wounded in sup[erior] et [and] max[illa] bone [jaw] fracture – splints; arm amputated sup[erior] 3rd humerus; sent off August 6.
Glassell, James S.	Pvt.	Kemper's	11th Va. Inf.	I	wound to base brain; died July 5.
Furgason, James	Pvt.	Kemper's	11th Va. Inf.	K	chest wound; contusion; sent off July 29.
Roop, H.R.	Pvt.	Kemper's	11th Va. Inf.	F	leg wound; sent off July 22.
Hawkins, John W.	Pvt.	Kemper's	7th Va. Inf.	A	hip wound; severely; sent off July 23.
Johnston, David E.	Sgt. Maj.	Kemper's	7th Va. Inf.		wound to back; sent off July 14.[39]
Conway, Catlett	Pvt.	Kemper's	7th Va. Inf.	A	slight wound to side; sent off July 29.[40]
Elliote, William O.	Pvt.	Kemper's	7th Va. Inf.	B	thigh wound; sent off July 22.
Smith, Richard A.	Pvt.	Kemper's	7th Va. Inf.	C	thigh wound; sent off July 22.
Coleman, Thomas P.	Pvt.	Kemper's	7th Va. Inf.	C	leg wound; sent off July 22.
Coleman, Joseph A.	Pvt.	Kemper's	7th Va. Inf.	C	neck wound; sent off July 22.
Hull, John E.	Pvt.	Kemper's	7th Va. Inf.	C	slight thigh wound; sent off July 22.

Name	Rank	Brigade	Regiment	Company	Wound
Smith, Nathaniel	Pvt.	Kemper's	7th Va. Inf.	C	serious ankle wound; sent off July 29.
Fortner, James H.	Pvt.	Kemper's	7th Va. Inf.	D	slight thigh wound; sent off July 14.
Fielding, William B.	Pvt.	Kemper's	7th Va. Inf.	I	slight thigh wound; sent off July 29.
Davis, William	Pvt.	Kemper's	7th Va. Inf.	K	arm wound; amputated; sent off July 22.
Albert, Jacob A.	Sgt.	Kemper's	24th Va. Inf.	F	slight hip wound; sent off July 22.[41]
Peck, John H.	Cpl.	Kemper's	24th Va. Inf.	F	slight scalp wound; sent off July 24.[42]
Schockley, William H.	Cpl.	Kemper's	24th Va. Inf.	I	slight thigh wound; sent off July 22.[43]
Mays, George W.	Cpl.	Kemper's	24th Va. Inf.	K	wounds to both thighs; sent off July 29.[44]
White, Ira	Pvt.	Kemper's	24th Va. Inf.	C	wound to humerus; fracture; sent off July 29.
Ziegler, Thomas F.	Pvt.	Kemper's	24th Va. Inf.	D	slight thigh wound; tetanus; died July 16.
Tench, Edwin J.	Pvt.	Kemper's	24th Va. Inf.	D	slight leg wound; sent off July 22.
Vermillion, Levi H.	Pvt.	Kemper's	24th Va. Inf.	G	wound to ["skull" lined out] brain; died July 9.
Peay, Robert P.	Pvt.	Kemper's	24th Va. Inf.	H	wound to back; sent off July 29.
Edwards, Joseph W.	Pvt.	Kemper's	24th Va. Inf.	I	wound to breast; sent off July 22.
Vellines, Marsden J.	Sgt.	Armistead's	9th Va. Inf.	E	flesh wound to thigh; sent off July 22.[45]
Culpepper, William A.	Sgt.	Armistead's	9th Va. Inf.	D	wrist wound; sent off July 14.[46]
Beach, John T.	Cpl.	Armistead's	9th Va. Inf.	F	leg and arm wounds; sent off July 25.[47]
Urquhart, William J.	Pvt.	Armistead's	9th Va. Inf.	D	wound to side; sent off July 22.
Miltier, Daniel	Pvt.	Armistead's	9th Va. Inf.	D	contusio[n]; sent off July 22.
Taylor, Enos	Pvt.	Armistead's	9th Va. Inf.	E	back and arm wounds; sent off July 22.
Garner, David	Pvt.	Armistead's	9th Va. Inf.	E	shoulder wound; sent off July 14.
Walters, Edwin	Pvt.	Armistead's	9th Va. Inf.	E	foot and side wounds; sent off July 25.

Name	Rank	Brigade	Regiment	Company	Wound
Totty, John	Pvt.	Armistead's	9th Va. Inf.	C	hip wound; sent off July 14.
Hodsden, Wilfred J.	Pvt.	Armistead's	9th Va. Inf.	F	foot wound; sent off July 25.
Owens, Thomas C.	Pvt.	Armistead's	9th Va. Inf.	G	neck wound; died July 9.
Land, James W. T.	Pvt.	Armistead's	9th Va. Inf.	G	thigh wound; sent off July 22.
Boyed, Henry C.	Pvt.	Armistead's	9th Va. Inf.	G	knee wound; sent off July 23.
Phillips, Henry O.	Pvt.	Armistead's	9th Va. Inf.	G	abdomen wound; sent off July 23.
Nash, Richard J.	Pvt.	Armistead's	9th Va. Inf.	G	knee wound; sent off July 29.
Hargroves, John R.	Pvt.	Armistead's	9th Va. Inf.	G	chest wound; sent off July 25.
Walton, Henry	Pvt.	Armistead's	9th Va. Inf.	I	foot wound; sent off July 25.
Host, Andrew C.	Pvt.	Armistead's	9th Va. Inf.	K	leg wound; sent off July 25.
Dunderdale, John A. F.	Pvt.	Armistead's	9th Va. Inf.	K	groin wound; died July 21.
Seay, Philip G.	Lt.	Armistead's	14th Va. Inf.	C	abdomen wound; sent off July 22.
Chalkley, Gideon P.	Lt.	Armistead's	14th Va. Inf.	D	knee wound; thigh wound; sent off July 25.
Adkins, John T.	Sgt.	Armistead's	14th Va. Inf.	D	leg wound; sent off July 22.[48]
Talley, Henry M.	Sgt.	Armistead's	14th Va. Inf.	G	wounds to both feet; sent off July 22.[49]
Tinsley, Thomas H.	Sgt.	Armistead's	14th Va. Inf.	B	foot wound; sent off July 25.[50]
Ives, Richard W.	Cpl.	Armistead's	14th Va. Inf.	H	wound to jaw inf; sent off July 29.[51]
Seay, Richard D.	Pvt.	Armistead's	14th Va. Inf.	A	["shoulder" lined out] wound to humerus; shoulder amputated; sent off July 25.
Gills, Peter M.	Pvt.	Armistead's	14th Va. Inf.	A	thigh wound; sent off July 25.
Hackworth, Elijah	Pvt.	Armistead's	14th Va. Inf.	B	leg wound; sent off July 23.
Johnson, William W.	Pvt.	Armistead's	14th Va. Inf.	B	sick; chronic diarrhoea [sic]; sent off July 23.

Name	Rank	Brigade	Regiment	Company	Wound
Hughes, Anthony T.	Pvt.	Armistead's	14th Va. Inf.	D	leg, arm and thigh wounds; sent off July 22.
Winfree, Joseph	Pvt.	Armistead's	14th Va. Inf.	D	leg wound; sent off July 22.
Gill, William F.	Pvt.	Armistead's	14th Va. Inf.	D	shoulder wound; sent off July 14.
Jones, Walter, L.	Pvt.	Armistead's	14th Va. Inf.	F	thigh wound; sent off July 25.
Sizemore, Thomas L.	Pvt.	Armistead's	14th Va. Inf.	G	shoulder wound; sent off July 14.
Pinson, Allen	Pvt.	Armistead's	14th Va. Inf.	G	["head" lined out] wound to brain; died July 5. [52]
Matthews, J. Kemp	Pvt.	Armistead's	14th Va. Inf.	G	thigh wound; sent off July 22.
Chandler, M. C.	Pvt.	Armistead's	14th Va. Inf.	G	shoulder wound; sent off July 25.
Light, William S.	Pvt.	Armistead's	14th Va. Inf.	H	thigh wound; sent off July 22.
Womack, James K.	Pvt.	Armistead's	14th Va. Inf.	H	leg wound; sent off July 25.
Coleman, Samuel A.	Pvt.	Armistead's	14th Va. Inf.	I	thigh wound; sent off July 22 [53]
Boyd, James G.	Pvt.	Armistead's	14th Va. Inf.	K	sick; chr[onic] diarrhoea; sent off July 22.
Whitt, John A.	Pvt.	Armistead's	14th Va. Inf.	K	wound to back; sent off July 14.
Miller, Joseph T.	Lt.	Armistead's	38th Va. Inf.	E	leg wound; amputated; sent off July 22.
Carter, Edward A.	Sgt.	Armistead's	38th Va. Inf.	A	foot wound; sent off July 23.
Meade, Harrison W.	Cpl.	Armistead's	38th Va. Inf.	D	leg wound; sent off July 23. [54]
Brown, John T.	Cpl.	Armistead's	38th Va. Inf.	E	arm, leg and buttock wounds; sent off July 25. [55]
Roffe, Lewis J.	Cpl.	Armistead's	38th Va. Inf.	G	thigh wound; sent off July 23. [56]
Evans, Robert H.	Pvt.	Armistead's	38th Va. Inf.	A	back and shoulder wounds; sent off July 25.
Evans, William M.	Pvt.	Armistead's	38th Va. Inf.	A	leg wound; sent off July 25.
Gosney, James L.	Pvt.	Armistead's	38th Va. Inf.	A	thigh wound; sent off July 23.
Easley, James C.	Pvt.	Armistead's	38th Va. Inf.	B	humerus wound; fractured; sent off July 29. [57]
Nuchols, James A.	Pvt.	Armistead's	38th Va. Inf.	B	arm wound; amputated; sent off July 29.

Name	Rank	Brigade	Regiment	Company	Wound
Owen, David L.	Pvt.	Armistead's	38th Va. Inf.	B	["shoulder" lined out] humerus wound; amputated at shoulder joint; sent off July 25.
Oakes, James A.	Pvt.	Armistead's	38th Va. Inf.	B	leg wound; amputated secondary; irritative fever; died July 15.
Uhles, David	Cpl.	Armistead's	38th Va. Inf.	D	flesh wounds to leg and thigh; sent off July 23.[58]
Foust, Fountain J.	Pvt.	Armistead's	38th Va. Inf.	B	leg wound; sent off July 25.
Meadows, James R.	Pvt.	Armistead's	38th Va. Inf.	B	wound to clavicle; fracture; sent off July 25.
Blair, Suter F.	Pvt.	Armistead's	38th Va. Inf.	B	thigh wound; amputated secondary; irritative fever; died July 15.
McCormick, William L.	Pvt.	Armistead's	38th Va. Inf.	C	flesh wound to leg; sent off July 22.
McCormick, John B.	Pvt.	Armistead's	38th Va. Inf.	C	sick; diarrhoea; sent off July 22.
Bryant, Fleming B.W.	Pvt.	Armistead's	38th Va. Inf.	C	thigh wound; sent off July 22.
Bohannon, William	Pvt.	Armistead's	38th Va. Inf.	C	sent off July 22.
White, J.	Pvt.	Armistead's	38th Va. Inf.	C	leg and shoulder wounds; sent off July 25.
Dodson, Josephus B.	Pvt.	Armistead's	38th Va. Inf.	C	thigh wound; amputated; died July 6.[59]
Simpson, Archer M.	Pvt	Armistead's	38th Va. Inf.	C	abdomen and leg wounds; penetrating cavity; died July 6.
Walker, John	Pvt.	Armistead's	38th Va. Inf.	D	leg wound; sent off July 14.
Robinson, James C.	Pvt.	Armistead's	38th Va. Inf.	D	arm wound; amputated; sent off July 23.[60]
Burnett, Edwin H.	Pvt.	Armistead's	38th Va. Inf.	G	wound to side; sent off July 14.
Rice, James J.	Pvt.	Armistead's	38th Va. Inf.	H	chest wound; sent off July 25.
Gray, Thomas W.	Pvt.	Armistead's	38th Va. Inf.	K	shoulder and back wounds; sent off July 29.
McDowell, Robert B.	Pvt.	Armistead's	38th Va. Inf.	K	shoulder wound; died July 22.[61]
George, William H.	Sgt.	Armistead's	53rd Va. Inf.	D	leg wound; dysentery acute; died July 13.[62]

Name	Rank	Brigade	Regiment	Company	Wound
Ammons, George W.	Cpl.	Armistead's	53rd Va. Inf.	K	wounds to both thighs; sent off July 25. [63]
Blankenship, William W.	Pvt.	Armistead's	53rd Va. Inf.	B	foot wound; sent off July 22.
Finn, Percival	Pvt.	Armistead's	53rd Va. Inf.	C	facial wound; sent off July 14.
Duell, Littleton J.	Pvt.	Armistead's	53rd Va. Inf.	C	thigh wound; sent off July 25.
Padgett, John F.	Pvt.	Armistead's	53rd Va. Inf.	D	leg wound; fracture; sent off July 25.
Lewis, John R.	Pvt.	Armistead's	53rd Va. Inf.	D	[no wounds listed]; sent off July 22. [64]
Bendall, Benjamin F.	Pvt.	Armistead's	53rd Va. Inf.	F	arm and leg wounds; amputation leg and arm; sent off July 29.
Williams, David R.	Pvt.	Armistead's	53rd Va. Inf.	F	leg and arm wounds; arm amputated; sent off July 25.
Stith, Benjamin A.	Pvt.	Armistead's	53rd Va. Inf.	H	leg wound; sent off July 14. [65]
Simpson, William R.	Pvt.	Armistead's	53rd Va. Inf.	I	thigh wound; sent off July 22.
Riddle, Thomas C.	Pvt.	Armistead's	53rd Va. Inf.	I	thigh wound; sent off July 22
Binns, Major E.	Pvt.	Armistead's	53rd Va. Inf.	K	hand and knee wounds; amputation secondary; upper 3rd thigh; died July 23.
Haden, Thomas D.	Sgt.	Armistead's	57th Va. Inf.	D	facial wound; sent off July 14. [66]
Eddins, Theodore F.	Sgt.	Armistead's	57th Va. Inf.	H	shoulder wound; sent off July 25. [67]
Miles, William S.	Sgt.	Armistead's	57th Va. Inf.	G	back and shoulder wounds; sent off July 25.
Martin, John C.	Sgt.	Armistead's	57th Va. Inf.	G	leg wound; sent off July 14.
Young, Charles P.	Cpl.	Armistead's	57th Va. Inf.	E	arm wound; amputated; sent off July 25. [68]
Elliot, Abraham F.	Cpl.	Armistead's	57th Va. Inf.	F	leg wound; ["tetanus" lined out]; sent off July 14. [69]
Drake, Robert B.	Pvt.	Armistead's	57th Va. Inf.	A	thigh wound; fract[ure]; sent off July 23. [70]
Smith, Arthur L.	Pvt.	Armistead's	57th Va. Inf.	A	side and arm wounds; sent off July 25.
McMellon, John W.	Pvt.	Armistead's	57th Va. Inf.	B	side wound; sent off July 14.

Name	Rank	Brigade	Regiment	Company	Wound
Vest, Willis M.	Pvt.	Armistead's	57th Va. Inf.	C	shoulder and side wounds; sent off July 25. [71]
Shelton, William T.	Pvt.	Armistead's	57th Va. Inf.	D	side wound; sent off July 25.
Meador, Jesse L.	Pvt.	Armistead's	57th Va. Inf.	E	abdomen wound; penetrating cavity; died July 9, '63. [72]
Young, George W.	Pvt.	Armistead's	57th Va. Inf.	E	back wound; sent off July 25.
McGhee, William H.	Pvt.	Armistead's	57th Va. Inf.	E	leg wound; sent off July 22.
Blankenship, Elijah P.	Pvt.	Armistead's	57th Va. Inf.	E	leg wound; sent off July 22.
George, William	Pvt.	Armistead's	57th Va. Inf.	E	both legs wounded; tetanus; died July 17. [73]
Crider, John H.	Pvt.	Armistead's	57th Va. Inf.	E	shoulder wound; sent off July 14.
Murphy, Pleasant	Pvt.	Armistead's	57th Va. Inf.	F	penis wound; sent off July 22.
Law, Peter C.	Pvt.	Armistead's	57th Va. Inf.	G	thigh wound; sent off July 14.
Bennett, Franklin	Pvt.	Armistead's	57th Va. Inf.	G	leg wound; sent off July 25.
Reinhart, William W.	Pvt.	Armistead's	57th Va. Inf.	H	wounds to both thighs; sent off July 25.
Martin, Richard S.	Pvt.	Armistead's	57th Va. Inf.	I	knee wound; sent off July 22. [74]
McAlister, Jehu H.	Pvt.	Armistead's	57th Va. Inf.	K	side and arm wounds; amputated; sent off July 25.
Huse, Samuel B.	Pvt.	Armistead's	57th Va. Inf.	K	leg wound; amputated finger; sent off July 29.
Peery, John M.	Pvt.	Armistead's	57th Va. Inf.	K	arm and hand wounds; sent off July 14.
Booze, William H.	Pvt.	Armistead's	57th Va. Inf.	K	thigh and foot wounds; sent off July 23.
McCommac, James M.	Pvt.	Armistead's	57th Va. Inf.	K	testicles wounded; sent off July 14.
Lemon, William	Pvt.	Armistead's	57th Va. Inf.	K	sent off July 23.

Stragglers

Name	Rank	Brigade	Regiment	Company	Wound
Hurst, William A.	Pvt.	[Semmes]	10th Ga.		sent off July 14th.
Watts, J. R.		[Wofford]	3rd Ga. Batt. [75]		cook; sent off July 25.
Ewing, J. W.		[Pettigrew]	52nd N.C.	E	knee wound; sent off July 22nd.

248 cases   34 deaths   36 amputations   20 upper extremity; 12 lower extremity;
2 at shoulder joint; 4 at surg neck humerus; 8 humerus; 6 forearm

6 Tetanus died
8 abdominal wounds died
5 lung   "   "
3 Head   "   "
1 Dysentery   "   "
2 Exhaustion   "   "
1 Erysipelas   "   "
1 ["both legs" lined out]
1 Neck   "   "
5 Irritative fever "   "
32 [33]

Cases
men   off.
238   10
deaths
32   2
amputations
30   4 [sic]

List of Surgeons, Nurses, and Attendants at Pickett's Division Hospital near Gettysburg, Pa.

Name	Rank	Brigade	Regiment	Company	Wound
Edward Rives	Surg. in Charge	Garnett's	28th Va. Inf.		
Thomas P. Mayo	Surg.	Kemper's	3rd Va. Inf.		
Alexander Grigsby	Surg.	Kemper's	1st Va. Inf.		
B. C. Harrison	Asst. Surg.	Garnett's	56th Va. Inf.		
William S. Nowlin	Asst. Surg.	Armistead's	38th Va. Inf.		
Walter L. Withers	Hosp. Steward	Kemper's	11th Va. Inf.		
Peter Tinsley	Chaplain	Garnett's	28th Va. Inf.		
Moore, M. J.	Pvt.	Garnett's	18th Va. Inf.	E	sent off July 24.
Harvey,[76]	Pvt.	Garnett's	18th Va. Inf.	F	
Houchens, Thomas W.	Pvt.	Garnett's	19th Va. Inf.	A	
Ware, Paulus M.[77]	Pvt.	Garnett's	19th Va. Inf.	K	
Durrett, John D.	Pvt.	Garnett's	19th Va. Inf.	[A]	sent off July 24. [note]
Huffman, Joseph	Pvt.	Garnett's	28th Va. Inf.	C	
Howard, Samuel J.	Pvt.	Garnett's	28th Va. Inf.	F	
Brown, Samuel M.	Pvt.	Garnett's	28th Va. Inf.	I	
Clark, Alexander	Pvt.	Garnett's	56th Va. Inf.	A	sent with wounded to Gen[l.] Hospital July 22.
Blackwell, [?][78]	Pvt.	Garnett's	56th Va. Inf.	[?]	
McGhee, Peter C.	Pvt.	Garnett's	56th Va. Inf.	K	
Harris, James W.	Pvt.	Garnett's	56th Va. Inf.	C	sent off July 24.
Stagg, James	Pvt.	Kemper's	1st Va. Inf.	B	sent off July 29.

["Owens, John" lined out]

["sent off to Gen[l.] Hospital with wound July 23" see p. 164]

Name	Rank	Brigade	Regiment	Company	Wound
Bowe, N. W.	Pvt.	Kemper's	1st Va. Inf.	D	sent off July 29.
Epps, James R.	Pvt.	Kemper's	1st Va. Inf.	G	
Hord, William F.	Pvt.	Kemper's	1st Va. Inf.	G	
Anderson, Charles E.	Pvt.	Kemper's	3rd Va. Inf.	B	
Ghent, Emmet M.	Pvt.	Kemper's	3rd Va. Inf.	C	sent off July 24.[79]
Holland, Matthew	Pvt.	Kemper's	3rd Va. Inf.	F	
Richardson, John W.	Musician	Kemper's	3rd Va. Inf.	F	sent off July 29.
Oden, Alexander	Pvt.	Kemper's	7th Va. Inf.	C	
Brown, J. V.	Pvt.	Kemper's	7th Va. Inf.	G	deserted 16th July[,] 1863.
Wolfe, Ezra M.	Pvt.	Kemper's	7th Va. Inf.	I	transferred to hospital in Gettysburg to nurse members of 7th Va. Inf.
Grubbs, John W.	Pvt.	Kemper's	7th Va. Inf.	B	sent off July 24.
Hume, William S.	Pvt.	Kemper's	7th Va. Inf.	A	nurse for Gen[l.] Kemper; sent off July 29.
Bowler, Napoleon B.	Pvt.	Kemper's	7th Va. Inf.	A	nurse for Gen[l.] Kemper.
Davis, John W.	Pvt.	Kemper's	7th Va. Inf.	A	
Percival, C. Dabney	Pvt.	Kemper's	11th Va. Inf.	G	
Parrish, Booker S.	Pvt.	Kemper's	11th Va. Inf.	A	sent off July 29.
Horton, Edwin R.	Pvt.	Kemper's	11th Va. Inf.	D	sent to General Hospital[80]
Wilcher, J.[81]	Pvt.	Kemper's	11th Va. Inf.	K	
Albert, George A.	Pvt.	Kemper's	24th Va. Inf.	F	sent off [n.d.][82]
Bell, James W.	Pvt.	Kemper's	24th Va. Inf.	C	sent off [n.d.]
Phillips, Charles T.	Sgt. Maj.	Armistead's	9th Va. Inf.		
Johnston, Theophilus	Pvt.	Armistead's	9th Va. Inf.	G	sent off July 29.

Name	Rank	Brigade	Regiment	Company	Wound
Earles, Rufus	Pvt.	Armistead's	14th Va. Inf.	G	sent to Genl. Hospital with wounded July 23.
Easley, Henry W.	Pvt.	Armistead's	38th Va. Inf.	D	
Barker, Josiah	Pvt.	Armistead's	38th Va. Inf.	C	sent off July 29.
White, Abram	Pvt.	Armistead's	38th Va. Inf.	C	
Murrell, James W.	Pvt.	Armistead's	38th Va. Inf.	A	
Wynn, Robert S.[83]	Pvt.	Armistead's	38th Va. Inf.	E	
Fuller, Brittain	Pvt.	Armistead's	38th Va. Inf.	B	
Binns, E.F.[84]	Pvt.	Armistead's	53rd Va. Inf.	K	
Riddle, George W.	Pvt.	Armistead's	53rd Va. Inf.	G	sent to Genl[.] Hospital with wounded July 22.[85]
Owens, William T.	Pvt.	Armistead's	57th Va. Inf.	E	
Snow, Pulaski P.	Pvt.	Armistead's	57th Va. Inf.	H	
Wingo, Lawrence H.	Pvt.	Armistead's	53rd Va. Inf.	C	
Tinsley, Samuel H.	Pvt.	Armistead's	57th Va. Inf.	D	
Puckett, James A.	Pvt.	Armistead's	14th Va. Inf.	I	

Recapitulation

Garnett's Brigade		Brotover	298
Wounded	56	Hosp Steward	1
Surgeons & Asst	2	Chaplain	1
Nurses & att	13		300
Kemper's Brigade			
Wounded	76		
Surgs	2		
Nurses & Attends	21	wounded remaining	
Armistead's		July 19 181	
Wounded	114		
Surg Asst	1		
Nurses	13		
	298		

List of wounded of Pickett's Division at 3rd Corps Hospital (Federal)

Walker, Nathan W.	Pvt.	Co. I 18th Va.	severe leg wound.
Reed, Charles W.	Pvt.	Co. G 8th Va.	left arm amputated; died July 17.[86]
Embrey, James T.	Pvt.	Co. I 11th Va.	thigh and knee wounds.
Jennings, J. T.	Pvt.	Co. G 11th Va.	left leg amputated; died July 18.[87]
Hughes, Jospeh H.	Pvt.	Co. A 28th Va.	left leg amputated.
Bowen, John	Pvt.	Co. B 7th Va.	fractured thigh.
Wilson, Richard	Pvt.	Co. G 14th Va.	ankle and thigh wounds.
Robinson, R. A.	Pvt.	Co. C 18th Va.	right leg amputated.[88]
Powell, C.	Pvt.	Co. E 9th Va.	left leg amputated.[89]
Jones, I. T.[90]	Pvt.	Co. D 7th Va.	ankle wound.
Bragg, Henry L.	Pvt.	Co. H 57th Va.	breast and arm wounds.
Hewn, N.	Pvt.	Co. I 7th Va.	left leg amputated.[91]
Chinn, Francis, W.	Pvt.	Co. D 8th Va.	neck and leg wounds.
Moon, Julian K.	Pvt.	Co. C 14th Va.	thigh wound.
Burchett, James M.	Pvt.	Co. K 8th Va.	left leg amputated.
Phillips, John E.	Sgt.	Co. B 11th Va.	slight head wound.[92]
Ramsey, James Y.	Pvt.	Co. E 14th Va.	knee wound.
Burroughs, G. W.	Pvt.	Co. G 24th Va.	knee wound.
Watson, John S.[93]	Cpl.	Co. I 57th Va.	wound to breast.
Gaulding, John R.	Pvt.	Co. I 57th Va.	wound to breast.
Maloney, Clem H.	Pvt.	Co. K 18th Va.	thigh wound.
Bresnaham, Mathew	Pvt.	Co. H 1st Va.	thigh wound.
Bausey, W. B.	Pvt.	Co. E 14th Va.	fractured thigh.
Gaskins, William H.[94]	Sgt.	Co. K 8th Va.	foot wound.

Ray, F. J.	Pvt.	Co. B 24th Va.	knee wound.
Bowen, Henry L.	Pvt.	Co. A. 8th Va.	foot wound.
Haley, Samuel H.	Pvt.	Co. I 24th Va.	leg wound.
Parker, E. L.	Sgt.	Co. I 1st Va.	left leg amputated.
Davis, Philip	Pvt.	Co. I 14th Va.	thigh wound.
Worsham, John B.[95]	Sgt.	Co. D 24th Va.	knee wound.
Goodson, Calvin	Pvt.	Co. H 3rd Va.	knee wound.
Milton, Calvin A.	Pvt.	Co. B 8th Va.	slight thigh wound.
Rowland, Rufus F.[96]	Sgt.	Co. G 24th Va.	leg wound.
Raber, Henry L.[97]	Pvt.	Co. A 8th Va.	wounded [in] 13 places in back and chest.
Robey, C. Ozias	Cpl.	Co. G 8th Va.	leg and arm wounds.
Stanley, S. R.	Pvt.	Co. D 57th Va.	thigh wound.
Shelton, Josiah W.	Pvt.	Co. B 57th Va.	thigh wound.
Barnett, J. P. [M.?][98]	Pvt.	Co. F 14th Va.	thigh wound.
Stokes, Collins	Pvt.	Co. K 38th Va.	wound to breast.
Keeling, William H.	Pvt.	Co. H 3rd Va.	head wound.
Dunston, James H.	Pvt.	Co. D 14th Va.	hip wound.
Dalton, Francis W.	Sgt.	Co. C 24th Va.	wounds to both legs.
Alley, D. S.	Pvt.	Co. F 11th Va.	thigh wound.
Kirkland, James M.	Pvt.	Co. F 53rd Va.	leg and thigh wounds.[99]
Black, Nicholas[100]	Sgt.	Co. K 19th Va.	thigh wound.
Taylor, Eugene G.[101]	Pvt.	Co. B 19th Va.	thigh wound.
Jennings, Henry C.	Pvt.	Co. H 18th Va.	frac[ture] right forearm.
Pollard, George M.	Sgt.	Co. H 18th Va.	wounds to right leg and both hands.[102]
Ferguson, Robert R.	Lt.	Co. K 53rd Va.	thigh wound.
Moore, James M.	Pvt.	Co. G 11th Va.	thigh wound; died July 19.
Blanton, Zachaiah A.[103]	Cpl.	Co. F 18th Va.	facial wound.
Miles, F. W.	Pvt.	Co. F 11th Va.	wound to breast.
Chapman, Gustavus A.	Pvt.	Co. G 1st Va.	arm wound.
Leftwich, James P.	Sgt.	Co. G 28th Va.	neck and arm wounds.[104]
James, Cornelius E.	Pvt.	Co. F 3rd Va.	arm wound.
Ehart, Adam G.	Pvt.	Co. E 19th Va.	leg wound.
Mahone, L. O.	Pvt.	Co. H 19th Va.	neck wound.
Waddle, William D.	Pvt.	Co. H 1st Va.	ankle wound.
Heath, George R.	Pvt.	Co. B 1st Va.	wound to side.

["Farley, James C." lined out][105]

Deaths Heard Of

Rhodes, Robert P.	Pvt.	Co. F 19th Va.	thigh wound; died July 15.[106]
Pillow, Daniel A.	Pvt.	Co. C 19th Va.	leg wound; died July 15.
McLaughlan, Hugh	Pvt.	Co. I 1st Va.	leg wound; died July 16.
Jennings, James[107]	Pvt.	Co. I 18th Va.	right leg amputated; died July 16.

An account of the wounds of Pickett's Division (Longstreet's Corps) at the battle of Gettysburg[.] Exclusive of those who fell into the hands of Federal Surgeons <u>immediately after</u> the fight <u>Ed Rives</u>

The subjoined account so far as it goes is correct being taken from the original report made by myself to the Surg. Genl of C.S.A. Of course in the necessary disorder and confusion of a Camp Hospital established ["immediately" lined out] during & after a great battle there is a want of fullness at least in reports & on this account the accompanying paper lacks the detailed of each ["important" lined out] case. The main facts however have been carefully preserved and by this much will add to statistical information of gunshot wounds The first object to be attained in presenting such a paper to the profession is I think 1st to construct a tabular statement of wounds of ["the" lined out] different region and the percentage of deaths to each region ——— 2nd To particularize so far as lies in my power each case of wound & the missile producing it & mode of death. This ["illegible"] I fear will be very imperfect except in a few instances which particularly attracted attention 3<u>d</u> To note by tabular form the character of all operative interference and the results of such procedure - the number & percentage of deaths in each & mode 4th To draw such conclusions from the whole as were common to my colleagues and myself ___ I ask the indulgence of the profession for ["illegible" lined out] whatever imperfections may exist, on the ground of the great difficulty of making and preserving records under such circumstances On the 3<u>d</u> of July at 3 o'clock 1863, Picketts Division 7000 strong were subjected to a heavy shelling and subsequently charged the Federal position _ ascending a declivity for the space of half a mile in the face of a heavy fire of artillery and small arms. The result of this charge in wounds which reached the field Hospital was as follows[:]

	Wounds	Deaths	Percent of Deaths
Head	6	3	50
Face	9	0	0
Neck	7	1	14.3
Shoulder	13	3	23.09

	Wounds	Deaths	Percent of Deaths
Sup. Extremity	40	2	.05
Chest	29	5	17.24
Back	12	1	08.33
Abdomen	16	8	50
Testicle	2	0	0
Penis	1	0	0
Buttock	8	0	0
Perineum	1	0	0
Inf Extremity	127	14	11.02
Total =	271	37	13.7

It will be seen from the foregoing table that the several regions bear a certain relation to each other in the probability of injury The following order exists in this table __ 1 Inf Extr. 2 Sup Extremity 3d Chest 4th Abdomen 5th ["Back" lined out] Shoulder 6th ["Face" written over] Back 7th ["Buttock" written over] Face 8th ["Neck" written over] Buttock 9th ["Head" written over] 10th Head 11th Testicle 12th Penis[.]

...to me the exaggerated irreverance of the present times is the root from which will spring a poison which may embitter the mortal days of generations to come.

Margaret Rives King

Cover of the ledger book

Name	Rank	Brigade	Regt	Co	Wound
Loving C.	Private	Garnetts	8th Va Inf	C	Abdomen ✓
Saunders G.	"	"	"	"	Leg
Oliver	Captain	"	18th	J	Arm
Jones	Lieut	"	"	"	Leg
Baugh W.	Sergt	"	"	A	Arm
Lafargue H	Private	"	"	A	Face
Lipscomb G.D.	"	"	"	C	Arm
Glenn J B	"	"	"	D	Humerus
French H.H.	"	"	"	C	Testicle Thy
Webb L E	"	"	"	G	Thigh
Hamilton A	"	"	"	H	" ✓
Fox J L	"	"	"	"	Perineum Bla
Garrett J W	"	"	"	"	Foot ✓
Harvey A	"	"	"	"	Thigh ✓
Fitzgerald J	"	"	"	J	" ✓
Roach W.S.	"	"	"	K	Arm
Durrett G.D.	"	"	19th	A	Back ✓
Jones C H	"	"	"	C	Abdn
Herndon C J	"	"	"	K	R.Lung
Jennings L O	"	"	"	J	L Lung ✓
Leathers J H	"	"	"	K	Ankle ✓
Debt R P	Sergt	"	28th	G	Thigh ✓
Tucker A	Private	"	"	B	" ✓
Starks W E	"	"	"	C	" ✓
Camper P.A.	"	"	"	C	Leg Back
Payne J H	"	"	"	K	Leg
Knight O.P.	"	"	"	F	Arm ✓
Mooreman W H	"	"	"	K	Thigh ✓
Skinner J H	"	"	"	F	Hip ✓
Wilson G W E	"	"	"	F	Thigh ✓
Wilson Jno R	"	"	"	F	Leg
Ayliff P C	"	"	"	G	Shoulder ✓
Drury C D	"	"	"	"	Lung ✓
Barker W H	"	"	"	"	Leg ✓
Hubbard Wm	"	"	"	"	"
Dowdy J T	"	"	"	"	Abdomen
Vineyard N	"	"	"	J	Thigh ✓
Prins Jno	"	"	"	"	Contusio ✓

Page 1 of ledger book

Names	Rank	Brigade	Reg't	Co	Wound
Fields R	Serg't	Garnett	56th Va	C	Hip
Deadman J H	Private	"	"	A	Leg
Williams D	"	"	"	B	Hip
Purdy W S				B	Face & Foot
Clark Wm				A	Thigh
Trainum D.C.				C	R Lung
Brown R				D	Scalp
Davis J J				D	Thigh
Denton T				A	Breast
Williams C				C	Arm
Craig J M				H	Thigh
Gibson H. J.				H	Humerus
Blackwell J				A	Groin
Lawson G				"	Thigh
Handman J C				"	
Heath R.W.				K	
Fields J A				K	Heel
Tucker B H				K	Humerus

Kemper's 1st Va

Kemper Jas L	Brig Gen'l	"			Groin
Moriarty J	Serg't	"	"	C	Back
Miller W	Corp'l	"	"	G	Leg
Overstreet	Private	"	"	B	Arm – Leg
Johnson G W	"			B	Arm
McCary B J				C	Thigh
Clark J D				C	Scalp
Davis C. W.				C	R Side & arm
Gill R. C.				C	L Breast
Wingfield L R				D	Chest
Thorton T S				D	Neck & Breast
Keiningham J				D	
Edward D				D	Arm
Ferguson H				G	Shoulder Humerus
Hode B H				G	Chest
Anderson W				H	Neck
Mosby W B				.	Side
Payne J W				.	Shoulder
Neal J J				J	Groin
Griffin C J				.	Arm & Knee

Page 3 of ledger book; note name of General Kemper.

186

Names	Rank	Brigade	Regt	Co	Wounds
Simpson A. Os.	Private	Armistead	38th Va Reg	C	Abdomen Leg √
Walker J H				D	Leg √
Robinson Jas				D	Arm √
Bennett C. H.				G	Side √
Rice J. J.				H	Chest √
Gray J W				K	Shoulder & Back √
McDowell R B					Shoulder √
George Wm H	Sergt	53rd Va Inf	D	Leg √
~~Davis~~ G. W	Corpl			✗	Both Thighs √
Blankenship Wm	Private			13	Foot √
Finn P	"			C	Face √
Duel L J	"				Thigh √
Padgett J F	"			D	Leg √
Bandale B. F.	"			H	Arm & Leg √
Williams D R	"			"	Leg & Arm
Stith B A	"			H	Leg √
Simpson W R	"			J	Thigh √
Riddle Thos E	"			"	" √
Binns M E	"			K	Hand & Knee √
Haden J D	Sergt	57th Va Inf	D	Face √
Eddins J F	"			H	Shoulder √
Myers W S	"			G	Back & Shoulder √
Martin J C	"			G	Leg
Young C W	Corpl			C	Arm √
Elliott A J				H	Leg √
Drake A B	Private			A	Thigh √
Smith A L	"				Side & Arm √
McMillen W	"			B	Side
West W M	"			C	Shoulder & Side √
Shelton J H	"			D	Side √
Meadow J L	"			C	Abdomen √
Young G W	"			C	Back √
McGee W H	"			C	Leg
Blankenship C P	"			C	Leg √
George W	"			C	Both Legs √
Gorden J H	"			C	Shoulder √
Murphy P	"			F	Penis √
Law P	"			G	Thigh √
Bennett J H	"			G	Leg √

Names	Rank	Brigade	Reg!	Co	Wound
Reinhart W	Private	Armistead	57th V Inf	H	Both Thighs ✓
Martin R S				J	Knee ✓
Mc Allister J H				K	Side ✓
Hughes S B				"	Leg ✓
Perry J				"	Arm & hand ✓
Booze W H				"	Thigh & Foot ✓
Mc Cormick J M				"	Fistules
Lemon Wm				"	Foot ✓

Stragglers

Hurst Wm A	Private		10th Ga		
Watts J K.			32d Ga Batt		
Ewing J W.			52 N.C.	Co E	Knee

5 4

5

Remarks   Cut off Died

Amputated
"   Finger

July 14th

July 14th

July 14th

List of Surgeons Nurses and Attendants at

Names	Rank	Brigade	Regiment	Co
Edward Rives	Surgeon in chg	Garnetts	28th Va Infy	
Theo P Mayo	Surg	Kempers	3rd " "	
A. S. Grigsby	Surg	"	1st " "	
B L Harrison	Asst Surg	Garnetts	56th " "	
Wm J Nowlin	Asst Surg	Armisteads	38th " "	
W L Withers	Hosp Steward	Kempers	11th " "	
P Tinsley	Chaplain	Garnetts	28th " "	
Moore	Private	Garnetts	18th Va Infy	
Harvey				
Richine			19th	
Ware				
Durritt				
Huffman J			28th	C
Wen Jno				J
Howard				I
Brown				C
Clark			56th	
Blackwell				
McGee				
Harris				
Stagg Jas	Private	Kempers	1st Va Infy	B
Bowe A W	"			D
Epps R.	"			G
Horde J	"			G
Anderson C C	"		3rd Va Infy	B
Ghent C R	"			C
Holland Thos	"			I
Richardson J	Musician			I
Oden	Private		7th Va Infy	C
Brown	"			G
Wolfe	"			J
Goutts	"			B
Hume	"			A
Bolu	"			A
Dans	"			A
Percival C D	"		11th Va Infy	G
Parrish B	"			A
Horton B	"			D

Page 15 of ledger book

Appendix

ORDER OF BATTLE
Gettysburg, Pennsylvania July 1–3, 1863
Army of the Potomac
Maj. Gen. George Gordon Meade

I Corps
Maj. Gen. Abner Doubleday / Maj. Gen. John Newton

First Division
Brig. Gen. James S. Wadsworth

Brig. Gen. Solomon Meredith / Col. William W. Robinson
Iron Brigade: 19th Indiana 24th Michigan 2nd Wisconsin 6th Wisconsin 7th Wisconsin **1829** / 63%[1]

Brig. Gen. Lysander Cutler
Second Brigade: 7th Indiana 76th New York 84th New York (14th Brooklyn) 95th New York 147th New York 56th Pennsylvania **2017** / 49.7%

Second Division
Brig. Gen. John C. Robinson

Brig. Gen. Gabriel R. Paul / Col. S. H. Leonard / Col. Adrian Root/ Col. Richard Coulter / Col. Peter Lyle
First Brigade: 16th Maine 13th Massachusetts 94th New York 104th New York 107th Pennsylvania **1537** / 66.8%

Brig. Gen. Henry Baxter
Second Brigade: 12th Massachusetts 83rd New York 97th New York 11th Pennsylvania 88th Pennsylvania 90th Pennsylvania **1452** / 44.7%

Third Division
Brig. Gen. Thomas A. Rowley / Maj. Gen Abner Doubleday

Col. Chapman Biddle
First Brigade: 80th New York 121st Pennsylvania 142nd Pennsylvania 151st Pennsylvania **1361** / 66%

Col. Roy Stone / Col. L. Wister / Col. Edmund Dana
Second Brigade: 143rd Pennsylvania 149th Pennsylvania 150th Pennsylvania **1317** / 64.8%

Brig. Gen. George J. Stannard / Col. F. V. Randall
Third Brigade: 12th Vermont 13th Vermont 14th Vermont 15th Vermont 16th Vermont **1950** / 18%[2]

Col. Charles S. Wainwright
Artillery Brigade: Battery B, 2nd Maine Light Artillery Battery E, 5th Maine Light Artillery Batteries E and L, 1st New York Light Artillery Battery B, 1st Pennsylvania Light Artillery Battery B, 4th United States Artillery **596** / 16.8%

II Corps
Maj. Gen. Winfield S. Hancock / Brig. Gen. John Gibbon

First Division
Brig. Gen. John C. Caldwell

Col. Edward E. Cross / Col. H. Boyd McKeen
First Brigade: 5th New Hampshire 61st New York 81st Pennsylvania 148th Pennsylvania **853** / 38.7%

Col. Patrick Kelly
Second Brigade: 28th Massachusetts 63rd New York (2 cos) 69th New York (2 cos) 88th New York (2 cos) 116th Pennsylvania (4 cos) **532** / 37.2%

Brig. Gen. Samuel K. Zook / Lt. Col. John Fraser
Third Brigade: 52nd New York 57th New York 66th New York 140th Pennsylvania **975** / 36.7%

Col. John R. Brooke
Fourth Brigade: 27th Connecticut (2 cos) 2nd Delaware 64th New York 53rd Pennsylvania 145th Pennsylvania (7 cos) **851** / 45.7%

Second Division
Brig. Gen. John Gibbon / Brig. Gen. William Harrow

Brig. Gen. William Harrow / Col. Franis E. Heath
First Brigade: 19th Maine 15th Massachusetts 1st Minnesota 82nd New York **1366** / 56.2%

Brig. Gen. Alexander S. Webb
Second Brigade: 69th Pennsylvania 71st Pennsylvania 72nd Pennsylvania 106th Pennsylvania **1244** / 39.5%

Col. Norman J. Hall
Third Brigade: 19th Massachusetts 20th Massachusetts 7th Michigan 42nd New York 59th New York (four cos) **922** / 40.9%

Capt. William Plummer
1st Company Massachusetts Sharpshooters **42** / 19%

Third Division
Brig. Gen. Alexander Hays

Col. Samuel S. Carroll
First Brigade: 14th Indiana 4th Ohio 8th Ohio 7th West Virginia **977** / 21.6%

Col. Thomas A. Smyth / Lt. Col. Francis E. Pierce
Second Brigade: 14th Connecticut 1st Delaware 12th New Jersey 10th New York (bn) 108th New York **1069** / 33.8%[3]

Col. George L. Willard / Col. Eliakim Sherrill / Lt. Col. James M. Bull
Third Brigade: 39th New York (4 cos) 111th New York 125th New York 126th New York **1508** / 47.3%

Capt. John G. Hazard
Artillery Brigade: Battery B, 1st New York Light Artillery Battery A, 1st Rhode Island Light Artillery Battery B, 1st Rhode Island Artillery Battery I, 1st United States Artillery Battery A, 4th United States Artillery **605** / 24.6%

III Corps
Maj. Gen. Daniel E. Sickles / Maj. Gen. David B. Birney

First Division
Maj. Gen. David B. Birney / Brig. Gen. J. H. Hobart Ward

Brig. Gen. Charles K. Graham / Col. Andrew H. Tippin
First Brigade: 57th Pennsylvania (8 cos) 63rd Pennsylvania 68th Pennsylvania 105th Pennsylvania 114th Pennsylvania 141st Pennsylvania **1516** / 48.8%

Brig. Gen. J. H. Hobart Ward / Col. Hiram Berdan
Second Brigade: 20th Indiana 3rd Maine 4th Maine 86th New York 124th New York 99th Pennsylvania 1st United States Sharpshooters 2nd United States Sharpshooters **2188** / 35.7%

Col. P. Regis De Trobriand
Third Brigade: 17th Maine 3rd Michigan 5th Michigan 40th New York 110th Pennsylvania (6 cos) **1387** / 35.2%

Second Division
Brig. Gen. Andrew A. Humphreys

Brig. Gen. Joseph B. Carr
First Brigade: 1st Massachusetts 11th Massachusetts 16th Massachusetts 12th New Hampshire 11th New Jersey 26th Pennsylvania 84th Pennsylvania[4] **1718** / 46%

Col. William R. Brewster
Second Brigade: 70th New York 71st New York 72nd New York 73rd New York 74th New York 120th New York **1837** / 42.4%

Col. George C. Burling
Third Brigade: 2nd New Hampshire 5th New Jersey 6th New Jersey 7th New Jersey 8th New Jersey 115th Pennsylvania **1365** / 37.6%

Capt. George E. Randolph / Capt. A. Judson Clark
Artillery Brigade: 2nd Battery, New Jersey Light Artillery Battery D, 1st New York Light Artillery 4th Battery, New York Light Artillery Battery E, 1st Rhode Island Light Artillery **596** / 17.8%

V Corps
Maj. Gen. George Sykes

First Division
Brig. Gen. James Barnes

Col. William S. Tilton
First Brigade: 18th Massachusetts 22nd Massachusetts 1st Michigan 118th Pennsylvania **655** / 19.1%

Col. Jacob B. Sweitzer
Second Brigade: 9th Massachusetts 32nd Massachusetts 4th Michigan 62nd Pennsylvania **1423** / 30%

Col. Strong Vincent / Col. James C. Rice
Third Brigade: 20th Maine 16th Michigan 44th New York 16th Michigan **1336** / 26.3%

Second Division
Brig. Gen. Romeyn B. Ayers

Col. Hannibal Day
First Brigade: 3rd United States Infantry (6 cos) 4th United States Infantry (4 cos) 6th United States Infantry (5 cos) 12th United States Infantry (8 cos) 14th United States Infantry (8 cos) **1553** / 24.6%

Col. Sidney Burbank
Second Brigade: 2nd United States Infantry (6 cos) 7th United States Infantry (4 cos) 10th United States Infantry (3 cos) 11th United States Infantry (6 cos) 17th United States Infantry (7 cos) **954** / 46.9%

Brig. Gen. Stephen H. Weed / Col. Kenner Garrard
Third Brigade: 140th New York 146th New York 91st Pennsylvania 155th Pennsylvania **1491** / 13.4%

Third Division
Brig. Gen. Samuel W. Crawford

Col. William McCandless
First Brigade: 1st Pennsylvania Reserves (9 cos) 2nd Pennsylvania Reserves 6th Pennsylvania Reserves 13th Pennsylvania Reserves **1248** / 12.4%

Col. Joseph W. Fisher
Second Brigade: 5th Pennsylvania Reserves 9th Pennsylvania Reserves 10th Pennsylvania Reserves 11th Pennsylvania Reserves 12th Pennsylvania Reserves (9 cos) **1609** / 3.4%

Capt. Augustus P. Martin
Artillery Brigade: 3rd Battery, Massachusetts Light Artillery Battery C, 1st New York Light Artillery Battery L, 1st Ohio Light Artillery Battery D, 5th United States Artillery Battery I, 5th United States Artillery **432** / 10%

VI Corps
Maj. Gen. John Sedgwick

First Division
Brig. Gen. Horatio G. Wright

Brig. Gen. Alfred T. A. Torbert
First Brigade: 1st New Jersey 2nd New Jersey 3rd New Jersey 15th New Jersey **1320** / .8%

Brig. Gen. Joseph J. Bartlett
Second Brigade: 5th Maine 121st New York 95th Pennsylvania 96th Pennsylvania **1325** / .4%

Brig. Gen. David A. Russell
Third Brigade: 6th Maine 49th Pennsylvania (4 cos) 119th Pennsylvania 5th Wisconsin **1484** / .1%

Second Division
Brig. Gen. Albion Howe

Col. Lewis A. Grant
Vermont Brigade: 2nd Vermont 3rd Vermont 4th Vermont 5th Vermont 6th Vermont **1832** / .5%

Brig. Gen. Thomas H. Neill
Third Brigade: 7th Maine (6 cos) 33rd New York (detachment) 43rd New York 49th New York 77th New York 61st Pennsylvania **1775** / .8%

Third Division
Maj. Gen. John Newton / Brig. Gen. Frank Wheaton

Brig. Gen. Alexander Shaler
First Brigade: 65th New York 67th New York 122nd New York 23rd New York 82nd Pennsylvania **1770** / 4.2%

Col. Henry L. Eustis
Second Brigade: 7th Massachusetts 10th Massachusetts 37th Massachusetts 2nd Rhode Island **1595** / 4.3%

Brig. Gen. Frank Wheaton / Col. David J. Nevin
Third Brigade: 62nd New York 93rd Pennsylvania 98th Pennsylvania 102nd Pennsylvania[5] 139th Pennsylvania **1369** / 3.9%

Col. Charles H. Tompkins
Artillery Brigade: Battery A, 1st Massachusetts Light Artillery 1st Battery, New York Light Artillery 3rd Battery, New York Light Artillery Battery C, 1st Rhode Island Light Artillery Battery G, 1st Rhode Island Artillery Battery D, 2nd United States Artillery Battery G, 2nd United States Artillery Battery F, 5th United States Artillery **937** / 1.3%

XI Corps
Maj. Gen. Oliver O. Howard

First Division
Brig. Gen. Francis C. Barlow / Brig. Gen. Adelbert Ames

Col. Leopold von Gilsa
First Brigade: 41st New York 54th New York 68th New York 153rd Pennsylvania **1136** / 46.4%

Brig. Gen. Adelbert Ames / Col. Andrew L. Harris
Ohio Brigade: 17th Connecticut 25th Ohio 75th Ohio 107th Ohio **1337** / 58.2%

Second Division
Brig. Gen. Adolph von Steinwher

Col. Charles R. Coster
First Brigade: 134th New York 154th New York 27th Pennsylvania
73rd Pennsylvania **1217** / 49.1%

Col. Orland Smith
Second Brigade: 33rd Massachusetts 136th New York 55th Ohio
73rd Ohio **1639** / 21.2%

Third Division
Maj. Gen. Carl Schurz

Brig. Gen. Alexander Schimmelfennig / Col. George von Amsberg
First Brigade: 82nd Illinois 45th New York 157th New York 61st
Ohio 74th Pennsylvania **1683** / 48%

Col. Wladimir Krzyzanowski
Second Brigade: 58th New York 119th New York 82nd Ohio 75th
Pennsylvania 26th Wisconsin **1420** / 47.1%

Maj. Thomas W. Osborn
Artillery Brigade: Battery I, 1st New York Light Artillery 13th Battery,
New York Light Artillery Battery I, 1st Ohio Light Artillery Battery K, 1st
Ohio Light Artillery Battery G, 4th United States Artillery **604** / 11.4%

XII Corps
Maj. Gen. Henry W. Slocum / Brig. Gen. Alpheus S. Williams

First Division
Brig. Gen. Alpheus S. Williams / Brig. Gen. Thomas H. Ruger

Col. Archibald L. McDougall
First Brigade: 5th Connecticut 20th Connecticut 3rd Maryland
123rd New York 145th New York 46th Pennsylvania **1835** / 4.4%

Brig. Gen. Henry H. Lockwood
Second Brigade: 1st Maryland Potomac Home Brigade 1st Maryland Eastern Shore 150th New York **1818** / 9.6%

Brig. Gen. Thomas H. Ruger / Col. Silas Colgrove
Third Brigade: 27th Indiana 2nd Massachusetts 13th New Jersey
107th New York 3rd Wisconsin **1598** / 17.5%

Second Division
Brig. Gen. John W. Geary

Col. Charles Candy
First Brigade: 5th Ohio 7th Ohio 29th Ohio 66th Ohio 28th Pennsylvania 147th Pennsylvania (8 cos) **1798** / 7.7%

Col. George A. Cobham Jr. / Brig. Gen. Thomas L. Kane / Col. George A. Cobham, Jr.
Second Brigade: 29th Pennsylvania 109th Pennsylvania 111th Pennsylvania **700** / 14%

Brig. George Sears Greene
Third Brigade: 60th New York 78th New York 102nd New York 137th New York 149th New York **1424** / 21.3%

Lt. Edward D. Muhlenberg
Artillery Brigade: Battery M, 1st New York Light Artillery Battery E, Pennsylvania Light Artillery Battery F, 4th United States Artillery Battery K, 5th United States Artillery **391** / 2.3%

Cavalry Corps
Maj. Gen. Alfred Pleasonton

First Division
Brig. Gen. John Buford

Col. William Gamble
First Brigade: 8th Illinois 12th Illinois (4 cos) 3rd Indiana (6 cos) 8th New York **1600** / 6.2%

Col. Thomas C. Devin
Second Brigade: 6th New York 9th New York 17th Pennsylvania 3rd West Virginia (2 cos) **1148** / 2.4%

Brig. Gen. Wesley Merritt
Reserve Brigade: 6th Pennsylvania 1st United States Cavalry 2nd United States Cavalry 5th United States Cavalry 6th United States Cavalry **1321** / 3.7%[6]

Second Division[7]
Brig. Gen. David McM. Gregg

Col. John B. McIntosh
First Brigade: 1st Maryland (11 cos) Company A, Purnell (Maryland) Legion 1st Massachusetts 1st New Jersey 1st Pennsylvania 3rd Pennsylvania Section, Battery H, 3rd Pennsylvania Heavy Artillery (serving as light arty) **1311** / 2.7%

Col. Pennock Huey
Second Brigade: 2nd New York 44th New York 6th Ohio (10 cos) 8th Pennsylvania

Col. J. Irvin Gregg
Third Brigade: 1st Maine (10 cos) 10th New York 4th Pennsylvania 16th Pennsylvania **1263** / 1.7%

Third Division
Brig. Gen. Judson Kilpatrick

Brig. Gen. Elon J. Farnsworth / Col. Nathaniel Richmond
First Brigade: 5th New York 18th Pennsylvania 1st Vermont 1st West Virginia (10 cos) **1925** / 5.1%

Brig. Gen. George A. Custer
Wolverine Brigade: 1st Michigan 5th Michigan 6th Michigan 7th Michigan **1934** / 13.3%

Horse Artillery

Capt. James M. Robertson
First Brigade: 9th Michigan Battery 6th New York Battery Batteries B and L, 2nd United States Artillery Battery M, 2nd United States Artillery Battery E, 4th United States Artillery **493** / 1.6%

Capt. John C. Tidball
Second Brigade: Batteries E and G, 1st U.S. Artillery Battery K 1st U.S. Artillery Battery A, 2nd U.S. Artillery Battery C, 3rd U.S. Artillery **276** / 5.4%[8]

Artillery Reserve
Brig. Gen. Robert O. Tyler / Capt. James M. Robertson

Capt. Dunbar R. Ransom
First Regular Brigade: Battery H, 1st United States Artillery Batteries F and K, 3rd United States Artillery Battery C, 4th United States Artillery Battery C, 5th United States Artillery **445** / 15.3%

Lt. Col. Freeman McGilvery
First Volunteer Brigade: 5th Battery, Massachusetts Light Artillery 9th Battery, Massachusetts Light Artillery 15th Battery, New York Light Artillery Batteries C and F, Pennsylvania Light Artillery **385** / 24.2%

Capt. Elijah D. Taft
Second Volunteer Brigade: Battery B, 1st Connecticut Heavy Artillery Battery M, 1st Connecticut Heavy Artillery 2nd Battery, Connecticut Light Artillery 5th Battery, New York Light Artillery **241** / 3.3%

Capt. James F. Huntington
Third Volunteer Brigade: 1st Battery, New Hampshire Light Artillery Battery H, 1st Ohio Light Artillery, Batteries F and G, 1st Pennsylvania Light Artillery, Battery C, West Virginia Light Artillery **431** / 8.6%

Capt. Robert H. Fitzhugh
Fourth Volunteer Brigade: 6th Battery, Maine Light Artillery Battery A, Maryland Light Artillery 1st Battery, New Jersey Light Artillery Battery K, 1st New York Light Artillery **499** / 7.2%

Army of Northern Virginia
Gen. Robert Edward Lee

First Corps
Lt. Gen. James Longstreet

McLaws' Division
Maj. Gen. Lafayette McLaws

Brig. Gen. Joseph B. Kershaw
Kershaw's Brigade: 2nd South Carolina 3rd South Carolina 7th South Carolina 15th South Carolina 3rd South Carolina Bn **2183** / 29.7%

Brig. Gen. Paul J. Semmes / Col. Goode Bryan
Semmes' Brigade: 10th Georgia 50th Georgia 51st Georgia 53rd Georgia **1334** / 32.4%

Brig. Gen. William Barksdale / Col. Benjamin G. Humphreys
Barksdale's Brigade: 13th Mississippi 17th Mississippi 18th Mississippi 21st Mississippi **1620** / 49.6%

Brig. Gen. William T. Wofford
Wofford's Brigade: 16th Georgia 18th Georgia 24th Georgia Cobb's (Georgia) Legion Phillips' (Georgia) Legion 3rd Georgia Bn Sharpshooters **1627** / 22.7%

Col. Henry G. Cabell
Cabell's Battalion: Ellis (North Carolina) Light Artillery Pulaski (Georgia) Artillery 1st Richmond Howitzers Troup County (Georgia) Artillery **378** / 13.8%

Pickett's Division[9]
Maj. Gen. George E. Pickett

Brig. Gen. Richard B. Garnett / Maj. Charles S. Peyton
Garnett's Brigade: 8th Virginia 18th Virginia 19th Virginia 28th Virginia 56th Virginia **1851** / 48.9%

Brig. Gen. James L. Kemper / Col. Joseph Mayo
Kemper's Brigade: 1st Virginia 3rd Virginia 7th Virginia 11th Virginia 24th Virginia **1781** / 38.1%

Brig. Gen. Lewis A. Armistead / Col. William R. Aylett
Armistead's Brigade: 9th Virginia 14th Virginia 38th Virginia 53rd Virginia 57th Virginia **2188** / 48.3%

Maj. James Dearing
Dearing's Battalion: Fauquier (Virginia) Artillery Richmond Hampden Artillery Richmond Fayette Artillery Lynchburg (Virginia) Artillery **430** / 3.5%

Hood's Division
Maj. Gen. John Bell Hood / Brig. Gen. Evander M. Law

Brig. Gen. Evander M. Law / Col. James L. Sheffield
Law's Brigade: 4th Alabama 15th Alabama 44th Alabama 47th Alabama 48th Alabama **1933** / 25.9%

Brig. Gen. Jerome B. Robertson
Texas Brigade: 3rd Arkansas 1st Texas 4th Texas 5th Texas **1734** / 34.8%

Brig. Gen. George T. Anderson / Lt. Col. William Luffman
Anderson's Brigade: 7th Georgia 8th Georgia 9th Georgia 11th Georgia 59th Georgia **1874** / 38.5%

Brig. Gen. Henry L. Benning
Benning's Brigade: 2nd Georgia 15th Georgia 17th Georgia 20th Georgia **1420** / 36.5%

Maj. Mathias W. Henry
Henry's Battalion: Branch (North Carolina) Artillery Charleston (South Carolina) German Artillery Palmetto (South Carolina) Artillery Rowan (North Carolina) Artillery **403** / 6.7%

Artillery Reserve
Col. James B. Walton

Col. E. Porter Alexander
Alexander's Battalion: Ashland (Virginia) Artillery Bedford (Virginia) Artillery Brooks (South Carolina) Artillery Madison (Louisiana) Light Artillery Richmond Battery Bath (Virginia) Artillery **576** / 24.1%

Maj. Benjamin F. Eshleman
Washington (Louisiana) Artillery: First Company Second Company Third Company Fourth Company **338** / 8.9%

Second Corps
Lt. Gen. Richard S. Ewell

Early's Division
Maj. Gen. Jubal A. Early

Brig. Gen. Harry T. Hays
Louisiana Tigers: 5th Louisiana 6th Louisiana 7th Louisiana 8th Louisiana 9th Louisiana **1295** / 26%

Brig. Gen. William Smith
Smith's Brigade: 31st Virginia 49th Virginia 52nd Virginia **806** / 26.4%

Col. Isaac E. Avery / Col. Archibald C. Godwin
Hoke's Brigade: 6th North Carolina 21st North Carolina 57th North Carolina **1244** / 33.1%

Brig. Gen. John B. Gordon
Gordon's Brigade: 13th Georgia 26th Georgia 31st Georgia 38th Georgia 60th Georgia 61st Georgia **1813** / 29.6%

Lt. Col. H. P. Jones
Jones' Artillery Battalion: Charlottesville (Virginia) Artillery Richmond Courtney Artillery Louisiana Guard Artillery Staunton (Virginia) Artillery **290** / 4.1%

Stonewall Division
Maj. Gen. Edward Johnson

Brig. Gen. George H. Steuart
Steuart's Brigade: 2nd Maryland Bn 1st North Carolina 3rd North Carolina 10th Virginia 23rd Virginia 37th Virginia **2121** / 36.3%

Col. Jesse M. Williams
Nicholl's Brigade: 1st Louisiana 2nd Louisiana 10th Louisiana 14th Louisiana 15th Louisiana **1104** / 35.2%

Brig. Gen. James A. Walker
Stonewall Brigade: 2nd Virginia 4th Virginia 5th Virginia 27th Virginia 33rd Virginia **1323** / 25.5%

Brig. Gen. John M. Jones / Lt. Col. R. H. Dungan
Jones' Brigade: 21st Virginia 25th Virginia 42nd Virginia 44th Virginia 48th Virginia 50th Virginia **1520** / 29.8%

Maj. Joseph W. Latimer / Capt. Charles I. Raine
Latimer's Artillery Battalion: 1st Maryland Battery Alleghany (Virginia) Artillery 4th Maryland Chesapeake Artillery Lynchburg (Virginia) Lee Battery **356** / 14.3%

Rodes' Division
Maj. Gen. Robert E. Rodes

Brig. Gen. Junius Daniel
Daniel's Brigade: 32nd North Carolina 43rd North Carolina 45th North Carolina 53rd North Carolina 2nd North Carolina Bn **2052** / 45.1%

Brig. Gen. Alfred Iverson Jr.
Iverson's Brigade: 5th North Carolina 12th North Carolina 20th North Carolina 23rd North Carolina **1384** / 65.2%

Brig. Gen. George Doles
Doles' Brigade: 4th Georgia 12th Georgia 21st Georgia 44th Georgia **1323** / 16.6%

Brig. Gen. Stephen D. Ramseur
Ramseur's Brigade: 2nd North Carolina 4th North Carolina 14th North Carolina 30th North Carolina **1027** / 26.8%

Col. Edward A. O'Neal
O'Neal's Brigade: 3rd Alabama 5th Alabama 6th Alabama 12th Alabama 26th Alabama **1688** / 41.2%

Lt. Col. Thomas H. Carter
Carter's Artillery Battalion: Jeff Davis (Alabama) Artillery King William (Virginia) Artillery Louisa (Virginia) Morris Artillery Richmond Orange Artillery **385** / 20%

Artillery Reserve
Col. J. Thompson Brown

Capt. Willis J. Dance
First Virginia Artillery: 2nd Richmond Howitzers 3rd Richmond Howitzers Powhatan (Virginia) Artillery 1st Rockbridge Artillery Salem (Virginia) Flying Artillery **367** / 13.6%

Lieut. Col. William Nelson
Nelson's Artillery Battalion: Amherst (Virginia) Artillery Fluvanna (Virginia) Consolidated Artillery Georgia Regular Battery **277** / 8.7%

Third Corps
Lt. Gen. Ambrose P. Hill

Anderson's Division
Maj. Gen. Richard H. Anderson

Brig. Gen. Cadmus M. Wilcox
Wilcox's Brigade: 8th Alabama 9th Alabama 10th Alabama 11th Alabama 14th Alabama **1726** / 45.1%

Brig. Gen. Ambrose R. Wright / Col. William Gibson
Wright's Brigade: 3rd Georgia 22nd Georgia 48th Georgia 2nd Georgia Bn **1413** / 49.3%

Brig. Gen. William Mahone
Mahone's Brigade: 6th Virginia 12th Virginia 16th Virginia 41st Virginia 61st Virginia **1542** / 6.7%

Col. David Lang
Perry's Brigade: 2nd Florida 5th Florida 8th Florida **742** / 61.3%

Brig. Gen. Carnot Posey
Posey's Brigade: 12th Mississippi 16th Mississippi 19th Mississippi 48th Mississippi **1322** / 8.5%

Maj. John Lane
Sumter (Georgia) **Artillery Battalion**: Cos A, B, C **384** / 10.9%

Heth's Division
Maj. Gen. Henry Heth / Brig. Gen. J. Johnston Pettigrew

Brig. Gen. J. Johnston Pettigrew / Col. J. K. Marshall
Pettigrew's Brigade: 11th North Carolina 26th North Carolina 47th North Carolina 52nd North Carolina **2581** / 56.2%

Brig. Gen. James J. Archer / Col. Birkett D. Fry / Lt. Col. Samuel G. Shepard
Archer's Brigade: 13th Alabama 5th Alabama Bn 1st Tennessee (Provisional Army) 7th Tennessee 14th Tennessee **1197** / 57.1%

Col. John M. Brockenbrough
Brockenbrough's Brigade: 40th Virginia 47th Virginia 55th Virginia 22nd Virginia Bn **971** / 19.2%

Brig. Gen. Joseph R. Davis
Davis' Brigade: 2nd Mississippi 11th Mississippi 42nd Mississippi 55th North Carolina **2305** / 44.7%

Lt. Col. John J. Garnett
Garnett's Artillery Battalion: Donaldsonville (Louisiana) Artillery Norfolk (Virginia) Artillery Norfolk Light Artillery Blues Pittsylvania (Virginia) Artillery **396** / 5.6%

Pender's Division
Maj. Gen. W. Dorsey Pender / Brig. Gen. James H. Lane / Maj. Gen. Isaac R. Trimble

Col. Abner Perrin
Perrin's Brigade: 1st South Carolina (Provisional Army) 1st South Carolina Rifles 12th South Carolina 13th South Carolina 14th South Carolina **1882** / 31.5%

Brig. Gen. James H. Lane / Col. Clarke M. Avery
Lane's Brigade: 7th North Carolina 18th North Carolina 28th North Carolina 33rd North Carolina 37th North Carolina **1734** / 45.7%

Brig. Gen. Edward L. Thomas
Thomas' Brigade: 14th Georgia 45th Georgia 45th Georgia 49th Georgia **1326** / 19.9%

Brig. Gen. Alfred M. Scales / Lt. Col. G. T. Gordon / Col. Lee J. Lowrance
Scales' Brigade: 13th North Carolina 16th North Carolina 22nd North Carolina 34th North Carolina 38th North Carolina **1351** / 52.1%

Maj. William T. Poague
Poague's Artillery Battalion: Albermarle (Virginia) Artillery Charlotte (North Carolina) Artillery Madison (Mississippi) Light Artillery Warrenton (Virginia) Artillery **377** / 9%

Artillery Reserve
Col. R. Lindsay Walker

Maj. D. G. McIntosh
McIntosh's Battalion: Danville (Virginia) Artillery Hardaway (Alabama) Artillery 2nd Rockbridge Artillery Richmond Battery **357** / 13.4%

Maj. William J. Pegram / Capt. E. B. Brunson
Pegram's Battalion: Crenshaw's Richmond Battery Fredericksburg Artillery Richmond Letcher Artillery Pee Dee (South Carolina) Artillery Richmond Purcell Artillery **375** / 13.6%

Stuart's Division
Maj. Gen. J. E. B. Stuart

Brig. Gen. Wade Hampton / Col. Lawrence S. Baker
Hampton's Brigade: 1st North Carolina 1st South Carolina 2nd South Carolina Cobb's (Georgia) Legion Jeff. Davis (Mississippi) Legion Phillips (Georgia) Legion **1751** / 6.4%

Brig. Gen. Fitzhugh Lee
Lee's Brigade: 1st Maryland Bn 1st Virginia 2nd Virginia 3rd Virginia 4th Virginia 5th Virginia **1913** / 5%

Brig. Gen. Albert G. Jenkins / Col. M. J. Ferguson
Jenkins' Brigade: 14th Virginia 16th Virginia 17th Virginia 34th Virginia Bn 36th Virginia Bn Charlottesville (Virginia) Horse Battery **1179** / 1.5%

Col. John R. Chambliss
Lee's Brigade: 2nd North Carolina 9th Virginia 10th Virginia 13th Virginia **1173** / 4.8%

Horse Artillery
Maj. R. F. Beckham

1st Stuart Horse Artillery 2nd Baltimore Battery Washington's (South Carolina) Horse Artillery 2nd Stuart Horse Artillery **434** / .9%

Brig. Gen. Beverly H. Robertson
Robertson's Brigade: 4th North Carolina 5th North Carolina

Brig. Gen William E. "Grumble" Jones
Laurel Brigade: 6th Virginia 7th Virginia 11th Virginia

Imboden's Command
Brig. Gen. John D. Imboden

18th Virginia 62nd Virginia Mounted Infantry McNeill's Partisan Rangers McClanahan's Virginia Artillery

Notes

PREFACE

1. George R. Stewart, *Pickett's Charge: A Microhistory of the Final Attack at Gettysburg, July 3, 1863* (Boston: Houghton Mifflin Company, 1959), 199.

2. W. H. Andrews, *Footprints of a Regiment: Recollections of the 1st Georgia Regulars* (Atlanta: Longstreet Press, 1992); William B. Jordan Jr., *Red Diamond Regiment: The 17th Maine Infantry, 1862–1865* (Shippensburg, Pa.: White Mane Publishing Company, Inc., 1996).

3. Kathy Georg Harrison, comp., *The Location of the Monuments, Markers, and Tablets on Gettysburg Battlefield* (Gettysburg: Thomas Publications, 1993), 25.

4. Warren W. Hassler Jr., *Crisis at the Crossroads: The First Day at Gettysburg* (Tuscaloosa: University of Alabama Press, 1970), 60–61.

5. David L. and Audrey J. Ladd, eds., *The Bachelder Papers: Gettysburg in Their Own Words,* 3 vols. (Dayton: Morningside, 1994), 1:141. Of the heroic John Burns, Sgt. George Eustice, Company F, 7th Wisconsin, wrote: "...he was true blue and grit to the backbone, and fought until he was wounded three times." Henry J. Hunt, "The First Day at Gettysburg," *Battles and Leaders of the Civil War,* ed. Robert Underwood Johnson and Clarence Clough Buell, 4 vols. (New York: The Century Co., 1887), 3:276. Hereafter *B&L.*

6. Gary W. Gallagher, "The Autumn of 1862: A Season of Opportunity," *Antietam: Essays on the 1862 Maryland Campaign,* ed. Gary W. Gallagher (Kent, Ohio: The Kent State University Press, 1989), 1. See also Thomas L. Connelly, *Army of the Heartland: The Army of the Tennessee, 1861–1862,* and *Autumn of Glory: The Army of Tennessee, 1862–1865* (Baton Rouge: Louisiana State University Press, 1967 and 1971).

7. Albert Castel, *Decision in the West: The Atlanta Campaign of 1864* (Lawrence: The University Press of Kansas, 1992), 475–79, 543–47; James A. Rawley, *Turning Points of the Civil War* (Lincoln: University of Nebraska Press, 1966), 171–204.

CHAPTER 1

1. James I. Robertson Jr., *Stonewall Jackson: The Man, The Soldier, The Legend* (New York: Macmillan Publishing USA, 1997), 726–29, 737, 742, 745, 746, 752.

2. Clifford Dowdey and Louis H. Manarin, eds., *The Wartime Papers of R. E. Lee* (Boston: Little, Brown and Company, 1961), 484.

3. Robert K. Krick, "Lee at Chancellorsville," in *Lee the Soldier,* ed. Gary W. Gallagher (Lincoln: University of Nebraska Press, 1996), 374.

4. Robertson, *Stonewall Jackson,* 234, 280, 508–9, 583. See also T. Michael Parrish, *Richard Taylor: Soldier Prince of Dixie* (Chapel Hill: University of North Carolina Press, 1995), 224.

5. *The War of the Rebellion: A Compilation of the Official Records of the Union and Confederate Armies*, 70 vols. in 128 parts (Government Printing Office: Washington D.C., 1880–1901), ser. 1, vol. 9, pt. 2:590. Hereafter OR.

6. OR, vol. 19, pt. 2:594.

7. Ibid., pt. 1:144.

8. Gallagher, "A Season of Opportunity," 3–5.

9. OR, vol. 19, pt. 1:145.

10. John G. Walker, "Jackson's Capture of Harpers Ferry," *B&L*, 2:605.

11. See Stephen W. Sears, *Landscape Turned Red: The Battle of Antietam* (New Haven and New York: Ticknor & Fields, 1983).

12. Dowdey and Manarin, *Wartime Papers of R. E. Lee*, 183–84; Hotchkiss completed the map on March 10; Edwin B. Coddington, *The Gettysburg Campaign: A Study in Command* (New York: Charles Scribner's Sons, 1984 edition), 8, 600 n. 11; Edward Porter Alexander, *Military Memoirs of a Confederate: A Critical Narrative* (New York: Da Capo Press, 1993 reprint), 322.

13. The following geographical features described the Department of the West. Commencing with the Blue Ridge Mountains running through the western portions of North Carolina, and following the line of said mountains through the northern part of Georgia to the railroad south from Chattanooga; thence by that road to West Point, and down the west bank of the Chattahoochee River to the boundary of Alabama and Florida; following that boundary to the Choctawhatchee River, and down that river to Choctawhatchee Bay (including the waters of that bay) to the Gulf of Mexico.
All that portion west of said line to the Mississippi River is included in the above command. OR, vol. 25, pt. 2:713–14, 724–26; vol. 17, pt. 2:757–78.

14. OR, vol. 25, pt. 2:725.

15. Edwin C. Bearss, *Decision in Mississippi: Mississippi's Important Role in the War Between the States* (Little Rock: Pioneer Press, 1962).

16. Steven E. Woodworth, *Davis And Lee At War* (Lawrence: University Press of Kansas, 1995), 230.

17. OR, vol. 27, pt. 2:313.

18. Archer Jones, *Confederate Strategy from Shiloh to Vicksburg* (Baton Rouge: Louisiana State University Press, 1961), 213–16; Woodworth, *Davis and Lee*, 231, 234.

19. Letter, Henry Heth to J. William Jones, June 1877, "Causes of Lee's Defeat at Gettysburg," *The Southern Historical Society Papers*, William Jones et al., eds., 1876–1930, Richmond, 4 (1877):153–54. Hereafter *SHSP*; "General Lee had surely won the battle, a North Carolinian observed, but he wondered to what purpose. Here were the armies in their old camps on opposite sides of the river, very much as if nothing had happened, and 'how much more does it look like peace than before....'" Stephen W. Sears, *Chancellorsville* (Boston and New York: Houghton Mifflin Company, 1996), x.

20. OR, vol. 25, pt. 2:790.

21. Dowdey and Manarin, *Wartime Papers of R. E. Lee*, 508.

22. OR, vol. 27, pt. 3:882; William Allan, "Memoranda of Conversations with General Robert E. Lee, reprinted in *Lee, the Soldier*, ed. Gary W. Gallagher (Lincoln: University of Nebraska Press, 1996), 14; "The Gettysburg campaign followed Chancellorsville even more naturally than the Maryland campaign of 1862 followed Manassas. Hooker's defeat was an extremely bitter blow to the North not so much in the actual losses, serious though they were, as in the confirmation it gave to the widespread belief that the South could not be

subdued. Never had the spirit of the North sunk so low as when Hooker's broken corps limped back to safety across the Rappahannock. Many who had frantically proposed opposition to peaceable secession in 1863 were willing, in June 1863, to the let the 'erring sisters go in peace.'" *Lee's Dispatches: Unpublished Letters of General Robert E. Lee, C. S. A., to Jefferson Davis and the War Department of the Confederate States of America, 1862–65*, Douglas S. Freeman, ed., with additional dispatches and foreword by Grady McWhiney (New York: G. P. Putnam's Sons, 1957 edition), 103–4 n. 3.

23. James Longstreet, "Lee In Pennsylvania," *Annals of the War, Written by Leading Participants, North and South* (Philadelphia: The Times Publishing Company, 1879), 416–17.

24. James Longstreet to Lafayette McLaws, July 25, 1873, reprinted in Richard Rollins, "'The Ruling Ideas' of the Pennsylvania Campaign: James Longstreet's 1873 Letter to Lafayette McLaws," *Gettysburg Magazine* 17 (July 1997): 15. See also James Longstreet, "Lee's Invasion of Pennsylvania," *B&L*, 3:246–47.

25. "The army, therefore, moved forward, as a man might walk over strange ground with his eyes shut." Longstreet, "Lee in Pennsylvania," *Annals of the War,* 416.

26. Letter, Heth to Jones, "Causes of Lee's Defeat," 154.

27. Dowdey and Manarin, *Wartime Papers of R. E. Lee,* 487–89.

28. OR, vol. 25, pt. 2:840, 842; Dowdey and Manarin, *Wartime Papers of R. E. Lee,* 489; Freeman, *Lee's Dispatches,* 91.

29. OR, vol. 25, pt. 2:845.

30. Dowdey and Manarin, *Wartime Papers of R. E. Lee,* 489.

31. Douglas S. Freeman, *Lee's Lieutenants: A Study in Command,* 3 vols. (New York: Charles Scribner's Sons, 1942–44), 2:661–62.

32. Edward G. Longacre, *Pickett, Leader of the Charge: A Biography of General George E. Pickett, C. S. A.* (Shippensburg, Pa.: White Mane Publishing Company, Inc., 1995), 61–111.

33. OR, vol. 25, pt. 1:803.

34. Ibid., pt. 2:787; Freeman, *Lee's Lieutenant's,* 2:508–9. General Lee urged promotion of Johnson to major general. OR, vol. 19, pt. 2:677.

35. OR, vol. 27, pt. 2:614–19, 625–26.

36. Jennings C. Wise, *The Long Arm of Lee,* 2 vols. (Lincoln: University of Nebraska Press, 1991, reprint), 2:548, 551, 554.

37. OR, vol. 25, pt. 2:850–51.

38. Alexander, *Military Memoirs,* 370.

39. OR, vol. 25, pt. 1:825–26.

40. OR, vol. 27, pt. 2:291.

41. Freeman, *Lee's Lieutenant's,* 2:711–13. Joseph Davis had served with the rank of colonel on Jefferson Davis' staff since September 1861. Mark M. Boatner III, *The Civil War Dictionary* (New York: David McKay Company, Inc., 1988 edition), 226.

42. Douglas S. Freeman, *R. E. Lee: A Biography,* 4 vols. (New York: Charles Scribner's Sons, 1936), 3:153.

43. OR, vol. 51, pt. 2:717; vol. 24, pt. 1:5–6.

44. Freeman, *Lee's Dispatches,* 98.

45. OR, vol. 14:923–26; vol. 24, pt. 1:192–94; pt. 2:814. The combined strength of Johnston's "Army of Relief" and the Vicksburg garrison, commanded by

Lt. Gen. John C. Pemberton, exceeded Grant's 51,000 men. Bearss, *Decision in Mississippi*, 337, 346–47.

46. OR, vol. 25, pt. 2:843.

47. Ibid., 849.

48. Ibid., 293.

49. *Jefferson Davis Constitutionalist: His Letters Papers & Speeches*, 10 vols., Dunbar Rowland, ed. (Jackson: Mississippi Department of Archives and History, 1923), 5:506.

50. Dowdey and Manarin, *Wartime Papers of R. E. Lee*, 501–3. The 1st Vermont Brigade and the 26th New Jersey conducted the June 5 reconnaissance. OR, vol. 27, pt. 1:676.

51. OR, vol. 27, pt. 2:313.

52. Mark Nesbitt, *Saber and Scapegoat: J.E.B. Stuart and the Gettysburg Controversy* (Mechanicsburg, Pa.: Stackpole Books, 1994), 38.

53. Hooker's believed Stuart intended to conduct a raid into Maryland. OR, vol. 27, pt. 1:32–34.

54. Edward G. Longacre, *The Cavalry at Gettysburg: A Tactical Study of Mounted Operations during the Civil War's Pivotal Campaign, 9 June–14 July 1863* (Lincoln: University of Nebraska Press, 1986, reprint), 65–81.

55. Freeman, *Lee's Lieutenants*, 3:13. Casualty figures at Brandy Station vary widely. See "Notes and Queries," Boyd Stalter, ed., *Civil War History*, vol. 7 (1962), 331.

56. Edward G. Longacre, *General John Buford: A Military Biography* (Conshohocken, Pa.: Combined Books, 1995), 167.

57. Longacre, *Cavalry at Gettysburg*, 87.

58. Nesbitt, *Saber and Scapegoat*, 23–25, 30–33.

59. Freeman, *Lee's Lieutenants*, 3:18.

60. Emory M. Thomas, *Bold Dragoon: The Life of J.E.B. Stuart* (New York: Harper & Row, 1986), 226–31. For Stuart's report, see OR, vol. 27, pt. 2:679–85.

61. Quoted in Coddington, *Gettysburg Campaign*, 60, 617 n. 43.

62. OR, vol. 27, pt. 2:43, 440.

63. Ibid., 108–9, 547.

64. Ibid., 42–46, 182.

65. Charles S. Grunder and Brandon H. Beck, *The Second Battle of Winchester: June 12–15, 1863* (Lynchburg, Va.: H. E. Howard, Inc., 1989), 36.

66. Jubal A. Early, *Jubal Early's Memoirs: Autobiographical Sketch and Narrative of the War Between the States* (Baltimore: The Nautical & Aviation Publishing Company of America, 1989, reprint), 246–47; OR, vol. 27, pt. 2:60–61, 74, 494.

67. Grunder and Beck, *Second Battle of Winchester*, 40–41; OR, vol. 27, pt. 2:477, 494.

68. OR, vol. 27, pt. 2:61, 74.

69. Ibid., 47.

70. Ibid., 501–2; Grunder and Beck, *Second Battle of Winchester*, 48–51; Wilbur Sturtevant Nye, *Here Come the Rebels!* (Baton Rouge: Louisiana State University Press, 1965), 112–13. Harpers Ferry was evacuated. The garrison and Milroy's survivors retired to Maryland Heights. OR, vol. 27, pt. 3:126.

71. OR, vol. 27, pt. 2:442, 456.

72. Ibid., 186, 464.

73. Ibid., 548–49.

74. Ibid., 442–43.

75. OR, vol. 27, pt. 1:38–39.

76. Ibid., 31.

77. Ibid., 35.

78. William Swinton, *Campaigns of the Army of the Potomac* (Secaucus, N.J.: The Blue & Grey Press, 1988, reprint), 316; OR, vol. 27, pt. 1:31.

79. OR, vol. 27, pt. 1:38.

80. Ibid., 44–45.

81. OR, vol. 27, pt. 2:315; pt. 3:887–88.

82. Ibid., pt. 1:43; pt. 2:610, 613; pt. 3:896.

83. Ibid., pt. 2:316, 613.

84. Author's emphasis. OR, vol. 27, pt. 2:316; "Stuart himself says that General Lee directed him, 'after crossing to proceed with all dispatch to join the right of the army in Pennsylvania.'" T. M. R. Talcott, "Stuart's Cavalry in the Gettysburg Campaign," *SHSP* 38 (1910): 198.

85. OR, vol. 27, pt. 1:972, 979–80; pt. 2:688, 691.

86. Longacre, *Cavalry at Gettysburg*, 110–12; Thomas, *Bold Dragoon*, 234–35; OR, vol. 27, pt. 2:687, 758; pt. 1:363–64; pt. 3:226.

87. OR, vol. 27, pt. 3:195.

88. Ibid., pt. 2:689–90; pt. 1:953; Longacre, *Cavalry at Gettysburg*, 123–24.

89. Ibid., pt. 1:598, 911; Longacre, *Cavalry at Gettysburg*, 125.

90. Ibid., 614. Concerning the loss to Hart's battery, Stuart wrote: "...*the first piece of my horse artillery which has ever fallen into the enemy's hands.* Its full value was paid in the slaughter it made in the enemy's ranks, and it was well sold." OR, vol. 27, pt. 2:690.

91. Longacre, *Cavalry at Gettysburg*, 127–29; OR, vol. 27, pt. 1:947.

92. Longacre, *General John Buford*, 173; OR, vol. 27, pt. 1:920–21.

93. Longacre, *Cavalry at Gettysburg*, 130–32. Jones' brigade, camped in Loudoun Valley since June 18, had seen little action. OR, vol. 27, pt. 2:759. Robert E. Lee's son, W. H. F. "Rooney" Lee, wounded at Brandy Station, was captured while recuperating with in-laws. Thomas, *Bold Dragoon*, 259.

94. Longacre, *General John Buford*, 175.

95. Nesbitt, *Saber and Scapegoat*, 54–55.

96. Thomas, *Bold Dragoon*, 239.

97. OR, vol. 27, pt. 2:306.

98. Coddington, *Gettysburg Campaign*, 120–21.

99. OR, vol. 27, pt. 3:248–50.

100. Ibid., 255.

101. OR, vol. 27, pt. 1:913. Buford's scouts saw McLaws' division. OR, vol. 27, pt. 3:914.

102. Ibid., pt. 3:285, 295.

103. Ibid., 307, 309. See also Coddington, *Gettysburg Campaign*, 122.

104. Thomas, *Bold Dragoon*, 241; OR, vol. 27, pt. 2:316. Kicked by a horse before leaving Virginia, Fitzhugh Lee was unable to perform his duty as brigade commander. He accompanied his command in an ambulance "until we got well into Maryland." Ladd and Ladd, *The Bachelder Papers*, 2:1201.

CHAPTER 2

1. OR, vol. 27, pt. 2:307, 443; pt. 3:914.

2. Coddington, *Gettysburg Campaign*, 107.

3. Harry W. Pfanz, *Gettysburg: The Second Day* (Chapel Hill: The University of North Carolina Press, 1987), 8.

4. OR, vol. 27, pt. 3:912–13.

5. Roger Long, "General Orders No. 72: 'By Command of Gen. R. E. Lee,'" *Gettysburg Magazine* 7 (July 1992): 22.

6. John O. Casler, *Four Years in the Stonewall Brigade*, ed. James I. Robertson Jr. (Dayton: Morningside Bookshop, 1971, reprint), 168.

7. The Caledonia iron works were burned on Early's own responsibility. Early, *Memoirs*, 255–56; OR, vol. 27, pt. 2:464–65; Boatner, *Civil War Dictionary*, 797.

8. Nye, *Here Come the Rebels!*, 271–76.

9. Early, *Memoirs*, 257.

10. William H. Allison, *A Short Story of the Battle of Gettysburg* (n.p., n.d.), 28; Robert L. Bloom, *A History of Adams County, Pennsylvania: 1700–1990* (Adams County Historical Society: 1992), 192; I. Daniel Rupp, *History and Topography of Dauphin, Cumberland, Franklin, Bedford, Adams and Perry Counties* (Lancaster, Pa.: Gilbert Hills Proprietor & Publisher, 1846), 522, 526–27; Adams County reputedly grows more fruit than any other U.S. county. *Atlas Plat Book, Adams County, Pennsylvania* (Rockford, Ill.: Rockford Map Publishers), 1977.

11. John M. Vanderslice, *Gettysburg: Where and How the Regiments Fought and the Troops they Encountered* (Philadelphia: n.p., 1897), 21.

12. Early, *Memoirs*, 258; Nye, *Here Come the Rebels!*, 275. According to General Buford, "Early's people seized every [horse] shoe and nail they could find." OR, vol. 27, pt. 1:923. See also Linda J. Black, "Gettysburg's Preview of War: Early's June 26, 1863, Raid," *Gettysburg Magazine* 3 (July, 1990).

13. Early, *Memoirs*, 258.

14. OR, vol. 27, pt. 2:491, 492, 498; Early, *Memoirs*, 260.

15. Early, *Memoirs*, 260–61; *The Story of Gettysburg: Its Heroes, Its Monuments, Its Consecrated Fields* (General Passenger Department, Philadelphia and Reading Railroad, 1896), notation, 7.

16. OR, vol. 27, pt. 2:466.

17. Ibid., 307, 358; "Dear Children," Memoir of Howard Malcolm Walthall, Richmond, May 1913, Marshall County Historical Museum, Holly Springs, Mississippi, 27.

18. William S. Christian, "My Own Darling Wife," *The Rebellion Record: A Diary of American Events*, 11 vols., ed. Frank Moore (New York: D. Van Norstrand, 1861–1864), 7:325. Greenwood, Pennsylvania is seven miles east of Chambersburg. OR, vol. 51, pt. 2:129.

19. OR, vol. 27, pt. 2:307; Coddington, *Gettysburg Campaign*, 126.

20. Coddington, *Gettysburg Campaign*, 129. On June 24, Brig. Gen. Gouverneur K. Warren sent Hooker a proposal to relocate the Army of the Potomac to Harpers Ferry in order to "paralyze" Lee's movements while the Federals collected reinforcements "sufficient to render us the stronger army of the two, if we are not already." OR, vol. 27, pt. 3:292.

21. OR, vol. 27, pt. 1:58–59; pt. 3:354, 444.

22. OR, vol. 27, pt. 1:59.

23. Ibid., 60.

24. Francis Marshal, *The Battle of Gettysburg: The Crest-Wave of the American Civil War* (Gaithersburg, Md.: Olde Soldier Books, 1987, reprint), 85; John Gibbon, *Personal Recollections of the Civil War* (Dayton: Press of Morningside

Bookshop, 1978, reprint), 122. Secretary of War Edwin Stanton and President Lincoln concluded "that Hooker must not be intrusted with the conduct of another battle." Charles P. Benjamin, "Hooker's Appointment and Removal," *B&L*, 3:241.

25. Swinton, *Army of the Potomac*, 323.

26. OR, vol. 27, pt. 1:61; pt. 3:369.

27. Coddington, *Gettysburg Campaign*, 209.

28. Gibbon, *Personal Recollections*, 129–30.

29. Henry Heth, "The Memoirs of Henry Heth," ed. James L. Morrison Jr., *Civil War History*, vol. 8 (September 1962): 304. See also, James P. Smith, "With Stonewall Jackson in the Army of Northern Virginia," *SHSP* 43 (1920): 56.

30. OR, vol. 27, pt. 3:914, 923.

31. Ibid., pt. 3:914–15.

32. Ibid., pt. 3:913.

33. Longacre, *Cavalry at Gettysburg*, 148–50.

34. OR, vol. 27, pt. 3:915.

35. Freeman, *Lee's Lieutenants*, 3:51–52. "The Richmond papers of the 13th blame Stuart much for allowing himself to be surprised in his camp by Pleasonton, and call upon him to do something to retrieve his reputation." OR, vol. 27, pt. 1:41.

36. Robertson was promoted to brigadier general on June 9, 1862. Jones' commission as brigadier general ranked from September 19, 1862. Ezra J. Warner, *Generals in Gray: Lives of the Confederate Commanders* (Baton Rouge: Louisiana State University Press, 1988 edition), 122, 167.

37. OR, vol. 27, pt. 3:927–28.

38. Freeman, *Lee's Lieutenants*, 3:59. "During the first two years of the Civil War, Robertson commanded a regiment of Confederate cavalry and cavalry brigades in both Virginia and North Carolina. While serving in these capacities, he failed to win the confidence of any of his direct superiors." Patrick A. Bowmaster, "Beverly H. Robertson and the Battle of Brandy Station," *Blue & Gray Magazine*, vol. 14, 1:21.

39. Thomas, *Bold Dragoon*, 69, 140, 173, 202.

40. OR, vol. 27, pt. 2:687, 758.

41. Ibid., pt. 3:915. See also, Longstreet, "Lee's Invasion of Pennsylvania," *B&L*, 3:249. Millwood was army headquarters. Dowdey and Manarin, *Wartime Papers of R. E. Lee*, 520.

42. Warner, *Generals in Gray*, 122, 260.

43. Nesbitt, *Saber and Scapegoat*, 70.

44. General Stuart had recently nominated Baker for promotion. Thomas, *Bold Dragoon*, 202. Hampton was severely wounded on July 3 and during his absence Baker led the brigade. According to General Lee, Baker "acquitted himself well." Dowdey and Manarin, *Wartime Papers of R. E. Lee*, 567.

45. Longacre, *Cavalry at Gettysburg*, 233–34; OR, vol. 27, pt. 3:927.

46. Nesbitt, *Saber and Scapegoat*, 69–70.

47. Longacre, *Cavalry at Gettysburg*, 151.

48. OR, vol. 27, pt. 1:143; pt. 2:692.

49. Longacre, *Cavalry at Gettysburg*, 149, 152.

50. OR, vol. 27, pt. 2:692–93; Longacre, *Cavalry at Gettysburg*, 153.

51. Nesbitt, *Saber and Scapegoat*, 59.

52. Longacre, *General John Buford*, 180.

53. Nye, *Here Come the Rebels!*, 313.

54. Emphasis John S. Mosby, "The Confederate Cavalry in the Gettysburg Campaign," *B&L*, 3:251–52.

55. Nesbitt, *Saber and Scapegoat*, 71.

56. OR, vol. 27, pt. 2:694.

57. OR, vol. 27, pt. 1:114.

58. Freeman, *Lee's Lieutenants*, 3:57–58. See also OR, vol. 27, pt. 2:707.

59. OR, vol. 27, pt. 2:694.

60. Freeman, *Lee's Lieutenants*, 3:66.

61. A participant in Stuart's operation characterized it as "...the grandest raid of the war." Terrence J. Winschel, "The Jeff Davis Legion at Gettysburg," *Gettysburg Magazine* 12 (January 1995): 73. Maj. William A. Morgan, 1st Va. (Lee), also characterized Stuart's operation as a raid. Ladd and Ladd, *The Bachelder Papers*, 2:1276–277.

62. Longacre, *Cavalry at Gettysburg*, 156.

63. OR, vol. 27, pt. 2:694–95; Freeman, *Lee's Lieutenants*, 3:67.

64. Longacre, *Cavalry at Gettysburg*, 157–58.

65. OR, vol. 27, pt. 2:695.

66. Ibid., pt. 3:64.

67. Longacre, *Cavalry at Gettysburg*, 61, 161.

68. Stahel was reassigned to the Department of the Susquehanna. OR, vol. 27, pt. 3:376, 496.

69. OR, vol. 27, pt. 1:991–92, 1005.

70. Ibid., 1008; pt. 2:695.

71. OR, vol. 27, pt. 1:992, 1012.

72. Longacre, *Cavalry at Gettysburg*, 175; "The foe turned and fled. He had for the first and last time polluted with his presence the loyal town of Hanover." OR, vol. 27, pt. 1:992.

73. Thomas, *Bold Dragoon*, 244.

74. Freeman, *Lee's Lieutenants*, 3:70–71. "If my command had been well closed now, this cavalry column, which we had struck near its rear, would have been at our mercy; but, owing to the great elongation of the column by reason of the 200 wagons and hilly roads, Hampton was a long way behind, and Lee was not yet heard from on the left." OR, vol. 27, pt. 2:695.

75. Longacre, *Cavalry at Gettysburg*, 176–78; Nesbitt, *Saber and Scapegoat*, 67. Company A, 6th Michigan, reconnoitered to Westminster and was not engaged at Hanover. OR, vol. 27, pt. 3:999.

76. Paul M. Shevchuk, "The Battle of Hunterstown, Pennsylvania, July 2, 1863," *Gettysburg Magazine* 1 (July 1989): 94.

77. Thomas, *Bold Dragoon*, 244.

78. OR, vol. 27, pt. 2:696.

79. "They got 125 new wagons, loaded with oats, corn, hams, hardtack, bacon and whiskey, with fresh mules and harness. In light of Lee's repeated orders to gather supplies, Stuart must have been elated." Nesbitt, *Saber and Scapegoat*, 76, 84.

80. Dowdey and Manarin, *Wartime Papers of R. E. Lee*, 525.

81. OR, vol. 27, pt. 3:914.

82. Ibid., 421.

83. Thomas, *Bold Dragoon*, 245; OR, vol. 27, pt. 2:696.

84. Longacre, *Cavalry at Gettysburg*, 193–94; OR, vol. 27, pt. 2:696.

85. OR, vol. 27, pt. 1:992.

86. Nesbitt, *Saber and Scapegoat*, 87–88; OR, vol. 27, pt. 2:697; George W. Beale, "A Soldier's Account of the Gettysburg Campaign," *SHSP* 11 (1883): 323.

87. Coddington, *Gettysburg Campaign*, 206–7.

88. Nesbitt, *Saber and Scapegoat*, 69–70.

89. OR, vol. 27, pt. 2:307, 313, 316; pt. 3:948; John D. Imboden, "The Confederate Retreat from Gettysburg," *B&L*, 3:420.

90. George F. R. Henderson, *The Science of War: A Collection of Essays and Lectures 1892–1903*, ed. Neill Malclom (New York and London: Longmans, Green, and Co., 1905), 303. For Stuart's explicit instructions to Robertson, see OR, vol. 27, pt. 3:927–28.

CHAPTER 3

1. Longstreet, *Annals of the War,* 419; Longstreet, "Lee's Invasion of Pennsylvania," *B&L*, 3:249–50.

2. Tony Trimble, "Harrison: Spy for Longstreet at Gettysburg," *Gettysburg Magazine* 17 (July 1997): 17. For the Army of the Potomac's disposition on June 28, see OR, vol. 27, pt. 1:143–44.

3. Freeman, *Lee's Lieutenants*, 3:49 n. 52.

4. Dowdey and Manarin, *Wartime Papers of R. E. Lee*, 529.

5. OR, vol. 27, pt. 2:316.

6. Ibid., 692, 699.

7. Longstreet, "Lee's Invasion of Pennsylvania," *B&L*, 3:251.

8. Nye, *Here Come the Rebels!*, 345–46.

9. OR, vol. 27, pt. 2:316–17.

10. Ibid., pt. 3:943–44. "This version of Lee's dispatch was recorded from memory into Lee's order book and contains at least two errors: the date of the letter, June 28, should be June 29, and the next-to-last sentence should read, 'move directly on Cashtown or turn down to Gettysburg.'" Nye, *Here Come the Rebels!*, 345.

11. Henry Heth, "The Memoirs of Henry Heth," 303. Pettigrew took three regiments to Gettysburg. Coddington, *Gettysburg Campaign*, 683 n. 17.

12. OR, vol. 27, pt. 2:317, 607; pt. 1:923.

13. Ibid., pt. 2:637; Heth, "Memoirs of Henry Heth," 303–4.

14. OR, vol. 27, pt. 2:607.

15. Alexander, *Military Memoirs*, 381. "No one claims, I believe, that the commander-in-chief ordered this advance of Lieutenant-General Hill." Randolph H. McKim, *A Soldier's Recollections: Leaves from the Diary of a Young Confederate* (New York: Longmans, Green, and Co., 1910), 172.

16. Hassler, *Crisis at the Crossroads*, 19. The total does not include the cavalry brigades of Hampton, Chambliss, Fitzhugh Lee, Robertson, Jones, or Imboden. John W. Busey and David G. Martin, *Regimental Strengths and Losses at Gettysburg* (Hightstown, N.J.: Longstreet House, 1994 edition), 129, 194.

17. McKim, *A Soldier's Recollections*, 170.

18. OR, vol. 27, pt. 3:415–16.

19. Buford's Reserve Brigade guarded his wagon train. OR, vol. 27, pt. 1:923; pt. 3:417, 420–21.

20. OR, vol. 27, pt. 3:416, 419–20, 422.

21. OR, vol. 27, pt. 1:114; pt. 3:416–17. The figure for the Army of the Potomac is the number engaged rather than total strength, 112,735. Busey and Martin, *Regimental Strengths*, 16.

22. James C. Biddle, "General Meade at Gettysburg," *Annals of the War*, 207–8; OR, vol. 27, pt. 3:358.

23. Warren W. Hassler Jr., "The First Day's Battle of Gettysburg," *Civil War History*, vol. 6 (September 1960): 261.

24. OR, vol. 27, pt. 2:637; Marc and Beth Storch, "'What a Deadly Trap We Were In': Archer's Brigade on July 1, 1863," *Gettysburg Magazine* 6 (January 1992): 14. The 11th Mississippi was detached to guard the division wagon train. Baxter McFarland, "The Eleventh Mississippi Regiment at Gettysburg," ed. Dunbar Rowland, *Publications of the Mississippi Historical Society Centenary Series* (Jackson), vol. 2 (1918): 550.

25. OR, vol. 27, pt. 1:927, 934. The myth that Buford's regiments carried "Spencer repeating carbines" at Gettysburg. Hassler, "The First Day's Battle of Gettysburg," 265, et al., is dispelled in D. Alexander Watson, "The Spencer Repeating Rifle at Gettysburg," *Gettysburg Magazine* 15 (July 1996).

26. General Reynolds' command was I Corps. OR, vol. 27, pt. 3:148, 414–15.

27. Coddington, *Gettysburg Campaign*, 682 n. 14.

28. Hassler, "The First Day's Battle of Gettysburg," 265; Coddington, *Gettysburg Campaign*, 267.

29. Reynolds knew in all probability that he would face Hill's entire corps. Douglas Craig Haines, "A. P. Hill's Advance to Gettysburg," *Gettysburg Magazine* 5 (July 1991): 8.

30. Hassler, "The First Day's Battle of Gettysburg," 265–66. General Meade also planned "falling upon some portion of Lee's army in detail." OR, vol. 27, pt. 1:67.

31. Trimble noted that Stuart "had never failed to report the condition of things every twenty-four hours or oftener..." Ladd, *The Bachelder Papers*, 2:925–26. In his conversation with General Lee in 1868, George Allan noted: "He did not want to fight, unless he could get a good opportunity to hit them in detail." Allan, "Memoranda of Conversations with Lee," *Lee the Soldier*, 14.

32. OR, vol. 27, pt. 1:273, 278; Coddington, *Gettysburg Campaign*, 685 n. 38.

33. Coddington, *Gettysburg Campaign*, 268; Haines, "A. P. Hill's Advance," 8. The 7th Indiana "was on duty in the rear..." OR, vol. 27, pt. 1:281.

34. Terrence J. Winschel, "Part 1: Heavy Was Their Loss: Joe Davis's Brigade at Gettysburg," *Gettysburg Magazine* 2 (January 1990): 8, 10.

35. Robert K. Krick, "Three Confederate Disasters on Oak Ridge: Failures of Brigade Leadership on the First Day at Gettysburg," *The First Day at Gettysburg: Essays on Confederate and Union Leadership*, ed. Gary W. Gallagher (Kent, Ohio: The Kent State University Press, 1992), 106.

36. OR, vol. 27, pt. 1:245, 266, 282; Ladd and Ladd, *The Bachelder Papers*, 2:911. The 147th New York lost 296 men out of 380 engaged: 77.9 percent. Busey and Martin, *Regimental Strengths*, 239.

37. Storch, "What a Deadly Trap We Were In," 22.

38. Krick, "Failures of Brigade Leadership," 99.

39. Coddington, *Gettysburg Campaign*, 269.

40. OR, vol. 27, pt. 1:245.

41. Ibid., 1031.

42. Ibid., 273; pt. 2:646.

43. Storch, "What a Deadly Trap We Were In," 22.

44. Coddington, *Gettysburg Campaign*, 269.

45. Michael Jacobs, *Rebel Invasion of Maryland and Pennsylvania and the Battle of Gettysburg July 1st, 2d and 3d, 1863* (Philadelphia: J. B. Lippincott & Co., 1864), 26. Facts pertaining to General Reynolds' death wound and his last moments remain disputed. See Steve Sanders, "Enduring Tales of Gettysburg: The Death of Reynolds," *Gettysburg Magazine* 14 (January 1996).

46. OR, vol. 27, pt. 1:273–74.

47. Ibid., pt. 2:646.

48. Storch, "What a Deadly Trap We Were In," 25.

49. OR, vol. 27, pt. 1:274; pt. 2:646.

50. Private Mahoney was killed later in the day. OR, vol. 27, pt. 1:245; Freeman, *Lee's Lieutenant's*, 3:80.

51. Coddington, *Gettysburg Campaign*, 271.

52. Storch, "What a Deadly Trap We Were In," 17, 24–25.

53. OR, vol. 27, pt. 1:279.

54. The exact number of captures from Archer's brigade on July 1 is unknown. Coddington, *Gettysburg Campaign*, 271, 687–88 n. 61.

55. OR, vol. 27, 1:245, 275.

56. Winschel, "Heavy Was Their Loss," 11.

57. Coddington, *Gettysburg Campaign*, 271; D. Scott Hartwig, "Guts and Good Leadership; The Action at the Railroad Cut, July 1, 1863," *Gettysburg Magazine* 1 (July 1989): 11.

58. "The Battle of Gettysburg," Sumner A. Cunningham publisher, Nashville, 1894–1932, *Confederate Veteran* 8 (April 1900): 165. Hereafter *CV*.

59. Dawes divided the brigade guard into two companies, which were deployed on each flank of his regiment. Ladd and Ladd, *The Bachelder Papers*, 1:323–24. See also "With the Iron Brigade Guard at Gettysburg," Lloyd G. Harris, Lance J. Herdegen and William J. K. Beaudot, eds., *Gettysburg Magazine* 1 (July 1989).

60. Winschel, "Heavy Was Their Loss," 11.

61. Krick, "Failures of Brigade Leadership," 108.

62. OR, vol. 27, pt. 1:276.

63. Terrence J. Winschel, "The Colors Are Shrouded in Mystery," *Gettysburg Magazine* 6 (January 1992): 78, 80.

64. Winschel, "Heavy Was Their Loss," 11.

65. Ladd and Ladd, *The Bachelder Papers*, 1:324–25.

66. OR, vol. 27, pt. 1:276.

67. OR, vol. 27, pt. 2:638; Freeman, *Lee's Lieutenants*, 3:81.

68. Coddington, *Gettysburg Campaign*, 272.

69. Ladd and Ladd, *The Bachelder Papers*, 2:912.

70. OR, vol. 27, pt. 1:246.

71. Hassler, "The First Day's Battle of Gettysburg," 268; OR, vol. 27, pt. 1:268.

72. Hassler, "The First Day's Battle of Gettysburg," 268–70; OR, vol. 27, pt. 1:727, 734. Following Union victory, a controversy developed over who decided to occupy Cemetery Hill, Reynolds or Howard. See Coddington, *Gettysburg Campaign*, 302–3.

73. OR, vol. 27, pt. 3:948; Coddington, *Gettysburg Campaign*, 280.

74. Haines, "A. P. Hill's Advance to Gettysburg," 10; Longstreet, "Lee in Pennsylvania," *Annals of the War,* 420.

75. Allan, "Memoranda of Conversations with Lee," *Lee the Soldier*, 13–14.

76. OR, vol. 27, pt. 2:613. "And here the absence of Stuart, with the bulk of the cavalry, does seem to me to cut some figure. Had they been with us Gen. Lee would doubtless have been too well informed of the enemy's exact location to have permitted two divisions to blunder into an attack upon two corps & a division of cavalry." Edward Porter Alexander, *Fighting for the Confederacy: The Personal Recollections of General Edward Porter Alexander*, ed. Gary W. Gallagher (Chapel Hill: The University of North Carolina Press, 1989), 231–32.

77. OR, vol. 27, pt. 2:444, 552.

78. Massy Griffin, "Rodes on Oak Hill: A Study of Rodes' Division on the First Day of Gettysburg," *Gettysburg Magazine* 4 (January 1991): 34.

79. OR, vol. 27, pt. 2:552.

80. Coddington, *Gettysburg Campaign*, 695 n. 2; OR, vol. 27, pt. 1:248.

81. Krick, "Failures of Brigade Leadership," 117.

82. Coddington, *Gettysburg Campaign*, 286.

83. OR, vol. 27, pt. 1:248.

84. Gary G. Lash, "Brigadier General Henry Baxter's Brigade at Gettysburg, July 1," *Gettysburg Magazine* 10 (January 1994): 9, 13, 15.

85. OR, vol. 27, pt. 1:282.

86. Ibid., pt. 2:553; Griffin, "Rodes on Oak Hill," 36.

87. Krick, "Failures of Brigade Leadership," 124, 126. "The right regiment (Third Alabama) was, under my [Rodes] order, placed on a line with Daniel's brigade, Colonel O'Neal being instructed to form the balance of the brigade upon it." OR, vol. 27, pt. 2:553, 592.

88. OR, vol. 27, pt. 2:607.

89. Lash, "Baxter's Brigade at Gettysburg," 14; OR, vol. 27, pt. 1:734. See also Kenneth M. Kepf, "Dilger's Battery at Gettysburg," *Gettysburg Magazine* 4 (January 1991).

90. OR, vol. 27, pt. 2:553.

91. Krick, "Failures of Brigade Leadership," 128; OR, vol. 27, pt. 2:601.

92. Griffin, "Rodes on Oak Hill," 38.

93. OR, vol. 27, pt. 2:592–93, 601.

94. OR, vol. 27, pt. 2:579; Krick, "Failures of Brigade Leadership," 128.

95. Hassler, "The First Day's Battle of Gettysburg," 272.

96. Lash, "Baxter's Brigade at Gettysburg," 16.

97. Gerald A. Patterson, "The Death of Iverson's Brigade," *Gettysburg Magazine* 5 (July 1991): 15; Ladd and Ladd, *The Bachelder Papers*, 2:1062.

98. Griffin, "Rodes on Oak Hill," 40.

99. Walter Clark, ed., *Histories of the Several Regiments and Battalions from North Carolina in the Great War 1861–1865*, 5 vols. (Wilmington: Broadfoot Publishing Company, 1992, reprint), 1:637. Hereafter *North Carolina Regiments*.

100. Lash, "Baxter's Brigade at Gettysburg," 18; OR, vol. 27, 1:282.

101. Clark, *North Carolina Regiments*, 2:235–36.

102. OR, vol. 27, pt. 2:579.

103. Clark, *North Carolina Regiments*, 1:287.

104. OR, vol. 27, pt. 2:580.

105. Ibid., 444.

106. Patterson, "The Death of Iverson's Brigade," 16.

107. OR, vol. 27, pt. 1:307.

108. Lash, "Baxter's Brigade at Gettysburg," 21.
109. Richard A. Sauers, "The 16th Maine Volunteer Infantry at Gettysburg," *Gettysburg Magazine* 13 (July 1995): 36.
110. OR, vol. 27, pt. 2:587.
111. Ibid., 444.
112. Clark, *North Carolina Regiments*, 1:637; OR, vol. 27, pt. 2:580, 587.
113. OR, vol. 27, pt. 2:554.
114. Ibid., 595.
115. Gary W. Gallagher, *Stephen Dodson Ramseur: Lee's Gallant General* (Chapel Hill: The University of North Carolina Press, 1985), 72. "It is said that Lt. Crowder, of Company A, and Lt. Dugger, of another regiment, ran back and advised him [Ramseur] to file off to the left and strike the Federal right." Clark, *North Carolina Regiments*, 2:237.
116. Lash, "Baxter's Brigade at Gettysburg," 22; OR, vol. 27, pt. 1:307.
117. Sauers, "The 16th Maine Volunteer Infantry," 36.
118. Hassler, "The First Day's Battle of Gettysburg," 273.
119. Griffin, "Rodes on Oak Hill," 46–47; Gallagher, *Stephen Dodson Ramseur*, 72. General Paul, shot in both eyes during the fighting, was reported killed. Charles E. Davis Jr., *Three Years in the Army: The Story of the Thirteenth Massachusetts Volunteers from July 16, 1861, to August 1, 1864* (Boston: Estes and Lauriat, 1894), 272; OR, vol. 27, pt. 1:72, 290.
120. Krick, "Failures of Brigade Leadership," 120; Warren W. Hassler, Jr., *Crisis at the Crossroads: The First Day at Gettysburg* (Tuscaloosa: University of Alabama Press, 1970), 93, 99.
121. Coddington, *Gettysburg Campaign*, 289; Freeman, *Lee's Lieutenants*, 3:83.
122. OR, vol. 11, pt. 2:365; OR, vol. 19, pt. 1:1028.
123. OR, vol. 25, pt. 1:948.
124. Jerry Frey, *In The Woods Before Dawn: The Samuel Richey Collection of the Southern Confederacy* (Gettysburg: Thomas Publications, 1994), 93–95.
125. OR, vol. 51, pt. 2:844.
126. Ibid., 684, 699.
127. Gary Kross, "That One Error Fills Him with Faults: Gen. Alfred Iverson and His Brigade at Gettysburg," *Blue & Gray Magazine*, vol. 12, 3 (February 1995): 24, 48, 52.
128. Alexander, *Fighting for the Confederacy*, 293.
129. Robertson, *Stonewall Jackson*, 678; Warner, *Generals in Gray*, 137.
130. Allan, "Memoranda of Conversations with Lee," *Lee the Soldier*, 8, 9.
131. Coddington, *Gettysburg Campaign*, 292.
132. Griffin, "Rodes on Oak Hill," 44.
133. OR, vol. 27, pt. 1:266, 356; pt. 2:566.
134. Hassler, "The First Day Battle of Gettysburg," 273–74.
135. D. Scott Hartwig, "The Defense of McPherson's Ridge," *Gettysburg Magazine* 1 (July 1989): 23; OR, vol. 27, pt. 2:643.
136. Craig L. Dunn, *Iron Men, Iron Will: The Nineteenth Indiana Regiment of the Iron Brigade* (Indianapolis: Guild Press of Indiana, Inc., 1995), 190.
137. Ladd and Ladd, *The Bachelder Papers*, 2:941.
138. OR, vol. 27, pt. 1:268; Dunn, *Nineteenth Indiana Regiment*, 191.
139. R. Lee Haden, "The Deadly Embrace: The Meeting of the Twenty-fourth Regiment, Michigan Infantry and the Twenty-sixth Regiment of North Carolina

Troops, at McPherson's Woods, Gettysburg, Pennsylvania, July 1, 1863," *Gettysburg Magazine* 5 (July 1991): 28–31.

140. Clark, *North Carolina Regiments*, 5:120, 131.

141. Busey and Martin, *Regimental Strengths*, 264–65.

142. Heth, "Memoirs of Henry Heth," 305.

143. Hassler, "The First Day's Battle of Gettysburg," 274.

144. OR, vol. 27, pt. 2:469; Early, *Memoirs*, 267.

145. D. Scott Hartwig, "The 11th Army Corps on July 1, 1863—'The Unlucky 11th,'" *Gettysburg Magazine* 2 (January 1990): 44–47; OR, vol. 27, pt. 1:712, 745; Ezra J. Warner, *Generals in Blue: Lives of the Union Commanders* (Baton Rouge: Louisiana State University Press, 1986 edition), 19.

146. OR, vol. 27, pt. 1:703, 721; pt. 2:484.

147. Brig. Gen. Robert F. Hoke had been badly wounded in the shoulder during the Chancellorsville campaign. The 54th North Carolina conducted prisoners to Staunton. Early, *Memoirs*, 229, 253, 268.

148. A detachment from the 154th New York returned in the evening to raise regimental strength "to about 75 men..." Mark H. Dunkelman and Michael J. Winey, "The Hardtack Regiment in the Brickyard Fight," *Gettysburg Magazine* 8 (January 1993): 20–21, 23; Hartwig, "The 11th Army Corps," 48. Company K lost two Napoleons, taken by the 6th North Carolina. OR, vol. 27, pt. 2:484.

149. Hartwig, "The 11th Army Corps," 48; Hassler, "The First Day's Battle of Gettysburg," 274.

150. OR, vol. 27, pt. 1:290, 293, 307; Hassler, *Crisis at the Crossroads*, 98.

151. Sauers, "The 16th Maine Volunteer Infantry," 39–40; Hassler, "The First Day's Battle of Gettysburg," 273; OR, vol. 27, pt. 1:295. The 16th Maine's losses were 77.9 percent. Busey and Martin, *Regimental Losses*, 240.

152. Davis, *Three Years in the Army*, 272–73. The 13th Massachusetts' losses were 65.1 percent. Busey and Martin, *Regimental Losses*, 240.

153. OR, vol. 27, pt. 1:283.

154. Kepf, "Dilger's Battery," 60.

155. Hassler, *Crisis at the Crossroads*, 84.

156. OR, vol. 27, pt. 1:735.

157. The 154th New York lost 178 missing and captured. Busey and Martin, *Regimental Losses*, 254, 313.

158. James Stuart Montgomery, *The Shaping of a Battle: Gettysburg* (Philadelphia: Chilton Company—Book Division, 1959), 65–66. Other sources say Schimmelfennig spent two days in either a pigsty or stable. Warner, *Generals in Blue*, 424; Boatner, *Civil War Dictionary*, 725.

159. Hassler, *Crisis at the Crossroads*, 127; Busey and Martin, *Regimental Strengths*, 270.

160. OR, vol. 1, pt. 1:269, 280, 289, 299.

161. J. Michael Miller, "Perrin's Brigade on July 1, 1863" *Gettysburg Magazine* 13 (July 1995): 25. Colonel Stone had been "severely wounded" and his successor, Col. Langhorne Wister, 150th Pennsylvania, "was also disabled...." OR, vol. 27, pt. 1:330.

162. OR, vol. 27, pt. 2:668.

163. Ibid., 657, 665; pt. 1:934.

164. Henry J. Hunt, "The First Day At Gettysburg," B&L, 3:282; OR, vol. 27, pt. 1:357.

165. OR, vol. 27, pt. 2:670.

166. Ibid., 658, 671.

167. OR, vol. 27, pt. 1:250.

168. OR, vol. 27, pt. 2:660, 662–63; Ladd and Ladd, *The Bachelder Papers*, 2:903.

169. Sauers, "Perrin's Brigade," 28; OR, vol. 27, pt. 2:662.

170. OR, vol. 27, pt. 1:250, 269; Ladd and Ladd, *The Bachelder Papers*, 2:942; Hassler, "The First Day's Battle of Gettysburg," 275.

171. OR, vol. 27, pt. 1:266, 280.

172. William H. Swallow, "The First Day at Gettysburg," *The Southern Bivouac*, ed. Basil W. Duke and R. W. Knott, Louisville 1882–1887, vol. 1, 7 (December 1885): 440; Hassler, *Crisis at the Crossroads*, 127.

173. Hassler, "The First Day's Battle of Gettysburg," 275; OR, vol. 27, pt. 1:721.

174. Rufus R. Dawes, "With the Sixth Wisconsin at Gettysburg," *Sketches of War History: 1861–1865, Papers Prepared for the Ohio Commandery of the Military Order of the Loyal Legion of fhe United States*, ed. Robert Hunter, 3 vols. (Cincinnati: Robert Clarke & Co., Cincinnati, 1890), 3:382.

175. Coddington, *Gettysburg Campaign*, 318, 713 n. 188.

176. Glenn Tucker, *High Tide at Gettysburg: The Campaign in Pennsylvania* (Indianapolis: The Bobbs-Merrill Company, Inc., 1958), 173–74.

177. The same obstacles did not deter Early's troops the following evening when the defenders were better prepared. Early, *Memoirs*, 269–70.

178. OR, vol. 27, pt. 2:469. The 58th Virginia conducted prisoners to Staunton. The 13th Virginia garrisoned Winchester. Early, *Memoirs*, 253.

179. Gary Kross, "At the Time Impracticable: Dick Ewell's Decision on the First Day at Gettysburg with Excerpts from Campbell Brown's Journal," *Blue & Gray Magazine*, vol. 12 (February 1995): 56. See also OR, vol. 27, pt. 1:771.

180. "Early...did not understand or have the energy for the Stonewall Jackson technique, the relentless follow-up and hot pursuit." Glenn Tucker, *Lee and Longstreet at Gettysburg* (Indianapolis: The Bobbs-Merrill Company, Inc., 1968), 36.

181. Coddington, *Gettysburg Campaign*, 700 n. 64.

182. Ladd and Ladd, *The Bachelder Papers*, 3:1350; Hassler, "The First Day's Battle of Gettysburg," 276; OR, vol. 27, pt. 1:368.

183. Tucker, *Lee and Longstreet*, 17.

184. Carl Schurz, *Reminiscences of Carl Schurz*, 3 vols. (New York: The McClure Co., 1907–1908), 3:14.

185. Ladd and Ladd, *The Bachelder Papers*, 3:1351. "He [the enemy] made a single attempt to turn our right, ascending the slope east of Gettysburg..." OR, vol. 27, pt. 1:368, 704.

186. Swallow, "The First Day at Gettysburg," *Southern Bivouac*, 441, 442. In a postwar conversation with Cousin Cassius Lee, Robert E. Lee "said that Ewell was a fine officer, but would never take responsibility of exceeding his orders, and having been ordered to Gettysburg, he would not go farther and hold the heights beyond the town." Robert E. Lee (son), *Recollections and Letters of General Robert E. Lee* (New York: Doubleday Company, 1924 edition), 415.

187. OR, vol. 27, pt. 1:284; Coddington, *Gettysburg Campaign*, 712 n. 182.

188. Ibid., 351. The Vermonters had been assigned to the Third Division, I Corps, July 1. The 12th Vermont and 15th Vermont remained in the rear as I Corps wagon train guards. Ladd and Ladd, *The Bachelder Papers*, 1:53. See also Christopher C. Dickson, "The Flying Brigade: Brig. Gen. George Stannard and the Road to Gettysburg," *Gettysburg Magazine* 16 (January 1997).

189. OR, vol. 27, pt. 1:366, 368, 825, 836. The exact position taken by the 5th Ohio and 147th Pennsylvania is unknown. Pfanz, *Gettysburg: The Second Day*, 60.

190. Ibid., pt. 1:252, 290, 704–5; Harry W. Pfanz, *Gettysburg: Culp's Hill and Cemetery Hill* (Chapel Hill: The University of North Carolina Press, 1993), 102–3.

191. Ibid., pt. 1:115, 368–69; pt. 3:465.

192. Coddington, *Gettysburg Campaign*, 310; Freeman, *Lee's Lieutenant's*, 3:86.

193. Freeman, *R. E. Lee*, 3:68.

194. Coddington, *Gettysburg Campaign*, 316–17; OR, vol. 27, pt. 2:317.

195. Ladd and Ladd, *The Bachelder Papers*, 3:1903.

196. James Longstreet, "Lee's Right Wing at Gettysburg," *B&L*, 3:339.

197. Longstreet, "Lee in Pennsylvania," *Annals of the War*, 421.

198. Longstreet, "Lee's Right Wing at Gettysburg," *B&L*, 3:340.

199. Pfanz, *Gettysburg: Culp's Hill and Cemetery Hill*, 72; Douglas C. Haines, "R. S. Ewell's Command, June 29–July 1, 1863," *Gettysburg Magazine* 9 (July 1993): 28; OR, vol. 27, pt. 2:318.

200. Pfanz, *Gettysburg: Culp's Hill and Cemetery Hill*, 76–77.

201. Haines, "R. S. Ewell's Command," 28.

202. Kross, "At the Time Impracticable," 56.

203. Isaac R. Trimble, "The Campaign and Battle of Gettysburg," *CV* 25 (1917): 212.

204. Ladd and Ladd, *The Bachelder Papers*, 2:932.

205. Early also advised Ewell that Culp's Hill should be occupied "because it commanded the enemy's position..." Freeman, *Lee's Lieutenant's*, 3:95–96.

206. George G. Meade, "The Meade-Sickles Controversy," *B&L*, 3:412.

207. OR, vol. 27, pt. 2:503–4, 537.

208. Ibid., 445.

209. Pfanz, *Gettysburg: Culp's Hill and Cemetery Hill*, 78–79; OR, vol. 27, pt. 2:504.

210. Haines, "R. S. Ewell's Command," 30; See also Pfanz, *Gettysburg: Culp's Hill and Cemetery Hill*, 420 n. 19.

211. Freeman, *Lee's Lieutenant's*, 3:100.

212. Freeman, *R. E. Lee*, 3:79–80.

213. Alexander, *Fighting for the Confederacy*, 234–35, 242.

214. Freeman, *Lee's Lieutenant's*, 3:102.

215. OR, vol. 27, pt. 2:504.

216. Ibid., 446.

217. Kross, "At the Time Impracticable," 57.

218. Pfanz, *Gettysburg: Culp's Hill and Cemetery Hill*, 86; OR, vol. 27, pt. 1:285.

219. OR, vol. 27, pt. 2:446, pt. 3:483; Pfanz, *Gettysburg: Culp's Hill and Cemetery Hill*, 87.

CHAPTER 4

1. OR, vol. 27, pt. 1:115; Pfanz, *Gettysburg: Culp's Hill and Cemetery Hill*, 107, 426 n. 2.

2. Coddington, *Gettysburg Campaign*, 330–32. It is uncertain whether General Sickles obtained a sketch map. Richard A. Sauers, *A Caspian Sea of Ink: The Meade-Sickles Controversy* (Baltimore: Butternut and Blue, 1989), 26, 117.

3. Pfanz, *Gettysburg: Culp's Hill and Cemetery Hill*, 111.

4. OR, vol. 27, pt. 1:759, 765, 825. The 1st Maryland Eastern Shore arrived July 3. A. Wilson Greene, "'A Step All-Important and Essential to Victory': Henry W. Slocum and the Twelfth Corps on July 1-2, 1863," *The Second Day at Gettysburg: Essays on Confederate and Union Leadership*, ed. Gary W. Gallagher (Kent, Ohio: The Kent State University Press), 1993, 104-5.

5. Coddington, *Gettysburg Campaign*, 333.

6. OR, vol. 27, pt. 1:416, pt. 3:1087. See also Pfanz, *Gettysburg: The Second Day*, 64, 72.

7. Ibid., pt. 1:116.

8. *Greene and His New York Troops at Gettysburg*, New York Monuments Commission (Albany: J. B. Lyon Company State Printers, 1909), 82; OR, vol. 27, pt. 1:855.

9. OR, vol. 27, pt. 1:826.

10. Jesse H. Jones, "The Breastworks at Culp's Hill," *B&L*, 3:316; OR, vol. 27, pt. 1:778, 856.

11. McKim, *A Soldier's Recollections*, 196.

12. Coddington, *Gettysburg Campaign*, 337-38; OR, vol. 27, pt. 1:759-60.

13. OR, vol. 27, pt. 1:765, 769; Greene, "Henry W. Slocum," 107-8.

14. Coddington, *Gettysburg Campaign*, 333.

15. OR, vol. 27, pt. 1:116, 621, 633; Pfanz, *Gettysburg: The Second Day*, 63; Oliver Wilcox Norton, *The Attack and Defense of Little Round Top: Gettysburg, July 2, 1863* (New York: The Neale Publishing Company, 1913), 246.

16. Sauers, *Caspian Sea*, 27-28; OR, vol. 27, pt. 1:482, 532.

17. Pfanz, *Gettysburg: The Second Day*, 125.

18. W. A. Swanberg, *Sickles The Incredible* (New York: Charles Scribner's Sons, 1956,) 185-87. See also Alexander, *Fighting for the Confederacy*, 209.

19. William Glenn Robertson, "The Peach Orchard Revisted: Daniel E. Sickles and the Third Corps on July 2, 1863," *The Second Day at Gettysburg: Essays on Confederate and Union Leadership*, ed. Gary W. Gallagher (Kent, Ohio: The Kent State University Press, 1993), 47.

20. Henry J. Hunt, "The Second Day at Gettysburg," *B&L*, 3:302-3; Sauers, *Caspian Sea*, 29-30; Coddington, *Gettysburg Campaign*, 351-52.

21. Sauers, *Caspian Sea*, 30, 99; OR, vol. 27, pt. 1:825.

22. OR, vol. 27, pt. 2:318.

23. Herman Hattaway and Archer Jones, *How the North Won: A Military History of the Civil War* (Urbana: University of Illinois Press, 1983), 398. Perhaps the best appraisal of Lee's thought process and decision to accept battle is the following: "It should not be forgotten that a general battle was not in Lee's design in going into Pennsylvania. He repeatedly stated that in consequence of the absence of Stuart with the cavalry he was unaware of the near proximity of the Federal army, and when Hill reported that a large force of infantry in his front on July 1st, did not believe it. It was only the fight of that afternoon that convinced him that Meade was near at hand, and he then deemed it injudicious to decline battle." Letter, William Allan to William Jones, April 27, 1877, "Causes of Lee's Defeat at Gettysburg," *SHSP* 4 (1877): 80. See also Freeman, *Lee's Lieutenant's*, 3:107-8 n. 7.

24. Walter H. Taylor, Memorandum, "Causes of Lee's Defeat at Gettysburg," *SHSP* 4 (1877): 82.

25. OR, vol. 27, pt. 2:318. For an analysis of General Lee's options on July 2, see Alexander, *Fighting for the Confederacy*, 233-34.

26. William Allan, "A Reply to General Longstreet," *B&L*, 3:355.

27. Pfanz, *Gettysburg: The Second Day*, 105–7. See also Freeman, *Lee's Lieutenant's*, 3:174, 755–56.

28. OR, vol. 27, pt. 2:318–19; Pfanz, *Gettysburg: The Second Day*, 150.

29. Glenn Tucker, *Lee and Longstreet at Gettysburg*, 2–5, 38, 45. For a thorough review of this vacuous dispute see Thomas L. Connelly, *The Marble Man: Robert E. Lee and His Image in American Society* (Baton Rouge: Louisiana State University Press), 83–90.

30. Longstreet, "Lee in Pennsylvania," *Annals of the War*, 437–39.

31. Freeman, *Lee's Lieutenants*, 3:175; Tucker, *Lee and Longstreet*, 16–17.

32. Coddington, *Gettysburg Campaign*, 371. For a concise summary of Longstreet's strategic thinking, see James Longstreet, "Causes of Lee's Defeat at Gettysburg," *SHSP* 5 (1878): 54–55.

33. John B. Hood, *Advance and Retreat: Personal Experiences in the United States & Confederate States Armies* (Philadelphia: Press of Buck and McFetridge, 1880), 57.

34. Jeffrey D. Wert, *General James Longstreet: The Confederacy's Most Controversial Soldier—A Biography* (New York: Simon & Schuster, 1993), 262–65.

35. OR, vol. 27, pt. 2:358; J. Gary Laine and Morris M. Penny, *Law's Alabama Brigade in the War Between the Union and the Confederacy* (Shippensburg, Pa.: White Mane Publishing Co., Inc., 1996), 76–77.

36. Longstreet, "Lee in Pennsylvania," *Annals of the War*, 422.

37. Coddington, *Gettysburg Campaign*, 376.

38. OR, vol. 27, pt. 2:358; Longstreet, "Lee's Right Wing at Gettysburg," *B&L*, 3:340.

39. Moxley Sorrel, *Recollections of a Confederate Staff Officer*, ed. Bell Irvin Wiley (Wilmington, N.C.: Broadfoot Publishing Company, 1987, reprint), 163–64. For a detailed analysis of Longstreet's attitude on July 2, see Robert K. Krick, "If Longstreet...Says So, It Is Most Likely Not True: James Longstreet and the Second Day at Gettysburg," *The Second Day at Gettysburg: Essays on Confederate and Union Leadership*, ed. Gary W. Gallagher (Kent, Ohio: The Kent State University Press, 1993), 69–74.

40. "Longstreet in History, Lee in the Balance: Dissection of 'The Lost Cause,'" Interview with Jeffrey D. Wert, William J. Miller, *Civil War Magazine* 45 (June 1994): 46.

41. OR, vol. 27, pt. 2:308, 318; Coddington, *Gettysburg Campaign*, 736 n. 90.

42. Coddington, *Gettysburg Campaign*, 378–82; OR, vol. 27, pt. 2:367.

43. Lafayette McLaws, "Gettysburg," *SHSP* 7 (1879): 70–71.

44. Robertson, "The Peach Orchard," 48, 50.

45. Hunt, "Second Day," *B&L*, 3:304; Map, "Confrontation on the Federal Left Hood's Division Advances," Pfanz, *Gettysburg: The Second Day*, 170–71. The 84th Pennsylvania (Carr) was III Corps wagon train guard at Westminster, Maryland. OR, vol. 27, pt. 1:160, 557.

46. Coddington, *Gettysburg Campaign*, 354–55, 720 n. 81; Sauers, *Caspian Sea*, 119, 147. See also Ladd and Ladd, *The Bachelder Papers*, 1:670–71.

47. Conversation with Edwin C. Bearss, Perryville, Kentucky, May 31, 1997.

48. "What if Sickles had obeyed Meade's orders and simply prolonged the Federal line southward along Cemetery Ridge? Any answer to this hypothetical question must be purely speculative, but some results seem probable. First, Sickles's corps likely would not have occupied Little Round Top in strength...Second, the flaws on the left of Meade's line probably would not have been addressed in a timely fashion. Thus Warren might not have visited

Little Round Top and brought forward the reinforcements that saved the position. Third, much of the ground on the Federal left for which Longstreet's men fought fiercely would have fallen to the Confederates with only the slightest resistance." Robertson, "The Peach Orchard," 55.

49. Ladd and Ladd, *The Bachelder Papers*, 1:672.

50. "The Seventeenth Maine took a strong position behind a stone wall, and did good service at this point." OR, vol. 27, pt. 1:493, 520. See also OR, vol. 27, pt. 2:318, 368, 397, 404.

51. Ladd and Ladd, *The Bachelder Papers*, 995. "...the Third Corps absorbed the shock of Longstreet's assault and disrupted it so much that the grayclad attackers failed to reach Cemetery Ridge with sufficient force to capture and hold the ridge." Sauers, *Caspian Sea*, 60. For criticism of Sickles' forward position, see Coddington, *Gettysburg Campaign*, 723 n. 130.

52. Contrary to Richard Sauers' assertion. "...the question of what the result might have been had Sickles remained in position on Cemetery Ridge is one that cannot be answered." Sauers, *Caspian Sea*, 60. "This advanced position, in my judgment, saved the day, indirectly, for although we were driven, the Rebels suffered so severely in driving us, and became so used up that they were utterly unfit to continue their progress, when they encountered the 6th [V] Corps. My opinion is, that if the Confederates had come upon us fresh with the force we first encountered at or near the proper place on line they would have walked right over all the troops we could have thrown in at that point, and Round Top and Little Round Top would have been in their possession— and of course the whole line would have been at their mercy." Ladd and Ladd, *The Bachelder Papers*, 2:837.

53. Col. Francis E. Heath, 19th Maine (Harrow), ordered by General Humphreys to "stop his men with fixed bayonets...refused...fearing my command would be carried off with the disordered crowd that was at that time very near us—" Ladd and Ladd, *The Bachelder Papers*, 1:257 3:1651.

54. Alexander, *Fighting for the Confederacy*, 235, 238; OR, vol. 27, pt. 2:429. "Colonel Batchelder, the Government Gettysburg Historian, said once in the hearing of the writer, that he had consulted fifty-six general officers who participated in the Battle of Gettysburg, as to Sickles' position, and they were about equally divided in their opinion regarding it." Jacob Hoke, *The Great Invasion of 1863* (New York: Thomas Yosseloff, 1959, reprint), 570. "...Wellington occupied Hougoumont, an advanced post, which bore very much the same relation to the British main line that the Peach Orchard did at Gettysburg." John Watts De Peyster, "The Third Corps and Sickles: An Address," reprinted in *Gettysburg Sources*, 3 vols., comp. James L. and Judy W. McLean (Baltimore: Butternut and Blue, 1987), 2:55. The Duke of Wellington's victory at Waterloo was gained in great measure due to the forward outposts of Hougoumont and La Haye Sainte before his main line which disrupted Napoleon's attacks, buying time for the Prussians to intervene. See David Hamilton Williams, *Waterloo New Perspectives: The Great Battle Reappraised* (New York: John Wiley & Sons, Inc.), 1994.

55. OR, vol. 27, pt. 3:1086.

56. Robertson, "Peach Orchard," 50.

57. Tucker, *High Tide*, 243; OR, vol. 27, pt. 1:131–32.

58. OR, vol. 27, pt. 881; Paul J. Lader, "The 7th New Jersey in the Gettysburg Campaign," *Gettysburg Magazine* 16 (January 1997): 59.

59. Pfanz, *Gettysburg: The Second Day*, 153–54; Tucker, *Lee and Longstreet*, 34.

60. Hood, *Advance and Retreat*, 57–59; E. M. Law, "The Struggle for 'Round Top'" *B&L*, 3:321–22.

61. OR, vol. 27, pt. 2:408.

62. Daniel M. Laney, "Wasted Gallantry: Hood's Texas Brigade at Gettysburg," *Gettysburg Magazine* 16 (January 1997): 36.

63. OR, vol. 27, pt. 2:391, 393, 404, 407.

64. Company D, 1st New York Artillery, positioned in the Wheatfield, fired solid shot into the woods. OR, vol. 27, pt. 1:586, 588.

65. Ladd and Ladd, *The Bachelder Papers*, 2:860–61; OR, vol. 27, pt. 2:404.

66. Kathleen Georg Harrison, "Our Principal Loss Was in this Place, Action at the Slaughter Pen and at South End of Houck's Ridge, Gettysburg, Pennsylvania, 2 July 1863," *Gettysburg Magazine* 1 (July 1989): 52.

67. Hood, *Advance and Retreat*, 59; Pfanz, *Gettysburg: The Second Day*, 172–73; J. S. McNeily, "Barksdale's Mississippi Brigade at Gettysburg," ed. Franklin L. Riley, Oxford: *Publications of the Mississippi Historical Society*, 14 (1914): 235.

68. Map, "Longstreet's Corps Opens the Attack," Pfanz, *Gettysburg: The Second Day*, 170–71. Lee's plan to attack up the Emmitsburg Road could have resulted in disaster if III Corps had remained on Cemetery Ridge, "but Lee's plan was the proper one to follow after Sickles had made his advance to the Peach Orchard and stretched one division, facing mainly southwest from the Peach Orchard to the Devil's Den, and the other along the Emmitsburg Road, facing northwest." Tucker, *Lee and Longstreet*, 34.

69. James R. Wright, "Time on Little Round Top," *Gettysburg Magazine* 2 (January 1990): 53.

70. Coddington, *Gettysburg Campaign*, 388–89; Norton, *Little Round Top*, 264, 287–88.

71. Pfanz, *Gettysburg: The Second Day*, 169, 173; Laine and Penny, *Law's Alabama Brigade*, 87, 90, 93.

72. Mauriel P. Joslyn, "'For Ninety Nine Years or the War': The Story of the 3rd Arkansas at Gettysburg," *Gettysburg Magazine* 14 (January 1996): 57.

73. Harrison, "Our Principal Loss," 55. The 3rd Maine did not rejoin the Second Brigade until the end of the day, having sustained heavy losses at the Peach Orchard fighting with the First Brigade. OR, vol. 27, pt. 1:507–8.

74. Laney, "Wasted Gallantry," 40.

75. Pfanz, *Gettysburg: The Second Day*, 181, 185.

76. Ladd and Ladd, *The Bachelder Papers*, 2:1023–24.

77. Kevin O'Brien, "Valley of the Shadow of Death: Col. Strong Vincent and the Eighty-third Pennsylvania Infantry at Little Round Top," *Gettysburg Magazine* 7 (July 1992): 44–5.

78. Harrison, "Our Principal Loss," 57.

79. OR, vol. 27, pt. 1:588.

80. "I always have and ever shall regret that I obeyed the order and moved my command [4th Maine] into that Den (Devil's Den) which caused our entire loss of prisoners and most of the casualties." Ladd, *The Bachelder Papers*, 2:1094–95.

81. Harrison, "Our Principal Loss," 62.

82. OR, vol. 27, pt. 1:510. In 1891, Colonel Walker wrote: "If it was not for the heel cord of my left leg being replaced which was severed at Gettysburg July 2, 1863 (my 45th birthday) I should sometimes almost think my being in the great battle was but a dream." Ladd and Ladd, *The Bachelder Papers*, 3:1783–84.

83. OR, vol. 27, pt. 1:396.

84. Ibid., pt. 2:394.

85. Pfanz, *Gettysburg: The Second Day*, 184.

86. Laney, "Wasted Gallantry," 40–41.

87. J. W. Lokey, "Wounded at Gettysburg," *CV* 22 (September 1914): 400.

88. Pfanz, *Gettysburg: The Second Day*, 191–92; OR, vol. 27, pt. 1:493.

89. Harrison, "Our Principal Loss," 64–65; OR, vol. 27, pt. 1:589. The 1st Texas should be credited with capturing Smith's guns since Colonel Work detailed two companies to remove three recoverable pieces; OR, vol. 27, pt. 2:409. See also Pfanz, *Gettysburg: The Second Day*, 553 n. 9. Colonel Walker believed that if Benning had gone to Law's support rather than Robertson's, the Confederates would have carried Little Round Top as they did Devil's Den. Tucker, *High Tide*, 266.

90. Pfanz, *Gettysburg: The Second Day*, 194; OR, vol. 27, pt. 1:494.

91. Laney, "Wasted Gallantry," 42; Pfanz, Gettysburg: *The Second Day*, 196.

92. OR, vol. 27, pt. 1:589.

93. Ibid., pt. 2:414.

94. Harrison, "Our Principal Loss," 65.

95. OR, vol. 27, pt. 1:526–27, 577–78, 589.

96. Pfanz, *Gettysburg: The Second Day*, 213.

97. O'Brien, "Valley of the Shadow of Death," 46.

98. Pfanz, *Gettysburg: The Second Day*, 221; O'Brien, "Stubborn Bravery," 39–40.

99. Coddington, *Gettysburg Campaign*, 395; OR, vol. 27, pt. 1:619.

100. Norton, *Little Round Top*, 259; Pfanz, *Gettysburg: The Second Day*, 227.

101. O'Brien, "Valley of the Shadow of Death," 46; Ladd and Ladd, *The Bachelder Papers*, 1:244. See also OR, vol. 27, pt. 1:628.

102. Pfanz, *Gettysburg: The Second Day*, 223, 225. Weed was absent selecting a position for his brigade. Ladd and Ladd, *The Bachelder Papers*, 2:895–96.

103. Brian A. Bennett, "The Supreme Event in Its Existence—The 140th New York on Little Round Top," *Gettysburg Magazine* 3 (July 1990): 23–25.

104. Pfanz, *Gettysburg: The Second Day*, 230; Norton, *Little Round Top*, 260.

105. OR, vol. 27, pt. 1:653.

106. Coddington, *Gettysburg Campaign*, 391.

107. OR, vol. 27, pt. 2:392.

108. Laine and Penny, *Law's Alabama Brigade*, 101.

109. Ladd and Ladd, *The Bachelder Papers*, 1:465.

110. Pfanz, *Gettysburg: The Second Day*, 231.

111. Coddington, *Gettysburg Campaign*, 393.

112. Pfanz, *Gettysburg: The Second Day*, 231–32.

113. OR, vol. 27, pt. 1:603, 623–24.

114. Laine and Penny, *Law's Alabama Brigade*, 104.

115. OR, vol. 27, pt. 1:603.

116. Ibid., 624; Ladd and Ladd, *The Bachelder Papers*, 3:1885.

117. OR, vol. 27, pt. 1:623–24. The 15th Alabama lost 172 men at Gettysburg. In contrast, the 47th Alabama lost 67 men. Laine and Penny, *Law's Alabama Brigade*, 107, 369.

118. Ladd and Ladd, *The Bachelder Papers*, 3:1871.

119. Jay Jorgensen, "Anderson Attacks the Wheatfield," *Gettysburg Magazine* 14 (January 1996): 68–69. The 7th Georgia was detached to provide flank security for the division against Federal cavalry. OR, vol. 27, pt. 2:396, 407.

120. Mac Wyckoff, "Kershaw's Brigade at Gettysburg," *Gettysburg Magazine* 5 (July 1991):41; Ladd and Ladd, *The Bachelder Papers*, 1:470.

121. Pfanz, *Gettysburg: The Second Day*, 255.

122. OR, vol. 27, pt. 2:372.

123. Ladd and Ladd, *The Bachelder Papers*, 1:455–56; Wyckoff, "Kershaw's Brigade," 42.

124. OR, vol. 27, pt. 2:367.

125. Pfanz, *Gettysburg: The Second Day*, 320. In his battle report, McGilvery noted: "After the battle, I...found 120 odd dead, belonging to three South Carolina regiments. This mortality was no doubt from the effect of the artillery fire." OR, vol. 27, pt. 1:882.

126. McLaws, "Gettysburg," 73; Gary G. Lash, "'A Pathetic Story': The 141st Pennsylvania (Graham's Brigade) at Gettysburg," *Gettysburg Magazine* 14 (January 1996): 90.

127. Lash, "A Pathetic Story," 92; Coddington, *Gettysburg Campaign*, 405.

128. John Heiser, "Action on the Emmitsburg Road, Gettysburg, Pennsylvania, July 2, 1863," *Gettysburg Magazine* 1 (July 1989): 80.

129. McNeily, "Barksdale's Mississippi Brigade," 238.

130. Terrence J. Winschel, "Their Supreme Moment: Barksdale's Brigade at Gettysburg," *Gettysburg Magazine* 1 (July 1989): 74.

131. Ladd and Ladd, *The Bachelder Papers*, 1:176, 480–81; Pfanz, *Gettysburg: The Second Day*, 256.

132. Lader, "The 7th New Jersey," 62; OR, vol. 27, pt. 1:885, 889.

133. Pfanz, *Gettysburg: The Second Day*, 329, 338.

134. OR, vol. 27, pt. 1:882; Ladd and Ladd, *The Bachelder Papers*, 3:1973.

135. Eric Campbell, "Baptism of Fire: The Ninth Massachusetts Battery at Gettysburg, July 2, 1863," *Gettysburg Magazine* 5 (July 1991): 69–71.

136. Campbell, "Baptism of Fire," 72–76; McNeily, "Barksdale's Brigade at Gettysburg," 249.

137. Coddington, *Gettysburg Campaign*, 417, 756 n. 41.

138. Ladd and Ladd, *The Bachelder Papers*, 1:177, 216, 622–23.

139. Pfanz, *Gettysburg: The Second Day*, 252. The combined strength of the First and Second Brigades, First Division, V Corps, approximated 1,664 officers and men; OR, vol. 27, pt. 1:601.

140. Jorgensen, "Anderson Attacks," 70, 72; Pfanz, *Gettysburg: The Second Day*, 257, 259.

141. Pfanz, *Gettysburg: The Second Day*, 262, 265; OR, vol. 27, pt. 1:520.

142. OR, vol. 27, pt. 1:369, 379.

143. Eric Campbell, "Caldwell Clears the Wheatfield," *Gettysburg Magazine* 3 (July 1990): 35; OR, vol. 27, pt. 1:175.

144. Wyckoff, "Kershaw's Brigade," 42.

145. OR, vol. 27, pt. 2:397; J. B. Kershaw, "Kershaw's Brigade at Gettysburg," *B&L*, 3:336.

146. D. Scott Hartwig, "'No Troops on the Field Had Done Better': John C. Caldwell's Division in the Wheatfield, July 2, 1863," *The Second Day at Gettysburg: Essays on Confederate and Union Leadership*, ed. Gary W. Gallagher (Kent, Ohio: The Kent State University Press, 1993), 159.

147. Campbell, "Caldwell Clears the Wheatfield," 40.

148. Hartwig, "John C. Caldwell's Division," 160.

149. Jorgensen, "Anderson Attacks the Wheatfield," 73–74.

150. Wyckoff, "Kershaw's Brigade," 44–45; Pfanz, *Gettysburg: The Second Day*, 282; Ladd and Ladd, *The Bachelder Papers*, 1:473.

151. OR, vol. 27, pt. 1:379.

152. Ibid., 400.

153. Ibid., 379–80.

154. Pfanz, *Gettysburg: The Second Day*, 327–28.

155. Campbell, "Caldwell Clears the Wheatfield," 47.

156. Lieutenant Colonel Fraser commanded the brigade by day's end. OR, vol. 27, pt. 1:369, 393–95.

157. Ladd and Ladd, *The Bachelder Papers*, 2:1102; OR, vol. 27, pt. 1:175, 394. "The One Hundred and Fortieth sustained the greatest percentage of loss in action [during the war] of any regiment from Pennsylvania." William F. Fox, *Regimental Losses in the American Civil War* (Albany: Albany Publishing Co., 1898 edition), 297.

158. Putnam lay in the Wheatfield 30 hours. On July 3, he received a second wound in the right shin. Ladd and Ladd, *The Bachelder Papers*, 1:412, 418–19.

159. Ladd and Ladd, *The Bachelder Papers*, 2:1233.

160. Campbell, "Caldwell Clears the Wheatfield," 48; Colonel Morgan, Hancock's chief of staff, encountered the First Division "flying to the rear, without [sic] no shadow of an organization." Ladd and Ladd, *The Bachelder Papers*, 3:1355.

161. OR, vol. 27, pt. 1:386.

162. The 9th Massachusetts was absent on picket duty. Ibid., 600, 610, 612, 662.

163. General Weed's Third Brigade belonged to Ayers' division. Ibid., 634, 646.

164. Wyckoff, "Kershaw's Brigade," 45.

165. Jorgensen, "Anderson Attacks the Wheatfield," 74.

166. Campbell, "Caldwell Clears the Wheatfield," 49; OR, vol. 27, pt. 2:400; Kershaw, "Kershaw's Brigade at Gettysburg," *B&L*, 3:337.

167. George Hillyer, "Battle of Gettysburg." Address before the Walton County, Georgia, Confederate Veterans, August 2, 1904. Captain Hillyer commanded the brigade at day's end. OR, vol. 27, pt. 2:401.

168. OR, vol. 27, pt. 1:133; James A. Woods, "Defending Watson's Battery," *Gettysburg Magazine* 9 (July 1993): 45.

169. OR, vol. 27, pt. 1:483, 533; Pfanz, *Gettysburg: The Second Day*, 346–47.

170. Kevin E. O'Brien, "To Unflinchingly Face Danger and Death: Carr's Brigade Defends Emmitsburg Road," *Gettysburg Magazine* 12 (January 1995): 16.

171. Pfanz, *Gettysburg: The Second Day*, 348.

172. O'Brien, "Carr's Brigade," 17; OR, vol. 27, pt. 1:554.

173. Heiser, "Action on the Emmitsburg Road," 81; Pfanz, *Gettysburg: The Second Day*, 348–49; OR, vol. 27, pt. 1:568.

174. OR, vol. 27, pt. 1:422, 426. See also pt. 2:608, 614, 618, 631.

175. O'Brien, "Carr's Brigade," 18.

176. Thomas L. Elmore, "The Florida Brigade at Gettysburg," *Gettysburg Magazine* 15 (July 1996): 48; Pfanz, *Gettysburg: The Second Day*, 374.

177. Heiser, "Action on the Emmitsburg Road," 83; OR, vol. 27, pt. 1:543.

178. O'Brien, "Carr's Brigade," 19.

179. OR, vol. 27, pt. 1:370, 533.

180. Letter, David Lang to Edward A. Perry, July 19, 1863, reprinted in Francis P. Fleming, "Florida Brigade at Gettysburg," *SHSP* 27 (1899): 195.

181. Pfanz, *Gettysburg: The Second Day*, 376.

182. Elmore, "The Florida Brigade," 48; OR, vol. 27, pt. 1:880.

183. Elmore, "The Florida Brigade," 50; Ladd and Ladd, *The Bachelder Papers*, 3:1652.

184. Pfanz, *Gettysburg: The Second Day*, 377; Winschel, "Their Supreme Moment," 76.

185. McNeily, "Barksdale's Brigade at Gettysburg," 236, 243.

186. OR, vol. 27, pt. 2:623.

187. Pfanz, *Gettysburg: The Second Day*, 384; Heiser, "Action on the Emmitsburg Road," 83; OR, vol. 27, pt. 1:426.

188. OR, vol. 27, pt. 1:423.

189. OR, vol. 27, pt. 2:629.

190. OR, vol. 27, pt. 1:478; Pfanz, *Gettysburg: The Second Day*, 287.

191. OR, vol. 27, pt. 1:436.

192. Ibid., 417.

193. Ladd and Ladd, *The Bachelder Papers*, 1:339; 2:1134–35.

194. Ladd and Ladd, *The Bachelder Papers*, 1:340; William A. Love, "Mississippi at Gettysburg," ed. Franklin L. Riley, Oxford: Publications of the Mississippi Historical Society, 9 (1906): 32.

195. Winschel, "Their Supreme Moment," 76.

196. Pfanz, *Gettysburg: The Second Day*, 404–5; OR, vol. 27, pt. 1:475.

197. Ladd and Ladd, *The Bachelder Papers*, 1:339–40, 481.

198. Robert A. Moore, *A Life for the Confederacy*, ed. James W. Silver (Wilmington, N.C.: Broadfoot Publishing Company, 1991, reprint), 153. See also Ladd and Ladd, *The Bachelder Papers*, 1:481.

199. Eric Campbell, "'Remember Harper's Ferry': The Degradation, Humiliation, and Redemption of Col. George L. Willard's Brigade," *Gettysburg Magazine* 7 (July 1992): 69–73; OR, vol. 27, pt. 1:472, 475.

200. Ladd and Ladd, *The Bachelder Papers*, 1:315; OR, vol. 27, 1:474.

201. Ladd and Ladd, *The Bachelder Papers*, 1:481. Longstreet ordered Wofford's withdrawal. Tucker, *Lee and Longstreet*, 66.

202. Coddington, *Gettysburg Campaign*, 418.

203. General Williams stated in his report that he received the order between 5:00 and 6:00 P.M. OR, vol. 27, pt. 1:759, 773; Ladd and Ladd, *The Bachelder Papers*, 1:215; Pfanz, *Gettysburg: Culp's Hill and Cemetery Hill*, 195.

204. OR, vol. 27, pt. 1:826, 856. For a review of the decision to denude Culp's Hill of its defenders, see A. Wilson Greene, "Henry W. Slocum and the Twelfth Corps," *The Second Day at Gettysburg: Essays on Confederate and Union Leadership* (Kent, Ohio: The Kent State University Press, 1993), 113–17.

205. Pfanz, *Gettysburg: Culp's Hill and Cemetery Hill*, 197–98.

206. Greene, "Henry W. Slocum and the Twelfth Corps," 120–21.

207. Robert W. Meinhard, "The First Minnesota at Gettysburg," *Gettysburg Magazine* 5 (July 1991): 81. Company F had been detached to serve as skirmishers. OR, vol. 27, pt. 1:424. Company L, 2nd Minnesota Sharpshooters, attached to the 1st Minnesota, fought in the area of Ziegler's Grove. Pfanz, *Gettysburg: The Second Day*, 550 n. 85. Company C served as division provost guard. Ladd and Ladd, *The Bachelder Papers*, 1:258.

208. Ladd and Ladd, *The Bachelder Papers*, 1:257; 2:1135; OR, vol. 27, pt. 1:371; Glenn Tucker, *Hancock The Superb* (Indianapolis: The Bobbs-Merrill Company, Inc., 1960), 145.

209. OR, vol. 27, pt. 1:425; Richard Moe, *The Last Full Measure: The Life and Death of the First Minnesota Volunteers* (New York: Henry Holt and Company, 1993), 269–70.

210. Meinhard, "The First Minnesota at Gettysburg," 82–83; Ladd and Ladd, *The Bachelder Papers*, 1:257–58.

211. Ladd and Ladd, *The Bachelder Papers*, 1:258; 2:960, 962. The 1st Minnesota lost 82 percent of its members who participated in the critical charge and though Ken Burns claims it suffered the highest rate of loss in the battle, the regiment's actual percentage of loss was 67.9 percent. The 24th Michigan and 25th Ohio lost 83.7 percent and 83.6 percent respectively. Busey and Martin, *Regimental Strengths*, 262.

212. OR, vol. 27, pt. 2:618.

213. Terrence J. Winschel, "Posey's Brigade at Gettysburg, Part 2," *Gettysburg Magazine* 5 (July 1991): 90–98; OR, vol. 27, pt. 2:633.

214. Freeman, *Lee's Lieutenants*, 3:125.

215. Freeman, *Lee's Lieutenants*, 3:127–28. Mahone's battle report begins: "The operations of this brigade in the battle of Gettysburg, Pa., may be summed up in a few brief remarks." Six succinct sentences follow. By comparison, the reports of Wright and Wilcox cover four pages. OR, vol. 27, pt. 2:616–25. For an examination of Mahone's conduct, see Bradley M. Gottfried, "Mahone's Brigade: Insubordination or Miscommunication?", *Gettysburg Magazine* 18 (January 1998).

216. Sorrel, *Confederate Staff Officer*, 242.

217. Coddington, *Gettysburg Campaign*, 421, 425. For a discussion of scenarios where Mahone's brigade could have assisted Wilcox, Lang, and Wright see Gottfried, "Mahone's Brigade," 74.

218. Tucker, *High Tide*, 288–89.

219. General Newton previously commanded the Third Division, VI Corps. OR, vol. 27, pt. 1:163, 258, 261.

220. OR, vol. 27, pt. 1:371.

221. Ibid., 1:258. The 13th Vermont's right wing consisted of Companies A, B, C, E and G. Pfanz, *Gettysburg: The Second Day*, 551 n. 97. The 13th Vermont's left wing remained on Cemetery Hill supporting a battery. OR, vol. 27, pt. 1:349.

222. Ibid., 351–52.

223. Pfanz, *Gettysburg: The Second Day*, 417, 422; OR, vol. 27, pt. 1:352, pt. 2:624.

224. OR, vol. 27, pt. 1:533.

225. Ibid., 608.

226. OR, vol. 27, pt. 2:631–32. Lang may have been misled by the movement of Willard's brigade as it passed across his front. Campbell, "Remember Harper's Ferry," 73.

227. OR, vol. 27, pt. 2:618.

228. Heiser, "Action on the Emmitsburg Road," 84.

229. OR, vol. 27, pt. 2:624.

230. Ibid., 343, 624, 629.

231. Anthony W. McDermott, *A Brief History of the 69th Regiment Pennsylvania Veteran Volunteers, from its Formation Until Final Muster Out of the U.S. Service* (Philadelphia: D. J. Gallagher & Company, 1889), 28.

232. OR, vol. 27, pt. 1:553, 559.

233. O'Brien, "Carr's Brigade," 21–22.

234. Pfanz, *Gettysburg: The Second Day*, 423–24.

235. General Meade used this term for Little Round Top in his report. OR, vol. 27, pt. 116.

CHAPTER 5

1. Joseph C. Mayo, "Pickett's Charge at Gettysburg," *SHSP* 34 (1906): 328.

2. David E. Johnston, *The Story of a Confederate Boy in the Civil War* (Radford, Va.: Commonwealth Press, Inc., 1980, reprint), 197–98.

3. John H. Lewis, *Recollections from 1860 to 1865: With Incidents of Camp Life, Descriptions of Battles, the Life of the Southern Soldier, His Hardships and Sufferings, and the Life of a Prisoner of War in the Northern Prisons* (Dayton: Morningside, 1983, reprint), 80; Johnston, *Confederate Boy*, 198.

4. Walter Harrison, *Pickett's Men: A Fragment of War History* (New York: D. Van Norstrand, 1870, reprint), 88.

5. Charles. T. Loehr, *War History of the Old First Virginia Regiment, Army of Northern Virginia* (Richmond: Wm. Ellis Jones, Book and Job Printer, 1884, reprint), 36.

6. Tucker, *Lee and Longstreet*, 68–70. "Pickett's men could have gone into battle...when they reached Gettysburg." Charles T. Loehr, "The First Virginia Infantry at the Battle of Gettysburg, and the Charge of Pickett's Division," *SHSP* 32 (1904): 40. "As events of the battle of the 2d passed, it seems fair to claim that with Pickett's brigades present at the moment of Wofford's advance for the gorge at Little Round Top, we would have had it before Crawford was there." James Longstreet, *From Manassas to Appomattox, Memoirs of the Civil War in America* (Philadelphia: J. B. Lippincott Company, 1896), 377.

7. Harrison, *Pickett's Men*, 88.

8. Early, *Memoirs*, 272.

9. OR, vol. 27, pt. 2:446.

10. Freeman, *Lee's Lieutenants*, 3:128–29. "As events finally unfolded, however, Ewell neither planned nor fought well." Coddington, *Gettysburg Campaign*, 428.

11. OR, vol. 27, pt. 2:446. Due to a lack of suitable positions, only 32 of approximately 80 Second Corps cannon became "actively engaged on July 2." Coddington, *Gettysburg Campaign*, 428.

12. Pfanz, *Gettysburg: Culp's Hill and Cemetery Hill*, 169–70. Andrews was wounded at Winchester. OR, vol. 27, pt. 2:442, 542.

13. Jay Jorgensen, "Joseph W. Latimer, 'The Boy Major,' at Gettysburg," *Gettysburg Magazine* 10 (January 1994): 32–33. See also Ladd and Ladd, *The Bachelder Papers*, 3:1621.

14. Pfanz, *Gettysburg: Culp's Hill and Cemetery Hill*, 170–71.

15. Jorgensen, "The Boy Major," 33; Pfanz, *Gettysburg: Culp's Hill and Cemetery Hill*, 171; Robert Stiles, *Four Years under Marse Robert* (Dayton: Morningside, 1977, reprint), 217–18; OR, vol. 27, pt. 2:456, 504, 542.

16. Coddington, *Gettysburg Campaign*, 428–29.

17. OR, vol. 27, pt. 2:447.

18. Marshall D. Krolick, "Forgotten Field: The Cavalry Battle East of Gettysburg on July 3, 1863," *Gettysburg Magazine* 4 (January 1991): 76, 78; Pfanz, *Gettysburg: Culp's Hill and Cemetery Hill*, 162–64.

19. OR, vol. 27, pt. 2:544.

20. Transported back to Virginia, Latimer died August 1, less than a month before his 20th birthday. Jorgensen, "The Boy Major," 29, 33–34.

21. OR, vol. 27, pt. 2:539; Wayne E. Motts, "To Gain a Second Star: The Forgotten George S. Greene," *Gettysburg Magazine* 3 (July 1990): 71.

22. Ibid. See also Ladd and Ladd, *The Bachelder Papers*, 1:294.

23. OR, vol. 27, pt. 2:537–38.

24. OR, vol. 27, pt. 1:861; pt. 2:537.

25. Mott, "The Forgotten George S. Greene," 71; Pfanz, *Gettysburg: Culp's Hill and Cemetery Hill*, 216; OR, vol. 27, pt. 2:513.

26. OR, vol. 27, pt. 1:731, 856–57. Rufus Dawes opined: "The breastworks on Culp[']s Hill undoubtedly saved us a great disaster on the night of the second day." Ladd and Ladd, *The Bachelder Papers*, 1:326.

27. Pfanz, *Gettysburg: Culp's Hill and Cemetery Hill*, 217–18, 221.

28. OR, vol. 27, pt. 1:372; Ladd and Ladd, *The Bachelder Papers*, 1:294–95.

29. OR, vol. 27, pt. 1:427, 432.

30. Thomas L. Elmore, "Courage Against the Trenches: The Attack and Repulse of Steuart's Brigade on Culp's Hill," *Gettysburg Magazine* 7 (July 1992): 85–86; George A. Thayer, "Gettysburg, as We Men on the Right Saw It," *Sketches of War History: 1861–1865, Papers Prepared for the Ohio Commandery of the Military Order of the Loyal Legion of the United States*, 3 vols., ed. Robert Hunter (Cincinnati: Robert Clarke & Co., 1890), 3:37.

31. Jay Jorgensen, "Holding the Right: The 137th New York Regiment at Gettysburg," *Gettysburg Magazine* 15 (July 1996): 66.

32. Pfanz, *Gettysburg: Culp's Hill and Cemetery Hill*, 222.

33. Ladd and Ladd, *The Bachelder Papers*, 1:326.

34. Elmore, "Courage Against the Trenches," 88.

35. OR, vol. 27, pt. 1:774, 865; pt. 2:510.

36. OR, vol. 27, pt. 1:847, 857, 867.

37. Jorgensen, "Holding the Right," 60, 67. The 137th New York and 20th Maine both lost 32.4 percent of their strength. Busey and Martin, *Regimental Strengths*, 248, 257.

38. OR, vol. 27, pt. 1:780, 813, 870; Ladd and Ladd, *The Bachelder Papers*, 1:219.

39. Pfanz, *Gettysburg: Culp's Hill and Cemetery Hill*, 167.

40. OR, vol. 27, pt. 2:470; Early, *Memoirs*, 273.

41. OR, vol. 27, pt. 2:480; pt. 1:718; Pfanz, *Gettysburg: Culp's Hill and Cemetery Hill*, 235, 244, 251–52.

42. General Ames took command of the First Division when Barlow was wounded. OR, vol. 27, pt. 1:706, 712–13.

43. Ladd and Ladd, *The Bachelder Papers*, 2:745. Colonel Harris assumed brigade command when Adelbert Ames took over the division. OR, vol. 27, pt. 1:713.

44. OR, vol. 27, pt. 2:480; Thomas E. Causby, "Storming the Stone Fence at Gettysburg," *SHSP* 29 (1901): 340.

45. Terry L. Jones, *Lee's Tigers: The Louisiana Infantry in the Army of Northern Virginia* (Baton Rouge: Louisiana State University Press, 1987), 172; OR, vol. 27, pt. 2:471.

46. Ladd and Ladd, *The Bachelder Papers*, 2:746.

47. Pfanz, *Gettysburg: Culp's Hill and Cemetery Hill*, Map, 238, 256–58; Eric A. Campbell, "'A Field Made Glorious': Cemetery Hill: From Battlefield to Sacred Ground," *Gettysburg Magazine* 15 (July 1996): 115 n. 46.

48. Pfanz, *Gettysburg: Culp's Hill and Cemetery Hill*, 260–61. The New Yorkers apparently abandoned the wall without discharging a volley. Ladd and Ladd, *The Bachelder Papers*, 1:236.

49. OR, vol. 27, pt. 2:484–86.

50. Ladd and Ladd, *The Bachelder Papers*, 1:236–38; 2:980.

51. Pfanz, *Gettysburg: Culp's Hill and Cemetery Hill*, 269; Ladd and Ladd, *The Bachelder Papers*, 1:311–12.

52. In General Ames' opinion, the Second and Third Divisions contributed nothing to the defense of Cemetery Hill. Ladd and Ladd, *The Bachelder Papers*, 1:149, 236. Capt. Emil Koenig, 58th New York, reported that the enemy column "was repulsed before we arrived." Maj. Benjamin A. Willis, 119th New York, remembered circumstances differently. "It is needless for me to say, general [Schurz], for you led us in person, with what alacrity the regiment responded, and with what determination it moved forward, and with what courage it met the foe, and, in conjunction with the gallant Fifty-eighth, drove him back, saved the position, and thus secured the army from irreparable disaster." OR, vol. 27, pt. 1:706, 731, 740, 743.

53. Ladd and Ladd, *The Bachelder Papers*, 3:1359. See also 1:236; OR, vol. 27, pt. 1:372.

54. Gibbon, *Personal Recollections*, 138.

55. OR, vol. 27, pt. 1:126, 417.

56. Ibid., 127. Gibbon also sent the 71st Pennsylvania, which wandered over to Culp's Hill instead. The 106th Pennsylvania arrived on the scene when the fight was over. Pfanz, *Gettysburg: Culp's Hill and Cemetery Hill*, 264.

57. Ladd and Ladd, *The Bachelder Papers*, 3:1419; Tucker, *High Tide*, 289.

58. Letter, Capt. David E. Beem, Company H, 14th Indiana, to his wife, July 5, 1863. Box 1, Folder 9, Indiana Historical Society, Indianapolis; OR, vol. 27, pt. 1:460, 463; Pfanz, *Gettysburg: Culp's Hill and Cemetery Hill*, 268.

59. According to Capt. James F. Huntington, who commanded a brigade of Reserve Artillery on Cemetery Hill: "I say and I believe it can be *proved* that the prompt and gallant action of Col. Carroll *saved the Hill* that Thursday evening and the value of that service it is hard to overestimate." Quoted in Gibbon, *Personal Recollections*, 206. Captain Weidrich credited Ames' two brigades for saving his guns. Ladd and Ladd, *The Bachelder Papers*, 2:1182.

60. OR, vol. 27, pt. 1:457.

61. Ibid., 372. Captain Ricketts professed that Carroll "arrived at the moment, when, if I had received no support, my men would have been overpowered…all the credit due to the infantry in that affair is due to Carroll's brigade alone." Ladd and Ladd, *The Bachelder Papers*, 1:236.

62. Ladd and Ladd, *The Bachelder Papers*, 2:977; The 8th Ohio had been detached to reinforce XI Corps' skirmish line on the left. OR, vol. 27, pt. 1:457, 459, 461.

63. OR, vol. 27, pt. 2:486.

64. Pfanz, *Gettysburg: Culp's and Cemetery Hill*, 271–72.

65. Jones, *Lee's Tigers*, 173.

66. Letter, Captain Beem to his wife, July 5, 1863. General Howard told Hancock afterwards that Carroll's brigade reached Cemetery Hill "'just in the nick of time,' and undoubtedly saved the hill from falling into possession of the enemy." Ladd and Ladd, *The Bachelder Papers*, 3:1359. See also OR, vol. 27, pt. 1:127, 873.

67. OR, vol. 27, pt. 2:481.

68. Ibid., pt. 1:457, 459.

69. "They said it was always so; if there was any hard fighting, they were always the first to be brought in, and then there was no help given them. They said their officers didn't care how many were killed, and especially old Hays, who was receiving his share of the curses. The truth of the story I can't vouch for;

I only tell it as it was told me..." Austin C. Stearns, 13th Massachusetts, was captured July 1 while trying to make Cemetery Hill. Austin C. Stearns, *Three Years with Company K*, ed. Arthur A. Kent (Cranbury, N.J.: Associated University Presses, Inc., 1976), 191–92.

70. Freeman, *Lee's Lieutenants*, 3:134; OR, vol. 27, pt. 2:485.

71. OR, vol. pt. 2:447, 470.

72. Freeman, *Lee's Lieutenants*, 3:177. "...Rodes failed to synchronize the movement of his division with the rest of Ewell's corps." Coddington, *Gettysburg Campaign*, 429.

73. Due to infection, Pender's leg was amputated; he died at Staunton, Virginia, July 18. Warner, *Generals in Gray*, 233–34.

74. OR, vol. 27, pt. 2:556, 665–66.

75. Ibid., 556, 587–88.

76. Ibid., 470; Pfanz, *Gettysburg: Culp's Hill and Cemetery Hill*, 276. "Extra Billy" Smith's three regiments remained isolated from the division and "...along with Gordon, might have been sent in with Avery and Hays, or at least in support of them. Since two brigades achieved a near success unaided, it is not unreasonable to believe that four brigades could have carried and held Cemetery Hill." Tucker, *Lee and Longstreet*, 48, 243.

77. Freeman, *Lee's Lieutenants*, 135 n. 34, 178.

78. Freeman, *R. E. Lee*, 3:102. See also Coddington, *Gettysburg Campaign*, 439–40.

79. Montgomery, *Shaping of a Battle*, 120.

80. Coddington, *Gettysburg Campaign*, 444–45.

81. Arthur J. L. Fremantle, *Three Months in the Southern States* (Lincoln: University of Nebraska Press, 1991, reprint), 259–60.

82. Tucker, *Lee and Longstreet*, 237.

83. Pfanz, *Gettysburg: The Second Day*, 414.

84. Walter H. Taylor, "The Campaign In Pennsylvania," *Annals of the War*, 311.

85. Coddington, *Gettysburg Campaign*, 449–51.

86. John Gibbon, "The Council of War on the Second Day," *B&L*, 3:313.

CHAPTER 6

1. Coddington, *Gettysburg Campaign*, 443, 768 n. 4.

2. OR, vol. 27, pt. 2:308.

3. Ibid., 308, 320.

4. Ibid., 320.

5. William Garrett Piston, "Longstreet, Lee, and Confederate Plans for July 3 at Gettysburg," *The Third Day at Gettysburg & Beyond: Essays on Confederate and Union Leadership*, ed. Gary W. Gallagher (Chapel Hill: The University of North Carolina Press, 1994), 45–46; OR, vol. 27, pt. 2:447.

6. Pfanz, *Gettysburg: Culp's Hill and Cemetery Hill*, 287–89. The 5th Alabama remained on guard duty in Gettysburg. OR, vol. 27, pt. 2:596.

7. OR, vol. 27, pt. 1:780, 870.

8. Kevin O'Brien, "'A Perfect Roar of Musketry': Candy's Brigade in the Fight for Culp's Hill," *Gettysburg Magazine* 9 (July 1993): 87–90; OR, vol. 27, pt. 2:519. "The hillside was considered too steep and its approaches too difficult to drag guns into position or to bring them to bear from the east side of Rock Creek." Fairfax Downey, *The Guns at Gettysburg* (New York: David McKay Company, Inc., 1958), 115.

9. OR, vol. 27, pt. 1:844; Pfanz, *Gettysburg: Culp's Hill and Cemetery Hill*, 295–96.

10. O'Brien, "'A Perfect Roar of Musketry,'" 92.

11. Elmore, "Courage Against the Trenches," 94.

12. George Thomas, "The Maryland Confederate Monument at Gettysburg: Address of Captain Thomas," *SHSP* 14 (1886): 45–46.

13. Pfanz, *Gettysburg: Culp's Hill and Cemetery Hill*, 316–18; OR, vol. 27, pt. 1:846. Four companies of the 1st North Carolina and the 10th Virginia did not participate in the charge. OR, vol. 27, pt. 2:511.

14. Elmore, "Courage Against the Trenches," 94.

15. Clark, *North Carolina Regiments*, 1:195.

16. Pfanz, *Gettysburg: Culp's Hill and Cemetery Hill*, 320.

17. OR, vol. 27, pt. 2:504.

18. Ibid., pt. 1:777, 781.

19. Ibid., pt. 2:505; pt. 1:814.

20. Elmore, "Courage Against the Trenches," 94.

21. Thomas, "The Maryland Confederate Monument," 46.

22. OR, vol. 27, pt. 1:808.

23. Ladd and Ladd, *The Bachelder Papers,* 1:636. In 1861, when the Eastern Shore Regiment was ordered into eastern Virginia, members of Company A refused. Capt. John C. Henry led away a group of men who enlisted in the Southern ranks. John E. Rastall, "Union Soldier Slave Owners," *CV* 7 (September 1899): 408.

24. Armistead L. Long, *Memoirs of Robert E. Lee* (New York: J. M. Stoddart & Company, 1887), 287–88. Porter Alexander commented: "It seems remarkable that the assumption of Col. Long so easily passed unchallenged that Confederate guns in open and inferior positions could 'suppress' Federal artillery fortified upon commanding ridges." Alexander, *Military Memoirs*, 416. "General Lee did not consider the Federal position at Gettysburg stronger than many others that army had occupied…" Letter, William Allan to William Jones, April 27, 1877, *SHSP* 80.

25. Longstreet, *From Manassas to Appomattox*, 386. For a summary of the impracticality of utilizing McLaws and Hood in Longstreet's assault, see Benjamin G. Humphreys, "Delayed Report of an Important Eyewitness to Gettysburg," *The Journal of Mississippi History,* vol. 46, 4 (November 1984): 314–17.

26. Longstreet, "Lee in Pennsylvania," *Annals of the War,* 429; Longstreet, "Lee's Right Wing at Gettysburg," *B&L,* 3:342–43.

27. William H. Palmer to T. M. R. Talcott, April 11, 1916, "The Third Day At Gettysburg," *SHSP* 41 (1916): 40.

28. Freeman, *R. E. Lee*, 3:108. Discussion between Longstreet and Lee concerning employment of the entire First Corps must have entered only a preliminary stage. According to Lafayette McLaws: "I was not notified that it was in contemplation even to make any further attack by either Hood's or my division, nor was I informed that it was the intention to assault the enemy's centre with Pickett's division, with the assistance of troops from other corps. I was not told to be ready to assist, should the assault be successful, nor instructed what to do should the assault fail and the enemy advance." McLaws, "Gettysburg," 79.

29. OR, vol. 27, pt. 2:320.

30. Ibid., 650.

31. Stewart, *Pickett's Charge*, 38–39; Love, "Mississippi at Gettysburg," 44.

32. James I. Metts, *Longstreet's Charge at Gettysburg, Pa. Pickett's, Pettigrew's and Trimble's Divs.* (Wilmington, N.C.: *Morning Star Press*, 1899), 9–10; Clark, *North Carolina Regiments*, 5:125.

33. OR, vol. 27, pt. 2:650.

34. Stewart, *Pickett's Charge*, 40.

35. OR, vol. 27, pt. 2:670–71.

36. Ibid., 665, 667.

37. Colonel Perrin described the action on Pender's front as "the heaviest skirmishing I have ever witnessed..." OR, vol. 27, pt. 2:659, 663, 666–67, 669. Lt. Thomas F. Galwey, Company B, 8th Ohio, related an incident on the skirmish line. A solitary tree stood between the lines "which became conspicuous on account of the well-aimed shots that came from it."

    We soon became aware that a couple of bold enemy sharpshooters had crawled up to it and were now practicing on any thoughtless man who offered himself as a mark. About the middle of the forenoon a cry of, "Don't fire, Yanks!" rang out, and we all got up to see what was coming. A man with his gun slung across his shoulder came out from the tree. Several of our fellows aimed at him but the others checked them, to see what would follow. The man had a canteen in his hand and, when he had come about half-way to us, we saw him (God bless him) kneel down and give a drink to one of our wounded who lay there beyond us. Of course we cheered the Reb, and someone shouted, "Bully for you! Johnny!" Whilst this was going on, we had all risen to our feet. The enemy too, having ceased to fire, were also standing. As soon as the sharpshooter had finished his generous work, he turned around and went back to the tree, and then at the top of his voice shouted, "Down Yanks, we're going to fire." And down we lay again.

    Thomas Francis Galwey, *The Valiant Hours: An Irishman in the Civil War*, ed. Wilbur S. Nye (Harrisburg: The Stackpole Company, 1961), 110–11. Before noon, the 8th Ohio lost four killed and 41 wounded. OR, vol. 27, pt. 1:461.

38. Freeman, *Lee's Lieutenants*, 2:182 n. 67; OR, vol. 27, pt. 608.

39. Clark, *North Carolina Regiments*, 5:661.

40. Longstreet, "Lee's Right Wing at Gettysburg," *B&L*, 3:343.

41. Ladd and Ladd, *The Bachelder Papers*, 3:1899; Johnston, *Confederate Boy*, 203.

42. Harrison, *Pickett's Men*, 90–91. The number given for troops committed by Pickett to Longstreet's Assault is derived from the total strength of the division, minus Maj. James Dearing's Artillery Battalion and divisional staff. Kathy Georg Harrison and John W. Busey, *Nothing But Glory: Pickett's Division at Gettysburg* (Gettysburg: Thomas Publications, 1993 edition), 452, 467.

43. OR, vol. 27, pt. 2:320, 619, 632.

44. Wert, *General James Longstreet*, 286–87.

45. Randolph A. Shotwell, *Three Years in Battle and Three in Federal Prisons*, 3 vols. (Raleigh: The North Carolina Historical Commission, 1931), 2:4; OR, vol. 27, pt. 2:385.

46. Rawley W. Martin and John H. Smith, "The Battle of Gettysburg and the Charge of Pickett's Division," *SHSP* 32 (1904): 184; *Supplement to the Official Records of the Union and Confederate Armies*, pt. 1–reports, vol. 5, ser. 5, Janet B. Hewett et al., eds. (Wilmington, N.C.: Broadfoot Publishing Company, 1995), 327. Hereafter *Supplement*.

47. Ladd and Ladd, *The Bachelder Papers*, 2:776.

48. OR, vol. 27, pt. 1:417.

49. Clark, *North Carolina Regiments*, 5:104; Coddington, *Gettysburg Campaign*, 476. Carroll's brigade—less the 8th Ohio—remained at Cemetery Hill. OR, vol. 27, pt. 1:261, 457, 472–73.

50. Gary G. Lash, "The Philadelphia Brigade at Gettysburg," *Gettysburg Magazine* 7 (July 1992): 102. Most of the 106th Pennsylvania remained with XI Corps. OR, vol. 27, pt. 1:434.

51. Edmund Rice, "Repelling Lee's Last Blow at Gettysburg," *B&L*, 3:387; OR, vol. 27, pt. 1:420.

52. OR, vol. 27, pt. 1:427.

53. Ladd and Ladd, *The Bachelder Papers*, 3:1403.

54. OR, vol. 27, pt. 1:419, 423, 445.

55. Ibid., pt. 1:238, 478–79; Hunt, "The Third Day at Gettysburg," *B&L*, 3:371.

56. Lt. Louis G. Young was aide-de-camp to General Pettigrew. *Supplement*, 416, 418–19.

57. Birkett D. Fry, "Pettigrew's Charge at Gettysburg," *SHSP* 7 (1879): 92.

58. Freeman, *R. E. Lee*, 3:111. See also Alexander, *Fighting for the Confederacy*, 280.

59. Longstreet, "Lee's Right Wing at Gettysburg," *B&L*, 3:343; OR, vol. 27, pt. 2:320, 678.

60. OR, vol. 27, pt. 2:320, 678.

61. Alexander, *Military Memoirs*, 418.

62. Alexander, *Fighting for the Confederacy*, 247. Alexander mistakenly added two guns in his memoir. Ladd and Ladd, *The Bachelder Papers*, 1:486.

63. Alexander, *Military Memoirs*, 419.

64. Downey, *Guns at Gettysburg*, 117. After Major Latimer was incapacitated, his battalion was commanded by Capt. Charles I. Raine. OR, vol. 27, pt. 2:544, 675.

65. Alexander, *Military Memoirs*, 419; Wise, *The Long Arm of Lee*, 2:666–67. The precise number of Confederate guns involved in the preliminary cannonade is unknown. Coddington, *Gettysburg Campaign*, 785 n. 94.

66. Ladd and Ladd, *The Bachelder Papers*, 1:484.

67. Letter, Edward P. Alexander to J. William Jones, March 17, 1872, "Causes of Lee's Defeat at Gettysburg," *SHSP* 4 (1877): 104.

68. Freeman, *R. E. Lee*, 3:109.

69. Longstreet, "Lee in Pennsylvania," *Annals of the War,* 430.

70. Alexander, *Fighting for the Confederacy*, 254.

71. Alexander, "Causes of Lee's Defeat at Gettysburg," 104.

72. Alexander, *Fighting for the Confederacy*, 255.

73. Alexander, *Military Memoirs*, 421.

74. Alexander, *Fighting for the Confederacy*, 255. For a slightly different version of General Wright's views on the attack, see Alexander, *Military Memoirs*, 422; Ladd and Ladd, *The Bachelder Papers*, 1:486.

75. Capt. Merritt B. Miller commanded the Third Company, Washington Artillery. Downey, *Guns at Gettysburg*, 127–28; Wise, *Long Arm of Lee*, 677.

76. OR, vol. 27, pt. 1:239; Alexander, *Fighting for the Confederacy*, 257. General Hunt's count does not include batteries on Cemetery Hill. The exact number of Union guns that dueled with the Confederates is impossible to ascertain because batteries were replaced during the cannonade. See Coddington, *Gettysburg Campaign*, 789 n. 24.

77. A. H. Moore, "Heth's Division at Gettysburg," *The Southern Bivouac* 3 (May 1885): 389–90.

78. Hunt, "The Third Day at Gettysburg," *B&L*, 3:371–72. Hazlett died on the evening of July 2. OR, vol. 27, pt. 1:238–39, 660.

79. Francis A. Walker, "General Hancock and the Artillery at Gettysburg," *B&L*, 3:385–86; Ladd and Ladd, *The Bachelder Papers*, 3:1361; Henry J. Hunt, "Rejoinder by Henry J. Hunt," *B&L*, 3:386–87.

80. Frank Haskell, *The Battle of Gettysburg*, ed. Bruce Catton (Boston: Houghton Mifflin Company, 1958, reprint), 88.

81. Gibbon, *Personal Recollections*, 149.

82. Haskell, *The Battle of Gettysburg*, 90. Rebel cannoneers in Hill's Corps cut their fuses a quarter mile too long. Stewart, *Pickett's Charge*, 145–46.

83. Hunt, "The Third Day at Gettysburg," *B&L*, 3:373; OR, vol. 27, pt. 1:239.

84. Ernest Linden Waitt, *History of the Nineteenth Regiment Massachusetts Volunteer Infantry, 1861–1865* (Salem: Salem Press Company, 1905), 235.

85. Gibbon, *Personal Recollections*, 147.

86. Waitt, *History of the Nineteenth Regiment*, 238.

87. John W. Plummer, "John W. Plummer's Account," *Rebellion Record*, 10:180.

88. Gibbon, *Personal Recollections*, 147–49.

89. Charles P. Page, *History of the Fourteenth Regiment, Connecticut Volunteer Infantry* (Meriden: Horton Printing Company, 1906), 149.

90. George H. Washburn, *A Complete Military History and Record of the 108th Regiment N.Y. Volunteers, from 1862 to 1894, Together with Roster, Letters, Rebel Oaths of Allegiance, Rebel Passes, Reminiscences, Life Sketches, Photographs, Etc.* (Rochester: E. R. Andrews, 1894), 50.

91. Galwey, *The Valiant Hours*, 106, 113.

92. Franklin Sawyer, *8th Ohio Volunteer Infantry: Gibraltar Brigade Army of the Potomac* (Huntington, W.Va.: Blue Acorn, 1994, reprint), 130.

93. Richard Irby, *Historical Sketch of the Nottoway Grays, Afterwards Company G, Eighteenth Virginia Regiment, Army of Northern Virginia* (Richmond: J. W. Ferguson & Son, 1878), 27.

94. Shotwell, *Three Years in Battle*, 2:12; Walthall, "Dear Children," 28. David S. Edwards, Company D, 1st Virginia "received a *wound* which fractured his right arm..." Captured at the division field hospital, Edwards was transferred to Letterman Hospital, July 12, and died, September 11. Tazewell S. Morton, Company D, 1st Virginia "received *wounds* which fractured his lower jaw and injured his left arm." Harrison and Busey, *Nothing But Glory*, 185–86. During the charge, Walthall crawled to the top of a hill with 15 other members of Company D. Loehr, *War History*, 36.

95. Johnston, *Confederate Boy*, 206; *Supplement*, 308, 311.

96. "Report of Col. Joseph Mayo, 3rd Virginia, July 25, 1863," reprinted in *Pickett's Charge!: Eyewitness Accounts*, ed. Richard Rollins (Redondo Beach, Ca.: Rank and File Publications, 1996 edition), 156.

97. Johnston, *Confederate Boy*, 207, 217.

98. Joseph C. Mayo, "Pickett's Charge at Gettysburg," *SHSP* 34 (1906): 330; Harrison and Busey, *Nothing But Glory*, 199. Mayo states that the legs of Lt. Azra P. Gomer were shattered. Rather, Gomer was severely wounded in the leg during the assault. See Azra P. Gomer, "Service of Third Virginia Infantry," *CV* 18 (May 1910): 228.

99. OR, vol. 27, pt. 2:999.

100. "Col. and Dr. R. W. Martin, of Virginia," *CV* 5 (February 1897): 70.

101. Alexander Iredell, *Historical Sketches of the Seventh Regiment North Carolina Troops* (Mooresville: Mooresville Publishing Company, 1893,) 35. Brigade reports for Pettigrew, Archer, Lane, and Scales do not mention casualties during the cannonade. Davis' brigade lost two men killed and 21 wounded. See OR, vol. pt. 2:643, 647, 650, 666, 671.

102. Johnston, *Confederate Boy*, 207; Shotwell, *Three Years in Battle*, 2:8.

103. Ladd and Ladd, *The Bachelder Papers*, 1:489.

104. Alexander, *Military Memoirs*, 422–23.

105. Alexander, *Fighting for the Confederacy*, 259. The most effective Confederate fire of the barrage was delivered against batteries on Cemetery Hill. See Coddington, *Gettysburg Campaign*, 494–95.

106. Tucker, *Hancock the Superb*, 149.

107. OR, vol. 27, pt. 1:239, 480.

108. Kent Masterson Brown, *Cushing of Gettysburg: The Story of a Union Artillery Commander* (Lexington: University Press of Kentucky, 1993), 235–36, 238; OR, vol. 27, pt. 1:480.

109. OR, vol. 27, pt. 1:883, 885, 888–98.

110. Writing in 1901, Louis E. Pattison, a former member of the 5th Massachusetts Battery, offered a high private's opinion. "Had Hancock let Hunt manage the whole line of artillery, the rebel column would never have reached the copse of trees, and a counter charge should then have been made by our Army, which would have been successful, and much of the slaughter of 1864, would have been avoided." Luther E. Cowles, *History of the Fifth Massachusetts Battery* (Boston, n.p., 1902), 652, 654. Colonel Alexander believed General Hancock's decision was correct. Alexander, *Fighting for the Confederacy*, 260.

111. OR, vol. 27, pt. 1:884.

112. Ibid., 239, 376; Hunt, "The Third Day at Gettysburg," *B&L*, 3:374.

113. McDermott, *A Brief History of the 69th Regiment*, 30; Brown, *Cushing of Gettysburg*, 241.

114. OR, vol. 27, pt. 1:432; Frederick Fuger, "Cushing's Battery at Gettysburg," *Journal of the Military Service Institution of the United States*, 41 (1907): 408, Gettysburg National Military Park; D. Scott Hartwig, "It Struck Horror To Us All," *Gettysburg Magazine* 4 (January 1991): 97.

115. OR, vol. 27, pt. 1:239, 428, 480, 690, 899; Hunt, "The Third Day at Gettysburg," *B&L*, 3:374; "One or two pieces which had been pushed out further to the front were left behind." Page, *History of the Fourteenth Regiment*, 150.

116. Alexander wrote that he sent the first note at 1:25 P.M. and the second note 10 minutes later. It is more likely that he misrecollected the time and it was closer to 2:30 P.M. Alexander, *Fighting for the Confederacy*, 258; Coddington, *Gettysburg Campaign*, 499–500.

117. Stewart, *Pickett's Charge*, 160–61.

118. The "come quick" note arrived after the decision to advance. Alexander, *Fighting for the Confederacy*, 260; Longstreet, "Lee's Right Wing at Gettysburg," *B&L*, 3:344–45; Longstreet, "Lee in Pennsylvania," *Annals of the War*, 430–31.

119. Longstreet, "Lee's Right Wing at Gettysburg," *B&L*, 3:355; Alexander, *Fighting for the Confederacy*, 261. Concerning the disappearance of the howitzers, Alexander believed: "It would not have made any difference in the result of the battle...but I feel bitterly about that to this day. It was such a beautiful chance to handle Arty & to show what it can do & I was only a fool not to have selected

some of my own old battalion for it, being tempted to try this [other] command as their guns were better adapted to close quarters." Ladd and Ladd, *The Bachelder Papers*, 1:488.

120. George W. Finley, "Bloody Angle," *Buffalo Evening News*, May 29, 1894, Gettysburg Newspaper Clippings, vol. 4, Gettysburg National Military Park; Johnston, *Confederate Boy*, 207. Alexander recollected the beginning of the assault as no later than 2:00 P.M., at variance with other accounts. Alexander, *Fighting for the Confederacy*, 261.

121. Henry T. Owen, "Pickett at Gettysburg," *Philadelphia Weekly Times*, March 26, 1881.

122. Mayo, "Pickett's Charge," 331.

123. Johnston, *Confederate Boy*, 207.

124. Martin and Smith, "The Battle of Gettysburg," 188.

125. James E. Poindexter, "General Lewis Addison Armistead," *CV* 22 (November 1914): 503; Harrison and Busey, *Nothing But Glory*, 398.

126. Lewis, *Recollections from 1860 to 1865*, 82; OR, vol. 27, pt. 2:1000. Sergeant Blackburn was mortally wounded. Harrison and Busey, *Nothing But Glory*, 398.

127. For a list of mounted personnel during the attack see Harrison and Busey, *Nothing But Glory*, 137.

128. Finley, "Bloody Angle."

129. Stewart, *Pickett's Charge*, 300–301.

130. OR, vol. 27, pt. 1:448.

131. Waitt, *History of the Nineteenth Regiment*, 237–38; Andrew E. Ford, *The Story of the Fifteenth Massachusetts Volunteer Infantry in the Civil War, 1861–1864* (Clinton: Press of W. J. Coulter, 1898), 276.

132. Ladd and Ladd, *The Bachelder Papers*, 3:1409. "None who saw this magnificent charge of Pickett's column...could refrain from admiring its splendor." Charles P. Banes, *History of the Philadelphia Brigade, Sixty-Ninth, Seventy-First, Seventy-Second and One Hundred Sixth Pennsylvania Volunteers* (Philadelphia: J. B. Lippincott & Co., 1876), 190.

133. Freeman, *Lee's Lieutenants*, 3:182–86. "Heth's division was much larger than Lowrance's brigade and my own [Lane's], which were its only support, and there was consequently no second line in rear of its left." OR, vol. 27, pt. 2:666.

134. Stewart, *Pickett's Charge*, 87.

135. Shotwell, *Three Years in Battle*, 2:17.

136. Alexander, *Fighting for the Confederacy*, 258; Ladd and Ladd, *The Bachelder Papers*, 1:522.

137. Clark, *North Carolina Regiments*, 2:365; Michael W. Taylor, "Col. James Keith Marshall: One of the Three Brigade Commanders Killed in the Pickett-Pettigrew-Trimble Charge," *Gettysburg Magazine* 15 (July 1996): 87.

138. William P. Haines, *History of the Men of Company F, with Description of the Marches and Battles of the 12th New Jersey Volunteers* (Camden: C. S. McGrath, 1897), 41.

139. Washburn, *Record of the 108th Regiment*, 52.

140. OR, vol. 27, pt. 1:467. "...a magnificent sight met my eyes." Gibbon, *Personal Recollections*, 150.

141. Page, *History of the Fourteenth Regiment*, 151.

142. Haskell, *Gettysburg*, 96.

143. OR, vol. 27, pt. 1:431.

144. Ladd and Ladd, *The Bachelder Papers*, 3:1410; McDermott, *A Brief History of the 69th Regiment*, 31.

145. Ibid., 3:1899.

146. OR, vol. 27, 1:239, 885, 888.

147. Ibid., pt. 2:386; *Supplement*, 310.

148. Owen, "Pickett at Gettysburg."

149. Irby, *Historical Sketch*, 27.

150. Shotwell, *Three Years in Battle*, 2:12.

151. Alexander, *Fighting for the Confederacy*, 262; E. Porter Alexander, "The Great Charge and Artillery Fighting at Gettysburg," *B&L*, 3:365.

152. Loehr, "The First Virginia Infantry," 40. Kemper's skirmishers continued forward when the rest of the brigade obliqued. Howard Malcolm Walthall realized that when "my part" reached the top of Rodgers' Hill, "the trial had gone against us." Walthall, "Dear Children," 29.

153. Martin and Smith, "The Battle of Gettysburg," 191; Ladd and Ladd, *The Bachelder Papers*, 3:1900.

154. Clark, *North Carolina Regiments*, 5:105; William H. Swallow, "The Third Day at Gettysburg," *The Southern Bivouac*, vol. 1, 9 (February 1886): 567.

155. Coddington, *Gettysburg Campaign*, 503; Stewart, *Pickett's Charge*, 184; OR, vol. 27, pt. 2:359.

156. Ladd and Ladd, *The Bachelder Papers*, 3:1899.

157. Finley, "Bloody Angle"; Edmund Rice, "Repelling Lee's Last Blow at Gettysburg," *B&L*, 3:387; Lash, "The Philadelphia Brigade," 104.

158. Stewart, *Pickett's Charge*, 187–88; Finley, "Bloody Angle"; OR, vol. 27, 1:428.

159. Moore, "Heth's Division at Gettysburg," *The Southern Bivouac*, 390; OR, vol. 27, pt. 2:644, 647.

160. Fry, "Pettigrew's Charge at Gettysburg," 93.

161. Clark, *North Carolina Regiments*, 5:146.

162. Ibid., 3:108.

163. Letter, J. McLeod Turner, published in the *Raleigh Observer*, November 30, 1877, reprinted in Michael W. Taylor, "North Carolina in the Pickett-Pettigrew-Trimble Charge at Gettysburg," *Gettysburg Magazine* 8 (January 1993): 78, 79.

164. Sawyer, *8th Ohio Volunteer Infantry*, 130.

165. Roger Long, "Dr. Billy's Battles," *Gettysburg Magazine* 16 (January 1997): 90.

166. OR, vol. 27, pt. 1:750, 893.

167. Galwey, *The Valiant Hours*, 116. See also Taylor, "Pickett-Pettigrew-Trimble Charge," 76.

168. Long, "Dr. Billy's Battles," 91–92.

169. Clark, *North Carolina Regiments*, 5:146.

170. Coddington, *Gettysburg Campaign*, 507.

171. Metts, "Longstreet's Charge at Gettysburg," 10; Letters, James H. Lane and W. G. Morris, published in the *Raleigh Observer*, November 30, 1877, reprinted in Taylor, "Pickett-Pettigrew-Trimble Charge," 76, 77. "Soon after we emerged from the woods, Davis' Brigade in front of us [37th North Carolina] became engaged with the enemy but, being exposed to a heavy flanking fire both of infantry and artillery, was forced back." *Supplement*, 457.

172. Love, "Mississippi at Gettysburg," 44, 47; Clark, *North Carolina Regiments*, 5:126. Baker claimed that "some" of the 11th Mississippi "went over the stone fence and upon the ridge" where the Federal batteries were located. Untitled, *CV* 4 (April 1896): 101.

173. McFarland, "Eleventh Mississippi at Gettysburg," 553.

174. Alfred H. Belo, *Memoirs of Alfred Horatio Belo* (Boston: Alfred Mudge & Son Inc., 1902), 33; Map, "Farthest to the Front," Clark, *North Carolina Regiments*, 3:299–300; 5:110–11.

175. Rice, "Repelling Lee's Last Blow," *B&L*, 3:388.

176. Owen, "Pickett at Gettysburg." "I have always thought that Garnet[t] perhaps saw this flanking party but there is no way now of ever deciding the point." Letter, Henry T. Owen to Col. H. A. Carrington, January 27, 1878, reprinted in Rollins, *Pickett's Charge!*, 175.

177. Fuger, "Cushing's Battery at Gettysburg," 408; OR, vol. 27, pt. 1:690.

178. Ibid., 880.

179. Ibid., 439; R. Steuart Latrobe, "The Pinch of the Fight at Gettysburg," *Baltimore American and Commercial Advertiser*, August 6, 1863.

180. Shotwell, *Three Years in Battle*, 2:13.

181. Lash, "The Philadelphia Brigade," 104.

182. Latrobe, "The Pinch of the Fight"; OR, vol. 27, pt. 1:373.

CHAPTER 7

1. Longacre, *Pickett Leader of the Charge*, 125; Robert A. Bright, "Pickett's Charge at Gettysburg," *CV* 38 (July 1930): 265.

2. "The General told me that Pickett's division had succeeded in carrying the enemy's position and capturing his guns, but after remaining there twenty minutes, it had been forced to retire, on the retreat of Heth and Pettigrew on its left." Longstreet must have related this to Fremantle after the assault. Fremantle, *Three Months*, 265–66. Longstreet certainly saw Virginians walking dejectedly toward him and Fremantle. John Michael Priest, "Lee's Gallant 6000?" *North & South*, vol. 1, 6:46.

3. Bright, "Pickett's Charge at Gettysburg," 265. Longstreet remembered that "Pickett had reached a point near the Federal lines." Longstreet, "Lee's Right Wing at Gettysburg," *B&L*, 3:346.

4. Bright, "Pickett's Charge at Gettysburg," 265.

5. OR, vol. 27, pt. 2:620, 632; C. M. Wilcox, "General C. M. Wilcox on the Battle of Gettysburg," *SHSP* 6 (1878): 119. See also T. M. R. Talcott, "The Third Day at Gettysburg," *SHSP* 41 (1916): 41.

6. Bright, "Pickett's Charge at Gettysburg," 265.

7. Letter, Lang to Perry, July 19, 1863, *SHSP* 27 (1899): 196.

8. OR, vol. 27, pt. 1:350, 353, 373, 1042. Stannard claimed he ordered the flank attack but it probably originated with Hancock. See Coddington, *Gettysburg Campaign*, 799 n. 123.

9. Bright, "Pickett's Charge at Gettysburg," 265; Owen, "Pickett at Gettysburg." "[The Vermonters] poured in volleys of musketry which the enemy from their formation could not return. The result was that they huddled up towards the center and the impetus of the charge was lost." "Journal of Major-General Abner Doubleday, U.S. Army, from June 4–August 1863," *Supplement*, 118–19.

10. Alexander, *Military Memoirs*, 420.

11. OR, vol. 27, 2:321; Alexander, *Military Memoirs*, 424. "One-half hour before Pickett's Division was put in motion, almost all the artillery ammunition was

exhausted all along the line, and none could be obtained from the ordnance train in time to be of service." Unsigned report, Fauquier Artillery, Dearing's Battalion. *Supplement*, 341.

12. Alexander, *Fighting for the Confederacy*, 262; Wise, *Long Arm of Lee*, 684–85.

13. Alexander, *Military Memoirs*, 428–29; OR, vol. 27, pt. 1:885, 888.

14. Stewart, *Pickett's Charge*, 204–6; Ladd and Ladd, *The Bachelder Papers*, 3:1900–1901.

15. "Report of Col. Joseph Mayo," reprinted in Rollins, *Pickett's Charge!*, 156. Harrison and Busey, *Nothing But Glory*, 178.

16. Mayo, "Pickett's Charge at Gettysburg," 333.

17. Ladd and Ladd, *The Bachelder Papers*, 2:1192; Johnston, *Confederate Boy*, 211.

18. Finley, "Bloody Angle." The 71st Pennsylvania's Roll of Honor indicates more men were killed at Ball's Bluff, Virginia, October 21, 1861, than at Gettysburg; Bane, *History of the Philadelphia Brigade*, 301–5.

19. Ladd and Ladd, *The Bachelder Papers*, 1:282; OR, vol. 27, pt. 1:439, 690.

20. Martin and Smith, "The Battle of Gettysburg," SHSP 32 (1904): 191–92; Harrison and Busey, *Nothing But Glory*, 179.

21. "Report of Col. Joseph Mayo," reprinted in Rollins, *Pickett's Charge!*, 156.

22. Mayo, "Pickett's Charge at Gettysburg," SHSP 34 (1906): 333. Colonel Mayo refers to Col. Walter T. Patton, 7th Virginia; Lt. Col. Alexander D. Callcote, 3rd Virginia; and Capt. C. Crawley Phillips, Company F, 3rd Virginia. Harrison and Busey, *Nothing But Glory*, 193, 199, 207.

23. Shotwell, *Three Years in Battle*, 2:14; Owen, "Pickett's Charge."

24. Hartwig, "It Struck Horror To Us All," 97; McDermott, *A Brief History of the 69th Regiment*, 31.

25. Brown, *Cushing of Gettysburg*, 251. Sergeant Fuger stated that Cushing fell as the enemy "came within about 100 yards from the battery..." Fuger, "Cushing's Battery at Gettysburg," 408.

26. Smith, "Christopher Smith Account."

27. Finley, Bloody Angle"; Ida Lee Johnson, "Over the Stone Wall at Gettysburg," CV (July 1923): 249; Harrison and Busey, *Nothing But Glory*, 84.

28. Swallow, "The Third Day At Gettysburg," 568.

29. Washburn, *Record of the 108th Regiment*, 50; OR, vol. 27, pt. 1:465. "...a battery that almost enfiladed us from the right as we neared the lane—a battery that seemed not to have been engaged in the first fire." Moore, "Heth's Division at Gettysburg," 392.

30. Metts, "Longstreet's Charge at Gettysburg," 10; Swallow, "The Third Day at Gettysburg," 567.

31. Coddington, *Gettysburg Campaign*, 507; Robert L. Bee, "Frederickburg on the Other Leg: Sergeant Ben Hirst's Narrative of Important Events, Gettysburg, July 3, 1863," *The Third Day at Gettysburg & Beyond: Essays on Confederate and Union Leadership*, ed. Gary W. Gallagher (Chapel Hill: The University of North Carolina Press, 1994), 148.

32. OR, vol. 27, pt. 1:454, pt. 2:644.

33. Page, *History of the Fourteenth Regiment*, 151–52.

34. Taylor, "Col. James Keith Marshall," 87.

35. Moore, "Heth's Division at Gettysburg," 391.

36. Lieutenant Moore admitted that the Yankees fought "with more than their usual determination." Ladd and Ladd, *The Bachelder Papers*, 2:914.

37. Owen, "Pickett at Gettysburg."

38. Stewart, *Pickett's Charge*, 212–13; Swallow, "The Third Day at Gettysburg," 568.

39. Clay was told Garnett had been killed by artillery fire. Winfield Peters, "The Lost Sword of General Richard B. Garnett, Who Fell at Gettysburg," *SHSP* 33 (1905): 28–29. Maj. Edmund Berkeley, 8th Virginia, wrote that Garnett was "shot through the brain..." *Supplement*, 311. Garnett's body was not identified for burial. "Maryland" Steuart recovered General Garnett's sword in a Baltimore pawn shop after the war. Stephen Davis, "The Death and Burials of General Richard Brooke Garnett," *Gettysburg Magazine* 5 (July 1991): 114–15.

40. Finley, "Bloody Angle"; Stewart, *Pickett's Charge*, 213.

41. Coddington, *Gettysburg Campaign*, 516–17.

42. Latrobe, "The Pinch of the Fight."

43. Gibbon, *Personal Recollections*, 152–53.

44. Haskell, *Gettysburg*, 103–4.

45. Lash, "Philadelphia Brigade," 106, 108. General Webb assumed command of the Philadelphia Brigade at the end of June. Edwin Coddington speculated that the 72nd Pennsylvania refused to advance on Webb's order because they were unfamiliar with him. Moreover, Webb appealed directly to the ranks instead of going through the chain of command. Coddington, *Gettysburg Campaign*, 517.

46. Mayo, "Pickett's Charge," 334; Martin and Smith, "The Battle of Gettysburg," *SHSP* 32 (1904): 192; Harrison and Busey, *Nothing But Glory*, 137, 239.

47. OR, vol. 27, pt. 2:360.

48. Ibid., 615.

49. Ibid., 320.

50. Ibid., 308.

51. A. T. Watts, "Something More About Gettysburg," *CV* 5 (February 1897): 67. See also David E. Holt, *A Mississippi Rebel in the Army of Northern Virginia: The Civil War Memoirs of Private David Holt*, eds. Thomas D. Cockrell and Michael B. Ballard (Baton Rouge: Louisiana State University Press, 1995).

52. Letter, James Longstreet to Emerson L. Bicknell, January 4, 1884, *B&L*, 3:392. See also Ladd and Ladd, *The Bachelder Papers*, 2:984–85. In his battle report, Col. Samuel E. Baker, 16th Mississippi, wrote: "On July 3, five companies of my regiment were out to the front skirmishing and when General Heth's Division advanced, the remaining five companies were ordered to form and be ready to advance. This was promptly done, and when the order came we moved steadily to the front under the most terrible cannonading I have ever experienced. After we had advanced about fifty yards, the order was given to halt and fall back to our position..." *Supplement*, 407.

53. OR, vol. 27, pt. 2:360. James Longstreet's tendency to avoid the truth is corroborated by the following: "I had offered my objections to Pickett's battle and had been over-ruled, and I was in the immediate presence of the commanding general when the order was given for Pickett to advance." Longstreet, "Lee's Right Wing at Gettysburg," *B&L* 3:345.

54. Long, *Memoirs of Robert E. Lee*, 290; Taylor, "The Campaign in Pennsylvania," 315. See also Carol Reardon, "Pickett's Charge: The Convergence of History and Myth in the Southern Past," *The Third Day at Gettysburg & Beyond: Essays on Confederate and Union Leadership*, ed. Gary W. Gallagher (Chapel Hill: The University of North Carolina Press), 1994.

55. Ladd and Ladd, *The Bachelder Papers*, 1:523. "Heth's Division was a part of the column of attack, and must not be regarded as a mere support to Pickett."

Martin W. Hazelwood, "Gettysburg Charge. Paper as to Pickett's Men," *SHSP* 23 (1895): 230.

56. Clark, *North Carolina Regiments*, 3:108.

57. Stewart, *Pickett's Charge*, 226, 256; Letter, William B. Shepard, published in the *Raleigh Observer*, November 30, 1877, reprinted in Taylor, "Pickett-Pettigrew-Trimble Charge," 83.

58. OR, vol. 27, pt. 2:645.

59. Page, *History of the Fourteenth Regiment*, 152. The 14th Tennessee lost four color-bearers while the 13th Alabama, 1st and 7th Tennessee, lost three each. OR, vol. 27, pt. 2:647.

60. Haines, *History of the Men of Company F*, 41.

61. Moore, "Heth's Division at Gettysburg," 391.

62. Letter from William G. Morris published in the *Raleigh Observer*, November 30, 1877, reprinted in Taylor, "Pickett-Pettigrew-Trimble Charge," 77.

63. Page, *History of the Fourteenth Regiment*, 156; OR, vol. 27, pt. 1:468.

64. OR, vol. 27, pt. 2:672.

65. Letter, Joseph J. Davis, published in the *Raleigh Observer*, November 30, 1877, reprinted in Taylor, "Pickett-Pettigrew-Trimble Charge," 85.

66. Letter, Henry C. Moore, published in the *Raleigh Observer*, reprinted in Taylor, "Pickett-Pettigrew-Trimble Charge," 90.

67. George W. Flowers, "The Thirty Eighth N.C. Regiment," *SHSP* 25 (1897): 260; Letter, Henry C. Moore, published in the *Raleigh Observer*, November 30, 1877, reprinted in Taylor, "Pickett-Pettigrew-Trimble Charge," 91.

68. Bruce A. Trinque, "Arnold's Battery and the 26th North Carolina," *Gettysburg Magazine* 12 (January 1995): 61–67.

69. Letters, James. H. Lane and Joseph H. Saunders, published in the *Raleigh Observer*, November 30, 1877, reprinted in Taylor, "Pickett-Pettigrew-Trimble Charge," 76–77.

70. Turner was captured and exchanged on September 18, 1864; Letter, J. McLeod Turner, published in the *Raleigh Observer*, November 30, 1877, reprinted in Taylor, "Pickett-Pettigrew-Trimble Charge," 79, 92.

71. Iredell, *Historical Sketches of the Seventh Regiment*, 37; Letter, Thomas L. Norwood, published in the *Raleigh Observer*, November 30, 1877, reprinted in Taylor, "Pickett-Pettigrew-Trimble Charge," 77–78.

72. Clark, *North Carolina Regiments*, 5:108. According to Lt. David Shields, aide-de-camp to General Hays, "the most successful" Confederate reached a point "within fifteen or twenty yards of our front where he fell, a bullet passing through his head, throwing him prone on his back, his feet towards his foe. He was unconscious but alive the next day, as could be seen from the blubbers on his lips." *Supplement*, 168–69.

73. Lewis, *Recollections from 1861 to 1865*, 85.

74. James E. Poindexter, "General Armistead's Portrait Presented," *SHSP* 37 (1909): 148–49; Harrison and Busey, *Nothing But Glory*, 412.

75. Ladd and Ladd, *The Bachelder Papers* 3:1411, 1902.

76. Poindexter, "General Armistead's Portrait," *SHSP* 37 (1909): 149; "Col & Dr. R. W. Martin," 70; Martin and Smith, "The Battle of Gettysburg," 187; Ladd and Ladd, *The Bachelder Papers*, 3:1901. A variation of Armistead's exhortation is: "Come on boys, we must give them the cold steel; who will follow me?" Swallow, "The Third Day at Gettysburg," 569.

77. James Carter, "Flag of the Fifty-Third Va. Regiment," *CV* 10 (June 1902): 263; Harrison and Busey, *Nothing But Glory*, 399, 412; *Supplement*, 336.

78. Roger Long, "Over The Wall," *Gettysburg Magazine* 13 (July 1995): 71; Stewart, *Pickett's Charge*, 217.

79. Lash, "Philadelphia Brigade," 109–10.

80. Owen, "Pickett at Gettysburg."

81. Ladd and Ladd, *The Bachelder Papers*, 3:1609.

82. McDermott, *A Brief History of the 69th Regiment*, 31–32; Hartwig, "It Struck Horror To Us All," 98; Ladd and Ladd, *The Bachelder Papers*, 3:1411.

83. Ladd and Ladd, *The Bachelder Papers*, 2:777–78.

84. Ibid., 3:1609, 1879.

85. Rice, "Repelling Lee's Last Blow," *B&L*, 3:388.

86. Ladd and Ladd, *The Bachelder Papers*, 3:1902; Coddington, *Gettysburg Campaign*, 518.

87. OR, vol. 27, pt. 1:374.

88. Ford, *Fifteenth Massachusetts*, 276.

89. OR, vol. 27, pt. 1:425; Moe, *The Last Full Measure*, 290.

90. Ladd and Ladd, *The Bachelder Papers*, 3:1363; *Supplement*, 214.

91. Martin and Smith, "The Battle of Gettysburg," 192–94.

92. Mayo, "Pickett's Charge at Gettysburg," *SHSP* 32 (1904): 335.

93. McDermott, *A Brief History of the 69th Regiment*, 32.

94. "Col. & Dr. R. W. Martin," 70.

95. D. B. Easley, "With Armistead When He Was Killed," *CV* 20 (August 1912): 379; Stewart, *Pickett's Charge*, 218.

96. Finley, "Bloody Angle"; Long, "Over the Wall," 71.

97. Easley, "With Armistead," 379.

98. Ladd and Ladd, *The Bachelder Papers*, 3:1413, 1628; *Supplement*, 336.

99. Finley, "Bloody Angle."

100. Tucker, *Hancock the Superb*, 155.

101. George G. Benedict, *Army Life in Virginia. Letters from the Twelfth Vermont Regiment and Personal Experiences of Volunteer Service in the War for the Union, 1862–1863* (Burlington: Free Press Association, 1895), 182–83.

102. Ladd and Ladd, *The Bachelder Papers*, 3:1364.

103. Rice, "Repelling Lee's Last Blow," *B&L*, 3:389.

104. Harrison and Busey, *Nothing But Glory*, 353.

105. Lewis, *Recollections from 1860 to 1865*, 85.

106. OR, vol. 27, pt. 2:1000; George K. Griggs, "Memoranda of the Thirty-Eighth Virginia Infantry," *SHSP* 14 (1886): 253; Ladd and Ladd, *The Bachelder Papers*, 2:1192; 3:1364. In 1889, the Philadelphia Brigade hosted survivors of Pickett's division. A hospitality tent was erected near the Copse of Trees with casks of beer provided. An old Johnny drained a tin cup and remarked to his hosts: "If you all had this up here that hot day in July, 1863, we would have stayed here." William T. Poague, *Gunner with Stonewall: Reminiscences of William Thomas Poague*, ed. Monroe F. Cockrell (Jackson, Tenn.: McCowat-Mercer Press, 1957, reprint), 76–77.

107. Finley, "Bloody Angle."

108. Lash, "Philadelphia Brigade," 109–10.

109. *Supplement*, 336–37.

110. Easley, "With Armistead," 379; "Echoes of Gettysburg," *CV* 21 (September 1913): 431.

111. OR, vol. 27, pt. 1:440.

112. Stewart, *Pickett's Charge*, 247.

113. OR, vol. 27, pt. 1:444; Ladd and Ladd, *The Bachelder Papers*, 3:1880.

114. Letter, Henry C. Moore, published in the *Raleigh Observer*, November, 30, 1877, reprinted in Taylor, "Pickett-Pettigrew-Trimble Charge," 91.

115. *Supplement*, 454; Ladd and Ladd, *The Bachelder Papers*, 2:1199; Isaac R. Trimble, "The Battle and Campaign of Gettysburg," *SHSP* 26 (1898): 126; Letter, Isaac R. Trimble to John W. Daniel, November 24, 1875, reprinted in *SHSP* 9 (1881): 35.

116. OR, vol. 27, pt. 2:659, 666; Letter, Joseph H. Saunders, published in the *Raleigh Observer*, November 30, 1877, reprinted in Taylor, "Picket-Pettigrew-Trimble-Charge," 77.

117. Eric Campbell, "'Remember Harper's Ferry': The Degradation, Humiliation, and Redemption of Col. George L. Willard's Brigade, Part 2," *Gettysburg Magazine* 8 (January 1993): 107.

118. Letter, James H. Lane, published in the *Raleigh Observer*, November 30, 1877, reprinted in Taylor, "Pickett-Pettigrew-Trimble Charge," 76.

119. Letter, William G. Morris, published in the *Raleigh Observer*, November 30, 1877, reprinted in Taylor, "Pickett-Pettigrew-Trimble Charge," 77.

120. OR, vol. 27, pt. 2:644; Letter, John T. Jones, July 30, 1863, published in the *Raleigh Observer*, November 30, 1877, reprinted in Taylor, "Pickett-Pettigrew-Trimble Charge," 82.

121. Clark, *North Carolina Regiments*, 5:152; Letter, William N. Snelling, published in the *Raleigh Observer*, reprinted in Taylor, "Pickett-Pettigrew-Trimble Charge," 86.

122. OR, vol. 27, pt. 2:672.

123. Ibid., 647.

124. "Typical of the Old South," *CV* 20 (May 1912): 202.

125. June Kimble, "Tennesseeans At Gettysburg—The Retreat," *CV* 18 (October 1910): 460–61; "Obituary of Junius Kimble," *CV* 19 (May 1911): 242; Galwey, *The Valiant Hours*, 118.

126. Washburn, *Record of the 108th Regiment*, 50, 53; Haines, *History of the Men of Company F*, 41.

127. OR, vol. 27, pt. 1:454.

128. Washburn, *Record of the 108th Regiment*, 53.

129. Clark, *North Carolina Regiments*, 5:108.

130. Watts, "Something More About Gettysburg," 67; *Supplement*, 430.

131. OR, vol. 27, pt. 3:1030.

132. Holt, *A Mississippi Rebel*, 198.

133. Busey and Martin, *Regimental Strengths*, 290.

134. Clark, *North Carolina Regiments*, 1:590.

135. OR, vol. 27, pt. 2:642, 651.

136. Moore, "Heth's Division at Gettysburg," 392.

137. OR, vol. 27, pt. 2:660.

138. Metts, "Longstreet's Charge at Gettysburg," 8.

139. Clark, *North Carolina Regiments*, 3:109.

140. William H. Morgan, *Personal Reminiscences of the War of 1861–65* (Lynchburg, Va.: J. P. Bell Co., Inc., 1911), 17, 167.

141. Gomer, "Service of Third Virginia Infantry," 228.

142. Ladd and Ladd, *The Bachelder Papers*, 2:778.

143. Shotwell, *Three Years in Battle*, 2:15; Marshal, *The Battle of Gettysburg*, 212.

144. OR, vol. 27, pt. 2:620, 632.

145. Ibid., pt. 1:1042.

146. Elmore, "The Florida Brigade," 54. Capture of the 8th Virginia's flag was credited to the 16th Vermont. OR, vol. 27, pt. 1:1042.

147. Letter, Lang to Perry, July 19, 1863, *SHSP* 27 (1899): 196.

148. OR, vol. 27, pt. 2:620.

149. Poague, *Gunner with Stonewall*, 74–75.

150. Ladd and Ladd, *The Bachelder Papers*, 1:778.

151. Coddington, *Gettysburg Campaign*, 531–32; Haskell, *Battle of Gettysburg*, 117–19.

152. Ladd and Ladd, *The Bachelder Papers*, 1:364, 366.

153. Coddington, *Gettysburg Campaign*, 532–33; Swinton, *Army of the Potomac*, 363.

154. Longstreet, "Lee in Pennsylvania," *Annals of the War*, 431.

155. Longstreet, "Lee's Right Wing at Gettysburg," *B&L*, 3:347.

156. Fremantle, *Three Months*, 268–69.

157. Longacre, *Leader of the Charge*, 127.

158. Losses averaged to Kemper, 38.1 percent; to Garnett, 48.9 percent; and Armistead, 48.3 percent. Harrison and Busey, *Nothing But Glory*, 456, 461, 467.

159. Harrison and Busey, *Nothing But Glory*, 457, 466.

160. Busey and Martin, *Regimental Strengths*, 292.

161. OR, vol. 27, pt. 1:454.

162. Busey and Martin, *Regimental Strengths*, 308.

163. Watts, "Something More About Gettysburg," 67. See also letter, Benjamin F. Carpenter, published in the *Raleigh Observer*, November 30, 1877, reprinted in Taylor, "Pickett-Pettigrew-Trimble Charge," 9. According to Maj. William McK. Robbins, 4th Alabama, who served as a Gettysburg Battlefield Commissioner: "...the left of Pickett & the right of Pettigrew and Trimble pushed forward & went equally far, as the testimony of impartial Union witnesses proves & the front lines of Confed. dead indicated to all observers...Yankees in that battle have told me that the commands from other states left their dead as far to the front & close to the Union lines as the Virginians." Reardon, *Pickett's Charge in History and Memory*, 151, 182–83.

164. Loehr, "The First Virginia Infantry," 35–36; Harrison and Busey, *Nothing But Glory*, 246.

165. Robert K. Krick, "The Parallel Lives of Two Virginia Soldiers: Armistead and Garnett," *The Third Day at Gettysburg & Beyond: Essays on Confederate and Union Leadership*, ed. Gary W. Gallagher (Chapel Hill: The University of North Carolina Press, 1994), 121–22; Harrison and Busey, *Nothing But Glory*, 343. Another source states General Armistead died at 9:00 A.M., July 5. See T. C. Holland, "With Armistead At Gettysburg," *CV* 29 (February 1921): 62.

166. OR, vol. 27, pt. 1:441, 444.

167. Ibid., 468.

168. A third flag, captured by the 8th Ohio, was confiscated by a staff officer. OR, vol. 27, pt. 1:462.

169. Ibid., 469–70.

170. Ibid., 432–33. The 53rd Virginia's flag was taken, possibly by the 71st Pennsylvania, at the rear section of Cushing's Battery. Harrison and Busey, *Nothing But Glory*, 113, 159, 160 n. 56.

171. McDermott, *A Brief History of the 69th Regiment*, 33; OR, vol. 27, pt. 1:428.

172. Ladd and Ladd, *The Bachelder Papers*, 2:1200.

173. The figure given for the assaulting column reflects Third Corps numbers given by George Stewart and more recent scholarship pertaining to Pickett's division. Stewart, *Pickett's Charge*, 172; Harrison and Busey, *Nothing But Glory*, 5–6. After the battle, Longstreet told Fremantle 30,000 men should have been committed instead of 15,000. Fremantle, *Three Months*, 274.

174. Long, *Memoirs of R. E. Lee*, 294–95; OR, vol. 27, pt. 3:1075.

175. LaSalle Corbell Pickett stated that she possessed a copy of her husband's report though it is not known to exist today. R. E. Stivers, "Notes and Queries," *Civil War History* 3 (September 1960): 304–6.

176. See Paul M. Shevchuk, "The 1st Texas Infantry and the Repulse of Farnsworth's Charge," *Gettysburg Magazine* 2 (January 1990).

177. See Paul M. Shevchuk, "Cut to Pieces: The Cavalry Fight at Fairfield, Pennsylvania, July 3, 1863," *Gettysburg Magazine* 1 (July 1989).

178. Longacre, *Cavalry at Gettysburg*, 220–21.

179. Coddington, *Gettysburg Campaign*, 521–22.

180. Longacre, *Cavalry at Gettysburg*, 244.

181. Wade Hampton returned to duty in November. Manly Wade Wellman, *Giant in Gray: A Biography of Wade Hampton of South Carolina* (New York: Charles Scribner's Sons, 1949), 127, 130.

182. Longstreet, "Lee's Right Wing at Gettysburg," *B&L*, 3:349.

183. OR, vol. 27, pt. 1:309, 310; Alexander, *Military Memoirs*, 435.

184. *Supplement*, 381; Imboden, "The Confederate Retreat From Gettysburg," *B&L*, 3:420–25. General Lee apparently believed that Pickett's division went unsupported because Pender's men were unfamiliar with General Trimble. Letter, Heth to Jones, June 1877, "Causes of Lee's Defeat at Gettysburg," *SHSP* 4 (1877): 154.

185. Imboden, "The Confederate Retreat from Gettysburg," *B&L*, 3:426–27.

186. OR, vol. 27, pt. 2:450.

187. OR, vol. 27, pt. 1:928.

188. Longacre, *Cavalry at Gettysburg*, 255–56.

189. Imboden, "The Confederate Retreat from Gettysburg," *B&L*, 3:427, 428; OR, vol. 27, pt. 1:928, 935.

190. Busey and Martin, *Regimental Strengths*, 312.

191. Alexander, *Military Memoirs*, 435.

192. OR, vol. 27, pt. 2:311, 360, 448.

193. Coddington, *Gettysburg Campaign*, 565–66.

194. Busey and Martin, *Regimental Strengths*, 312.

195. OR, vol. 27, pt. 1:117, 663.

196. Harry W. Pfanz, "The Gettysburg Campaign after Pickett's Charge," *Gettysburg Magazine* 1 (July 1989): 122; OR, vol. 27, pt. 1:81, 84, 86.

197. Alexander, *Fighting for the Confederacy*, 269.

198. OR, vol. 27, pt. 3:669, 998; Dowdey and Manarin, *Wartime Papers of R. E. Lee*, 545, 548.

199. OR, vol. 27, pt. 1:91–92.

200. OR, vol. 27, pt. 3:675.

201. Ibid., 683.

202. OR, vol. 27, pt. 2:323, 449.

203. Ibid., 362.

204. Ibid., 640.

205. OR, vol. 27, pt. 1:988, 990.

206. Ibid., pt. 2:640.

207. Longacre, *Cavalry at Gettysburg*, 268; OR, vol. 27, pt. 1:1000.

208. OR, vol. 27, pt. 2:640–41, 648; pt. 3:1016.

209. Ibid., pt. 2:641.

210. Ibid., pt. 1:991.

211. Ibid., pt. 1:92.

212. John G. Nicolay and John Hay, eds., *Complete Works of Abraham Lincoln*, 12 vols. (New York: The Lamb Publishing Company, 1905 edition), 9:18.

213. Nicolay and Hay, eds., *Complete Works of Abraham Lincoln*, 9:28–30. For a balanced review of Meade's conduct in pursuit of Lee, see A. Wilson Greene, "From Gettysburg to Falling Waters: Meade's Pursuit of Lee," *The Third Day at Gettysburg & Beyond: Essays on Confederate and Union Leadership*, ed. Gary W. Gallagher (Chapel Hill: The University of North Carolina Press, 1994).

214. Dowdey and Manarin, *The Wartime Papers of R. E. Lee*, 565.

215. Stanley F. Horn, ed. *The Robert E. Lee Reader* (Indianapolis: The Bobbs-Merrill Company, Inc.), 336–37. See also Lee, *Recollections and Letters*, 415.

216. Emphasis added. Dowdey and Manarin, *Wartime Papers of R. E. Lee*, 490.

217. Dowdey and Manarin, *Wartime Papers of R. E. Lee*, 589–90.

218. Ladd and Ladd, *The Bachelder Papers*, 3:1694–695.

219. Robert K. Murray and Warren W. Hassler, "Gettysburg Farmer," *Civil War History* 3 (June 1957): 180, 187.

CHAPTER 8

1. Otto Juettner, A.M., M.D., *Daniel Drake and His Followers: Historical and Biographical Sketches* (Cincinnati: Harvey Publishing Company, n.d.), 198–99; Margaret Rives King, *A Memento of Ancestors and Ancestral Homes, Written for Her Nieces and Nephews* (Cincinnati: Robert Clarke & Co., 1890), 26, 75–76, 109–16.

2. Juettner, *Daniel Drake*, 275. Margaret Rives, born July 1, 1819, died in 1924. Anna Maria Rives, born October 10, 1822, died in 1862. James Rives Childs, *Reliques of the Rives: Being Historical and Geneological Notes of the Ancient Family of Ryves of County Dorset and of the Rives of Virginia* (Lynchburg, Va.: J. P. Bell Company, Inc., 1929), 571–72.

3. King, *Ancestors and Ancestral Homes*, 10. Landon C. Rives was born June 30, 1825. Childs, *Reliques of the Rives*, 571. Field and Staff Muster Rolls indicate that Landon Rives was assigned to the 1st Virginia Cavalry: "...never reported for duty." *Compiled Service Records*, National Archives, Washington, D.C., Box 11. Rives died at Richmond from pneumonia, March 18, 1862. "Dr. Rives was a native of Virginia, and married and made the home of his later years there; but his youth and early manhood were identified with Cincinnati, and for some years he practised his profession here. His untimely & unexpected death brings sorrow and heaviness among a wide circle of associates and friends, deeply attached to him by his rare union of ardent, high-spirited nature, with the most gentle and generous qualities, and the invariable bearing of a gentleman." *Cincinnati Daily Commercial*, May 1, 1862.

4. A. H. Roller, "Muster-Roll of the Company and Some of Its Casualties," *SHSP* 24 (1896): 293. The Bedford Greys were originally Company G, 28th Virginia. Harrison and Busey, *Nothing But Glory*, 309, 317; *Compiled Service Records*, Box 747. In *The Roster of Confederate Soldiers*, there are two notations for Edward Rives. "28th Inf. Surg." Below it reads: "Pickett's Div. Surg." Janet B. Hewett, ed., *The Roster of Confederate Soldiers 1861–1865*, 16 vols. (Wilmington, N.C., Broadfoot Publishing Company, 1996), 13:192.

5. *Compiled Service Records*, Box 711; Frank E. Fields, *28th Virginia Infantry* (Lynchburg, Va.: H. E. Howard, Inc., 1985), 76. Joseph K. Barnes and George A. Otis, *Medical and Surgical History of the War of the Rebellion*, 16 vols. (Washington, D.C.: Government Printing Office, 1870–1888), 2:620.

6. Childs, *Reliques of the Rives*, 572. Rives' home address was 95 East 3rd Street, *Cincinnati City Directory*, 1869, 479.

7. Childs, *Reliques of the Rives*, 572; Elsie Johnson Ayres, *Highland Pioneer Sketches and Family Genealogies* (Springfield, Ohio: H. F. Skinner, 1971), 184, 212; *Hillsboro Gazette*, October 4, 1883. Among numerous Union generals buried in Spring Grove Cemetery are: Joseph Hooker, Godfrey Weitzel, Manning F. Force, Kenner Garrard and the poet William H. Lytle. Warner, *Generals in Blue*, 156, 168, 235, 288, 549.

8. William A. Baugh is listed as First Sergeant, Company A, 18th Virginia. Harrison and Busey, *Nothing But Glory*, 273.

9. Josiah B. Glenn is listed as Third Sergeant, Company D, 18th Virginia. Harrison and Busey, *Nothing But Glory*, 277.

10. Thomas Harvey is listed as Private, Company H, 18th Virginia, and was "*wounded...*" Harrison and Busey, *Nothing But Glory*, 285.

11. Samuel Fitzgerald, Jr., is listed as Fourth Corporal, Company I, 18th Virginia and suffered "a flesh *wound* in the thigh..." Harrison and Busey, *Nothing But Glory*, 287.

12. Elijah T. Roach is listed as a member of Company K, 18th Virginia. Ibid., 289.

13. E. H. Jones is not listed among the dead in *The Gettysburg Death Roster: The Confederate Dead at the Battle of Gettysburg* by Robert K. Krick (Dayton: Morningside, 1985 edition), 68.

14. Leroy P. Jennings is listed as Third Corporal, Company I, 19th Virginia, and was wounded "in the right lung..." Harrison and Busey, *Nothing But Glory*, 304.

15. Read P. Debo is listed as Fifth Sergeant, Company G, 28th Virginia. Harrison and Busey, *Nothing But Glory*, 319.

16. Joseph H. Payne is listed as First Corporal, Company D, 28th Virginia. Harrison and Busey, *Nothing But Glory*, 315.

17. M. R. Hubbard, listed as Private, Company G, 28th Virginia, was wounded "in the leg and buttock." Harrison and Busey, *Nothing But Glory*, 321.

18. Richard Field is listed as First Sergeant, Company E, 56th Virginia. Harrison and Busey, *Nothing But Glory*, 333.

19. Embren E. Williams is listed as Fifth Sergeant, Company E, 56th Virginia. Harrison and Busey, *Nothing But Glory*, 333.

20. Robert B. Blackwell is listed as Private, Company H, 56th Virginia, and was "*wounded...*" Harrison and Busey, *Nothing But Glory*, 338.

21. John E. Hardiman is listed as Third Corporal, Company E, 56th Virginia. Harrison and Busey, *Nothing But Glory*, 339.

22. Bentley H. Tucker is listed as Fourth Sergeant, Company K, 56th Virginia. Harrison and Busey, *Nothing But Glory*, 341.

23. John Moriarity is listed as Fifth Sergeant, Company C, 1st Virginia. Harrison and Busey, *Nothing But Glory*, 184.

24. William T. Miller is listed as First Corporal, Company G, 1st Virginia. Harrison and Busey, *Nothing But Glory*, 187. He is not listed among the dead in *The Gettysburg Death Roster*, 84.

25. George W. Johnson is listed as Private, Company D, 1st Virginia Infantry. Harrison and Busey, *Nothing But Glory*, 186.

26. Benjamin F. Ames is listed as Third Corporal, Company F, 3rd Virginia. Harrison and Busey, *Nothing But Glory*, 199.

27. Paul P. Tuck is listed as First Sergeant, Company K, 34th Virginia. Harrison and Busey, *Nothing But Glory*, 204.

28. William H. Murray is listed as Fifth Sergeant, Company K, 3rd Virginia. Harrison and Busey, *Nothing But Glory*, 204.

29. George T. Jackson is listed as Private, Company C, 3rd Virginia. Harrison and Busey, *Nothing But Glory*, 196.

30. Daniel B. Mitchell is listed as Private, Company C, 3rd Virginia. Harrison and Busey, *Nothing But Glory*, 196.

31. Joseph W. Pope is listed as Second Corporal, Company G, 3rd Virginia Infantry. Harrison and Busey, *Nothing But Glory*, 200.

32. John Kelly is listed as First Corporal, Company E, 11th Virginia. Harrison and Busey, *Nothing But Glory*, 228.

33. Thomas S. Rector is listed as First Corporal, Company A, 11th Virginia. Harrison and Busey, *Nothing But Glory*, 222.

34. John P. Daniel is listed as First Corporal, Company H, 11th Virginia. Harrison and Busey, *Nothing But Glory*, 233.

35. John N. Ammen is listed as First Corporal, Company D, 11th Virginia. Harrison and Busey, *Nothing But Glory*, 227.

36. George D. Tweedy is listed as Private, Company C, 11th Virginia. Harrison and Busey, *Nothing But Glory*, 226.

37. John Daprato is listed as Private, Company H, 11th Virginia. Harrison and Busey, *Nothing But Glory*, 233.

38. Robert G. Kyle is listed as First Corporal, Company F, 11th Virginia. Harrison and Busey, *Nothing But Glory*, 230.

39. David E. Johnston is listed as Color Corporal, 7th Virginia. Harrison and Busey, *Nothing But Glory*, 208.

40. Conway Catlett is listed as Fifth Sergeant, Company A, 7th Virginia. Harrison and Busey, *Nothing But Glory*, 209.

41. Jacob A. Albert is listed as Second Sergeant, Company F, 24th Virginia. Harrison and Busey, *Nothing But Glory*, 248.

42. John H. Peck is listed as Private, Company F, 24th Virginia. Harrison and Busey, *Nothing But Glory*, 249.

43. William H. Shockley is listed as First Corporal, Company I, 24th Virginia. Harrison and Busey, *Nothing But Glory*, 253.

44. George W. Mays is listed as Second Corporal, Company K, 24th Virginia. Harrison and Busey, *Nothing But Glory*, 254.

45. Marsden J. Vellines is listed as Second Sergeant, Company E, 9th Virginia. Harrison and Busey, *Nothing But Glory*, 351.

46. William A. Culpepper is listed as First Sergeant, Company D, 9th Virginia. Harrison and Busey, *Nothing But Glory*, 350.

47. John T. Beach is listed as Fourth Corporal, Company F, 95th Virginia. Harrison and Busey, *Nothing But Glory*, 352.

48. John T. Adkins is listed as Fifth Sergeant, Company D, 14th Virginia. Harrison and Busey, *Nothing But Glory*, 366.

49. Henry M. Talley is listed as First Sergeant, Company G, 14th Virginia. Harrison and Busey, *Nothing But Glory*, 370.

50. Thomas H. Tinsley is listed as Third Sergeant, Company B, 14th Virginia. Harrison and Busey, *Nothing But Glory*, 361.

51. Richard W. Ives is listed as First Corporal, Company H, 14th Virginia. Harrison and Busey, *Nothing But Glory*, 374.

52. Allen Pinson is not listed among the dead in *The Gettysburg Death Roster*, 94.

53. Samuel A. Coleman is listed as Second Corporal, Company I, 14th Virginia. Harrison and Busey, *Nothing But Glory*, 375.

54. Harrison W. Meade is listed as Private, Company D, 38th Virginia. Harrison and Busey, *Nothing But Glory*, 387.

55. John T. Brown is listed as First Corporal, Company E, 38th Virginia. Harrison and Busey, *Nothing But Glory*, 388.

56. Lewis J. Roffe is listed as First Corporal, Company G, 38th Virginia. Harrison and Busey, *Nothing But Glory*, 391.

57. James C. Easley is listed as a member of Company D, 39th Virginia. Harrison and Busey, *Nothing But Glory*, 386.

58. David Uhles is listed as Fourth Corporal, Company B, 38th Virginia. Harrison and Busey, *Nothing But Glory*, 382.

59. Josephus B. Dodson is not listed among the dead in *The Gettysburg Death Roster*, 44.

60. James C. Robinson is listed as Private, Company B, 38th Battalion Virginia Volunteer Light Artillery. Available records indicate he was unwounded. Harrison and Busey, *Nothing But Glory*, 444.

61. Robert B. McDowell is not listed among the dead in *The Gettysburg Death Roster*, 78.

62. William H. George is listed as Fifth Sergeant, Company D, 53rd Virginia. Harrison and Busey, *Nothing But Glory*, 404. He is not listed among the dead in *The Gettysburg Death Roster*, 53.

63. George W. Ammons is listed as Second Corporal, Company K, 53rd Virginia. Harrison and Busey, *Nothing But Glory*, 415.

64. John R. Lewis is listed as Private, Company D, 53rd Virginia, was "*shot* in the arm and right leg..." Harrison and Busey, *Nothing But Glory*, 405.

65. Benjamin A. Stith is listed as Fifth Sergeant, Company H, 53rd Virginia. Harrison and Busey, *Nothing But Glory*, 411.

66. Thomas D. Haden is listed as Fifth Sergeant, Company D, 57th Virginia. Harrison and Busey, *Nothing But Glory*, 425.

67. Theodore F. Eddins is listed as Fourth Sergeant, Company H, 57th Virginia. Harrison and Busey, *Nothing But Glory*, 432.

68. Charles P. Young is listed as Second Corporal, Company E, 57th Virginia. Harrison and Busey, *Nothing But Glory*, 426.

69. Elliot F. Abraham is listed as Fourth Corporal, Company F, 57th Virginia. Harrison and Busey, *Nothing But Glory*, 428.

70. The death of Robert B. Drake, Private, Company A, 57th Virginia, is recorded as July 8. Harrison and Busey, *Nothing But Glory*, 420.

71. Willis M. Vest is listed as Fourth Sergeant, Company C, 57th Virginia. Harrison and Busey, *Nothing But Glory*, 423.

72. Jesse L. Meador is listed as Private, Company A, 57th Virginia. Harrison and Busey, *Nothing But Glory*, 420.

73. William George is not listed among the dead in *The Gettysburg Death Roster*, 53.

74. Richard S. Martin is listed as First Sergeant, Company I, 57th Virginia. Harrison and Busey, *Nothing But Glory*, 433.

75. Watts was a member of the 3rd Georgia Sharpshooter Battalion. See Busey and Martin, *Regimental Strengths*, 141.

76. Surgeon Rives did not record the first name of "Harvey." Since wounded soldiers served in the hospital, A. Harvey, Company H, may have been meant. Four other unwounded candidates for hospital attendant are indicated by the division roster: Privates John S. and Henry H. of Company F; Thomas of Company H; J. C. of Company K. Harrison and Busey, *Nothing But Glory*, 281, 285, 289.

77. Paulus M. Ware is listed as Private, Company I, 19th Virginia. Harrison and Busey, *Nothing But Glory*, 306.

78. Robert B. Blackwell, listed as Private, Company H, 56th Virginia, was "*wounded...*" Harrison and Busey, *Nothing But Glory*, 338.

79. Emmet M. Ghent is listed as Third Corporal, Company C, 3rd Virginia. Harrison and Busey, *Nothing But Glory*, 194.

80. Edwin R. Horton is listed as Private, Company B, 11th Virginia. Harrison and Busey, *Nothing But Glory*, 224.

81. William J. Wilcher is listed as Private, Company K, 57th Virginia, and was reported "*killed...*" Harrison and Busey, *Nothing But Glory*, 437.

82. George A. Albert is listed as Third Corporal, Company F, 24th Virginia. Harrison and Busey, *Nothing But Glory*, 249.

83. Robert S. Wynn is listed as Musician, Company E, 38th Virginia. Harrison and Busey, *Nothing But Glory*, 388.

84. Benjamin F. Binns, Private, Company K, 53rd Virginia, was "probably *wounded...*" Harrison and Busey, *Nothing But Glory*, 415.

85. George W. Riddle is listed as Private, Company I, 53rd Virginia. Harrison and Busey, *Nothing But Glory*, 413.

86. Charles W. Reed is listed as First Sergeant, Company G, 8th Virginia. Harrison and Busey, *Nothing But Glory*, 267.

87. John T. Jennings, Private, Company H, 19th Virginia, is not listed as a casualty. Harrison and Busey, *Nothing But Glory*, 302.

88. Robert A. Robertson, listed as Corporal, Company C, 18th Virginia, was "*wounded* in the arm and leg..." Harrison and Busey, *Nothing But Glory*, 276.

89. Charles W. Powell, Private, Company E, 9th Virginia, is not listed as wounded and captured. Harrison and Busey, *Nothing But Glory*, 352.

90. John F. Jones, listed as Private, Company D, 7th Virginia, suffered a "*wound* which fractured his left ankle joint (leg amputated)..." Harrison and Busey, *Nothing But Glory*, 214.

91. N. B. Herring, listed as Private, Company I, 7th Virginia, was "*wounded* in the left leg (amputated)..." Harrison and Busey, *Nothing But Glory*, 218.

92. John E. Phillips is listed as Second Sergeant, Company B, 11th Virginia. Harrison and Busey, *Nothing But Glory*, 223.

93. John S. Watson is listed as Second Corporal, Company I, 57th Virginia. Harrison and Busey, *Nothing But Glory*, 433.

94. William H. Gaskins is listed as First Sergeant, Company K, 8th Virginia. Harrison and Busey, *Nothing But Glory*, 269.

95. John B. Worsham is listed as Fourth Sergeant, Company D, 24th Virginia. Harrison and Busey, *Nothing But Glory*, 246.

96. Rufus F. Rowland is listed as Fourth Sergeant, Company G, 24th Virginia. Harrison and Busey, *Nothing But Glory*, 250.

97. Henry L. Raber, who was probably struck by canister, lived until August 14. Harrison and Busey, *Nothing But Glory*, 261.

98. James A. Barnett, listed as Private, Company F, 19th Virginia, "received a shell *wound* in the right thigh..." Harrison and Busey, *Nothing But Glory*, 299.

99. James M. Kirkland is listed as Private, Company H, 53rd Virginia. Harrison and Busey, *Nothing But Glory*, 411.

100. Nicholas Black is listed as First Sergeant, Company K, 19th Virginia. Harrison and Busey, *Nothing But Glory*, 306.

101. Eugene G. Taylor is listed as First Sergeant, Company B, 19th Virginia. Harrison and Busey, *Nothing But Glory*, 293.

102. George M. Pollard is listed as Second Sergeant, Company H, 18th Virginia. Harrison and Busey, *Nothing But Glory*, 284.

103. Zachariah A. Blanton is listed as Captain, Company F, 18th Virginia. Harrison and Busey, *Nothing But Glory*, 281.

104. James P. Leftwich is listed as Second Sergeant, Company G, 28th Virginia. Harrison and Busey, *Nothing But Glory*, 319.

105. James C. Farley, listed as Private, Company G, 18th Virginia, was "*wounded.*". Harrison and Busey, *Nothing But Glory*, 283.

106. Robert P. Rhodes is not listed among the dead in *The Gettysburg Death Roster*, 98.

107. James Jennings is listed as Second Sergeant, Company I, 18th Virginia. Harrison and Busey, *Nothing But Glory*, 286.

APPENDIX

1. Numbers that succeed each brigade indicate officers and men actually engaged at Gettysburg. The percentage of loss follows. All numbers and percentages, unless otherwise stated, are taken from *Regimental Strengths and Losses at Gettysburg.*

2. Brigade strength and loss does not include 12th and 15th.

3. Brigade loss does not include the 10th New York: 82 / 7.3 percent.

4. Brigade loss does not include the 84th Pennsylvania on detached duty as III Corps wagon train guard.

5. Brigade loss does not include the 102nd Pennsylvania which was detached to guard Army of the Potomac trains at Westminster, Maryland.

6. Brigade loss does not include the 6th United States Cavalry which was engaged at Fairfield, July 3.

7. Col. Pennock Huey's brigade was detached to guard Army of the Potomac trains at Westminster, Maryland.

8. Brigade loss does not include Battery C, attached to Huey's brigade.

9. Brigade and artillery battalion strength and losses are taken from *Nothing But Glory.*

Bibliography

Alexander, Edward Porter. *Fighting for the Confederacy: The Personal Recollections of General Edward Porter Alexander.* Edited by Gary W. Gallagher. Chapel Hill: The University of North Carolina Press, 1989.

———. *Military Memoirs of a Confederate: A Critical Narrative.* Reprint, New York: Da Capo Press, 1993.

Allison, William H. *A Short Story of the Battle of Gettysburg.* N.p., n.d.

Annals of the War, Written by Leading Participants, North and South. Philadelphia: The Times Publishing Company, 1879.

Atlas Plat Book, Adams County, Pennsylvania. Rockford, Illinois: Rockford Map Publishers, 1977.

Ayres, Elsie Johnson. *Highland Pioneer Sketches and Family Genealogies.* Springfield, Ohio: H. F. Skinner, 1971.

Banes, Charles P. *History of the Philadelphia Brigade, Sixty Ninth, Seventy First, Seventy Second and One Hundred Sixth Pennsylvania Volunteers.* Philadelphia: J. B. Lippincott & Co., 1876.

Bearss, Edwin C. *Decision in Mississippi: Mississippi's Important Role in the War Between the States.* Little Rock: Pioneer Press, 1962.

Benedict, George G. *Army Life in Virginia. Letters from the Twelfth Vermont Regiment and Personal Experiences of Volunteer Service in the War for the Union, 1862–1863.* Burlington: Free Press Association, 1895.

Bloom, Robert L. *A History of Adams County, Pennsylvania: 1700–1990.* Adams County Historical Society, 1992, 192.

Brown, Kent Masterson. *Cushing of Gettysburg: The Story of a Union Artillery Commander.* Lexington: University Press of Kentucky, 1993.

Busey, John W., and David G. Martin. *Regimental Strengths and Losses at Gettysburg.* Hightstown, N.J.: Longstreet House, 1994 edition.

Casler, John O. *Four Years in the Stonewall Brigade.* Edited by James I. Robertson, Jr. Reprint, Dayton: Morningside, 1971.

Castel, Albert. *Decision in the West: The Atlanta Campaign of 1864.* Lawrence: The University Press of Kansas, 1992.

Cincinnati City Directory, 1869.

Clark, Walter, ed. *Histories of the Several Regiments and Battalions from North Carolina in the Great War, 1861–1865.* 5 vols. Reprint, Wilmington, N.C.: Broadfoot Publishing Company, 1991.

Coddington, Edwin B. *The Gettysburg Campaign: A Study in Command.* Reprint, New York: Charles Scribner's Sons, 1984.

Connelly, Thomas L. *Army of the Heartland: The Army of the Tennessee, 1861–1862.* Baton Rouge: Louisiana State University Press, 1967.

———. *Autumn of Glory: The Army of Tennessee, 1862–1865.* Baton Rouge: Louisiana State University Press, 1971.

———. *The Marble Man: Robert E. Lee and His Image in American Society.* Baton Rouge: Louisiana State University Press, 1977.

Cowles, Luther E. *History of the Fifth Massachusetts Battery.* Boston: n.p., 1902.

Davis, Charles E., Jr. *Three Years in the Army: The Story of the Thirteenth Massachusetts Volunteers from July 16, 1861, to August 1, 1864.* Boston: Estes and Lauriat, 1894.

Dowdey, Clifford, and Louis H. Manarin, eds. *The Wartime Papers of R. E. Lee.* Virginia Civil War Commission. Boston and Toronto: Little, Brown and Company, 1961.

Downey, Fairfax. *The Guns at Gettysburg.* New York: David McKay Company, Inc., 1958.

Dunn, Craig L. *Iron Men, Iron Will: The Nineteenth Indiana Regiment of the Iron Brigade.* Indianapolis: Guild Press of Indiana, Inc., 1995.

Early, Jubal A. *Jubal Early's Memoirs: Autobiographical Sketch and Narrative of the War Between the States.* Reprint, Baltimore: The Nautical & Aviation Publishing Company of America, 1989.

Fields, Frank E. *28th Virginia Infantry.* Lynchburg, Va.: H. E. Howard, Inc., 1985.

Ford, Andrew E. *The Story of the Fifteenth Massachusetts Volunteer Infantry in the Civil War, 1861–1864.* Clinton: Press of W. J. Coulter, 1898.

Fox, William F. *Regimental Losses in the American Civil War.* Albany, N.Y.: Albany Publishing Co., 1898 edition.

Freeman, Douglas S. *Lee's Lieutenant's: A Study in Command*. 3 vols. New York: Charles Scribner's Sons, 1942–44.

———. *R. E. Lee: A Biography*. 4 vols. New York: Charles Scribner's Sons, 1936.

Freeman, Douglas Southall, ed. *Lee's Dispatches: Unpublished Letters of General Robert E. Lee, C. S. A. to Jefferson Davis and the War Department of the Confederate States of America, 1862–65*. With additional dispatches and foreword by Grady McWhiney. New York: G. P. Putnam's Sons, 1957 edition.

Fremantle, Arthur J. L. *Three Months in the Southern States*. Reprint, Lincoln: University of Nebraska Press, 1991.

Frey, Jerry. *In the Woods before Dawn: The Samuel Richey of the Southern Confederacy*. Gettysburg: Thomas Publications, 1994.

Gallagher, Gary W. *Stephen Dodson Ramseur: Lee's Gallant General*. Chapel Hill: The University of North Carolina Press, 1985.

Gallagher, Gary W., ed. *Antietam: Essays on the 1862 Maryland Campaign*. Kent, Ohio: The Kent State University Press, 1989.

———. *The First Day at Gettysburg: Essays on Confederate and Union Leadership*. Kent, Ohio: The Kent State University Press, 1992.

———. *Lee the Soldier*. Lincoln: University of Nebraska Press, 1996.

———. *The Second Day at Gettysburg: Essays on Confederate and Union Leadership*, Kent, Ohio: The Kent State University Press, 1993.

———. *The Third Day at Gettysburg & Beyond*. Chapel Hill: The University of North Carolina Press, 1994.

Galwey, Thomas Francis. *The Valiant Hours: An Irishman in the Civil War*. Edited by Wilbur S. Nye. Harrisburg: The Stackpole Company, 1961.

Gibbon, John. *Personal Recollections of the Civil War*. Reprint, Dayton: Morningside, 1978.

Grunder, Charles S., and Brandon H. Beck. *The Second Battle of Winchester: June 12–15, 1863*. Lynchburg, Va.: H. E. Howard, Inc., 1989.

Haines, William P. *History of the Men of Company F, with Description of the Marches and Battles of the 12th New Jersey Volunteers*. Camden: C. S. McGrath, 1897.

Harrison, Kathy Georg, comp. *The Location of the Monuments, Markers, and Tablets on Gettysburg Battlefield*. Gettysburg: Thomas Publications, 1993.

Harrison, Kathy Georg, and John W. Busey. *Nothing But Glory: Pickett's Division at Gettysburg.* Gettysburg: Thomas Publications, 1993.

Harrison, Walter. *Pickett's Men: A Fragment of War History.* Reprint, New York: D. Van Norstrand, 1870.

Haskell, Frank. *The Battle of Gettysburg.* Edited by Bruce Catton. Reprint, Boston: Houghton Mifflin Company, 1958.

Hassler, Warren W., Jr. *Crisis at the Crossroads: The First Day at Gettysburg.* Tuscalsoosa: University of Alabama Press, 1970.

Hattaway, Herman, and Archer Jones. *How the North Won: A Military History of the Civil War.* Urbana: University of Illinois Press, 1983.

Henderson, George F. R. *The Science of War: A Collection of Essays and Lectures, 1892–1903.* Edited by Neill Malclom. New York and London: Longmans, Green, and Co., 1905.

Hewett, Janet B., ed. *The Roster of Confederate Soldiers 1861–1865.* 16 vols. Wilmington, N.C.: Broadfoot Publishing Company, 1996.

Hoke, Jacob. *The Great Invasion of 1863.* Reprint, New York and London: Thomas Yosseloff, 1959.

Holt, David E. *A Mississippi Rebel in the Army of Northern Virginia: The Civil War Memoirs of Private David Holt.* Edited by Thomas D. Cockrell and Michael B. Ballard. Baton Rouge: Louisiana State University Press, 1995.

Hood, John B. *Advance and Retreat: Personal Experiences in the United States & Confederate States Armies.* Philadelphia: Press of Buck and McFetridge, 1880.

Horn, Stanley F., ed. *The Robert E. Lee Reader.* Indianapolis: The Bobbs-Merrill Company, Inc., 1949.

Hunter, Robert, ed. *Sketches of War History: 1861–1865, Papers Prepared for the Ohio Commandery of the Military Order of the Loyal Legion of the United States.* 3 vols. Cincinnati: Robert Clarke & Co., 1890.

Irby, Richard. *Historical Sketch of the Nottoway Grays, afterwards Company G, Eighteenth Virginia Regiment, Army of Northern Virginia.* Richmond: J. W. Ferguson & Son, 1878.

Iredell, Alexander. *Historical Sketches of the Seventh Regiment North Carolina Troops.* Mooresville: Mooresville Publishing Company, 1893.

Jacobs, Michael. *Rebel Invasion of Maryland and Pennsylvania and the Battle of Gettysburg, July 1, 2, and 3, 1863.* Philadelphia: J. B. Lippincott & Co., 1864.

Johnson, Robert Underwood, and Clarence Clough Buell, eds. *Battles and Leaders of the Civil War.* 4 vols. New York: The Century Co., 1887.

Johnston, David E. *The Story of a Confederate Boy in the Civil War.* Reprint, Radford, Va.: Commonwealth Press, Inc., 1980.

Jones, Archer. *Confederate Strategy from Shiloh to Vicksburg.* Baton Rouge: Louisiana State University Press, 1961.

Jones, Terry L. *Lee's Tigers: The Louisiana Infantry in the Army of Northern Virginia.* Baton Rouge: Louisiana State University Press, 1987.

Juettner, Otto, A.M., M.D. *Daniel Drake and His Followers: Historical and Biographical Sketches.* Cincinnati: Harvey Publishing Company, n.d.

King, Margaret Rives. *A Memento of Ancestors and Ancestral Homes, Written for Her Nieces and Nephews.* Cincinnati: Robert Clarke & Co., 1890.

Krick, Robert K. *The Gettysburg Death Roster: The Confederate Dead at the Battle of Gettysburg.* Dayton: Morningside, 1985 edition.

Ladd, David L., and Audrey J., eds. *The Bachelder Papers: Gettysburg in Their Own Words.* 3 vols. Dayton: Morningside, 1994.

Laine, J. Gary, and Morris M. Penny. *Law's Alabama Brigade in the War Between the Union and the Confederacy.* Shippensburg, Pa.: White Mane Publishing Co., Inc., 1996.

Lee, Robert E. (son). *Recollections and Letters of General Robert E. Lee.* New York: Doubleday Company, 1924 edition.

Lewis, John H. *Recollections from 1860 to 1865: With Incidents of Camp Life, Descriptions of Battles, the Life of the Southern Soldier, His Hardships and Sufferings, and the Life of a Prisoner of War in the Northern Prisons.* Reprint, Dayton: Morningside, 1983.

Loehr, Charles T. *War History of the Old First Virginia Regiment, Army of Northern Virginia.* Reprint, Richmond: Wm. Ellis Jones, Book and Job Printer, 1884.

Longacre, Edward G. *The Cavalry at Gettysburg: A Tactical Study of Mounted Operations during the Civil War's Pivotal Campaign, 9 June–14 July 1863.* Reprint, Lincoln: University of Nebraska Press, 1986.

Longacre, Edward. *General John Buford: A Military Biography.* Conshohocken, Pa.: Combined Books, 1995.

———. *Leader of the Charge: A Biography of General George E. Pickett, C. S. A.* Shippensburg, Pa.: White Mane Publishing Company, Inc., 1995.

Long, Armistead L. *Memoirs of Robert E. Lee*. New York: J. M. Stoddart & Company, 1887.

Longstreet, James. *From Manassas to Appomattox: Memoirs of the Civil War in America*. Philadelphia: J. B. Lippincott Company, 1896.

Marshal, Francis. *The Battle of Gettysburg: The Crest-Wave of the American Civil War*. Reprint, Gaithersburg, Md.: Olde Soldier Books, 1987.

McDermott, Anthony W. *A Brief History of the 69th Regiment Pennsylvania Veteran Volunteers, from Its Formation until Final Muster Out of the U.S. Service*. Philadelphia: D. J. Gallagher & Company, 1889.

McKim, Randolph H. *A Soldier's Recollections: Leaves from the Diary of a Young Confederate*. New York: Longmans, Green, and Co., 1910.

McLean, James L., and Judy W., comps. *Gettysburg Sources*. 3 vols. Baltimore: Butternut and Blue, 1987.

Metts, James I. "Longstreet's Charge at Gettysburg, Pa. Pickett's, Pettigrew's and Trimble's Divs." Wilmington, N.C.: Morning Star Press, 1899.

Moe, Richard. *The Last Full Measure: The Life and Death of the First Minnesota Volunteers*. New York: Henry Holt and Company, 1993.

Montgomery, James Stuart. *The Shaping of a Battle: Gettysburg*. Philadelphia & New York: Chilton Company—Book Division, 1959.

Moore, Frank, ed. *The Rebellion Record: A Diary of American Events*. 11 vols. New York: D. Van Norstrand, 1861–1864.

Moore, Robert A. *A Life for the Confederacy*. Edited by James W. Silver. Reprint, Wilmington, N.C.: Broadfoot Publishing Company, 1991.

Morgan, William H. *Personal Reminiscences of the War of 1861–65*. Lynchburg, Va.: J. P. Bell Co., Inc., 1911.

Nesbitt, Mark. *Saber and Scapegoat: J.E.B. Stuart and the Gettysburg Controversy*. Mechanicsburg, Pa.: Stackpole Books, 1994.

New York Monuments Commission. *Greene and His New York Troops at Gettysburg*. Albany: J. B. Lyon Company State Printers, 1909.

Nicolay, John G., and John Hay, eds. *Complete Works of Abraham Lincoln*. 12 vols. New York: The Lamb Publishing Company, 1905 edition.

Norton, Oliver Wilcox. *The Attack and Defense of Little Round Top: Gettysburg, July 2, 1863*. New York: The Neale Publishing Company, 1913.

Nye, Wilbur Sturtevant. *Here Come the Rebels!* Baton Rouge: Louisiana State University Press, 1965.

Page, Charles P. *History of the Fourteenth Regiment, Connecticut Volunteer Infantry.* Meriden: Horton Printing Company, 1906.

Pfanz, Harry W. *Gettysburg: Culp's Hill and Cemetery Hill.* Chapel Hill: The University of North Carolina Press, 1993.

————. *Gettysburg: The Second Day.* Chapel Hill: The University of North Carolina Press, 1987.

Poague, William T. *Gunner with Stonewall: Reminiscences of William Thomas Poague.* Edited by Monroe F. Cockrell. Reprint, Jackson, Tenn.: McCowat-Mercer Press, 1957.

Riley, Franklin L., ed. *Publications of the Mississippi Historical Society,* Jackson.

Rawley, James A. *Turning Points of the Civil War.* Lincoln: University of Nebraska Press, 1989 edition.

Reardon, Carol. *Pickett's Charge in History and Memory.* Chapel Hill: University of North Carolina Press, 1997.

Robertson, James I., Jr. *Stonewall Jackson: The Man, the Soldier, the Legend.* New York: Macmillan Publishing USA, 1997.

Rollins, Richard, ed. *Pickett's Charge!: Eyewitness Accounts.* Redondo Beach, Ca.: Rank and File Publications, 1996 edition.

Rowland, Dunbar, ed. *Jefferson Davis Constitutionalist: His Letters Papers & Speeches.* 10 vols. Jackson: Mississippi Department of Archives and History, 1923.

Rozwenc, Edwin C., ed. *Slavery as a Cause of the Civil War.* Boston: D.C. Heath and Company, 1949.

Rupp, I. Daniel. *History and Topography of Dauphin, Cumberland, Franklin, Bedford, Adams and Perry Counties.* Lancaster, Pa.: Gilbert Hills Proprietor & Publisher, 1846.

Sauers, Richard A. *A Caspian Sea of Ink: The Meade-Sickles Controversy.* Baltimore: Butternut and Blue, 1989.

Sawyer, Franklin. *8th Ohio Volunteer Infantry: Gibraltar Brigade Army of the Potomac.* Reprint, Huntington, W.Va.: Blue Acorn, 1994.

Schurz, Carl. *Reminiscences of Carl Schurz.* 3 vols. New York: The McClure Co., 1907–1908.

Sears, Stephen W. *Chancellorsville.* Boston and New York: Houghton Mifflin Company, 1996.

————. *Landscape Turned Red: The Battle of Antietam.* New York: Ticknor & Fields, 1983.

Shotwell, Randolph A. *Three Years in Battle and Three in Federal Prisons*. 3 vols. Raleigh: The North Carolina Historical Commission, 1931.

Sifakis, Stewart. *Compendium of the Confederate Armies: Virginia*. New York: Facts on File, Inc., 1992.

Sorrel, Moxley. *Recollections of a Confederate Staff Officer*. Edited by Bell Irvin Wiley. Reprint, Wilmington, N.C.: Broadfoot Publishing Company, 1987.

Stearns, Austin C. *Three Years with Company K*. Edited by Arthur A. Kent. Cranbury, N.J.: Associated University Presses, Inc., 1976.

Stewart, George R. *Pickett's Charge: A Microhistory of the Final Attack at Gettysburg, July 3, 1863*. Boston: Houghton Mifflin Company, 1959.

Stiles, Robert. *Four Years under Marse Robert*. Reprint, Dayton: Morningside, 1977.

The Story of Gettysburg: Its Heroes, Its Monuments, Its Consecrated Fields. Philadelphia and Reading Railroad: General Passenger Department, 1896.

Swinton, William. *Campaigns of the Army of the Potomac*. Reprint, Secaucus, New Jersey: The Blue & Grey Press, 1988.

Thomas, Emory M. *Bold Dragoon: The Life of J.E.B. Stuart*. New York: Harper & Row, Publishers, 1986.

Tucker, Glenn. *Hancock the Superb*. Indianapolis: The Bobbs-Merrill Company, Inc., 1960.

———. *High Tide at Gettysburg: The Campaign in Campaign*. Reprint, Dayton: Morningside, 1973.

———. *Lee and Longstreet at Gettysburg*. Indianapolis: The Bobbs-Merrill Company, Inc., 1968.

Vanderslice, John M. *Gettysburg: Where and How the Regiments Fought and the Troops They Encountered*. Philadelphia: n.p., 1897.

Waitt, Ernest Linden. *History of the Nineteenth Regiment Massachusetts Volunteer Infantry, 1861–1865*. Salem: Salem Press Company, 1905.

Wallace, Lee A. Jr. *1st Virginia Infantry*. Lynchburg, Va.: H. E. Howard, Inc., 1985 edition.

Warner, Ezra J. *Generals in Blue: Lives of the Union Commanders*. Baton Rouge: Louisiana State University Press, 1986 edition.

———. *Generals in Gray: Lives of the Confederate Commanders*. Baton Rouge: Louisiana State University Press, 1988 edition.

Washburn, George H. *A Complete Military History and Record of the 108th Regiment N. Y. Volunteers, from 1862 to 1894, Together with Roster, Letters, Rebel Oaths of Allegiance, Rebel Passes, Reminiscences, Life Sketches, Photographs, Etc.* Rochester: E. R. Andrews, 1894.

Wellman, Manly Wade. *Giant in Gray: A Biography of Wade Hampton of South Carolina.* New York: Charles Scribner's Sons, 1949.

Wert, Jeffrey D. *General James Longstreet: The Confederacy's Most Controversial Soldier—A Biography.* New York: Simon & Schuster, 1993.

Williams, David Hamilton. *Waterloo New Perspectives: The Great Battle Reappraised.* New York: John Wiley & Sons, Inc., 1994.

Wise, Jennings C. *The Long Arm of Lee.* 2 vols. Reprint, Lincoln: University of Nebraska Press, 1991.

Woodworth, Steven E. *Davis and Lee at War.* Lawrence: University Press of Kansas, 1995.

Government Records

Compiled Service Records of Confederate Soldiers Who Served in Organizations from Virginia. National Archives, Washington, D.C.

Government Publications

Barnes, Joseph K., and George A. Otis. *Medical & Surgical History of the War of the Rebellion.* Vol. 2, pt. 2. Washington, D.C.: Government Printing Office, 1877.

United States War Department. *The War of the Rebellion: A Compilation of the Official Records of the Union and Confederate Armies,* 70 vols. in 128 pts. Washington, D.C.: Government Printing Office, 1880–1901.

Manuscript Sources

Capt. David E. Beem, Company H, 14th Indiana, to his wife, July 5, 1863. Box 1, Folder 9, Indiana Historical Society, Indianapolis.

"Dear Children." Memoir of Howard Malcolm Walthall. Marshall County Museum, Holly Springs, Mississippi. Richmond: 1913.

Newspapers

Baltimore American and Commercial Advertiser

Buffalo Evening News

Cincinnati Daily Commercial

Hillsboro Gazette

Philadelphia Weekly Times

Periodicals

Blue and Gray Magazine

Civil War History

Civil War Magazine

Confederate Veteran Magazine

Gettysburg Magazine

The Journal of Mississippi History

North & South Magazine

Southern Bivouac

Southern Historical Society Papers

INDEX